The *Arte of English Poesie*

Nowe because I am not well seen in
Englishe Meters my self, therfore I coulde
not, I confesse, wel exemplifye in Englishe
all these foresayde figures in Latin. . . .
Whoso can do it, is worthy prayse, and
worthy more praise yf he wyll doe it—
Richard Sherry, *A Treatise of the Figures
of Grammer and Rhetorike,* 1555.

The Arte of English Poesie

BY

GEORGE PUTTENHAM

Edited by

GLADYS DOIDGE WILLCOCK

and

ALICE WALKER

CAMBRIDGE
AT THE UNIVERSITY PRESS
1936
REPRINTED
1970

Published by the Syndics of the Cambridge University Press
Bentley House, 200 Euston Road, London, N.W.1
American Branch: 32 East 57th Street, New York, N.Y. 10022

PUBLISHER'S NOTE

Cambridge University Press Library Editions are re-issues of out-of-print standard works from the Cambridge catalogue. The texts are unrevised and, apart from minor corrections, reproduce the latest published edition.

Standard Book Number: 521 07782 6

First published 1936
Reprinted 1970

First printed in Great Britain at the University Press, Cambridge
Reprinted in Great Britain by John Dickens & Co. Ltd, Northampton

CONTENTS

PREFACE

The *Arte of English Poesie* is a work of proved usefulness. Contemporaries and seventeenth-century writers borrowed from it wholesale, and literary historians, critics and philologists still turn to it again and again; its *disiecta membra* meet one everywhere in Elizabethan studies. Yet, though much handled, it seems to have made little impression as a whole. It is in the conviction that the work deserves to be read and appreciated for itself, as a piece of lively exploration and the record of an interesting personality, that we have undertaken this edition and presented it in this form. The book would repay more detailed elucidation than the limits of this edition allow, but minute annotation of so lengthy a work would have put its price beyond the reach of the common reader. It is the object of the present edition to place the *Arte* before a wide circle of those interested in Elizabethan letters as a vivid record of Elizabethan critical and creative habits and to introduce its author as not only knowable but worth knowing.

It is our pleasant duty to thank Dr F. S. Boas for kindly interest at the beginning of this enterprise, Dr R. B. McKerrow for unfailing helpfulness and much wise counsel on our work in all its stages, and the Syndics of the Cambridge University Press for their courageous generosity in undertaking this publication. We should also like to record our appreciation of the help Miss Avery Woodward has given us on some Greek and

(vii)

Latin problems and of the courtesy and ungrudging assistance we have received from the staffs of the Public Record Office, the Bodleian Library and the British Museum. Finally, we should like Miss K. S. Block to look upon this edition as some recognition of the stimulus towards Tudor studies which both editors drew from her labours on their behalf many years ago.

Whether our estimate of the *Arte* is endorsed or not, it can at all events be claimed for it that it has supplied its editors with the perfect formula for submitting a new interpretation of the work: 'the election is the writers, the iudgement is the worlds'.

A. W.
G. D. W.

INTRODUCTION

PRELIMINARY

The main outlines of the story of Elizabethan criticism—
of the assimilation and translation into English thought
of the common Renaissance heritage of ideas—are well-
enough known. In works of reference, in source-books
and anthologies, the *Arte of English Poesie* has been
'placed' in its relationship to the main trend of English
and foreign criticism. In the following pages an attempt
will be made to develop the interest of author and book
in and for themselves. The *Arte* is not only the most
ambitious and comprehensive undertaking in Elizabethan criticism; it is also the expression of one of the
most alert and flexible Elizabethan minds. It is humanistic and also genially human.

One other work claimed by the writer of the *Arte*
survives—*Partheniades*, a brief collection of poems in
honour of Elizabeth, which can be assigned from internal evidence to *c.* 1581–2. These poems are not
easily accessible and have been very little read. They
provide interesting corroboration of the personality dis-
cerned in the *Arte* and even more incontestably reveal
it as endowed (for its time) with an unusually pene-
trating and courageous sense of reality. The rhythms,
as survivals of a simple early-Tudor syllabic prosody,
might well rouse the young Harington's scorn, but the
substance at its best reveals a mind of the type we like
to think of as modern.

It is unsatisfactory to leave such a writer with only
a vague and disputed title to a name. This Introduction
will attempt to justify and clarify the ascription of the
Arte to 'Puttenham' and to recall from his extant
writings some of the more interesting traits of a distinctive personality.

(ix)

There is evidence that the *Arte*, like the *Essais* of Montaigne, grew with its author's growth and that its apparent inconsistencies and indubitable reconsiderations are pointers to the processes by which an interesting mind arrived at its conclusions, as well as to vicissitudes and cross-currents in the Elizabethan world at large. The composition carries us from a man's prime to his old age and the *Arte* has, accordingly, a maturity and spaciousness possessed by no other critical work of its day. It embodies the results of experience in the world of men as well as of books and finds a unifying theme in the parallel between civilisation and art. 'Puttenham' cuts the gordian knot of the problem with which contemporary criticism wrestled so unprofitably by relating literature not to ethics but to life.

The *Arte* marks the culmination of a period of vigorous exploration in the field where language and literature meet. It shows how the origin of English criticism was bound up with the awakening of linguistic consciousness and constitutes our most fully documented guide to the Tudor approach to poetry. It is unconcerned with the abstract theories on which the bulk of Renaissance criticism was expended. After a short preliminary book, justifying the existence of poetry as the expression of social and individual needs, its writer addresses himself strenuously to untrodden paths—an examination of the Art of English Poetry— and the focussing of attention on the poet's medium and craft keeps us in immediate contact with the aims and problems of the day. Most of these are dead to us—they were dead even to Shakespeare—but the perspective of time should save us from concurring in the late-Elizabethan impatience with the soberer vein of mid-Tudor writers. From the prosodic experiments there emerged a gradual awareness of the stressed structure of English verse, from the Inkhorn term controversy an enhanced sense of the multiple texture of our language, magnificently exploited in the period that followed, and from the rhetorical cult (now deadest of all) a sort of religious industry in language that soon enabled it to throw away its crutches of schemes and tropes. The *Arte*, read strenuously and imaginatively, should make all these dry bones live. No one was less of a pedant than 'Puttenham'. Had these things been matters of pedantry he would not have handled them. They were objects of delight at a court which was a main growing point in the national life.

I. THE AUTHORSHIP

The *Arte of English Poesie* appeared anonymously, accompanied by a dedication in which Richard Field, its printer, professed ignorance of its authorship. It is quite clear, however, from the alterations made while the work was in the press,[1] that it was published with its author's co-operation and that its anonymity reflected the feeling that a gentleman should be 'dayntie of his doings' and not advertise his name in print. In the book itself no attempt is made to conceal its writer's identity. On the contrary, it is one of the most intimate works of its age and, from its autobiographical clues and numerous references to his earlier works, many contemporaries must have guessed its author without difficulty.

The two early references to the authorship of the *Arte* which have come to light agree in attributing it to 'Puttenham'.[2] Two years after its publication Harington (though he respected in print its author's anonymity by describing him as an 'unknowne'), in a private note to Field, referred to what is undoubtedly the *Arte* as 'Put-

1 *V*. Bibliographical Note, p. cv.
2 For a detailed account of early notices concerning the authorship of the *Arte*, *v*. Capt. B. M. Ward's article, 'The Authorship of the *Arte of English Poesie*: A suggestion', *Review of English Studies*, 1925, pp. 284–308.

nams book'. About twenty-five years later Bolton, in his *Hypercritica*, described it as the work 'as the fame is' of one of Elizabeth's Gentlemen Pensioners, 'Puttenham'. Another early reference to 'Puttenham' in a literary context occurs in Richard Carew's essay on 'The Excellencie of the English tongue' as printed in the 1614 edition of Camden's *Remaines*, where 'Maister Puttenham' is mentioned with Sidney and Stanyhurst as having demonstrated the 'copiousnesse' of English verse forms. This does not explicitly associate 'Puttenham' with the *Arte*, but it proves, at all events, the existence of a Puttenham with literary associations.

So far, efforts to identify the author of the *Arte* have proved inconclusive. Until recently, critical opinion wavered between George Puttenham (the candidate of the work's early editors) and Richard, his elder brother, whose claims were first canvassed by Croft in his edition of *The Governour* (1883).[1] Recently, both George and Richard have been discredited by Capt. B. M. Ward, who examined and dismissed as untenable the traditional belief that it was the work of a Puttenham and suggested Lord Lumley as its author.[2]

Capt. Ward's case was, on the face of it, strong and has received, in some quarters, unreserved acceptance. He collated the autobiographical references in the *Arte* with what is known of Lumley and, although on some points there was no evidence to show whether these tallied or not and Lumley was given the benefit of the doubt, no serious discrepancies appeared to exist. Five disturbing facts, however, raise grave doubts concerning his authorship. One of the strongest pieces of circumstantial evidence in his favour was the assumption that he was in Brussels in the spring of 1566 with his father-in-law, the Earl of Arundel, and attended the banquet at which the writer of the *Arte* 'stoode a beholder'

1 Vol. I, Introduction, pp. clxxxii–clxxxix.
2 *R.E.S., loc. cit.*

(p. 271).[1] Capt. Ward argued that Lumley, who on 17 March 1565/6 received a royal commission to transact certain business in Italy, left London with Arundel on 19 March. But Arundel 'went over Seas' on 16 March,[2] before the signing of this commission, and there is some evidence that Lumley was still in England three days later.[3] He appears to have been back by 24 May.[4] He had, therefore, rather less than nine weeks in which to reach Italy, complete his negotiations and return to England, so that it is very unlikely that he had the time for so long a détour as a visit to Brussels involved.

Secondly, Capt. Ward strengthened his case for Lumley by reference to his reputation as an antiquary and book-collector, but the catalogue of his library[5] reveals the fact that his books consisted mainly of Latin works on theology and history. Lumley's library cannot be taken as representative exclusively of his own literary tastes, since it comprised the spoils of various monastic libraries, some of Cranmer's books and the library of the Earl of Arundel, who was well known as a book-collector.[6] It is, therefore, not so much what the library contained as what it did not contain that is significant: and the only original works of contemporary

1 That Lumley, a man of thirty and Arundel's son-in-law, 'stoode a beholder' at a banquet where Arundel was the guest of honour is, in any case, highly improbable.

2 Murdin, *Burghley State Papers*, 1759, p. 761.

3 P.R.O., *Close Rolls*, C. 54/702, nos. 37 and 51. Unfortunately it appears not to be known whether the personal appearance recorded at the enrolment of a deed in Chancery was, in the sixteenth century, a fact or merely a legal formula. It is just possible that the enrolment was transacted by attorney. In any case, Lumley did not leave England with Arundel. [Descriptive titles of documents in the Public Record Office will be given with the first reference only. Subsequent references to the same class of documents will be by official numbers.]

4 P.R.O., C. 54/702, nos. 49 and 50.

5 The original catalogue (of which the British Museum possesses a modern transcript, MS. Add. 36659) is in the library of Trinity College, Cambridge.

6 Warner and Gilson, *Catalogue of Western MSS. in the old Royal and King's Collections in the British Museum*, 1921, Vol. I, Introduction, p. xix.

English poetry that Lumley possessed were the *Mirror for Magistrates* and the *Faerie Queene*.[1] As the equipment for writing the *Arte*, its author must have had by him the English poems of Gower, Tottel's *Miscellany*, Gascoigne's *Posies*, Turberville's *Epitaphes, Epigrams, Songs and Sonets*, Stanyhurst's *Aeneis*, Soowthern's *Pandora* and some manuscript containing lyrics of Dyer, Raleigh, Sidney and the Earl of Oxford;[2] but Lumley possessed none of these—not even Tottel's *Miscellany*. As the owner of a library of about seven thousand books he had remarkably few English works and apparently took not the slightest interest in the literature or the problems that inspired the *Arte*. His library is, indeed, that of a man for whom an Art of English Poetry did not exist.

Thirdly, Lumley preserved among his books the exercises of his boyhood,[3] his translation of a work of Erasmus,[4] and collections of moral maxims[5] and short prayers[6] 'gathered' by himself. If he was the author of the *Arte* and, therefore, of *Elpine, Ginecocratia, The Woer, Lustie London, De Decoro, Ierotekni* and *The Originals and Pedigree of the English Tong*,[7] why are these works, too, not in his library? If Lumley was the author of the *Arte*, his library is the place where these lost works should have been preserved.

Fourthly, even if we assume that, by some remarkable coincidence, Lumley failed to keep these manuscripts, there still exists a very serious difficulty, for his extant writings discredit the assumption that he was the writer of the *Arte*. It is impossible to believe that there

1 Lumley had a fair number of English translations from classical poets, but this seems to have been the only branch of contemporary verse activity that interested him.
2 *V.* Appendix III.
3 B.M., MS. Add. 36659, fol. 291ʳ.
4 B.M., MS. Royal 17A. xlix.
5 B.M., MS. Royal 17A. xxiv.
6 B.M., MS. Royal 18A. xviii.
7 *V.* Index, *s.v.* George Puttenham, *Lost Works*.

lies behind the orthodox, balanced platitudes he collected for Prince Henry, the unorthodox, enquiring mind of the *Arte* and *Partheniades*, to which, indeed, many of Lumley's religious views would have been definitely repulsive. The evidence of the library seems conclusive: whoever wrote the *Arte* it was not Lumley. If the *Arte* was his, his library would surely have contained some indication of literary interests and his extant works some traces of the mind and personality discernible in the *Arte* and *Partheniades*.

Lastly, contemporary evidence for 'Puttenham's' authorship cannot be dismissed lightly, for references to it, though few, are unanimous and appear to rest on independent authority. Harington's testimony, on account of its early date, is particularly weighty and one of three interpretations must be put upon it. First, that he was unwittingly deceived; and this, since he patronised the same printer and belonged to the same class as the writer of the *Arte*, is improbable. As a corollary it follows that 'fame' and Bolton were similarly misinformed. Or, secondly, if we accept Capt. Ward's hypothesis, we must assume that Lumley's desire for anonymity was so strong that he arranged, with Field's connivance, a Puttenham camouflage which Harington knew of and respected; and this is completely at variance with the self-revelation which is so characteristic a feature of the *Arte*.[1] Or, thirdly, we must assume that Harington was right. This is the natural interpretation to put on his ascription. The casual, but unhesitating, manner in which he refers to 'Putnams book' (when he could equally well have mentioned the work's title) indicates that he harboured no misgivings concerning the *Arte*'s writer. His attribution has the corroboration

---

1 Indeed, if Lumley thus conspired to mislead the public, then we can hardly accept the autobiographical references in the work itself at their face value. Logically, they too should be regarded as part of a false trail, so that the very evidence on which the case for his authorship rests becomes worthless by the conclusions that are drawn from it.

of the seventeenth-century tradition to which Bolton refers and we are not justified in departing from it unless it can be proved conclusively that no Puttenham was its author.

The case for the Puttenhams was dismissed on the evidence of the known facts concerning their lives. A good deal, however, can be added to their biographies, and a re-examination of their lives shows that there is no valid evidence against authorship by either George or Richard and a great deal which narrows the case very definitely in favour of George.

Richard's case can be briefly stated. Like the author of the *Arte* he had spent much time out of England. He was abroad from 1560 to 1567, when he paid a brief and secret visit to England,[1] sold his possessions[2] and then returned to the continent where he remained for some years. There is no evidence for his return until *c.* 1578.[3] He was a prisoner in the King's Bench from 1583 to May 1587,[4] but nothing has so far been produced to show that he was in prison when the *Arte*

1 P.R.O., *State Papers, Domestic, Elizabeth*, S.P. 12/66/53 and S.P. 12/176/45.

2 P.R.O., C. 54/743, no. 40.

3 Evidence for his return *c.* 1578 is contained in a document calendared in the Domestic State Papers for February 1569/70 (P.R.O., S.P. 12/66/53). This should be dated *c.* 1579. Richard had petitioned for the return of £900 paid into the Treasury by his son-in-law, Francis Morris. This sum represented nine yearly instalments of £100, beginning early in 1571, of which the ninth was paid on 12 February 1578/9 and the tenth on 23 April 1580 (P.R.O., S.P. 12/176/45). Richard's petition for the return of £900 should, therefore, be dated between February 1578/9 and April 1580. There is no evidence that he took advantage of the pardon granted (for his unauthorised absence from the country) in January 1569/70 (P.R.O., *Patent Rolls*, C. 66/1061, m. 24). This pardon was clearly prompted by legal considerations (P.R.O., S.P.12/66/53). The lawsuits in which George was involved in the early seventies definitely indicate that Richard was still abroad (P.R.O., *Star Chamber Proceedings*, St. Ch. 5/P 35/10, Interrogations to Sater, Item 67 and P.R.O., *Chancery Proceedings*, C. 2 Eliz./P 6/52). If, as seems very probable, the unsigned letter to George beginning 'Brother' (P.R.O., S.P. 12/127/32) was Richard's (cf. p. xxviii, n. 4), he was back in England towards the end of 1578.

4 P.R.O., *Court of Requests, Orders and Decrees*, Req. 1/14, fol. 279^r–279^v.

was published, as Capt. Ward contends. It is sometimes stated that he was a prisoner in 1588, but the
evidence rests on the misdating of a petition of 1585.[1]
According to Capt. Ward, he was in prison in October
1587, but this document is dated 12 October 28 Elizabeth, *i.e.* 1586.[2] The will of a Richard Puttenham who
was a prisoner in the King's Bench in 1597[3] is probably
his,[4] but this does not constitute evidence of continuous
imprisonment from 1583 to 1597. He was certainly
at liberty early in May 1587[5] and probably in October
and November the same year.[6] There is no evidence
that he filled the rôle of Gentleman Pensioner assigned
to the writer of the *Arte* by Bolton, but he describes himself as 'sworne servaunt'[7] to Elizabeth and speaks of
having served her 'in some degree'.[8] That he collected
an annuity at Chaucer's tomb[9] suggests some literary
interests, but there is nothing to show that he wrote,
or could have written, the *Arte*. His case, indeed, stands
where it stood before the Lumley challenge: the biographical evidence, so far as it goes, presents no serious
difficulties,[10] but the absence of any indication of literary
activities or intellectual interests renders his case both

1 Capt. Ward noted this error (*R.E.S.*, *loc. cit.*, p. 289, n. 1). The document is dated 1585 by the P.R.O. (S.P. 12/183/66) and the date is confirmed
by an accompanying letter from Sir Wolstan Dixie, Lord Mayor of London
in 1585.

2 P.R.O., Req. 1/14, fol. 181ʳ.

3 *Arte of English Poesie*, ed. Arber, p. 15.

4 As Collier noted, the burial of a Richard Puttenham, who was a Yeoman
of the Queen's Guard, was recorded in the parish register of St Clement
Danes on 2 July 1601. In the administration of this Richard Puttenham's
estate (Somerset House, 4 July 1601) he is described as of Amersham. As he
left a widow Mary Puttenham, whose Christian name was that of the Sher-
field Richard's wife, it is perhaps wise not to be too positive about the 1597
will.

5 P.R.O., Req. 1/14, fol. 279ʳ–279ᵛ.   6 *Ibid.* fol. 392ʳ–392ᵛ.

7 *Ibid.* fol. 279ʳ.   8 *Ibid.* fol. 279ᵛ.

9 P.R.O., C. 54/743, no. 40.

10 There still remains the fact that he was born *c.* 1520 and the writer of
the *Arte* was probably born between 1529 and 1535. A possible explanation
of this difficulty was suggested by Croft (*The Governour*, Introduction,
Vol. I, p. clxxxvii).

doubtful and problematic. He is a runner in the *Arte* stakes, but his chances can only appeal to a gambler who will take a risk on a dark horse at very long odds.

On George's behalf a much stronger claim can be made. Two lines of approach to the question of his authorship are open: the biographical and the literary. Information derived from the *Arte* can be compared with such facts of George Puttenham's life as are recoverable from contemporary records; and the existence of one sustained writing from George Puttenham's pen, *A Justificacion of Queene Elizabeth in Relacion to the Affaire of Mary Queene of Scottes*,[1] opens up a hitherto neglected avenue of literary investigation—a comparison of this work with the *Arte* and *Partheniades*. On the biographical evidence it can be shown that it is possible that George Puttenham wrote the *Arte*; on the literary evidence possibility becomes probability and approaches certainty.

From the *Arte* the following facts can be deduced with some certainty concerning its author's life and circumstances.

(1) He wrote a poem *Elpine*, at the age of eighteen, for Edward VI (p. 169) and was, therefore, in all probability born between 1529 and 1535.

In a letter written late in 1578 George Puttenham speaks of himself as 'beyinge now apon the poynt of fyftie yeares of age'.[2] He was born, therefore, *c.* 1529 and would be about eighteen when Edward VI succeeded to the throne, so that *Elpine*, if his, might have been written to celebrate Edward's accession. From

---

1 This was published, as an anonymous work, by the Camden Society in *Accounts and Papers Relating to Mary Queen of Scots*, 1867, pp. 65–134. At least eight MSS. survive (cf. p. xxiii, n. 1); some have no title and where titles exist they seem to have been supplied by copyists. The Camden Society's has been adopted for the sake of uniformity.

2 P.R.O., S.P. 12/126/17. The statement is repeated in another version of the same letter, S.P. 12/126/18.

what we are told of the poem it seems to have been an allegory of the ship of state (p. 169) and a fitting subject with which to greet the new king.

(2) The writer of the *Arte* was brought up in the courts of foreign countries (p. 302).

Of George Puttenham's early years very little has come to light. Concerning the first thirty years of his life very few facts appear to be recorded. We know roughly the date of his birth. He matriculated at Cambridge in 1546,[1] at the age of seventeen, but apparently left the university without taking a degree. He is mentioned in a licence of 12 April 1551, granted to Sir Thomas Elyot's widow and Sir James Dyer (to whom she was now married), concerning the temporary disposal of certain manors formerly belonging to Sir Thomas Elyot, but no light is shed on his whereabouts or circumstances.[2] In August 1556 he was admitted to the Middle Temple[3] at the unusually late age of twenty-seven. There are thus several long periods in his early life about which we know nothing and the chance of filling in these *lacunae* is exceedingly slight. No records exist to show what Englishmen were abroad at this period though it is quite clear, from the State Papers and from the lives of men who made their mark as divines, statesmen or men of letters, that there were hundreds of Englishmen abroad at any rate during Mary's reign. There is evidence that George Puttenham's environment later in life was more cosmopolitan than that of most Englishmen of his day[4] and there is no reason why his life should not have run on similar lines in his early years. The dominantly Italic character of his handwriting certainly suggests his having spent a considerable time abroad during his formative period.

1 J. and J. A. Venn, *Alumni Cantabrigienses*.
2 P.R.O., *Calendar of Patent Rolls, Edward VI*, Vol. 4, p. 42 (C. 66/835, m. 24).
3 *Middle Temple Records: Minutes of Parliament*, Vol. 1, p. 106.
4 *V. post*, p. xxvi.

When he writes hastily Secretary features become prominent;[1] when he writes with care his handwriting is
sufficiently modern for an eye accustomed merely to
Elizabethan spelling to read it.[2] For his generation
Puttenham's handwriting is unusual. By far the majority
of Englishmen born *c.* 1530 (and even much later) still
wrote a hand unaffected by foreign influence.

(3) It is generally believed that the writer of the *Arte*
was educated at Oxford, but this is not nearly so well-
established a fact as is generally assumed. The sentence
on which the assumption is based (p. 210) is, both in
its wording and its lack of punctuation, ambiguous. In
the absence of a comma in a sentence that demands one,
the reader is compelled to supply his own and it is as
possible to read

> when I was a scholler,   in Oxford they called euery such
> one *Iohannes ad oppositum*

(indicating that the writer was a Cambridge man) as it
is to read

> when I was a scholler in Oxford,   they called euery such
> one *Iohannes ad oppositum*

(indicating that he was an Oxford man). The use of the
pronoun *we* would definitely have identified the writer
with the latter university, but *they* implies detachment
from Oxford habits. The phrase *of Oxford* would equally
have avoided ambiguity. As the sentence stands, therefore, we are not justified in forcing its interpretation by
taking the words 'a scholler in Oxford' out of their context and the less so since the *Arte* itself, in the evidence
it affords of a knowledge of Greek and an interest in
English linguistic problems, definitely indicates a Cambridge stimulus.

---

1 *E.g.* Puttenham's MS. corrections in Bodl. MS. Add. C. 83 and P.R.O.,
St. Ch. 5/P 9/4 (Puttenham's additions to the list of obligations, etc. alleged
to be missing from his coffers).
2 *E.g.* P.R.O., S.P. 12/126/16.

George Puttenham matriculated as a pensioner of Christ's College, Cambridge, in November 1546. He may, of course, have migrated from the one university to the other like many contemporaries, but an education at the Cambridge of Cheke and Ascham is quite sufficient to explain the liberal and progressive spirit of the *Arte* and its linguistic bias. The Oxford of the forties, very definitely, could not have laid the foundations of such a work.

(4) The number of anecdotes relating to the law-courts and lawyers in the *Arte*[1] suggests that its writer had moved in legal circles and had received a legal training. A hint to this effect is perhaps to be found in Harington's Preface to *Orlando Furioso*:

> my cause I count so good, and the euidence so open, that I neither neede to vse the countenance of any great state to boulster it, nor the cunning of anie suttle lawyer to enforce it.[2]

This sentence is preceded by a summary of the subject-matter of Book I, Chs. viii and xvii of the *Arte* and is followed by a reference to the book by name. It affords, therefore, strong evidence that Harington intended by the 'suttle lawyer' the author of the book he had in mind and, therefore, the 'Putnam' of his note to Field.

George Puttenham was admitted to the Middle Temple in August 1556. His mother's family, the Elyots, had distinguished legal traditions and he was related to some of the most eminent lawyers of his day— Sir James Dyer and the Throckmortons. He felt no diffidence in instructing the Privy Council on a point of legal procedure[3] and at least on one occasion was accused of having taken advantage of his knowledge of

1 *V*. Index, *s.v.* lawcourts.
2 *Orlando Furioso*, 1591, Sig. ¶ ij^v. Gregory Smith (*Elizabethan Critical Essays*, Vol. 2, p. 196) reads 'little' for 'suttle'.
3 P.R.O., S.P. 12/126/16.

Latin and of the law for nefarious ends.[1] Among a class whose animosities found expression in physical violence and bloodshed Puttenham is distinguished by his preference for legal weapons. By his enemies he was consistently represented as a forger of deeds, addicted to 'covenous practyses', and an exploiter of legal graft and legal knowledge.

(5) The writer of the *Arte* was a fairly prolific 'manuscript' author. He wrote for the most part in the vernacular, but possibly also (as the title *De Decoro* suggests) in Latin.

George Puttenham's family traditions render some literary interests very probable. His mother, the sister of Sir Thomas Elyot, seems to have been an educated woman, since her father, Sir Richard Elyot, left her all his English books.[2] George Puttenham was at the Middle Temple in the late fifties when the Inns of Court were the chief centre of literary activity. That he had both an adequate knowledge of Latin and an interest in its literature is shown by some fragments of translation from Suetonius.[3] Further indication of intellectual interests is contained in a letter of 1578 to Sir John Throckmorton in which he writes:

> I haue resolved with my self to employ my tyme in Studyes and with conferens with the greatest lerned men I can fynde. Solitary Studyes avaylynge nothynge, and this can not I do at yowr howse.[4]

Conclusive proof both of his ability as a writer and of its recognition is provided by his *Justificacion*. The work belongs to the same class of official writing as Bacon's account of Essex's conspiracy and was undoubtedly undertaken at the Queen's request. The existence of at

1 P.R.O., St. Ch. 5/P 26/3.
2 *The Governour*, ed. Croft, Vol. 1, Appendix A, p. 312.
3 P.R.O., S.P. 12/126/67.
4 P.R.O., S.P. 12/126/64. Throughout this Introduction MS. contractions have been expanded in accordance with the writer's normal spelling.

least seven manuscripts, roughly contemporary with its writing,[1] points to an authorised circulation, and the manner in which Elizabeth's opinions and feelings are recorded renders it quite impossible that the work was written without her sanction. In passage after passage it is as Elizabeth's spokesman that Puttenham writes and he was undoubtedly her chosen advocate. This commission would never have been given to a man who had not already proved his ability with the pen, as well as his willingness to employ it in the Queen's service, and the *Justificacion* itself shows quite plainly that its writer was no novice, but was qualified by the mastery and confidence of a man who was used to marshalling his ideas and setting them down on paper. The *Justificacion* is a kind of *Areopagitica*, written with classical forensic traditions in mind, and shows that its writer was not only recognised as an able apologist of Elizabeth's cause but was also a man who had received and applied the rhetorical training the writer of the *Arte* admired. Like the *Arte* and *Partheniades*, the *Justificacion* appears to have circulated as an anonymous work. That it was Puttenham's there can be no doubt. It is attributed to him in MS. Harl. 831 and a note in the Calthorpe MS., in the handwriting of Robert Beale, describes it as 'made by Geo. Puttenham'. This testimony must be accepted as conclusive in view of the official nature of the work and Beale's position as Clerk to the Privy Council. The evidence of Bodl. MS. Add.

---

1 B.M., MS. Harl. 831.
 B.M., MS. Cotton Calig. D. 1, fols. 37ʳ–84ᵛ.
 Bodl., MS. Tanner 108.
 Bodl., MS. Add. C. 83 (imperf.).
 Camb. Univ. Library, MS. kk. 1. 3 (14) i.
 Calthorpe MS. (*Hist. MSS. Comm.*, 2nd *Report*, 1871, p. 41).
 Winnington MS. (Camden Society Preface, p. xxiii; cf. *supra*, p. xviii, n. 1).
 An eighth MS. (B.M., MS. Harl. 4647, fols. 143ᵛ–63ᵛ) is an early eighteenth-century transcript of Cotton Calig. D. 1. The last two MSS. were collated with the Winnington MS. for the Camden Society's publication. A transcript of Cotton Calig. D. 1 can be found in the P.R.O., *Calendar of Scottish Papers*, 1586–8, pp. 356–88.

C. 83, which contains corrections in Puttenham's own hand, puts his authorship beyond doubt.

(6) Although the writer of the *Arte* professes a slighter acquaintance with Elizabeth's than with foreign courts (p. 302), he undoubtedly moved among courtiers and men of affairs. He had been present when foreign ambassadors were entertained by the Queen (p. 291). He had heard and admired the eloquence of Sir Nicholas Bacon and had come upon him 'sitting in his gallery alone with the works of Quintilian before him' (p. 140). He was acquainted with the manuscript writings of Dyer, Raleigh, Sidney and the Earl of Oxford and was sufficiently in favour with Elizabeth to address his book to her, quote her opinions (p. 295) and offer advice on the conduct of foreign affairs (p. 314).

George Puttenham could certainly have filled this rôle. He was the nephew of Sir Thomas Elyot. His father, Robert Puttenham, had played a prominent part in country affairs and was related to some of the most influential Hampshire families. His brother-in-law, Sir John Throckmorton, was for twenty-three years Chief Justice of the County of Chester and a member of the Council of Wales. Sir John's brother, Sir Nicholas Throckmorton, held even more responsible posts under Mary and Elizabeth. George Puttenham's marriage to Lady Elizabeth Windsor, *c.* 1560, brought him into touch with families of considerable wealth and influence. His wife's first husband, Richard Paulet, was the brother of Sir William Paulet, Marquess of Winchester and Lord Treasurer. Her second husband was the wealthy William Windsor, second Baron Windsor, whose eldest son and heir by a former marriage married the half-sister of Edward de Vere, seventeenth Earl of Oxford. By virtue of his connections with Throckmortons, Paulets and Windsors, George Puttenham must have moved among men in the closest touch with the court and affairs of state and his *Justificacion* bears

witness to an intimate knowledge of the political events
of his day. He knows what has happened in Parliament
and the Privy Council. He narrates an anecdote concerning the reception of a French ambassador by 'the
gravest counsellors of this realme' (pp. 132–3).[1] In
1588 Elizabeth rewarded him in affectionate terms for
his 'good, true, faithful and acceptable service'.[2] There
is no difficulty in explaining his acquaintance with at
least the work of Dyer and the Earl of Oxford. To the
former he was related through the marriage of Sir
Thomas Elyot's widow to Sir James Dyer and to the
latter through the Windsors. It is useless, therefore,
to argue that George Puttenham had no courtly connections and, on this account, could not have written
the *Arte*. He was related to some of the most influential
men of his day and there is no difficulty in believing
that the writer of the *Justificacion* might have addressed
to Elizabeth another work which shows the same
familiarity with her views and interests and the same
loyal devotion.

(7) The writer of the *Arte* had seen 'the Courts of
Fraunce, Spaine, Italie, and that of the Empire, with
many inferior Courts' (p. 271). When he gained
this experience is not made clear; it may have been a
part of his early education or have been acquired later
in life.

It has already been noted that the character of George
Puttenham's handwriting leads one to suppose that he
had more than a 'tourist' acquaintance with the continent. The first record of his foreign travels which has
come to light is a statement in a deposition of Sir John
Throckmorton's that about the fifth year of Elizabeth's
reign Puttenham visited Flanders.[3] Puttenham speaks
of the same occasion as 'about the tyme of his first

1 References to the *Justificacion* are to the Camden Society edition.
2 P.R.O., C. 66/1315, m. 7.
3 P.R.O., S.P. 12/127/30.

going biyonde the seas'.[1] Since he is here replying to a demand for details of his transactions with Throckmorton within a specified period—

> What convayances hath passed between you and Sir Iohn Throgmorton ether for lands or goodes any tyme within these ten or twelve yeres[2]—

this does not necessarily preclude his having been abroad as a child or young man. That Puttenham was thinking strictly of the period affected by his financial dealings with Sir John is indicated by his amending the dates given in the interrogation to 'this xij or xv yeares' in his reply.[3] All that his statement can conclusively be taken to imply is, therefore, that within the period he had in mind, 'this xij or xv yeares' (1563–78), the 1563 visit to Flanders was the first of a number of journeys abroad. There is evidence that in England he moved in a somewhat cosmopolitan environment. He had an Italian servant, Julio Mantuano, in his employment in 1569.[4] When he was attempting to avoid arrest in 1578 'a lytell frenche boye' acted as messenger between him and his servants and it was 'in the frenche house' that he lay in hiding and was taken prisoner.[5]

Two anecdotes in the *Arte* go some way towards fixing the date of one of its writer's visits to the continent. These point to his presence in Flanders, probably in the spring of 1566. Unfortunately, neither anecdote can be dated precisely. The first (p. 271) indicates his presence in Brussels at a banquet given to the Earl of Arundel by Margaret, Duchess of Parma, and William

---

1 P.R.O., S.P. 12/127/27, Item 5.
2 P.R.O., S.P. 12/127/26, Item 5.
3 P.R.O., S.P. 12/127/27, Item 5.
4 P.R.O., S.P. Foreign, Elizabeth, S.P. 70/111/627 (olim 795).
5 P.R.O., S.P. 12/127/28, Item 2; that the Puttenham family had some connection with the continent earlier than any *recorded* visit is seen from the fact that a certain 'John ffrances mayanza' (or 'magansa') was in Richard's employment c. 1558 (P.R.O., C. 2 Eliz./R 10/27).

of Orange some time after 27 March;[1] the second (p. 279) points to his presence at Spa at the same time as 'a Marshall of Fraunce called *Monsieur de Sipier*', whose physicians 'had all giuen him vp'. The 'Marshall' has been identified with Philibert de Marcilly, seigneur de Cipièrre, who died at Liège in September 1566.[2]

George Puttenham appears to have been in England on 3 and 13 April and 23 July 1566.[3] It is possible that he visited the continent sometime this year, though there

1 The banquet cannot have taken place before this date since William of Orange was until then at Breda (*Correspondance de Guillaume le Taciturne*, ed. Gachard, 1850, Vol. 2, pp. 134–5). We accept, for the sake of argument, Capt. Ward's assumption that the Brussels banquet referred to in the *Arte* coincided with this particular visit of Arundel's to Italy, though there is no conclusive proof that it did.

2 This identification of Capt. Ward's (*v. R.E.S.*, *loc. cit.* p. 299) has been accepted provisionally, but it is far from conclusive and a great deal can still be said for Croft's identification of 'Monsieur de Sipier' with François de Scépeaux, Sire de Vieilleville (*The Governour*, Vol. 1, Introduction, p. clxxxvi), since the latter was a Marshal of France and Capt. Ward's candidate was not. Confusion between de Cipièrre and de Scépeaux, who were both distinguished soldiers, may have led the writer of the *Arte* to credit the former with the latter's rank, but the pension of 'six thousand crownes' referred to in the *Arte* (p. 279) is a crux, since no evidence is forthcoming that de Cipièrre received a reward for his services, while de Vieilleville received 10,000 écus in 1569 from Charles IX. The situation is then that de Cipièrre was not a Marshal of France and there is no evidence that he received a royal pension, but he died near Spa at a date conveniently close to the assumed date of the Brussels banquet to make identification with him tempting. De Vieilleville was a Marshal of France and received a royal pension, but died in France in 1571. The honours seem to be easy. We have, of course, no right to assume that the physicians' forebodings were speedily fulfilled and that a man who lay seriously ill at Spa necessarily died there. Spa waters and 'six thousand crownes' may have given the 'Marshall' a new lease of life and once this possibility is admitted the evidence for de Cipièrre's identification with the 'de Sipier' mentioned in the *Arte* is slight. Even if we accept Capt. Ward's identification, we have no warrant to assume (as Capt. Ward does) that the writer of the *Arte* was at Spa in September 1566. De Cipièrre may have been ill at Spa for months. The evidence is, indeed, so highly conflicting that it is rash to press identification on the present evidence and the absence of conclusive proof of the date of the Brussels banquet puts the whole question of the writer of the *Arte*'s presence in Flanders in 1566 on a purely hypothetical basis. In any case, it is unwise to attach too much importance to anecdotes introduced as illustration of a point rather than as the record of a fact.

3 P.R.O., C. 54/700, no. 62; C. 54/723, no. 37. The evidence for Puttenham's whereabouts at this time is, like that for Lumley's (cf. *supra*, p. xiii, n. 3), inconclusive.

is no evidence that he did. We know that he was in Flanders in 1563 and that he was abroad at least once between then and 1578. No licences to leave the country exist for 1566, but since Puttenham's name does not appear on the list for 1573–8 (the only Elizabethan list still extant) his undated second visit to the continent, which must have been between 1563 and 1573, may have been in 1566.

(8) The writer of the *Arte* was a friend of Sir John Throckmorton (p. 179).

George Puttenham was Throckmorton's brother-in-law and there is every indication of a firm and long-standing friendship between them. Capt. Ward argued that Puttenham could not have written the *Arte* in view of his quarrel with Sir John Throckmorton in 1578,[1] but the breach between them seems to have been only temporary. The friendship dated back to Puttenham's Inns of Court days[2] and for the next twenty years (until Throckmorton's death in 1580) Puttenham's debt of gratitude accumulated at compound interest. It was Sir John who rescued him from financial difficulties, who bailed him out of prison[3] and who acted as buffer between Puttenham and the Privy Council in the long dispute with Lady Elizabeth Windsor. Consideration for others was not, however, Puttenham's strong point and in 1578 he exhausted the patience of both Sir John and his brother, Richard. The latter wrote[4] abusing him roundly for his 'ingrate lettres' to Sir John, who had 'strayned him selfe, his purse, his creditt, yea his lande' on his behalf and reminded him that Throckmorton was the only friend he had and the only person

1 P.R.O., S.P. 12/126/64.
2 *Middle Temple Records: Minutes of Parliament*, Vol. I, p. 119.
3 P.R.O., S.P. 12/127/27, Item 5.
4 P.R.O., S.P. 12/127/32. The letter is unsigned but opens 'Brother'. Since it is clearly addressed to George Puttenham and since George and Richard were now the only surviving sons of Robert Puttenham (P.R.O., C. 2 Eliz./P 11/49) there is strong presumptive evidence that the writer was Richard.

likely to stand by him. Sir John was plainly at his wits'
end to know how to bring his brother-in-law to a more
reasonable frame of mind. For five years Puttenham
had ignored, or parried by excuses, orders from the
Archbishop of Canterbury and the Privy Council concerning his wife's allowance and, now that Fabian tactics
would no longer avail and the Privy Council had issued
a warrant for his arrest, he had gone into hiding and
could not be found. He refused to see Sir John, whom
the Privy Council had made responsible for his appearance, but addressed to him 'many frivolous notes'
which Throckmorton answered 'in some Collour'.[1]
Neither threats, promises nor persuasions could lure him
from his hiding-place and, in view of his conduct, Sir
John's comments on his ingratitude are mild. A desire
to do his best for his brother-in-law, however, outlived
his anger and, in spite of the difficulties in which
Puttenham had involved him, he continued to add to
his debt of gratitude. He effected his arrest (as the
Privy Council demanded), 'thoughe for allyance sake,
very loth to endanger him',[2] but he satisfied for the
time being Lady Windsor's financial needs[3] and six
months later, when an agreement in the long dispute
was reached, he stood as Puttenham's surety.[4] 'No
night that harbourd rankor in his breast' is a trait com-
mented on by the writer of the *Arte* in his epitaph on
Sir John Throckmorton (p. 179) and few men can
have had such cause as Puttenham to remember him
as 'a deere friend' and to record his 'many commendable vertues'.[5]

Two more references in the *Arte* have been invested
with some autobiographical significance by Capt. Ward.
Its writer narrates an anecdote concerning the first

---

1 P.R.O., S.P. 12/127/28, Item 1.
2 P.R.O., S.P. 12/127/25.   3 *Ibid.*
4 *Acts of the Privy Council*, 1578–80, pp. 189, 299.
5 Cf. 'Ne neuer were his values so well knowen,
     Whilest he liued here, as now that he is gone.'

2   (xxix)

parliament of Mary's reign. It opens with 'I remember in the first yeare of Queenes Maries raigne a Knight of Yorkshire was chosen speaker of the Parliament' (p. 139). From this Capt. Ward infers that the writer must have been present as a member of this parliament. The point of the anecdote, however, turns not so much on what happened in the parliament as on the comment on the speaker's oration of 'a bencher of the Temple both well learned and very eloquent, returning from the Parliament house'. The writer need, therefore, have known nothing more of the matter than the bencher's comment[1] and there is no more reason for supposing that he was a member of this parliament than that he was a member of the parliament of Henry VIII from which he reports a speech ostensibly *verbatim* (p. 192).

The second anecdote is assigned by Capt. Ward to the royal progress in Huntingdonshire in 1564, but, again, there is nothing to show that the writer was present when the incident he describes took place. According to Stow, 'in the yeere 1564 Guylliam Boonen, a dutchman, became the Queenes Coach manne and was the first that brought the vse of Coaches into England',[2] so that the story of the countryman who, seeing one for the first time, bade the Queen's coachman 'stay' his 'cart' (p. 259) might long have been remembered in connection with this progress and have come to the ears of many who were not present when the incident occurred. The fact that the writer of the *Arte* uses this anecdote as an illustration of *Tapinosis* and that Peacham gives as an example of the same figure 'to call...a Ladyes Coutch a Carte'[3] suggests that the anecdote

1 That the writer of the *Arte* had no very accurate memory of this parliament is seen in his confusion over the Speaker's identity (*v.* Gregory Smith, *Elizabethan Critical Essays*, Vol. 2, pp. 418-9).

2 *Annales*, 1615, p. 867.

3 *Garden of Eloquence,* 1577, Sig. Gij^r.

may owe more to tradition (and possibly literary suggestion) than appears on the surface.

On this biographical evidence it is impossible to establish George Puttenham's claim to the authorship of the *Arte* with any finality, although the majority of the facts concerning his life correspond fairly closely with what is known of the writer of the *Arte*. He was about eighteen when Edward VI came to the throne and may have written *Elpine* to celebrate his accession. There are indications that his environment was less insular than that of the average Englishman of his day and his handwriting points to his having spent a considerable time abroad in his early years. He had studied law and there is some evidence that Harington's 'Putnam' was a 'suttle lawyer'. He was well-connected both by birth and marriage. He was a friend of Sir John Throckmorton, was acquainted with the court, and related by marriage to Dyer and the Earl of Oxford. He was rewarded by Elizabeth for his services. He had intellectual interests and his *Justificacion* not only shows considerable ability but argues that he enjoyed a high reputation as a writer. There are, however, uncharted periods of his life and on some points, where evidence of his whereabouts at a particular time or stage in his career is lacking, uncertainties exist. There is no proof that he was educated abroad or that he was in Flanders in 1566. From such facts of his life as can be recovered, however, it can be claimed that it is possible that he was the author of the *Arte*. An examination of the non-biographical evidence provided by *Partheniades*, the *Arte* and the *Justificacion* offers convincing proof of common authorship.

Partheniades,[1] which has been curiously neglected in

---

1 B.M., MS. Cotton Vesp. E viii, fols. 169ʳ–78ʳ. The collection has been twice edited: by Haslewood (with the *Arte*) in 1811 and by W. R. Morfill, *Ballads from MSS.* (Ballad Soc. Publ.), 1873, Vol. 2, pp. 72–91. The latter text has been used throughout this Introduction.

attempts to identify the author of the *Arte*, sheds some very distinctive light on its anonymous writer, more particularly on his political and religious views. The first Partheniad introduces the collection as a New Year's gift to the Queen. The last, which refers to Elizabeth's twenty years' reign, suggests 1579 as the date when they were assembled.[1] 'Twentye yeare agon' may, of course, be only a rough estimate of the time that had elapsed since Elizabeth's accession, and a suspicion that too literal an interpretation of the round number cannot be pressed is confirmed by the opening lines of the first poem:

> Gracious Princesse, Where princes are in place
> To geue you gold, and plate, and perles of price,
> It seemeth this day.

This suggests the presence of royalty at court when it was written and points to the New Year of 1581–2, when Alençon was in England, rather than 1579, when the reference to 'princes' would have no point.[2] Capt. Ward argued that *Partheniades* could not be the work of a Puttenham since there is no record of either George or Richard ever having presented a New Year's gift to the Queen,[3] but too literal an interpretation of what was a recognised literary device cannot be pressed and the first Partheniad must be taken as the record of a complimentary intention rather than an actual fact. This is confirmed by the writer's own words, in which

---

1 It is unwise to assume that these poems were written at one time. Some wavering in the writer's point of view on Elizabeth's marriage problem suggests that their composition may have been spread over several years. In some poems Elizabeth's determination to remain single is praised; in others a French marriage alliance is urged.

2 Some support is lent to the theory of a date *c.* 1581–2 for some of these poems by the reference to Alençon as having 'bidd repulse of the great Britton Mayde' in Parth. 8 (*v. Partheniades*, ed. Morfill, p. 80, n. 1).

3 In any case, since the lists of New Year's gifts to Elizabeth are incomplete, generalisation is risky.

he introduces his collection as 'in nature of a New
yeares gifte' to the Queen, and its anonymity in itself
precluded its having been formally presented.[1] The
poems consist mainly of eulogies of Elizabeth but three
(3, 9 and 10) regret that she had no son to succeed
her and that the project of a French marriage alliance
had come to nothing. Two others (13 and 14) assess
the seriousness of the puritan menace to society and
the state. They make it clear that their writer was a man
of strong antipathy to puritanism on aesthetic and
social grounds. The 'pompe' of 'prelates' was a part
of the pageantry of life that he enjoyed. That he was
no 'papist' is clear from references in the *Arte* to the
'excessiue authoritie of Popes' (p. 12) and 'the rable
of Monkes' (p. 14), regarded as propagators of ignorance in the Dark Ages.

The eleventh Partheniad examines some pagan and
Christian notions concerning the origin and end of the
world. Its writer's unmistakable preference for the
atomic theory of 'praty moates' over belief in a deity
who had created, but would one day 'in his rage'
wantonly destroy, expresses as openly heterodox a criticism of popular Christian teaching as is to be found in
Elizabethan literature. The writer of *Partheniades* was,
therefore, a man who hated puritanism, desired a state
religion which was aesthetically satisfying and con-
ducive to political and social harmony, and in his heart
inclined to a roomy deism incompatible with strict
Christian orthodoxy.

George Puttenham's religious views were definitely
antagonistic to puritanism. There are records of clashes
with two reforming bishops—the Calvinistic Grindall,
Bishop of London, whose murder he was accused of

1 If in January 1579 books against a French alliance were found in the
Queen's Chamber (Neale, *Queen Elizabeth*, 1934, p. 240), there is no reason
why *Partheniades* should not have been brought to the Queen's notice in a
similar way.

having conspired in 1569,[1] and Robert Horne, Bishop
of Winchester, who on hearing that Puttenham had
been appointed to the Commission of the Peace for
Hampshire wrote to Cecil protesting that he was a man
of 'evil life' and a 'notorious enemye to God's Truthe'.[2]
That Puttenham did not share Horne's reforming zeal
is confirmed by a deposition in a lawsuit of a few years
later in which the deponent described how Puttenham
'hadd in certeine Coffers Lienge in Sherfeild. . . secretly
hidden and laied vpp to no good purpos', stoles, copes,
vestments, mass books, psalters 'and soche lyke trum-
perie fitt for the service of the masse and other Papisticall
Service'.[3] His *Justificacion*, however, is the work of a
loyal supporter of Elizabeth in Church as well as State,
with no sympathy for the 'follie and arrogancie' of
'papistes' and plotters (p. 99). There is thus strong
evidence for assuming that he was a man who combined
an acceptance of the Elizabethan church settlement with
a leaning towards traditional ritual and a hatred of
puritans. That his opinions were probably not merely
anti-puritan but, to a rigid mind, scandalously irreligious
is implied in Horne's denunciation, for his censure (in
the same letter) of the Catholics, Sir Robert Oxenbridge
and Ralph Scrope, is accompanied by no such horrified
condemnation of their views as of Puttenham's. Sug-
gestions such as those in the eleventh Partheniad would
certainly have seemed to Horne a flagrant denial of
'God's Truthe'.

The similarity between Puttenham's point of view
and that of the writer of *Partheniades* comes out even
more strongly in their attitude towards the practical
application of religion. The writer of *Partheniades* was
a man with a realist and tolerant outlook on the world

---

1 P.R.O., S.P. 70/111/627 (*olim* 795). This deposition, taken in April
1570, alleges that the murder of the Bishop of London was broached by
Puttenham five months earlier.
2 *Salisbury MSS.*, Pt. 1, p. 393.   3 P.R.O., C. 2 Eliz./P 11/49.

as it is. The purpose of the thirteenth Partheniad is to show 'What thinges in nature, common reason, and cyvill pollicye goe so faste linked together as they maye not easilye bee soonedred without preiudice to the politike bodye, whatsoever evill or absurditye seeme in them'. The maintenance of the state and even of religion, its writer argues, depends on a wise acceptance of the alloy in their currency. A strikingly similar point of view is expressed at the close of George Puttenham's *Justificacion*:

> yt is found that the law of God yt self doth often tymes, and in manie cases, dispence with such manner of fraielties as tend to the universall benifite of mankynd and manteinaunce of the civill societye, using a marvelous myld, and gentell tolleracion of them, knowinge [that] we be, where our lief and conversacion is to continew at his appoinctment, what our wekenes is, and the manifould impedimentes of our perfection, and for spetiall regardes importynge the universall comfort of man (pp. 133–4).

In *Partheniades* and this passage in the *Justificacion* there is the same stress on the prime importance of civilisation and society and both writers agree as to the expediency of tolerating necessary evils and recognise the rôle they play in holding together the social fabric. That evil is inherent in good is the argument of the thirteenth Partheniad; that good may come of evil is the explicit statement of the close of George Puttenham's *Justificacion*: 'God him self suffringe some few evelles to preferre manie goodes'. The arguments are not, of course, the same, but they spring from the same belief that good and evil are not necessarily irreconcilable and antithetical forces but in some measure inseparable and complementary. To most contemporaries this willingness to accept the alloy in the metal must have appeared dangerously unorthodox and the refusal to see good and evil as a simple problem that can be expressed in terms of black and white narrows the search for the writer of *Partheniades* to a very few. Of the few who might have shared this view, George Puttenham was certainly one.

Further, *Partheniades* and (to a lesser degree) the *Arte* are the work of a man who felt confident of his capacity to play the part of man of affairs as well as of man of letters. *Partheniades*, as has been seen, was not merely a formal contribution to the poet's chorus of praise of Elizabeth but was partly inspired by a desire to direct her policy in political and religious matters. The writer of the *Arte* breaks the thread of his argument to warn Elizabeth of the inadvisability of interfering in Dutch affairs (*v.* Appendix I, p. 314) and to comment on the 'wisdome and pacience' she had shown towards Mary, Queen of Scots (p. 248). This is compatible with George Puttenham's habits and political views. Too free an expression of his opinions on the Queen's counsellors (especially Leicester) involved him in serious charges in 1570,[1] so that it would be natural to find him advocating the French marriage and putting a spoke in Leicester's wheels by reviling the Dutch. The passage in the *Arte* on Mary, Queen of Scots, is entirely in keeping with the point of view of the lengthier *Justificacion* (cf. especially p. 80). Proof of the recognition of his ability to fill the dual rôle of man of affairs and letters is provided by Elizabeth's choice of him as her advocate.

In addition to these general points of similarity, there is a passage in the *Justificacion* which embodies both a striking parallel in idea and a sequence of verbal echoes reminiscent of one of the prose headings in *Partheniades*:

> others undeservedlie *maligning* her Highnes greate *prosperi-tyes* and glorie (such hath allways bene the nature of *envie*

1 P.R.O., S.P. 12/66/43, iii and iv, Items 16 and 17; S.P. 70/111/627 (*olim* 795).

and reward of the greatest and most excellent *vertue*.....
(*Justificacion*, p. 67.)

That *vertue* ys alwayes subiect to *envy* and many times to
perill; and yf her Maiesties most notable *prosperities* haue
ever beene *maligned*, the same hath beene for her only
vertues sake. (Partheniad 6.)

The same idea, applied to the same person, in the same
words, makes it seem impossible that this echo is
merely coincidence.

A comparison of the *Arte* and *Justificacion* yields
further evidence of common authorship. One of the
most striking features of the *Arte* is its 'copiousness'
of vocabulary. Many words which are now a part of
the current language—*multiformity, predatory, rotundity,
insect, grandiloquence, presupposal, reminiscence*[1]—are recorded as occurring here for the first time. The writer
recognises that many of the words he uses will be un-
familiar to his readers and he explains their meaning
and justifies their use. A similar 'copiousness' is quite
the most striking linguistic feature of the *Justificacion*.
It is impossible to read it without being struck continually by words which seem beyond the range of
sixteenth-century expression. Puttenham was not merely
abreast of his day but far ahead of it in the adequacy
of his vocabulary. Many of the words he uses anticipate
by some years (and one or two of them by many) the
first recorded use. Among these are *equitable* (first recorded by the *N.E.D.* in 1646), *equitably* (1663), *ir-
resolution* (1592), *negotiate* (1599), *infringement* (1593),
intertraffic (1603), *eminency* (1602), *competency* (1594),
incompetent (1597), *incompetency* (1611), *disproportioned*
(1597).[2] Two of these, *negotiate* and *disproportioned*,
occur in the *Arte*.[3] Another new word common to both
works is the noun *politian*.[4] The word was one which

1 Pp. 19, 38, 101, 150, 150, 196, 306.
2 Pp. 68, 107, 74, 78, 93, 97, 120, 121, 121, 121, 127.
3 Pp. 293 (*negotiate, negotiating*), 153 (*disproportioned*).
4 *Arte*, p. 146; *Justificacion*, p. 126.

(xxxvii)

the writer of the *Arte* picked out for special comment (p. 146). It was apparently just coming into use in the eighties and the first recorded use is from Lyly's *Sappho* (1584). No very great weight, therefore, can be attached to its appearance a few years later in both the *Arte* and the *Justificacion*. What is significant is that in the copy of the *Justificacion* which Puttenham corrected himself[1] and which can, therefore, be assumed to represent a copy of his own manuscript the word is italicised, indicating that he recognised it as a word not in general circulation. That it was not generally understood is seen from one manuscript in which the copyist took it as a proper name and altered it to 'Polinices'.[2]

There are hints that Puttenham was the same stickler for linguistic exactness as the writer of the *Arte*. In the *Justificacion* he pauses to point out his deliberate choice of the word *abode* rather than *captivity* or *restraint* (p. 78) and to gloss the word *incompetent* (first recorded in 1597)—'incompetent, that is, not fitt to be admitted to deeme of her fact' (p. 121). Further evidence that he paid a strict attention to the use of words is provided by his deposition concerning certain charges in 1570. To the question 'dyd not you speake anie thing of the great goodnes showed vnto the right honorable Therle of leycestre by the Quenes Maiestie'[3] he replied 'he can not tell what ys ment by the worde goodnesse'.[4] Whether his caustic reply was intended to pillory a euphemistic evasion in the word or merely its vagueness is not clear, but it shows the same fastening upon the word as we find in the *Arte* and it would not have occurred to the average Elizabethan to seize on this point.

The number of new words in the *Arte* and the *Justificacion* cannot, of course, be claimed as conclusive evidence of common authorship. English vocabulary was

1 Bodl., MS. Add. C. 83, fol. 28ᵛ. 2 Ed. Camden Society, p. 126, n. 1.
3 P.R.O., S.P. 12/66/43, iii, Item 16.
4 P.R.O., S.P. 12/66/43, iv, Reply to Item 16.

still expanding rapidly and any Elizabethan work of the eighties with pretence to 'copy' embodies a number of words not hitherto recorded. What is significant is that the vocabulary of the *Arte* and *Justificacion* is that of a man who, while he retained certain habits of speech acquired in his youth (e.g. expressions such as *acknowen* and *to weet*), had at the same time maintained a linguistically receptive mind that was still capable of absorbing new words. By the mid-eighties George Puttenham and the writer of the *Arte* were old men, yet their vocabulary, even when compared with that of much younger contemporaries, surprises by its adequacy and very modern ring. Moreover, the new words they use have the same flavour. They are not (like much of the new vocabulary of the eighties and early nineties) examples of linguistic extravagance which failed to survive their day, but words which exemplify the taste and fastidious discrimination on which the writer of the *Arte* lays such stress.

The style of the *Justificacion* is very similar to that of the *Arte*, but an almost complete absence of mannerisms makes it difficult to demonstrate wherein their similarity lies. Both are characterised by the somewhat loose and involved sentence structure of a man who, unlike most of his contemporaries, is concentrating on matter rather than manner. Both are remarkable for the absence of balancing, alliteration, translacing, antithesis and similar rhetorical devices which mark the more ambitious prose of the eighties. There is in both the same loose and easy sequence of clauses and the same lack of sentence finish. One noticeable trick of style, however, is common to both works. In both an adjective of foreign origin is frequently placed after the noun it qualifies. This is, of course, not exceptional. It occurs with fairly consistent regularity in early-Tudor works (e.g. *The Governour*), but it is comparatively rare by the eighties. The identity of George Puttenham and the writer of the *Arte* cannot, therefore, be argued from this, but that two works should exemplify as their most striking linguistic characteristics the survival of the same early-Tudor habit, the same disregard of the prevailing trend towards a deliberately patterned sentence-structure, and an easy manipulation of an amazingly up-to-date and discriminating vocabulary affords strong testimony of common authorship.

Behind these two works lie the same mental habits, the same personality and the same convictions. In both, 'nature' and 'common reason' are the authorities to which the writer defers and in both the ability to express an opinion without reference to 'authority' is remarkable. The author of the *Arte* can write on poetry without once referring to classical or patristic pronouncements either against it or in its favour. In the *Justificacion* Puttenham bases his arguments on 'the law of nature and reason, wherupon all other lawes ar grounded' (p. 107) rather than on 'texts, and authorities of Lawes' to whose absence he himself draws attention.[1] The arguments throughout the work are, indeed, prompted by the three considerations stressed in the thirteenth Partheniad: 'nature, common reason, and cyvill pollicye'. It cannot be claimed that these traits were unique, but minds of this calibre were exceedingly rare in Elizabethan England. A conviction that common sense is a better guide than accepted opinion or authority is, indeed, exceptional among serious thinkers of Puttenham's day.

Consequently the conclusions of the *Arte* and the *Justificacion* are personal and are frankly expressed as such:

> Yf the heraultes will saie otherwise by ther art and profession, I woulde be gladd to heare how they wilbe able to infirme my opinion. (*Justificacion*, p. 105.)

1 B.M., MS. Harl. 831, p. 132. The final peroration in which this statement is made (pp. 132–6, 'Now for the maintenance...death so long') is omitted in some MSS. and the Camden Society edition.

> Now againe at this time, the young Gentlemen of the Court haue taken vp the long haire trayling on their shoulders, and thinke it more decent: for what respect I would be glad to know. (*Arte*, p. 286.)

> And sence, in my humble conceit, they may be in both cases said the law of Armes...it is a meare follie for anie prisoner abusynge thone to appeale for helpe to thother. (*Justificacion*, p. 110.)

> ...the ancient guise in old times vsed at weddings (in my simple opinion) nothing reproueable. (*Arte*, p. 51.)

The same urbanely self-confident note is heard throughout these passages and the pleasantly personal strain that runs through the *Arte* and the ironic assurance of the *Justificacion* express the same, somewhat egotistic, personality.

Both works are marked by a love of analysis and distinctions. The writer of the *Arte* delights in linguistic 'niceties' (p. 251) and 'the differences of things' (p. 263):

> Therefore to discusse and make this point somewhat cleerer, to weete, where arte ought to appeare, and where not, and when the naturall is more commendable than the artificiall in any humane action or workmanship, we wil examine it further by this distinction. (p. 303.)

Puttenham responds with equal alacrity to opportunities for establishing a distinction:

> For clearinge of which poinct, and satisfaction of manie irresolute myndes, we must needes saie somewhat, and for manner sake more then for anie necessitie. (p. 118.)

> To which purpose we will explaine the matter better with this distinction. (p. 119.)

Both these sentences might have come from the *Arte* and might have been quoted as examples of the characteristic manner in which its writer drew attention to a problem and settled down to the congenial task of analysis.

Lastly, what is to Puttenham the final and conclusive justification of Elizabeth's action is the conviction which distinguishes the approach to poetry in the *Arte* from all contemporary works on the same theme. Elizabeth, Puttenham argues, has only done what everyone else would have done in similar circumstances 'and will not refuse to doo whiles the world contineweth, that is, rather to kill then to be killed' (p. 132). In this natural and universal instinct, 'growinge out of our owne willes, and beynge bred in our fleshe and bloud', he sees nothing 'straunge or horrible' (p. 133). An unwritten natural law based on universal human instinct is, he argues, as infallible a guide for human conduct as 'anie other ordinaunce or constitucion of man' (p. 133). That he attached considerable importance to this argument is seen by the manner in which he produces it as the final and clinching proof of his case. All other considerations (the legality of Mary's imprisonment, the justice of her trial) are brushed aside while he vindicates the right of human nature to control human affairs. It is this same refusal to see anything 'straunge or horrible' in the expression of human impulses which moulds and determines the conception of poetry underlying the *Arte*. Its writer refuses to be limited or baulked by the Renaissance interpretation of poetry from an ethical standpoint. He sees it as the expression of the whole range of human interests and needs. Consequently he is unconcerned with allegories and dark conceits. An allegory is to him merely a figure of speech and not a means of reconciling the poet and the moralist. Love poetry justifies itself because 'there is no frailtie in flesh and bloud so excusable' as love (p. 48). His point of view is epitomised in his brief but firm dismissal of Cicero's condemnation of dancing:

> but there by your leaue he failed, nor our young Courtiers will allow it, besides that it is the most decent and comely demeanour of all exultations and reioycements of the hart, which is no lesse naturall to man then to be wise or well learned, or sober. (p. 292.)

The voice of authority cannot shake his conviction that delight is as natural as sobriety and that what is natural is right. In the latter half of the sixteenth century this point of view was rare. Critics and writers tacked a heavy course against a widespread distrust of human nature, and this willingness to accept as legitimate the expression of natural instincts limits the search for the author of the *Arte* to a very small number of Elizabethans.

The similarity between these three works is all the more striking in view of the difference in their subject-matter. The *Arte* was originally composed, without thought of publication, for Elizabeth and a courtly circle and was, therefore, written with ease and intimacy. *Partheniades* is a collection of poems written with the threefold object of complimenting Elizabeth on her wise and moderate procedure in affairs of state and religion, of warning her of the social and aesthetic menace of puritanism, and of pointing out that her duty was to provide her subjects with an heir to the throne. The *Justificacion* is a serious piece of sustained argument written to convince 'persons, both princelie and private' of the justice and necessity of the execution of Mary, Queen of Scots. 'Decorum' had to be observed and the subject precluded the confidences and light-hearted excursions in which the writer of the *Arte* indulged. Superficially, therefore, the *Justificacion* offers so few points of contact with the *Arte* and *Partheniades* that the existence of so many common features in the three works cannot be lightly dismissed. These range from similarity in point of view and mental habits to details of style and verbal echoes and all three are linked by a common feature and a common impulse: each, in aim and execution, is the work of an adept apologist and all three are actuated by the same motive—duty and homage to Elizabeth. No one factor is in itself sufficient to prove George Puttenham's authorship of all three works, but the cumulative weight of the evidence seems conclusive. Two years after it appeared in print Harington described the *Arte* as 'Putnams book' and in view of the variety of the evidence in George Puttenham's favour it is impossible not to believe that he was the Puttenham to whom Harington referred. The *Arte* and *Partheniades* are not works which any Elizabethan might have written. They bear the stamp of a mind and personality sufficiently rare to make its expression quite distinctive. Such a mind and personality George Puttenham had.

II. THE DATE OF THE *ARTE*

Arber in 1869, after noting the inconclusive internal evidence for the *Arte*'s date, suggested that it was written about 1585 but partially revised before publication, and here the question of its date has generally been left. Though since the end of the eighteenth century there have been suspicions that the book may contain earlier material, it has not, in general, been pushed far enough back, and all attempts to assign it to any one year, or indeed any one decade, inevitably break down before conflicting evidence. In works of reference in current use the *Arte* is definitely placed in the post-Sidney tradition and is, as a rule, associated with Webbe's *Discourse* (1586).

When closely studied, however, the book recedes from this position. Large portions of it are difficult to blend with the spirit and activities of the 'busier pageant' of the eighties, whereas a student of mid-Tudor literature finds himself strangely at home. Once this impression of an earlier world has been recognised, corroboration springs up on every side to deepen impression into conviction.

The scope and solidity of the work at once mark it off from a literature of Apologies, Discourses and 'abiect abbreuiations of Arts'; its humanistic quality links it with Elyot's *Governour* (1531), Wilson's *Arte of Rhetorique* (1553) and Ascham's *Scholemaster* (1570). There is, too, an authentic note of pioneership, incompatible with composition between 1585 and 1589; as soon as he leaves classical or continental tradition for English ground the author claims to be the first in the field, an αὐτοδίδακτος. His world of poetry is dominated by the early-Tudor courtly makers. His textbook is the *Songes and Sonettes* (1557); no other work competes with this as a source of illustration. Drama is to him a matter of morality plays and interludes. The numerous quotations from his own works show him to have possessed an ear satisfied with the movements and phrasing bequeathed to the mid-century by early-Tudor drama and the *Songes and Sonettes*—movements which differ radically from the heavy iambic stroke of the Turberville-Gascoigne stage and from the more mellifluous cadences of the Sidney-Spenser group.

In still other respects the *Arte* detaches itself from the interests and activities of the eighties. It has no connection with the puritan attack on poetry, music or stage plays. The only hints of controversy or debate are the statement of its thesis 'That there may be an Art of our English Poesie, aswell as there is of the Latine and Greeke' (I, ii) and a few sentences in defence of wit, 'solace' and the Figures. This is all the more remarkable since in *Partheniades* (c. 1581–2) Puttenham showed himself more deeply and sensitively aware of the exact nature of the puritan menace to life and the arts than did the majority of the anti-Martinists.

He appears as unconscious of the Press as of the puritan. Though he is content that the people shall have their romances, ballads and pageants, he shows himself unaware of any popular invasion of the literary field. In the eighties, in the works of Webbe, Nashe and others, the recent increase of printing activity, the 'infinite fardles of printed pamphlets, wherewith thys Countrey is pestered', became a commonplace. Puttenham writes with a serene unconsciousness of both the opportunities and dangers of the Press. In this, it may be argued, he is merely maintaining the old tradition of aristocratic aloofness (an attitude that had become completely ostrich-like by 1585-9), but to refrain from rushing into print under one's own name is a different matter from affecting ignorance of the very existence of a popular press. Sidney maintains the aristocratic tradition, but he feels himself under no compulsion to feign ignorance of the printers' wares.

Again, as a survey of the *status quo* in the latter eighties, the *Arte* is surprisingly inadequate. This is strikingly illustrated by a comparison with the packed allusions of Nashe's Preface to *Menaphon* (1589) or even with Webbe's *Discourse* (1586). There is only a casual reference to the 'Gentleman who wrate the late shepheardes Callender' (p. 63), whereas to Nashe Spenser is England's defence against the foreigner's challenge and to Webbe the *Shepheardes Calender* is almost what the *Songes and Sonettes* was to Puttenham. There is no mention of Lyly, Fraunce or Watson. Though so keen a prosodist, Puttenham overlooks blank verse. The Theatre had been built since 1576, but the word *'theater'* only occurs in the *Arte* in an archaeological context. It requires italics as an incompletely denizened word and is carefully connected with *'theatrum,* as much to say as a beholding place' (p. 37).

The prose of the *Arte* speaks even more indubitably of an earlier and simpler world than that of the eighties. It is freer from any trace of 'euphuistic' patterning than the prose of Gascoigne. Though there is a fundamentally strenuous preoccupation with language, there is no hint of that emotional excitement over words and sentences which marks the post-Euphuistic phase. Puttenham disposes of an easy, ample and discriminating vocabu-

lary, but the monitory shadow of Sir John Cheke still
looms behind him. There is nothing to show that he
anticipated, or would have welcomed, the 'gold rush for
vocabulary' in which towards the end of the sixteenth
century England competed with other nations.

The inference from these facts is that the main lines
of the *Arte* were laid down before the puritan menace
materialised and before the popular invasion of the
literary field had attracted attention. Its writer naturally,
therefore, uses the quieter accents of a more slowly
moving world. The hypothesis of an old man setting
about the composition of a book in 1585 and, through
failure to adapt himself to the new age, overweighting
his work in the direction of the studies of his youth is
inadequate to explain the facts. There is no sign in the
Arte of any hardening of the mental arteries. It is,
moreover, a carefully planned book; had its scheme first
been thought out about 1585 the emphasis and proportions must have been different.

At the same time parts of the book undoubtedly date
from the eighties. If the more sustained passages re-
flecting the interests of this decade are carefully read
in their context, they reveal themselves as reconsiderations or interpolations and point irresistibly to the con-
clusion that shorter references to similar material are
likewise insertions in an earlier matrix that was once
complete without them. These islands of later reference,
with one important exception, group themselves into
an archipelago stretching over the latter part of Book II
and the whole of Book III.

Puttenham considered carefully the planning of his
book. He introduced and rounded off judiciously the
different phases of his subject and in particular he seems
to have wished to mark the transition from book to
book by a few words of summary and preparation.
Book I, Ch. xxx was evidently intended to wind up the
largely derivative treatment of the past and to prepare

for the pioneering Book II. The wording ('The part that next followeth') indicates that the new material ('Of Proportion') is to follow immediately. But in our version of the *Arte* we find instead a long chapter (xxxi) of roll-call appreciations of English poets. References to the work of Dyer, Sidney and Raleigh at once assign this chapter to the early eighties. It can unhesitatingly be dubbed an interpolation of *c.* 1585 or even later (cf. pp. cv–cvi). Even if there were no other evidence, the rejoicing over the new generation of courtly poets is incompatible with the gloomy description in Ch. viii of an inhospitable courtly soil. One is tempted to put almost a generation between the two chapters.

The original Book II seems to have ended with Ch. xi. The last paragraph opens with 'To finish the learning of this diuision' and concludes with three forcible repetitive sentences. Anyone who has absorbed Puttenham's style (or happy lack of it) will recognise that no merely stylistic consideration prompts this repetition. We find it because he is clinching his subject and dismissing his book. Ch. xi, however, is less than half-way through the present Book II. It is followed by a series of sections fire-new from the mint of the mid- and latter-eighties. They are concerned with 'courtly trifles' (shaped poems, *imprese*, anagrams) or 'scholastical toyes' (classical numbers in English verse). The section on shaped poems (the first part of Ch. xii) carries no internal evidence of date, but its subject and spirit link it with the effervescent ingenuity of the new courtly world portrayed by Lyly. It was appropriately into this chapter that in 1589, while the book was printing,[1] Puttenham inserted later collections of similar courtly trifles—*imprese* and anagrams. In the following chapters devoted to 'perfite versifying' we turn back four or five years. These chapters, provoked by Stanyhurst's *Aeneis* (1582) and stimulated by a temporary courtly vogue,

---

[1] *V.* Bibliographical Note, pp. civ–cv.

assign themselves without any difficulty to the early eighties. They are, moreover, indubitable reconsiderations, for they retract Puttenham's repeated refusals earlier to admit 'feet' in English measures. In the complete version of the *Arte* the eight inserted pages on *imprese* and anagrams are thus interpolation within interpolation.

In Book III there is no such simple stratification. Continuity with the earlier layer is shown by the use of the same basis of illustration from the *Songes and Sonettes* and the author's own works. We recognise the mid-Tudor quality and outlook in many contexts, notably in the passage on Inkhorn terms (III, iv). All this has been richly reinforced by material from the Gascoigne-layer and from the later courtly school. The book is thickly studded with references to works and personalities of the eighties; the writer quotes his epitaph on Sir John Throckmorton (d. 1580); he refers to the *Arcadia* (*c.* 1580); he quotes from the manuscript poems of Dyer, Sidney, Raleigh and Oxford; Raleigh is known to be knighted (Jan. 1584/5). There seems little doubt that Book III has been extensively reworked and amplified; it has swelled to the proportions of the two other books put together. It is pervaded by the new courtly tone. The single dominating figure of a humanist Queen has been supplemented by a circle of young gentlewomen and gentlemen united in a passionate curiosity concerning the Figures. There is a more fundamental change of tone and manner. Puttenham disposes now of so much material and so many ideas that he cannot be confined within the strict limits of his subject. The critic turns essayist; life and literature interpenetrate. Again, almost a generation seems to intervene between the sedate Book I and the ripest portions of Book III.

There is ample evidence that much new work was put into the book round about 1584 and bibliographical proof of further additions while the work was in the press. There may well be other insertions of different dates but, if so, they do not betray themselves by indubitable chronological signs. Certain small textual details suggest that Puttenham had a habit of working over his manuscript. On p. 86 there are a couple of lines ('And these ten litle meeters' etc.) which appear to have no context. Book II, Ch. ii seems to contain two drafts of the same material. On p. 173 for a prose example a verse piece has been substituted. On p. 185 there is a reference to 'these verses of ours' which should follow but do not. Certain repetitions (on pp. 248–9 of a sentence on p. 247 and on p. 274 of a short passage on p. 259) suggest that there has been some revising or moving about of material.

These major and minor revisions point to a long existence of the work in manuscript and to habits of altering and rearranging. They cannot be dismissed as signs of hasty or careless composition comparable to the symptoms of ill-digested work in Greene's romances and many Elizabethan plays. The *Arte* was not 'yarkt up' in haste; it deepens as it proceeds and the last book, so far from showing anxiety to be at the end, is the least hurried part of the book. How much solid work as well as zest and lively observation has been put into Book III can only be appreciated by comparison with the desiccated legion of Renaissance works on schemes and tropes. The reason why Puttenham revised this book, but in Books I and II was content to interpolate, is not difficult to find. Book III is a book of Language. The exploitation of language was going on at an accelerated pace in the world outside and language was, in any case, his master-interest. He was content to leave where it was the traditional material handled in the first thirty chapters of Book I. It was not now of vital moment. Language, however, he continually watched and studied. The original draft of Book III would seem meagre by the eighties; by then Puttenham had collected ample new material and could speak with the confidence and ease of one who knew himself to be thoroughly *en rapport* with a word- and figure-loving generation.

It has been suggested that nearly a generation lies between the earliest and latest layers. Certainly at least twenty years between the original mid-Tudor book and the post-Armada additions seems the shortest interval that will satisfy the conditions. On this subject a piece of corroborative external evidence seems to lurk in Drummond's confused report (*c.* 1619) of Ben Jonson's reference to the *Arte* as 'done 20 yeers since & Keept Long in wrytte as a secret'. There is manifest confusion here for '20 yeers since' does not correspond with the date of the *Arte*'s publication. The difficulty is generally cleared up by assuming that '20' is an error for '30', but the misunderstanding or misrepresentation may have been more fundamental and what Jonson may have intended to convey was that the *Arte* existed in manuscript twenty years before its publication. This would put the date of the first draft back to *c.* 1569. There was nothing to render unlikely such an undertaking in the sixties. A great deal of lively work in language was going on and Wilson's *Arte of Rhetorique* may well have inspired Puttenham to do for the poet what Wilson had done for the prose writer. There is nothing in the subject-matter of the first thirty chapters of Book I[1] or the first eleven chapters of Book II incompatible with this date. Jonson's '20' may well, of course, have been a round number. We shall not, however, be far wrong if we carry the shaping of the book back to the mid-sixties (the close of the Ascham period);

---

[1] On p. 46 there is a reference to the thirty-one years of Elizabeth's reign. This is almost undoubtedly a printer's correction for there is evidence that the MS. of the *Arte* went to the printer in the form it received *c.* 1585 (*v.* Bibliographical Note, p. cv). It was perhaps the printer who called attention to the anti-Dutch passage (irrelevant and tactless in 1589) and secured an alternative paragraph.

it is from the Cambridge humanists that its main stimulus appears to be derived.

The *Arte* gains enormously in interest from a recognition of its mid-Tudor provenance and of the stratification of the text. Its serenity, in an age so 'iron & malitious' to the arts, and the openness and freedom of its approach to its subject are proof of remarkable independence of temper. The works of Elyot, and still more of Cheke, Smith, Wilson and Ascham, interpreted humanism in a markedly didactic and utilitarian spirit. The *Arte* has its practical side, but its theory and appreciations offer us the least utilitarian, the least moralistic, and the nearest to an aesthetic, approach to poetry made in England in the sixteenth century. As a mid-Tudor work, it also lessens the time-lag in the English response to the more liberating and fruitful influences of the Renaissance spirit. Recognition of its pioneering quality should stimulate the reader to an alerter and more sympathetic appreciation of the originality of the work.

The *Arte* thus viewed illuminates an important formative (but still difficult and obscure) period in our literary history. It helps the whole course of Elizabethan criticism to fall into a more coherent and consistent pattern. It helps us to visualise more perfectly the earliest stages in our critical tradition when, following in the wake of the vernacular movements in Italy and France, Englishmen were roused to a devoted pre-occupation with the actual medium—the words and shapes—of prose and poetry, a more radical and productive interest than any discussion of 'kinds' and 'rules'. It allows us to estimate more precisely the damage done to the formation of a liberal and aesthetic tradition by the emergence of the puritan power at that particular stage in our history.

The apparent inconsistencies of the book now reveal themselves as indices of the growth of an open, flexible mind. The author, over a long period, was 'devising', experimenting and adapting like his age. The *Arte* is a cross-section of critical development. It takes us from one literary world to another and is at home in each. The new men of the eighties were fully aware of the quickening of pace and the complication of the pattern of existence going on all around them. Lyly has perfectly expressed the change in educated England that synchronised with his own emergence into the limelight:

> Trafficke and trauell hath wouen the nature of all Nations into ours, and made this land like Arras, full of deuise, which was Broade-cloth, full of workemanshippe. (Preface to *Midas*.)

The change from broadcloth to arras can actually be traced in the *Arte*. It thus reproduces in itself the patterns of evolution in the pre-Shakespearian Tudor world. By tracing out its earlier and later layers we can watch a revolution in the prosodic apprehension of English metres, we can take soundings of the deepening of the linguistic and literary currents and follow the growth of critical habit and independent judgment. What breadth and perspective this gives the book can only be fully grasped after comparison with, for example, Nashe's Preface to *Menaphon* which, overflowing as it is with vitality, is just the crest of the wave of 1589 and nothing more.

III. PUTTENHAM AS CRITIC

It is, perhaps, coincidence, but nevertheless a fact of considerable significance, that most Elizabethan works of criticism were the output of young men (Lodge, Sidney, Webbe, Nashe, Harington, Carew). The *Arte*, as has been seen, embodies a prolonged experience of Elizabethan life and letters. If it was in being as early as 1569, its author was then about forty and had made his literary début in the reign of Edward VI. The *Arte* is not to be regarded as the essay of a prentice hand in criticism; *De Decoro* and the *Originals and Pedigree of the English Tong* prepared the ground for it. The book is the design of a man's prime. Even in the early and largely derivative Book I we are, accordingly, aware of a firmness and maturity in sharp contrast with the timidity of Webbe or the crudeness of Lodge. It took maturity to draw with combined modesty and decision the line of demarcation between 'sources' and original observation (pp. 58–9) and no little firmness as well as critical sensitiveness to reject so roundly (p. 38) the traditional view of the eclogue as 'the first and most auncient forme of artificiall Poesie'. Puttenham rightly sees it as a product of sophistication and ulterior motives.

In Tudor times, apart from the information collected by chroniclers and antiquaries such as Leland and Bale, knowledge of the mediaeval past was thin and, though much mediaeval work was still circulating and mediaeval themes retained the affections of the populace, the Elizabethan critic was ignorant and scornful of mediaeval achievement. Puttenham approaches the native past with the equipment provided by a gentleman's library of the period and no more can be said for his knowledge than that it compares favourably with that of contemporary critics. He knew, as most Elizabethans did not, that *Piers Plowman* was the title, and not the author, of a work and had some notion of its contents. He recognised the large part played in mediaeval English verse by translation. He had a first-hand knowledge not only of Chaucer but of Gower. He perceived the stylistic importance of the poems of Wyatt and Surrey and saw that they formed a landmark for his century. He illustrates, however, many prevalent misconceptions and limitations. Apart from the chapter where he traces the spread of rhyming Latin in courts and monasteries (I, vii) he can carry the story of our literature no further back than Chaucer. He subscribes, though uncertainly, to the 'vulgar error' that Chaucer and Gower were knights. He fails to note the metrical principles of *Piers Plowman* and his mind was apparently closed to the achievement of Skelton, 'I wot not for what great worthines surnamed the Poet *Laureat*'. What distinguishes him in his review of the English heritage is not knowledge but some evidence of critical temper. He is prepared to accept mediaeval literature as, though benighted, existing in its own right. He refrains from poking superior fun at the romances, 'old aduentures & valiaunces of noble knights', and sees no reason why they should be made to conform to 'the nature & stile of large histories', 'for they be sundry formes of poems and not all one' (p. 42). He would not have wished to see Sidney's 'blinde Crowder' in the rôle of Pindar's ape. He did not grudge the people their 'fit of mirth for a groat' in taverns and alehouses. All he demanded was that the instructed poet should 'know to whose eare he maketh his rime' and not mix his genres as Skelton had done.

It is significant that Puttenham does not, like Webbe, look in Chaucer for morals or 'profitable knowledge' or laud his efficacy as a castigator of vice. He accepts, of course, but without emphasis, the moral and intellectual responsibility of the poet; with classical and Renaissance theory before him and a long series of works blending the *utile* with the *dulce* this was no more than a recognition of the facts. He was, indeed, perfectly prepared by temperament to welcome the Horatian view of poets as the first civilisers of the human race; this notion he elaborates in the early chapters of Book I. He liked to think of poetry as a civilising factor; the word *civil*, which appears so frequently in the *Arte*, clothes his ideal. But civilisation was as much an artistic concept to him as it was social or moral. It was an Art of Living. This comes out very clearly in the chapters on Decorum (III, xxiii–xxiv), where it soon becomes impossible to isolate the literary concept from the social. Each is a principle of adjustment in recognition of the variety of human situation and experience: it is the relativity, not the rigidity, of the notion of Decorum which interests him. It was for a chameleon poet that he collected forms, 'colours' and 'figures' to match the unplanned variety of experience and through art to 'civilise' it, *i.e.* make it pleasing to the senses and intelligible to the mind. Puttenham's way of looking at the Kinds is to see them as so many varieties of response to the whole gamut of human experience and to all the phases of human evolution. It is this which differentiates even the chapter headings in Book I (especially from xii onwards) from the Scaligerian enumeration of the 'revealed' Kinds and Forms. Poetry, as Puttenham shows it to us, wells up from the pressure of every human need and feeling. Thus love poetry follows all the April moods of that passion:

> the poore soules sometimes praying, beseeching, sometime honouring, auancing, praising: an other while railing, reuiling, and cursing: then sorrowing, weeping, lamenting: in the ende laughing, reioysing & solacing the beloued againe, with a thousand delicate deuises, odes, songs, elegies, ballads, sonets and other ditties, moouing one way and another to great compassion. (p. 45.)

There must even be a poetry of malice and irritation, bristling with 'bitter taunts, and priuy nips', because men 'must needs vtter their splenes...or else it seemed their bowels would burst' (p. 54). Puttenham was the last man to be afraid of laughter and his belief in 'Nature' was, unlike that of many Elizabethans, more than word-deep. He could never have been guilty of Ascham's attack on the 'bold bawdrye' of the *Morte d'Arthur*. After a slyly Chaucerian apology to 'chaste and honorable eares' he handles with honest enjoyment the subject of the *Epithalamium*. The problem of love poetry worried him not at all. He even attempts, though

with circumspection, to defend poetry containing matter
'not alwayes of the grauest, or of any great commoditie
or profit, but rather in some sort, vaine, dissolute, or
wanton' (p. 24). He delighted in ingenuity. The love
of this was abroad in his world and grew like a snowball
while the *Arte* was in the making. For his principal
excursion into witty and formal artifice—his 'Fuzie or
spindle', his 'Lozange rabbated', his 'egge displayed'—
he has been much laughed at. It is only fair to point
out, however, that this section (II, xii) is not so hackneyed
as his critics have supposed. These *geometrical* poems
have been cursorily identified with the shaped poems
(eggs, flowers, altars, wings, etc.) derived from the Greek
anthology. Puttenham was aware of these toys (he
mentions 'Anacreons egge') but, except perhaps for his
Pilaster where he notes an architectural analogy, his
shapes have an independent origin. They are mathe-
matical and are pure form. Like the arabesque, they are
of oriental origin. They are a waste of energy, no doubt,
but they testify to the possession of a valuable bump
of curiosity and illustrate the catholicity of Puttenham's
outlook on poetry. By 1589 he considered that the
courtly cult of *imprese* and anagrams required his blessing.
He got Field to insert it into the text in such a way that
the whole series of courtly trifles is covered by a general
defence of the poetry of pure wit and relaxation which
had originally been called forth by the shaped poems
alone. With doubtless intentional sarcasm he lumps together as 'reprehendours' the 'all holy and mortified',
the 'altogether graue and worldly' and those 'all giuen
to thrift and passing for none art that is not gainefull
and lucratiue'. He will suffer no 'seuere censor of the
ciuill maners of men' to curtail the 'conuenient solaces
and recreations of mans wit' (pp. 111–2).

Puttenham found the *dulce* more congenial than the
utile. He never mentions, neither did he share, Plato's
distrust of the moving and dazzling power of poetry.

He is fond of the word *inveigle* to describe its effects upon the mind. Poetry wears by natural right what Sidney calls 'masking raiment', but not necessarily for Sidney's reasons. He will not have the poet confounded with the judge and brushes aside as irrelevant the old distrust of the colours and figures (III, vii) which occasionally raised its head in the classical world. In this context Puttenham approaches a hedonistic view of poetry as the pleader 'of pleasant & louely causes and nothing perillous', disposing 'the hearers to mirth and sollace by pleasant conueyance and efficacy of speach'. For a complete statement of his views this description needs supplementing from the passages in Book I where he links poetry to the expression of life's tenser moments as well as wit's relaxation.

This inveigling power of poetry is partly exerted, of course, through invention and imagination but, though Puttenham had done a little mental wrestling with what he found in his classical guides on these subjects (I, viii), it was not this side of the poetic function that interested him. He was himself inveigled by 'gallant and harmonical accents', 'voluble and slipper vpon the tong', by 'stirring of tunes' and the neat clinching of sense and sound by rhyme. Above all he loved and watched language, the very texture of a poet's speech, 'more cleanly couched and more delicate to the eare' than prose can ever be. It was as craftsman and craft's teacher that he approached his subject. His eye (or ear) was always open for a point of technique or of literary medium. It was doubtless his individual recognition of the sensory apparatus by which poetry works her spell that emboldened him in Book III to throw overboard the consecrated classification of schemes and tropes in favour of his own subdivision into *auricular*, *sensable* and *sententious* by which this 'efficacy' of speech was given maximum importance.

Some portions of the *Arte* are, of necessity, derivative.

The least original part is Book I. Much of the information here and many of the leading ideas concerning the
antiquity and dignity of poetry had been set out before
(though not in English) and were to be again. Even so,
Book I is not a mere compilation; it is a genuine colla-
boration between 'any Renaissance critic' and George
Puttenham, who contributes humanity to humanism.
In Book II, in dealing with the metrical craft of English
poetry, he is compelled to stand on his own feet and
shows no false diffidence in doing so. In Book III he
is moving in one of the most sedulously cultivated
Renaissance fields. The chapters on style, the names of
the Figures and some of the examples have obviously a
textbook source—some rhetorical manual closely related to the popular work of Susenbrotus. But this is
merely the basis. Puttenham is face to face with his
own deeply studied language and roused to his maximum of independence and energy.

In general he is honest and consistent in distinguishing
between his debts and his own observations. Unfortunately for source-hunters, however, he considered it no
part of a gentleman's business to be pedantically explicit.
He is content with acknowledgments to the 'best clerks'
or 'learned Grammarians'. There is no scuttling to shelter
behind a barricade of impressive names. If there is a trace
of snobbery here, it is a less irritating form than that
which stuffed the margin with references derived at
second-hand. As regards modern ascriptions of facts
and ideas in the *Arte* to Scaliger, Du Bellay or others, it
is wise to maintain an attitude of reserve. It is easier to
find parallels than to be certain one has hit upon a 'source'.
Puttenham draws on no very recondite material and most
of his information was accessible in more than one textbook. Except perhaps in one or two chapters in Book I
there are few signs of that mosaic method by which
a writer like Lodge 'conveyed' passages from two or
three authors to his own pages with no intermediate

remaking. Puttenham was not hot from the university or from the challenge of a controversialist. A good deal of his material had probably been held in the mind for some time and freely combined and recombined before he set out on the *Arte*. It has at all events entered into some odd alliances. In Book I we recognise much familiar humanistic stuff, but it has been fitted into a naïve evolutionary scheme (particularly of the drama) which could be riddled by any one who had read the most garbled version of Aristotle's *Poetics*.

Puttenham, of course, finds it convenient to use precedent and example as argument, but he is less given to this than his contemporaries. It is characteristic of him to prefer example to mere authority. He seldom uses jargon and is rarely vague. His technical bias means that he really reads what occupies his attention. This is excellently seen in his criticism of Gower, where he could have no humanistic pointers. He has considered his verse ('homely and without good measure'), his vocabulary ('strained much deale out of the French writers'), his rhyme ('wrested') and his invention ('small subtillitie'). Gascoigne, 'who in most of his things wrote very well' (p. 258), is criticised for lack of attention to detail (p. 194) and for writing on occasions 'more curiously than needed' (p. 258). Turberville is censured for foolish epithets (pp. 255–6), ignorance and affectation (p. 252). Puttenham is careful to distinguish translation from original work. He 'spots' and scornfully exposes Soowthern's pilferings from Ronsard's *Odes*:

> this man deserues to be endited of pety *larceny* for pilfring other mens deuises...for in deede as I would wish euery inuētour which is the very Poet to receaue the prayses of his inuention, so would I not haue a trāslatour be ashamed to be acknowen of his translation. (p. 253.)

He had, like almost all educated Elizabethans, a bookish side, but he was willing, when occasion demanded, to trust to good sense, observation and the test of common experience:

> And yet if ye will aske me the reason, I can not tell it, but that it shapes so to myne eare, and as I thinke to euery other mans. (p. 132.)

The distinguishing quality of Puttenham as a critic is the directness and singleness of his approach to poetry. He is not, like Lodge, Webbe, Harington or even Sidney, compelled to approach poetry by a non-aesthetic détour. He could, like Aristotle, accept the notion that the objects of *mimesis* are the actions of men and that the test of excellence is craftsmanship. Poetry is to him the legitimate expression of all the moods and phases, the loves and hatreds, of the individual. It is also the *mimesis* of the changing states of society. This helps him to a certain historical and social perspective. He is tolerant of mediaeval literature as the mirror of its times. Since society consists of all conditions of men, the simple are entitled to their ballads and romances while the taste of the courtier will express itself in more sophisticated forms. The Poet 'by his many moodes of skill' serves 'the many humors of men' (p. 299).

This sentence from the last chapter of the *Arte* epitomises Puttenham's mature and very individual recognition of the relationship between Life and Poetry. Instinctively he looks behind the 'form' to some 'humor' or some emotional overflow which is to be expressed or communicated. Alert reading shows how frequently and vividly words of mood and feeling run from his pen: 'iolity of courage', 'moodes and pangs of louers', 'a peece of ioy to be able to lament with ease, and freely to poure forth a mans inward sorrowes', 'torment and canker to the minde', 'the boiling stomacke'. By stressing these emotional springs Puttenham vitalises the Kinds.

He saw no reason why there should not be all sorts

3   (lxi)

of poetry. Because man is, or hopes to be, a rational and moral being, Puttenham was willing, like all his contemporaries, to respect the strenuous and ethically minded poet. In several contexts he applies to a poem phrases like 'to none ill edification' or 'for...good instruction of the posteritie'. But man also eats, drinks, makes love, likes an ingenious puzzle and wears elaborate clothes to express his love of ornament and determination to secure a margin above the necessary. Just as there is an art of doing these things well (Decorum or the 'civil' life) so the art of poetry provided a means of expressing them well. If man is a microcosm, Puttenham claimed for Art also the right to be a little universe.[1]

The catholicity of Puttenham's outlook was in no way accompanied by lax or uncritical standards. The lines of the *Arte* follow easy curves but they are never woolly. There are reconsiderations but the scheme is never blurred; Puttenham valued his scheme and more than once in Book III recapitulated it for his reader's benefit. He never imagined that Art was an easy taskmistress and on points of craftsmanship he is clear-cut, even dogmatic. He fixed a gulf between the Poet and the Bungler. He was not content to leave Imagination, Phantasy, Art and Nature as hazy concepts. The last chapter of Book III on Art and Nature has a closeness of texture which shows that his mind was gripping on this well-worn classical theme.

Puttenham's conception of the relationship between life and art meant, of course, that he had no need of 'authority' as an interpreter or guide. Consequently the *Arte*, which is quite the most technical Renaissance survey of its subject, is quite the least bookish.

---

1 We hear a great deal of the poet as the mentor of society in the opening chapters of Book I. This is, of course, the orthodox opening gambit of the Renaissance critic. Puttenham arrives rapidly at a more independent standpoint and as soon as broadcloth turns to arras the poet is shown not as the mentor of primitive society but as the mouthpiece of the civil life.

IV. THE *ARTE* AS CRITICISM: MAIN CRITICAL TOPICS

Puttenham planned his book to proceed from the outside to the inside of his subject. In Book I he works out a survey of the Progress of Poesy and relates the larger kinds (Tragedy, Comedy, Epic, Pastoral, etc.) to various phases in a logical, rather than historical, evolution of human culture, and the smaller kinds (*Epithalamia, Dirae, Genethliaca,* etc.) to the turning-points in individual existence and the varying moods and passions of men. In Book II he reviews, from his own knowledge and observation, the metrical forms actually in use in England, passing from the standard measures to the trifles and toys which amused the fashionable world. In Book III he gets down to the basic medium of Language—Dialect, Vocabulary, Style and the whole armoury of the Figures. Here he finds himself in the heart of his subject.

The title *Arte* was not casually chosen. In Puttenham's day it was a matter of debate whether an Art of anything so apparently unstable and ungoverned as a modern vernacular could exist. It requires some imagination as well as study to recall from the hints of mid-Tudor writers the strength and influence of what seems to us unprogressive and doomed opinion; the tenacity of the conviction that Art was limited to the classical tongues can be gauged from the energy with which Mulcaster in his *Elementarie,* as late as 1582, lays about him on the progressive side. The significance of the title *Arte* and the view that Art and English Poesy are not incompatible terms are underlined by Puttenham in Book I, Ch. ii. After the introductory Book I, the work keeps strictly to its title. It not only describes and discusses, it teaches its particular craft. This keeps Puttenham close all the time to the technical side of his subject. Poetry is not surveyed from a cool distance;

it is a thing made and in the making; it is above all constantly heard. This perpetual closeness to the movement and texture of verse makes the *Arte* our best guide to the Elizabethan approach to poetry. We only half-read Gascoigne or Golding or Spenser if we fail to allow for the Elizabethan mind and ear. Elizabethan poetry was written primarily for Elizabethans to read and that they did not, in the most concrete sense, read poetry as we do, that indeed the actual reading differed markedly in early- and mid-Tudor times from late-Tudor times, is proved abundantly by the *Arte*. It is, therefore, as finger-posts to the Elizabethan reading and judging of poetry that certain topics from its abundant material have been selected for fuller consideration.

i. *Prosody*

Puttenham's second book, 'Of Proportion', with its indispensable minimum of technical terms and its diagrams, wears to many an uninviting look and has not been very diligently studied. It keeps, however, so close to the acoustic qualities of poetry that it provides an invaluable guide to the Tudor ear for those to whom Puttenham's parallel between proportion musical and poetical is not a dead or conventional formula.

The stratification of the text dictates the method of approach. It has been shown that the first eleven chapters constitute the earliest of the three chronological layers of which the complete text of this book consists. That these chapters represent the first English prosody and antedate Gascoigne's *Certayne Notes* is indicated by Puttenham's claim to be a first deviser in this field. It is in these eleven chapters that he is to be studied as an exponent of early- and mid-Tudor metrical knowledge, practice and preferences. The final chapters (xiii–end) were the fruit of a controversy most active in the early eighties and none of the prosodic concepts handled in them should be allowed to colour or disturb the picture of early-Tudor versification offered by the first eleven.

These early chapters introduce us to several clearly expressed and very significant metrical tastes of the author and his age. Puttenham loved best 'staffe' (or strophic form) and 'band' (that is, the fusing of all the lines of a stanza into a unity by 'entertangled' rhyme). His remarks on the subject of 'band' are thoroughly sound; he shows how for lack of it stanzas of inferior writers fall apart into two halves, and he remarks as a defect the independence of the final couplet in rhyme royal. For 'continuance' he notes the appropriateness of 'a *distick* or couple of verses'. The even number is always preferred to the odd. This is bound up with another preference—for clear, strong, masculine rhyme. Though Puttenham admits feminine rhymes he endeavours to minimise their effects: 'the sharpe accent falles vpon the *penultima* [*i.e.* the strong rhyming syllable]...which doth so drowne the last, as he seemeth to passe away in maner vnpronounced, & so make the verse seeme euen'. Measures of from eight to twelve syllables please him best (the fourteener 'kepeth the eare too long from his delight') and in the same way he prefers middle length stanzas: a piece of verse of more than ten lines is rather 'a whole ditty then properly a staffe'. There is some interesting comment on the difference between learned and popular taste. Some of this is what we should expect: the people, who *listen* to their poetry, must have quick returns of rhyme; longer 'distances' (between concords) involve more complex 'entertangling' and therefore more Art. Petrarch in his *canzoni* is the master here. The educated reader brings the eye as well as ear to bear on a poem and enjoys therefore the richer apprehension. The well-built strophe declares its pattern ('occular proportion') to the eye, while the ear records its chimes and echoes.

Another difference is less expected. The populace is more indulgent of rhyme on inkhorn polysyllables than the polite listener. It is a 'grosse' type of rhyme and will pass only among ignorant people who, at their interludes, have to concentrate upon what is actually happening on the stage.[1]

There are one or two unaccountable omissions from Puttenham's survey. He mentions the sonnet once or twice in the other books but he gives no prosodic account of it here, nor has he a word to say of blank verse. Earliness of date and his concentration on rhyme as the main pivot of metre may account for the latter omission, but no such explanation will do for the apparent failure to recognise the sonnet as a distinct metrical form. It is hard to believe that so keen a student of Petrarch could have shared in the popular confusion by which a sonnet was identified with any short love poem. It is possible that Puttenham considered the original sonnet as a 'huitain' plus a 'sizeine' (not linked by 'band' and therefore distinct) and sufficiently covered by what he says of each. In the same way, since there is even less 'band' in the English sonnet, what he had written of the 'quadrien' and 'distick' would serve.

Apart from these omissions, what he has to say in these eleven chapters about the forms and patterning of English verse is consistent in intention and in effect. He had dealt with subject-matter in Book I and has little to say here of gallant invention or brave conceit. Art tends to eclipse inspiration. These chapters portray a mid-Tudor studious poet, already verging on middle age, interpreting the standards of the Interludes and the *Songes and Sonettes*, although new men with new rhythms (or rather one rhythm, the 'olde Iambicke stroake') were probably already making their mark.

[1] In the terminology of the later-written chapters Puttenham refers again to this popular preference (p. 127). He now calls it *dactilique* verse and exemplifies by the rhyme *retribution/restitution*. These rhymes 'smatch more the schoole of common players than of any delicate Poet *Lyricke* or *Elegiacke*'.

When we turn to Puttenham's discussion of the internal structure of the English line, of the essential mechanism of English metrical speech, we are in deeper waters. His declarations, which can be abundantly corroborated from other sources, leave no possible doubt that we read early- and mid-Tudor verse from too modern a standpoint and judge it by largely irrelevant standards. Puttenham recognises two principles and two only—*number* and *rhyme*. The first he calls 'measure', the second 'concord' or 'symphonie'. The first is mechanical and requires little argument; all Puttenham's enthusiasm is expended on the second. It is rhyme which compensates for the lack of 'numerositie' and which offers to the English maker opportunities for the display of Art comparable to those enjoyed by the classical poet. The delight of the ear is the 'cadence or the tuneable accent in the ende of the verse'. It is the 'Poetes cheife Musicke'. Hence partly the preference for clear, strong rhymes. We must imagine the Tudor speaker making 'all the hast he can to be at an end of his verse' and then coming out with resonant emphasis on the 'cadence' (Puttenham's technical term for the rhyming portion of a line). Rhyme in this sense is, indeed, the rudder of verses. It was doubtless in this way that the often tumbling, internally chaotic, lines of early- and mid-Tudor drama were spoken. *Mutatis mutandis* the lines of courtly eclogues and sonnets were read in the same way. The rhyme was a resolution of all uncertainties.

The part that breath-emphasis necessarily plays in any metrical patterning of a strongly stressed language like English was, when Puttenham began to write, unrecognised and it is, therefore, irrelevant to apply to early-Tudor verse-making the stress principle as a clearly analysed concept. Nobody could be clearer on this subject than Puttenham and in one context (II, iii) he is so careful in contrasting the theoretically undifferentiated

English line (having 'no such feete or times or stirres') with the internal ripple of the classical line that we must believe him. In the course of this book and in Gascoigne, Harvey, Stanyhurst and Campion, we can watch the notion of emphasis or (breath) accent slowly coming to birth, very largely as the result of the clash between native and classical metres and the closer scrutiny of syllables involved. There is no sign that it was ever universally accepted during the Renaissance and Milton ignores it.

It was partly this failure to recognise any internal modulation of the line that led to the insistence not only on strong and obvious rhyme but also on a clear and fixed caesura. It was a further proof of Art to secure that no indivisible polysyllable fell just where the rule prescribed a pause; a break, moreover, helped to organise the welter of syllables and gave some design to the interior of the line. Puttenham is dogmatic on this point. He prescribes exactly where the caesura must fall in every 'measure'. He exalts it into a test of Art: 'in euery long verse the *Cesure* ought to be kept precisely, if it were but to serue as a law to correct the licentiousnesse of rymers'. This heavy pause is to us a part of the obviousness of early-Elizabethan versification. We are, indeed, unsympathetic towards the prosodic formalism of which it appears to speak and inclined to dismiss as pedantry or misguided zeal the comma after every fourth syllable with which the printer of Gascoigne's *Steele Glas* peppered his text. Puttenham's words, however, show that for the strong internal pause, as for the heavy final rhyme, there once existed a reason. It secured Art in the middle of the line as well as at the end.

It is true that Puttenham uses the word 'accent' frequently in these chapters. This might superficially make his prosody appear more modern than it is. With one exception, however, the word *when used of English metre* has no reference to the government of the whole line. The accented is the key-syllable which supports the cadence: in double or triple rhyme there is one strong syllable which rings out clearly; in masculine rhyme there is a single syllable to mark the pattern. There is no need to limit the meaning of 'accent' here to stress; it can include pitch, tone, singing quality. Puttenham derived the term, of course, from the Latin. He paraphrases at length the Latin rule for speech-accentuation and proceeds to apply it to English words like *áltitude* and *héaviness*. He was fascinated by Roman polysyllables—not by their magnificence but by their modulation. In this passage (p. 79) he is within an ace of being led by his comparative method to stating a principle of accentual modulation in English verse—but the final step is not taken.

There is one passage in these chapters (p. 73) where the matter is carried a stage further. Puttenham notes of a line of Surrey's—

Salomon Dauids sonne, king of Ierusalem—

that it is a 'very good' Alexandrine (*i.e.* it counts up accurately to twelve syllables and the caesura falls after the sixth) but his ear is conscious of something unsatisfactory in its rhythm. He uses the word 'accent' in his explanation, but can only analyse the error or difficulty in terms of *number*, not rhythm: *Salomon*, having the sharp accent on the *Sal*, 'runnes like a *Dactill*, and carries the two later sillables away so speedily as it seemes but one foote... *and by that meanes makes the verse seeme but of eleuen sillables*'. He tries as an alternative

Robóham Dauids sonne king of Ierusalem

and then suddenly emerges as the complete and clear-headed accentual prosodist: 'or thus

Restóre king Dáuids sónne vntó Ierúsalém'.

This is the only case in these early chapters where

(lxix)

Puttenham marks an accentual scheme throughout a line. If the last version be not an interpolation, it seems to have been arrived at by worrying at a difficulty until illumination came.

Puttenham's chapters on 'perfite versifying' can only be fully discussed in a wide context covering the whole movement to which they belong. The most dangerous error that is likely to be made concerning them is that of taking them too seriously, of going solemnly through them for misapprehension of Latin custom, failure of phonetic realism, inconsistencies, impossibilities, and so on. If Puttenham had girded up his loins to the task he could have talked as much sense as Harvey and more delightfully. He has not made the effort. He is using only the fringe of his mind; his wits play the contemporary game, but his heart remains with the *Songes and Sonettes*. His own words should warn off the heavy-footed critic. He introduces the subject as a 'scholastical' toy and strikes the key of the gay defender of Paradoxes: 'This is (ye will perchaunce say) my singular opinion: then ye shall see how well I can maintaine it' (p. 121). He exhibits an eel-like ingenuity and wriggles humorously out of one untenable position after another. At the end, when he is tired of going one better than Stanyhurst (a very difficult thing to do), he allows the whole fantastic structure of tribrachs, dactils and molossi to tumble over like a house of cards before the memory of 'the pleasant melody of our English meeter'.

Though for the strenuous thinking put into this controversy we must turn elsewhere (to Harvey, Stanyhurst and Campion), Puttenham's native awareness was such that in his idle chapters he registers the immense gain to critical perception and prosodic analysis which was won by the 'perfite' versifiers.

The essence of the new prosody was the study of the internal structure of the line. Out of the clash between the old and the new emerged, not of course the *fact*, but the *perception*, of stress as a means of differentiating between syllables and securing that 'stirre' within the line which Puttenham had earlier denied to English metres. This had been empirically demonstrated for years in the strong 'iambicke stroake' of the mid-century fourteener and poulter's measure, whence it spread into shorter lines. Gascoigne had found a name for it, 'natural *Emphasis*', and had associated it (doubtless with confusing results) with the 'three maner of accents', *i.e.* signs. None of those, however, who can be proved to have read the *Certayne Notes* (such as Gabriel Harvey and James VI of Scotland) seem to have divined the full importance of this; they certainly do nothing to improve upon it. It required more wrestling and experience before the idea clarified itself; this wrestling can be watched in Harvey's letters to Spenser (1580). When the idea was born it required a name, and it was inevitable that the name should be *accent* from the Latin and that the associated terminology (*acuta*, *gravis*, 'sharp', 'flat') should be from the same source.

Concept and name emerge in Puttenham's later chapters, though a general haziness of context may obscure definition. Since 1575 Gascoigne's *Certayne Notes* had been accessible and, not being tied (like Harvey) to grammarian's distinctions, Puttenham was in a better position to grasp the significance of Gascoigne's achievement, which his own comparative study of English and Latin polysyllables had already foreshadowed. Stanyhurst's Preface of 1582 had also made some points about accent clear, though it was confused or pedantic about others. When Puttenham recants his classical heresy at the end of Ch. xvi he announces that he is going to return to 'scanning our verse by sillables rather than by feete'. Some following elliptical words show, however, that he is not reverting to the simple early-Tudor prosody. He intends to use the *words* iambic, trochaic, and dactylic, to describe (presumably) certain metrical movements. These movements 'ye shall discerne by their accents', *i.e.* accent is the principle of government or modulation. It is to his credit, or to that of the Sidney-Spenser age, that he is not going to look for a steady stream of accentual 'iambs'; he is in no sense arrested at the early-Elizabethan phase of Gascoigne and Googe. The mid-century 'iambic' iteration was being loosened and suppled by the individual tastes and talents of a new generation of poets, by the coincident linguistic expansion, and by the prolonged and absorbed attention the Sidney group had given to all the principles of melodic variation *within* the Latin and English line.

We must imagine the reading and speaking of poetry as changing with all these variations in the poets' feeling for their medium, for poetry still maintained in part its ancient oral tradition. To the early-Tudor reliance on pause and rhyme succeeded an excessive feeling for mechanical internal regularity of a *ti túm ti túm* pattern, still strong in pause and heavy in rhyme. Of this we hear from Gascoigne and Webbe but not Puttenham,[1] for it is, as it were, lost in the chronological gap between his earlier and later layer. This satisfaction of the ear in regularity must have been instinctive before Gascoigne applied to it the iambic analogy. Regularity seems to have been native to the Alexandrine (and fourteener) from the beginning, perhaps as a kind of substitute for French smoothness. With the rise of the new poets the interior of the line is not left to simple arithmetic or simple instinct. English syllables had been drilled to march; they could now be trained to dance. The interior of the line grew more interesting than it had ever been before.[2] Very gradually, as verse was read, rhyme

---

1 Except perhaps in his scansion of Surrey's line quoted above.

2 A most striking example of the richer and more elastic prosodic apprehension won by *c.* 1585 is Puttenham's own poem 'Brittle beauty' (p. 123) and his comments thereon. Within the one 'measure' of the decasyllable

would slip from a main structural feature to an ornament, an added grace. As rhyme was more lightly
sounded *enjambement* and variety of pause would become more possible and new subtleties, less simply
mechanical and arithmetical, would be induced. The
stage was set for blank verse to come (ultimately) into
its own. In the meanwhile, Puttenham turned again to
his well-thumbed *Songes and Sonettes* and re-read its
contents on new principles (pp. 129–34).

ii. *The 'Figures'*

The third book of the *Arte*, 'Of Ornament', is really
concerned with Language—its study and organisation
for the poet's purposes. Puttenham ranges from practical injunctions concerning the choice of language to
discursive discussions of the dominating Renaissance
themes—Decorum, and Art and Nature. Here, at the
end of the book, only perfunctory efforts are made to
remember his ostensible subject, the Art of English
Poesy. The real theme is now Life; Puttenham is writing
in the tradition of the *Courtier*, even sometimes as one
who may already have read Montaigne.

The third book reveals none of the time-layers so
apparent in Book II. Some of the chapters (the more
obviously derivative such as v, vi and viii) are thinner
in texture than the majority and add little to the range
of idea and information that made an average equipment in Quintilian's time. These chapters may well be
survivals from the earliest version. The book as a whole,

(varied by an occasional feminine rhyme) he delights to find a wide variety
of rhythms and patterns and, in particular, traces with zest the differences
secured by the juxtaposition of monosyllables, bisyllables, polysyllables and
of different combinations of these:

Brittle beauty blossome daily fading (bisyllables: trochaic);
Morne, noone, and eue in age and eke in eld (monosyllables: iambic);
Dangerous disdainefull pleasantly perswading (polysyllables: dactylic).

however, has been extensively reworked. It must be thought of as the accumulated material of a lifetime. It takes us from the rhetorician's stock-in-trade, through the work of the *Songes and Sonettes* period and the Gascoigne-Turberville layer, down to the new makers, Sidney, Dyer, Raleigh and the Earl of Oxford. These last could only have been accessible to Puttenham in manuscript, and to the manuscript commonplace-books and songbooks he doubtless owed a number of quotations which have not been identified.

The Figures constitute the *pièce de résistance* of this book and here it is difficult for Puttenham to carry his modern reader with him. They have become typical of all that we distrust in rhetoric. Their studied application seems to make of poetry a synthetic, rather than a creative, art. The confusion of Poetry and Rhetoric was, however, no peculiar vice of the Elizabethans. It goes back to Greek antiquity and the Roman, coarser-grained than the Greek, inevitably responded more heartily to Rhetoric than Poetry. Virgil seems to have been well aware of the dividing line and to have stood firmly on the poet's side, but that did not prevent Quintilian from turning him to account, or Servius from writing a treatise on the Figures in Virgil. Changed conditions during the Middle Ages had broken the genuinely forensic Roman tradition and had thus emptied Rhetoric of its practical and solid content; by the fifteenth century it was equated with 'facund' or 'aureate' language.[1] In spite of the fact that the better textbooks circulating after the Revival of Learning used a sheep-and-goat principle, separating figures suitable for poetry from those suitable for prose, the Elizabethans, again inevitably, carried the confusion further still. As soon as the Renaissance even began to turn towards the Baroque, ornament became a passion and

1 D. L. Clark, *Rhetoric and Poetry in the Renaissance* (Columbia University Studies in English and Comparative Literature), New York, 1922.

poetry could escape no more than architecture, painting and dress. '[Sans] ornemens...toute oraison et poëme sont nuds, manques et debiles' (Du Bellay, *Défense*, I, v). As prose grew more elaborate the line between 'oraison' and 'poëme' became more difficult to draw. Gascoigne says, without a twinge of artistic conscience, that the Poet may use all the figures that are used in prose and Puttenham only intermittently remembers that Poetry is not Oratory.

To the stimulus which the Elizabethan mind, up to *c.* 1595, received from the Figures we have the testimony of a cloud of witnesses. Gascoigne asserts that 'to roll in pleasant woordes' was not enough: 'some figures also in the handlyng thereof' were essential, otherwise the result would seem 'to the skilfull Reader but a tale of a tubbe'. Although the hunting of schemes and tropes scarcely slackened during the Middle Ages, Elizabethans seem, to our minds, excessively sensitive to the difference between mediaeval rhetoric and their own. It was the absence either of their own baroque exuberance, or of the pressure and density which come from a close study of the packed Latin style, that chilled their appreciation of such mediaeval writers as they knew. 'Homely' (twice used by Puttenham of pre-Tottel verse) records their reaction. A spate of textbooks, some for the school, others for the world, stimulated and catered for the popular demand. With different degrees of freshness they expressed the prevailing conviction, shared by Italy (earlier), by Spain, France and Portugal, that the vernacular is 'bare', and that the study of schemes and tropes will show all patriots how to enrich their mother-tongue. A well-educated modern reader may confess without shame to momentary confusion between *Hypozeuxis* and *Hypozeugma*, but to his Elizabethan prototype the categories of the figures were, like the multiplication-tables, a part of his foundations. Schoolmasters were wont, says Sherry in his

Schemes and Tropes (1550), to point out to their scholars '*Hic est figura*: and sometyme to axe them, *Per quam figuram?*' (Sig. A6ᵛ). Sherry's pupils later in life would have no difficulty in seeing where the joke lay in almost every remark of Holofernes ('What is the figure? what is the figure?') and would have recognised in Pistol's 'He hears with ears' the stock example of *Pleonasmus*. The comic dramatist expected rhetorical jest and allusion to be taken as readily as a music-hall joke about the loss of King John's clothing in the Wash would be today.

This brings us once more to the question of Elizabethan reading and listening, as well as of the general criticism of poetry. If we suspend judgment as to the value of this pursuit of 'applied' rhetorical ornament and substitute for it a sort of detective interest—a nose to smell out the odiferous flowers of fancy, the jerks of invention—it is possible to approximate to the Elizabethan habit. Poets who took so much trouble to follow Art would not wish this Art to be ignored in the reading and would expect their listeners, and still more their readers, to respond with aural and mental agility. The 'schemes' are nothing but the organisation of patterning; this patterning contented the ear like rhyme and the identification of the patterns was a delight to the instructed mind. Such a response to poetry was never vague or half-awake.

Richard Sherry compared the reader ignorant of his figures 'to him whiche gooeth into a goodlye garden garnyshed wyth dyuers kindes of herbes and flowers, and that there doeth no more but beholde them, of whome it maye be sayde that he wente in for nothynge but that he wold come out', while the reader who knows his figures is like 'hym which be syde the corporall eie pleasure, knoeth of eueri one the name & propertye' (*Schemes and Tropes*, A8ʳ-A8ᵛ). To its first readers the *Shepheardes Calender* offered in the more elaborate

eclogues full measure of this combined 'corporall' and
intellectual delight. The stanza in the November ode
beginning

> Why doe we longer liue, (ah why liue we so long)

maintains an average of a figure a line. E. K., in his gloss
on the work, gives an excellent representation of the
Elizabethan reader. He notes at the end of January of

> I loue thilke lasse, (alas why doe I loue?)

'a prety Epanorthosis in these two verses, and withall
a Paronomasia or playing with the word'. In February
he finds 'a liuelye figure, whiche geueth sence and
feeling to vnsensible creatures', in October 'an Ironicall
Sarcasmus'. He considers that November with its
highly wrought Ode surpasses all the others in the
book and calls attention to 'an elegant Epanorthosis',
'a notable and sententious comparison A minore ad
maius', 'a gallant exclamation' and 'a liuely Icon'.
Shakespeare had absorbed the Art of Rhetoric and his
early plays, especially the Chronicles, are often dubbed
'rhetorical'. In any fully authenticated early Shake-
spearian play, however, we can see that the age of
rhetorical innocence is passing. Shakespeare can stand
both within and without the tradition. We find what
appears to be a naïver approach to the subject in the
Poems and Sonnets where he approximates himself most
closely to the courtly intelligentsia. Sonnet 66 ('Tired
with all these') is a study in *Anaphora* as thorough
as anything in Gascoigne (who hunted this figure most
industriously). 'Increasing store with loss, and loss with
store' is a neater example of '*Syneciosis*, or the Crosse
copling' than any that Puttenham gives. We are all
aware of the patterning in Elizabethan verse of this
period, but we are generally content to name the *genus*—
balance, antithesis, repetition, and so on. The educated

Elizabethan could give a name to every *species*. He would 'spot' the *Ploce* in

then you were

Yourself again after your self's decease

and would enjoy unravelling the complex of figure-within-figure in

Music to hear, why hear'st thou music sadly?
Sweets with sweets war not, joy delights in joy:
Why lov'st thou that which thou receiv'st not gladly,
Or else receiv'st with pleasure thine annoy?

It is characteristic of Puttenham's attitude towards his subject that he should modify (greatly daring) the traditional classification into one that gave him the fullest opportunity for analysing the sensory appeal of poetry. It is characteristic, too, of the critical turn of his mind that he was aware that the Figures (as poetical apparatus) needed some defence. He knew perfectly well that the best rhetorical tradition restricted to prose the so-called rhetorical or 'sententious' figures and left Poetry, to that extent, the purer and austerer art. But he is so much 'inveigled' by his Figures that he cannot stop when he has come to an end of his legitimate categories, *auricular* and *sensable*. There were still a number of fine Greek titles challenging the 'Anglesaxon' in him. A reason must be found for including in poetry the non-poetical. Neither in life nor letters was Puttenham ever gravelled for a reason. Since the sententious figures 'conteine a certaine sweet and melodious manner of speech' (pp. 196–7) they are 'after a sort' *auricular*. He goes further and executes a *volte face*. Eye and ear are merely avenues to the mind and 'what els is man but his minde?' Then, since a very large number of the prose figures to come are related to Amplification, he turns his back on the fine economy of poetry: 'one or two drops of water perce not the flint stone . . . the minde being no lesse vanquished with large loade of speech, than the limmes are with heauie burden'. The pressure behind Puttenham was, indeed, too great even for a more rigid mind to resist; these prose or rhetorical figures are (apart from the tried favourites like Metaphor and Simile) the most widely spread and easily recognised in Elizabethan poetry of this phase.[1]

No better illustration of the great dominating conception of style during this period can be found than Puttenham's defence and definition of the Figures in general. Classical antiquity had bequeathed the simple, but not unsatisfying, definition of style as *mentis imago* or *character*. This Puttenham knows and quotes (III, v). Partly cutting across this was the notion of three types of subject (high, mean and low) and the consequent existence of three styles. Style here *can* still be thought of as pressure from within shaping outward expression (though it very frequently was not). This Puttenham handles with unexpected rigidity in Ch. vi. Flexible and realist minds in classical antiquity had always felt this scheme too fixed and had urged the extension and blending of the styles. Puttenham, aware that he is defying certain most learned clerks, will have none of this, with the result that he blunders over Parody as a mixed kind. This, as has been said, is an early chapter; it obviously held no interest for the Puttenham of 1585. Thirdly, there were all the ramifications of rhetoric as an actual art of persuasion, to which public life in the Greek *polis* and Roman republic lent such sanctions that neither prose nor poetry could maintain its independence. Rhetoric was not an art of argument—that was logic; it was an art to dazzle and persuade. Its enemies said that it was a way of making the worse appear the better reason. Rhetoric as oratory (as distinct from an art of composition) cut through the *nexus* between personality and style or subject and ex-

---

[1] The figures we have quoted in this chapter from Spenser and Shakespeare are all *prose* figures.

pression. His profession prescribed for the pleader his topics and attitude towards them; if they required borrowed plumes it was his business to provide them. He turned up his 'places' and Figures. This could only induce a notion of style as 'clothes', differing in richness by the dictates of Decorum, collected and put on from outside. The attraction of classical precedent and the passion for ornament in itself replaced in the Elizabethan world the ancient practical sanctions. The analogy of clothing came all too easily; it occurs and recurs in Puttenham's general discussions. In his opening chapter ('Of Ornament Poeticall') style is compared to a lady of quality's 'courtly habillements', clothing a body that would be indecent without them. 'Silkes', 'tyssewes' and 'costly embroideries' occur to him in the same context. The setting of jewels, 'passements of gold vpon the stuffe of a Princely garment' and the 'Orient coulours' of a painter are further analogies. The thought that Art and tact are necessary suggests another comparison; rouge is for the lady's cheek, not her forehead or chin. Later (p. 159) he observes that language is never 'so well appointed for all purposes of the excellent Poet, as when it is gallātly *arrayed* in all his colours which figure can set vpon it'.

Though this may seem to foster and express an unduly 'detachable' view of style and though Puttenham, as his zeal carries him through the sententious figures, frequently either forgets the poet and substitutes the 'persuader' or clumsily combines them, yet, throughout his first two classes and in his general view, he keeps steadily to the fore the means, sensory and intellectual, by which poetry, as a unique art, attains its object. The figures are the sum of all the resources (other than metrical) by which poetry conveys its special overplus of excitement or stimulation; they are the sum, expressed in Elizabethan terms, of the types of ambiguity, the obliquities, the transferences, the echoes and con-

trolled associations, which lift poetry above mere statement and by which the poet lets odd and unexpected
lights into his subject, 'drawing it', says Puttenham,
'from plainnesse and simplicitie to a certaine double-
nesse' (p. 154). Poetry is not for tideless blood or the
literal mind. It is a 'guilefull & abusing talke', 'seeking
to inueigle and appassionate the mind'. Figurative
speech (p. 159) is a 'noueltie of language...estranged
from the ordinarie habite and manner of our dayly
talke and writing'. It gives ornament or efficacy by

> many maner of alterations in shape, in sounde, and also in
> sence, sometime by way of surplusage, sometime by defect,
> sometime by disorder, or mutation, & also by putting into
> our speaches more pithe and substance, subtilitie, quick-
> nesse, efficacie or moderation, in this or that sort tuning
> and tempring them, by amplification, abridgemēt, opening,
> closing, enforcing, meekening or otherwise disposing them
> to the best purpose.

Puttenham could not foretell how rapidly the life
would ebb from his subject. The rhetorical manuals,
and particularly the treatises of schemes and tropes,
have become to us conspicuous examples of *biblia a-
biblia*. It can be claimed without exaggeration that
Puttenham has left us the most readable account in
English. There are traces of the qualities by which
Quintilian kept his *Institutiones* above the textbook level.
There is, in fact, a good deal which recalls Quintilian.
Both he and Puttenham keep their exposition salted
with genuine criticism and maintain it as a humane
study, neither rigid nor spineless. Puttenham's age and
order were not over-given to recourse to originals, but
there is enough evidence of contact for us to credit him
with a share in Sir Nicholas Bacon's enthusiasm for the
Institutiones.

There is no short way of demonstrating the readable-
ness of Puttenham's treatment of the Figures. The only
convincing method is to read some twenty of the hand-

books in Latin and the modern vernaculars circulating in his time and to draw first-hand illustration of the difference between the critic's and the grammarian's touch. For one thing there is the almost conversational style, full of personal allusions and direct address to the reader. Then there is Puttenham's habit of talking about the figures as if they were alive. Many of the titles are very vigorous personifications—'the Changeling', 'the Ouer reacher, otherwise called the loud lyer', 'the Rerewarder', 'the Middle marcher' and a host beside. There is a high proportion of verbs and verbal nouns to adjectives, and of concrete words to abstract. Puttenham finds homely similes by which to display his figures in action: '*Sillepsis*, or the Double supply' 'may be likened to the man that serues many masters at once'; '*Prolepsis* or the Propounder' should rather be called 'the forestaller, for like as he that standes in the market way, and takes all vp before it come to the market in grosse and sells it by retaile, so by this maner of speach...'. The figures flash into gesture: the 'fleering frumpe' is accompanied by 'drawing the lippe awry, or shrinking vp the nose'. Puttenham has, moreover, put an immense amount of observation, reading and genuine work into his book. It is packed full of stuff. The English titles, lovingly designed to show some 'kick' or arresting quality in the Greek, are frequently odd but they are original. By all these means, as in Book II, he sticks close to the actual efficacy, the working, of poetry. By all these means, too, he keeps us aware of a mind perpetually in action. Large as are his debts, he is never merely transferring matter from one book to another. He conveys in his pages something of the quality of thought and idea in the making, not ready-made, that keeps Montaigne's *Essais* perpetually alive. The figures provoke lively anecdotes: of an old woman in his mother's nursery, of 'a mouthy Aduocate', of a 'sorrie man of law', of a lady who, on receiving a *Metalepsis* by way of compliment from a 'pleasant Gentleman' visiting her in her nursery, broke out

> Gods passion hourson...would thou haue me beare mo children yet.

One has to read these chapters with a very dull and unreceptive mind if at some point the figures do not step out of their pages and march, climb, turn, counter-turn, and exchange 'drie mocks' for 'fleering frumpes' before one's eyes.

Book III took its final shape about 1585, just at the topmost point of the rhetorical curve. The Art of Rhetoric had been expounded by serious humanists and public servants like Thomas Wilson, by schoolmasters like Richard Sherry and by ministers of religion like Henry Peacham. Arcadian rhetoric competed with classical prosody in the Countess of Pembroke's circle. Puttenham keeps up an air of writing for a circle of 'pretie amourets' hanging on his lips, or rather on his pen, for information on this subject. In the latter eighties and throughout the nineties the curve declines. Fewer new books and editions of older ones are called for. Rhetoric retreats from the world to the school. The support of classical precedent meant that it remained among an Englishman's foundations and continued to shape the prose sentences in English books for many years to come. But, except among the 'Spenserians', the alliance with poetry was gradually dissolved and the Figures were shorn of their glamour. The rhetorical conception of style as a shot and patterned material *applied to* a subject gradually gave way before another which is exemplified, rather than defined, in the poems of Donne and the mature plays of Shakespeare.

In *Hamlet* it is the old Polonius who entangles himself in the figures and the Queen's sharp reprimand

'More matter, with less art' may be taken as the motto of a new era. The movement had produced absurdities enough, but the devotion it expressed and engendered was expended on the language Shakespeare was to use. For thirty years unremitting attention was bestowed on the English language; there has been nothing like it since. It was not the cult of a clique but of educated England. The minutest details were weighed and studied—the choice of words, the shape and design of sentences, the use of ornament. An enormous number of indispensable words of criticism and intellectual or literary perception were, not necessarily invented, but extended in meaning and disseminated by the Arts of Rhetoric—words like *insinuation, explication, amplification, circumlocution.* The systematic nomenclature of so fundamental a thing as punctuation was largely bequeathed by the Arts. *Colon* is first recorded (by the *N.E.D.*) from Puttenham; *comma* from Angel Day's *English Secretorie* (1586). Words like *imitation, art, method* and *invention* were filled with new critical and literary content and left ready for the neo-classic age to come. The fruits of all this solid work remained when the day of taffeta phrases, silken terms precise and three-pil'd hyperboles was over.

iii. *Language*

For his day, Puttenham may be considered something of a language specialist. He had written a book on the *Originals and Pedigree of the English Tong* and *De Decoro* had probably some linguistic bearings. Though the detailed consideration of poetic speech is reserved for Book III, the whole of the *Arte* is unified by its consistent and ever watchful interest in language. A steady stream of linguistic comment runs through the book. Always at the back of the writer's mind is the thesis contained in his title: the book is to demonstrate the capacity of the English vernacular for Art. It is thus linked to the great battle of the modern vernaculars against the classical tongues which was being waged in every country of Europe to which the influence of the Renaissance had come. Awareness of language (its problems, its responsibilities, its care and study) was as much a humanist product as literary criticism. In Italy the contest was fought out first, but the position of Italy was unique; a line of great Tuscan poets stretching back to Dante, the sense of continuity with the Roman past, the lack of political unity, created a set of privileges and problems that could not exist elsewhere. In Spain, Portugal, France, England and to a certain extent in Germany, however, conditions reproduce themselves almost monotonously. Scholars assume or maintain that the vernaculars are bare and inadequate, not only limited by frontiers but incapable of carrying the heaviest guns. Sooner or later, poets and humanists of a different type, moved by national feeling as well as deeper instincts, rally to the defence of the vernaculars, of their potentialities, if not of their achievements, and set themselves to provide the means (Imitation, Ornament, Art) by which these potentialities may be realised. It is very noticeable how, particularly in the pamphlets of Du Bellay and Sidney, it is faith in the latent capacities of the language and in the native genius, rather than respect for past literary achievements, which provides the rock of their defence.

The invention of printing had exposed the weakness of the vernaculars. The very multiplication of books advertised the instability and the lack of uniformity in the modern tongues. Printers who produced vernacular works may well have felt that their output made a poor show and had a limited appeal against the standardised productions for international circulation pouring from the Aldine Press in Venice and the Officina Ascensiana in Paris. Formerly, as manuscripts found their way about the country they could be adapted by copyists to their own dialect and time, but how was a printer, producing a large number of books at once and relying on a wide sale to recoup himself, to be sure of satisfying those who wanted 'curious' terms and those who wanted simple, or of being even understood by those who said 'egges' and those who said 'eyren'? Caxton had shown himself vividly aware of these difficulties. They had not entirely disappeared by Mulcaster's time.

The first increase in knowledge did nothing to lessen these difficulties. A very little comparative study made it easy to dub the romance languages 'bastard', while the northern languages had not even the dubious distinction of the bar sinister. They were frankly 'barbarous' and cacophonous, spoken by the descendants of those responsible for the break-up of Roman civilisation. Hence the cultivators of English had a very uphill row to hoe and it is noticeable how consistently England is omitted from any review of the Republic of Letters made by Italian linguists and humanists in the sixteenth century. There was, indeed, every excuse for being at sea in early sixteenth-century England. There was no guidance at all except Custom and analogies (often misleading) in other languages. Orthography was chaos, prosody non-existent, accent in romance words was shifting and completely unstable in new polysyllables. Grammarians, rhetoricians, orthopeists, prosodists, mostly with an eye steadily fixed on Latin, rushed into the breach in an endeavour to establish the needed law and order.

It is sometimes forgotten that the weight of Latin authority on the English language during this period was by no means all dead weight. In its day, Latin had passed through a similar crisis and had waged an uphill fight with Greek for the right to become a literary and philosophical language. Consequently, in favourite Latin authors, particularly in Cicero who was the main champion in the battle, Renaissance patriots who had the eye could find incentives to progress and to national endeavour. In Cicero's *De Natura Deorum* (which Puttenham had read) we find passages of slightly astonished gratification at the advances made in one man's working years not unlike later Elizabethan complacencies. If, to some, Horace stood as the High Priest of a restrictive Decorum, by others (including Puttenham) he could be quoted as an upholder of the principle of linguistic growth and change. Owing perhaps to certain affinities between the Roman and the English mind, especially in practical gifts and power of compromise, the analogy between the ancient and the modern struggle was, possibly, particularly helpful in England. It was as a consistent Ciceronian that Ascham wrote English books for Englishmen; those who in Italy or elsewhere could consider no other prose medium than Ciceronian Latin were, ironically, no more than half-Ciceronians. It is interesting to compare the absoluteness of Du Bellay's rejections and acceptances with the characteristic English critical approach in Puttenham, Harvey and Daniel. In England the main battle was won by certain practical compromises, supported by the ardour of patriotism. While the compositors, in the humdrum pursuit of their calling, quietly and gradually settled the burning question of orthography, the country's will to expression found a way. 'It is a world to see', says Lyly, who was always ready with a neat critical touch, 'how English men desire to heare finer speach then the language will allow.' Translation, coinage and onomatopeic exuberance provided the language with fresh material, while the study of the Arts of Rhetoric and of foreign authors drilled writers in its management. A defeatist note regarding English as a medium for Art rapidly became impossible. Instead, it became the fashion to laud the 'copiousness' of English and to make quite uncritical claims on its behalf.

Puttenham approaches the all-enveloping subject with the conviction of the true-born Englishman but with the Roman *gravitas* of his more broad-cloth age. He makes no extravagant claims and has a clear realist sense of some of the essential differences between living English, as an amalgam of Saxon, Norman and 'altered Latines', and the classical (and dead) languages. He had himself a flair for linguistic fact (as distinct from speculation) and had made language a thing of aural and mental touch as well as of significance. The continuity of his linguistic studies, the length of time that the *Arte* was growing under his hand, combine to give the book balance and perspective. He is not rushing into a wordy contest with the latest patriotic battle cry on his lips. His handling of language, even in the latest layers, is in keeping with the mid-Tudor provenance of the book.

Puttenham has something to say on a very wide range of linguistic topics—on the mechanism of speech (the part played by lips, tongue and teeth), on the origin of quantity, on the acoustic qualities of certain vowels and consonants (*n*, *r*, *t*, *d*, *l* are 'most flowing and slipper vpon the toung'), on 'stirre' of polysyllables, on onomatopeic creation of new words, on imperfect rhymes and on 'ortographie'. He knows enough of the earlier history of our language to be aware of its stratification. His linguistic flair as well as curiosity is exemplified by what he says of the British language

> which as some will, is at this day, the Walsh, or as others affirme the Cornish: I for my part thinke neither of both, as they be now spoken and pronounced. (p. 144.)

He is the first to use in an English work the term 'Anglesaxon' (p. 144). He distinguishes between the Saxon layer and the Norman, and between this and later layers of importations direct from book-Latin (p. 117); he recognises very acutely not only the responsibility of clerks and secretaries for these adaptations but the fact that these late forms have come mainly from France or have been formed on a (learned) French model. He distinguishes them from genuine 'Norman' or old French as 'altered Latines, and without any imitation at all', *i.e.* without any attempt to assimilate them to the patterns of words which have been through the mill of oral tradition: *innombrable* is 'Norman' or French in origin, *innumerable* is 'altered Latine'.

Puttenham's chapter 'Of Language' (III, iv) contains the classical discussion for early modern English of the Standard Language. He first defines the general notion of a received standard language; it is 'a speech... fully fashioned to the common vnderstanding, & accepted by consent of a whole countrey'; this is the '*Idioma*' or 'mother speach' of a people. It is relatively not absolutely, fixed; it will receive alteration 'by extraordinary occasions by little & little, as it were insensibly bringing in of many corruptiōs that creepe along with the time'. The standard language of his own time Puttenham crisply defines as 'the vsuall speach of the Court, and that of London and the shires lying about London within lx. myles, and not much aboue'. He thus distinguishes his standard language partly on a regional and partly on a class basis. Puttenham's own fastidious but quite unforced sense of the chaste and normal in diction reflects itself in nearly everything he says in this connection. The poet must use the 'naturall, pure, and the most vsuall' speech of his country. If he does not haunt the Court, then he is more likely to find it in 'good townes and Cities' than in marches, frontiers and ports. He is warned against the universities where 'Schollers vse much peeuish affectation of words out of the primatiue languages'. He will not look for the best language close to the soil in any 'vplandish village' or find it in the 'strange accents or ill shapen soundes, and false ortographie' 'of the inferiour sort, though he be inhabitant or bred in the best towne and Citie'. The poet is to use the language of his own time; he 'shall not follow *Piers plowman* nor *Gower* nor *Lydgate* nor yet *Chaucer*'. Puttenham admits that, from the Saxon purist's point of view, Northern English is purer than the more mingled Southern; nevertheless, it is the Southern that the poet must use since it is more courtly and 'currant'. Puttenham is, of course, only concerned with the literary language of the poet; he is laying down no laws for ordinary communication. He accepts the fact that more people from every shire write Southern than speak it and that in daily intercourse gentlemen and even 'learned clarkes' will 'condescend' to their humbler neighbours and speak their dialect.

Puttenham exercised a discriminating connoisseur-ship in words and he expected the poet to do likewise. It was an instinct in him to watch words. He interrupts the summary of the kinds of poetry to note that of the terms 'enterlude, song, ballade, carroll and ditty' all except *song* ('our naturall Saxon English word') are borrowed from the French, while the names of other kinds, 'Comedie, Tragedie, Ode, Epitaphe, Elegie, Epigramme', are derived from Greek and Latin (p. 58). He guesses at a root relationship between 'weete, weene, wotte, witlesse, witty & wise' (p. 204). He likes to distinguish between shades of meaning, sometimes not without excusable self-commendation: 'this diuersitie in the termes perchance euery man hath not noted' (p. 20). He glosses new words (*scientific, rhythm, idiom*) and explains proverbial phrases and colloquial expres-sions (*Scarborough warning, to sit on his skirts, speak like Bishop Nicholas*). When he censures Turberville and Stanyhurst for lack of Decorum in their use of the words *pelf, trudge* and *tug* he is careful to point out their original meaning and exact significance. He notices current tendencies to distort or restrict the meaning of words (*paragon, fantastical, rascal*). He defends his own use of certain 'straunge and vnaccustomed wordes' (*politian*, *majordomo*) and explains their force and derivation.

Nothing more clearly points to the mid-Tudor critic than the seriousness with which Puttenham approaches the Inkhorn term controversy (III, iv). The movement for restricting the recruitment of vocabulary from Latin and Greek goes back to the Cambridge of the forties when Sir John Cheke translated the Gospel of St Matthew into 'Saxon' English and (later) advertised to educated England his restrictive views in a foreword to Hoby's *Courtier*. There is much to be said at all times in defence of the rights of our Anglo-Saxon inheritance, but Cheke expressed his views uncompromisingly and at a very unfortunate time. His own prestige and the currency of the *Courtier* gave them considerable potency. 'Down with the Inkhorn' became a parrot cry of mid-century criticism, though it was not difficult for men of sanely progressive views, like Richard Sherry and George Pettie, to expose the fallacy in Cheke's argument. Scholars like Ascham and Wilson offered, however, the Saxon side the support of precept or example and the easy link with patriotism gave it unexpected currency among the poets. Gascoigne advises his novice to shun polysyllables because 'the more monasyllables that you use, the truer Englishman you shall seeme, and the lesse you shall smell of the Inkehorne'. Saxon purism must bear a certain responsibility for drabness and lumpishness of diction in many of the mid-century translators and versifiers, such as Phaer, Churchyard, Googe, Turberville and Gascoigne himself, and must have been one of the factors that turned Spenser's face (though he was Mulcaster's pupil) to the native past as a linguistic mine. Puttenham opens his discussion (p. 145) in the tones of one of Cheke's disciples. The intending poet is warned against three classes of words: 'inkhorne termes so ill affected brought

(xci)

in by men of learning as preachers and schoolemasters: and many straunge termes of other languages by Secretaries and Marchaunts and trauailours, and many darke wordes and not vsuall nor well sounding, though they be dayly spoken in Court'. Immediately upon this Puttenham cries *Peccavi* and confesses to the use of a varied list of recent importations, among them *politian, idiom, mechanical, method, figurative*. These he discusses and justifies as supplying a need. Other words, *penetrate, penetrable, indignity*, Puttenham admits as denizens in the language, 'for our speach wanteth wordes to such sence'. Others, *audacious, facundity, egregious, implete, compatible*, he is less inclined to allow. That in general he was prepared to stand by reason and custom in this matter is shown by his citation of Horace as an authority to prove that vocabulary, like other things natural and human, has its cycles and that in the long run Use and Custom are the 'onely vmpiers'.

Puttenham's own list by no means exhausts the debt which English owes to the *Arte*. Literary criticism was a new activity and had to find its terms and method. Words like *ode, lyric, accent, stanza, idiom, method* were then new-comers. The *Arte* smoothed their passage. Other terms make their first appearance here: *epic, orthographical, epigrammatist, trisyllable*. The recent or new words which Puttenham employs are either semi-technical and critical (which 'cannot be refused, specially in this place for description of the arte') or they are of an unobtrusive type blending easily with the romance tradition in our language. They are the kind that steal insensibly upon a language and make themselves indispensable before they are recognised. Puttenham had a creative as well as a critical flair for language, but it is not shouted from the housetops like Nashe's neologism or the huffe-snuffe roystering terms of Stanyhurst's *Aeneis*.

The Elizabethan study, cult almost, of words did not

suffer from the whirligig of time like the rhetoric. It was concerned with essentials and it did not collapse. The late eighties and nineties were years of word-making and language-building which, as a result of the efforts of the critics and humanists, did not proceed altogether haphazard. The expansion was led by men who had acquired the 'feel' of the language, a sense of its warp and woof. The dramatists, especially Shakespeare, show how nation-wide was the interest in words. They assume that strenuous attention will be paid to them; punning and quibbling rest on this assumption. The Dogberrys and Dame Quicklys of Elizabethan England delighted (if we may argue from the stage to life) to steal the scraps from the almsbasket of words. That a country Justice should pounce on the etymology of a new term (*accomodate*) is not perhaps surprising; it is less expected that the Bardolphs of the Elizabethan world should be verbal and grammatical precisians.[1]

Language rose like a tide on all sides until the ghost of Sir John Cheke relinquished its Canute-like efforts. The very pressure of language must have done something to melt the formalism of mid-Tudor prosody. It is significant that when the language was sifted in the Augustan age it settled down again happily enough in limited prosodic forms.

The great linguistic expansion is not foreshadowed in the *Arte*. Nothing so popular, indeed, came within its writer's ken. The *Arte* retains the modesty of an earlier age and Puttenham takes up his humanist's duty by the language where his uncle, Sir Thomas Elyot, had left it off. No book illustrates better the sense of responsibility which is the distinguishing mark of the humanist approach. Camden in his *Remaines* displays far more knowledge than Puttenham can claim but his materials are set out with a collector's zeal. They are

1 *II Henry IV*, III, ii; Bardolph cannot let pass Shallow's misuse of 'phrase'.

antiquarian exhibits. The humanist impulse has petered out or been merged in other interests.

One of the most prevalent impressions of Elizabethan criticism is that of a marked misfit between criticism and creation. The juxtaposition of the paragraphs on drama in the *Apologie* with the output of the popular stage, or of Spenser's Letter to Raleigh with the baroque exuberance ('arras full of deuise') of the *Faerie Queene*, calls up the image of the hen when her ducklings take to water. This impression only corresponds with the facts as long as we fix the mind on certain over-debated topics and fit English criticism into a European sequence dealing with the shibboleths of the Forms, Rules and Unities. The *Arte*, if we will really read it, brings home to us the importance of a different great critical tradition which leaves no impression of misfit or futility. Linguistic criticism in mid- and late-Tudor England was, apart from some oddities and excesses, at the centre of things. It focussed, directed and expressed a national consciousness and enormously extended, enriched and disciplined the language itself. A host of ripe, sane, progressive opinions on the subject can be collected from prefaces to 'Arts', textbooks and translations. To this rich and expanding tradition Shakespeare owed more than to his poet-predecessors. How full his mind was of it can be seen in *Love's Labour's Lost*.

CONCLUSION

One of the main purposes of this Introduction has been to exhibit the author of the *Arte* not, of course, as a master-mind, but as a freely moving intelligence, recording itself over a period of twenty years or more. The book is unequal in value and interest—some chapters have been described by serious historians and philologists as tissues of absurdities—but whatever the subject the writer's handling of it gives a picture of a mind in action, not book-making but thinking, observing, reconsidering. The temperament which moulds the *Arte* into self-expression is not perhaps common at any time and could not have been fostered by an 'iron & malitious age'.

Its individuality can best be apprehended by considering its reaction to the threat of puritanism. In the mid-Elizabethan period the sectaries, as a subversive element, roused against themselves political and social, as well as religious, hatred. It was natural enough that courtiers, defenders of poetry and easy-going maintainers of the *status quo* should take sides against them; it was (and is) equally natural for the full-blooded man to have small use for the kill-joy who says 'Because I am virtuous there shall be no more cakes and ale'. Elizabethan Brownists and precisians were, however, merely local and partisan expressions of a perennial puritanism which was entrenched in the Catholic church and, indeed, both was and is entrenched in the hearts of a large proportion of the human race. It is the negative attitude and, in its black *versus* white approach to life, often barrenly schematic; it draws its strength from a passionate and exclusive idealism or, less nobly, from fear. It finds the fighting point of its Gospel in the parable advocating the laying of the axe to the root of the tree, while the Puttenham-type recalls that, according to another parable, the wheat and tares grow together until the harvest and that, in any case, to no one less than the angels is given the task of sorting one from the other. Most Elizabethans, whatever their creed, were too much under the shadow of this puritanism to see it detached and whole; they oscillated too much between extremes for any steady vision. Gascoigne must compensate for his *Dan Bartholmew* by his *Diet for Droonkardes*; Lyly is blown about like a feather by conflicting winds of opinion about love. Grass must have grown on the *via media* in Elizabethan times. It was, however, for many reasons, the way Elizabeth at her accession desired to tread and if there was one thing Puttenham prayed for, it was that, with the regal pace he admired so much, she might walk in it unhindered. In two very interesting companion poems (*Partheniades*, 13 and 14) he implores her not to let herself be deflected from it.

In the first poem puritanism is handled on two planes —the more complex or 'philosophical' and the simpler or partisan. The schematic approach is shown to be inapplicable to life as it is lived on this complicated planet. It is pure abstraction and a defiance of reality and Nature. There is no weeding process which can

> Remove misterye from religion,
> From godly feare all superstition,
> Idolatrye from deepe devotion.

After some partisan hits, Puttenham moves to a second big idea; this purgative creed is an impoverishment of the 'civil' life; it grudges all that margin which is the opportunity for civilisation; it finds no scope for 'atmosphere' and associations or the traditional decencies. It not only forbids peasants their country sports; it takes from

> olde reliques reverence,
> From publique shews magnificence.

It would shear the majesty from kings and 'solemne circumstance from all these worldly thinges'.

A second, conciser, poem shows an even more Baconian appreciation of the alloy which, though it 'embaseth', makes the metal work the better. The puritan creed, applied in logical severity, reduces humanity to 'unaccomodated man'; it would

> Pull out of clothe and comelye weede
> The nakt carcas of Adames seede.

The black *versus* white attitude endeavours to wed the practically impossible to the aesthetically undesirable. This idea inspires Puttenham to his finest couplet in the little envoy:

> Princesse, yt ys as if one take awaye
> Greene wooddes from forrests, and sunne-shine fro the daye.

The two poems together are a plea for freedom to work towards the perfection of the civil life by inclusion rather than exclusion. They take us far beyond the defence of cakes and ale.

In the *Arte* Puttenham has nothing to say of the puritan actually at the gates, but the same mind and the same discernment express themselves in the insistence upon margin as essential to the civil life and in the view of poetry as man's solace, conveying upon occasions profit for mind and spirit but needing no ulterior motive, existing in its own right as an art and finding place for toys and trifles, even for merriment not of the precisest. Puttenham saw, too, as clearly as Matthew Arnold, how easily this puritanism blends with utilitarian and, indeed, mere money-getting standards. The man who asks of art 'What is the message?' and the man who asks 'What is the use?' easily make common cause. The strength of the utilitarian distrust of poetry is explicit or implicit in numberless prefaces,[1] plays and pamphlets. In Elizabethan days the very identification of verse-making with youth was a way of discrediting it. The *Arte* holds out both hands to youth.

The outlook of the *Arte* is secular. Puttenham prefers to speak 'in phrase of the Gentiles'. He had given an intelligent man's consideration to some of the questions that arise where religion and philosophy meet and he seizes the opportunity afforded by the mention of heathen hymns in Book I to enter a protest against the anthropomorphism into which religious utterance so

---

1 It is amusing that Field in his Preface to the *Arte* provides an example of the slight estimation of the art of poetry.

easily slips. 'The Lord thy God is a jealous God' would have seemed to him (in his heart) a shocking statement only justifiable by some kind of Figure. The intelligent man's God is '*autharcos*' not '*anthropopathis*' (p. 28). In the eleventh Partheniad he shows that he has taken some interest in various Christian and pagan explanations of the origin and destiny of the world. It is difficult not to hear a note of ironic distaste in the description of the 'Day of Judgment' view:

> There bee agayne
> A secte of men, somewhat precise,
> Beleeue a godd did yt devise,
> And not in vayne,
>
> Nor longe agone,
> Onely to serue Adam's linage
> Some little while as for a stage
> To playe vpon;
>
> And by despighte
> One daye agayne will in his rage
> Crushe it all as a kicson cage
> And spill it quite.

The deepest, or at least the most plangent, note that Puttenham can strike is heard later in this poem where the outlook upon mortality is one which Odysseus could have shared:

> O bootlesse carke
> Of mortal men searchinge to knowe,
> Of this or that, since he must rowe
> The dolefull barke
>
> Which Charon guydes,
> Fraught ful of shadows colde and starke,
> That ferrye to the coontryes darke,
> Tendinge theyr tydes.

In view of the extreme tenderness of Elizabethan orthodoxy, these three poems sail very near the wind. A certain community of temper and common interest in critical speculation may explain the note of *empressement* which is heard in the majority of Puttenham's references to Raleigh.

The *Arte* is a tribute to enjoyment of the richness and variety of experience in this present life. It records the quips and jests Puttenham had appreciated and his observations of princes, courtiers, lawyers, ambassadors, gentlewomen in their nurseries and pretty mistresses at Court. Vivid vignettes speak of a man who kept his eyes open and relished life. He could take his ease in his inn, some place of 'common resort' where men come to 'chat and prate', where 'many merry heades meete', and where he could savour vigorous rhymes scribbled with ink, chalk or coal on walls and mantle-pieces (p. 54). He may easily have joined in the ballads and catches trolled in these resorts, not all of which were as respectable as the old song of Percy and Douglas to which the heroic chord in Sidney's heart vibrated. It was characteristic of Puttenham, when writing with gusto his chapter on the *Epithalamium*, to insert a sly biblical reference (*Sicut sponsa de thalamo*) and to refrain from prudish comment on the rites appropriate to 'widowes or such as had tasted the frutes of loue before, (we call them well experienced young women)'. At 'these midsommer pageants in London' Puttenham had watched with appreciation 'shrewd boyes' peeping under the imposing façade of 'great and vglie Gyants marching as if they were aliue, and armed at all points, but within...stuffed full of browne paper and tow'. He peered into rings for 'devices' and turned up fruit trenchers of wood to scan the posies painted on their backs. He could be so lost in spelling out an epitaph (the effusion of some 'bastard rimer') as to find himself locked in a church by the sexton (p. 56). He could apply himself with equal concentration to a matter of state.

The egotism of the man appears in the book 'civilised' in obedience to the prevailing theme. The egotist can take a detached view of the ego. In the chapters on classical metres he enjoys his own slipperiness; the zest with which his pen races is inspired not by the subject in itself but by delight in his successful impersonation of the 'perfite' versifier. He dismisses his book at the end with an apology to Elizabeth for having ridden his hobby-horse so long. We shall not look to such a character for rigorous judgments or unbending earnestness. The *Arte* is the expression of an urbane and flexible temperament, shrewd and critical in its judgments, but preferring with Democritus to say it with laughter rather than with Heraclitus in tears (p. 112).

Another method of appreciating the individual quality behind the *Arte* is by comparison with other contemporary workers in the same field. It is easy to contrast the courtly critic with the university product by the help of E. K. and Gabriel Harvey. The comparative bookishness, even pedantry, of E. K.'s critical gloss to the *Shepheardes Calender* is obvious enough. But there is more than this. In E. K.'s critical remarks and in the records of Gabriel Harvey's larger mind and wider interests, there are hints of still lingering obscurantism or capacity to join in some kind of witch-hunt. Even Spenser is not free from this. The mind of the writer of the *Arte* moves in open daylight. It sees no bogies and never once uses the accents of repression or fear. This is not coarseness of fibre, for there is no condonation of grossness or bluntness in the *Arte*; it is evenness of pulse. The *Justificacion* brings home this quality even more forcibly. As an *ex parte* presentation of events which roused contemporaries to frenzy and can still inspire a fiercely partisan spirit after more than three hundred years, its balance and its freedom from hysteria are remarkable.

The most interesting and profitable comparison is with Sidney. Here, since both writers belong to the

(c)

same class, we expect more common ground. *Arte* and
Apologie carry themselves with the same aristocratic
assurance and ease. Each critic stresses the 'moving'
power of poetry. Otherwise they have not much in
common. The *Apologie* is the poet's plea for his vocation; the *Arte* is the critic's analysis of the poet's craft.
Puttenham's time, his temperament and his object permitted him more freedom than the Apologist could
claim. He is less burdened by the weight of authority
than Sidney and the influence of Italian critics like
Daniello and Minturno, or scholars like Scaliger, is
much less traceable in him. Sidney has much ado to
square Plato's views of poetry with his thesis; Puttenham does not trouble to mention the exclusion of poets
from the Republic, but the manner in which he disposes
of the complaint of the old Areopagus against Rhetoric
shows how he could have dealt with Plato had he wished.
The author of *Astrophel and Stella* hedges a little on the
subject of love poetry: 'Alas Love, I would thou
couldest as wel defend thy selfe, as thou canst offend
others'. The topic gave Puttenham no qualms. He had
no misgivings about Ovid (Partheniad 2) or Lucian,
'the merry Greeke' (*Arte*, p. 260). He can dismiss
Cicero's condemnation of dancing with a terse 'but
there by your leaue he failed'. He did not need (like
Elyot) to buttress his opinion by the precedent of
David's dancing before the ark. As an intelligent man
he was prepared to absorb 'delightful teaching' but he
did not demand parables or dark conceits. Poetry, he
assumes, will find room for all. He did not share the
black and white point of view which was influential
enough with Sidney to cause him some hesitation. To
characterise the whole from a part—the persistent error
of the puritan schematic mind—was to Puttenham ad-
missible only as a figure of speech (*synecdoche*) and,
therefore, an 'abusion'. It was not a logical approach
to truth. To admit trifles or careless mirth into the

ample scope of poetry was not to make Art itself trifling or careless.

Sidney's *Apologie*, of course, soars to an *O altitudo* to which Puttenham does not climb. He strikes neither the Platonic nor the heroic note. It is his distinction, however, that, within the limits of his mundane vision, he had a clearer grasp of the independence and self-sufficiency of poetry than was possessed (or at least expressed) by any other Elizabethan critic. Spenser's prose conception in the letter to Raleigh moves in blinkers as compared with Puttenham's. One would have liked more evidence that he could bridge the gulf which separated the Elizabethan from Chaucer, for Chaucer was a poet after his own heart, with the same Horatian sense of 'the craft so long to lerne' and the same human suppleness—too 'civilised' for that high seriousness which speaks the accents of *Inferno* or *Paradiso* or the world of *Lear*.

BIBLIOGRAPHICAL NOTE

The *Arte of English Poesie* was entered on the Stationers' Register to Thomas Orwin on 9 November 1588.[1] On 7 April 1589 Orwin's rights were 'by his consent nowe putt ouer' to Richard Field[2] and the same year Field's edition was published. An examination of the ten copies of Field's quarto accessible in the public, university and college libraries of London, Oxford and Cambridge[3] shows that the text exists in three principal forms. A word for word collation has not been made. All that has been attempted is an account of the principal variants of Field's edition and an interpretation of the literary bearings of the bibliographical evidence.

At three points, revision involving substantial alteration was made while the work was in the press: (1) while the outer forme of N was printing four leaves were inserted between the N and O gatherings; (2) while the inner forme of Ee was printing a paragraph on Ee iv was cancelled and another substituted; (3) a number of corrections were made on Ee ij[r], probably at the same time as (2). Some copies (A) contain none of these revisions:

> B.M., C. 71.c.16.
> B.M., 239.k.7.
> Bodl., Douce, PP.206.
> Victoria and Albert Museum, Dyce, 7998.

Others (B) contain (2) and (3):

> Bodl., Art. 4⁰. P. 21.
> Trinity College, Cambridge, VI.2.8.
> Trinity College, Cambridge, Capell, R. 14.
> Cambridge University Library, SSS.24.24.

1 Fol. 236ᵛ; Arber's Transcript, Vol. 2, p. 506.
2 Fol. 242ᵛ; Arber's Transcript, Vol. 2, p. 518.
3 We should like to record our appreciation of the courtesy of the Cambridge University Library and Trinity College, Cambridge, in allowing us to examine their copies.

Others (C) contain (1), (2) and (3):

B.M., G. 11548.
B.M., C. 21.b.18.

If the law of permutations and combinations can be applied to Field's assembling of his sheets, it is likely that the text existed (and may still exist) in other forms. It is more especially probable that copies were put together containing (1) but not (2) and (3).

The so-called 'cancelled' leaves. The four additional leaves, to which Arber's description 'cancelled' is still very frequently applied, were inserted between the N and O gatherings while printing of these sheets was in progress. Their insertion involved the removal of the last thirteen lines of N iiij^v ('When I wrate...lucratiue, as the') and their resetting in the corresponding position on the last of the additional pages. That printing had got as far as the sheets of O but not beyond is shown by the signatures and pagination. The additional leaves are signed j, ij, iij, [iiij]. They are not paginated. N iiij^v is numbered 84. O i^r is numbered 85. Pagination is continuous as far as O iiij^v, which is numbered 92. P i^r is numbered 101. That a gap of eight was left in the pagination at this point to allow for the additional leaves shows that printing of P had not yet begun.

That these additional pages represented new material, rather than the rectification of a printer's omission, is shown by their contents. There is a reference to the Armada on ij^r and, on the evidence of the cancelled passage on Ee iv^v (v. p. cv), Puttenham's manuscript went to press in the form it had received before the autumn of 1585. Further, among the emblems described in these pages is that of Philip of Spain discovered by Drake at S. Domingo on his 1586–7 West India voyage. Latin and French accounts of the expedition were printed at Leyden in 1588 and an English version was published by Field in 1589. Puttenham's description of Philip's device is clearly based on that in the accounts of Drake's voyage[1] and it is, therefore, very likely that he had come across the work in Field's printing house. These additional pages are clearly by the same hand as the rest of the *Arte* and their insertion at this stage shows that Puttenham co-operated in its publication and that Field's protested ignorance of its writer was made in deference to Puttenham's wishes. His desire to remain anonymous may have come as a surprise to Field, who by beginning the printing of the text at C suggests that he expected fairly long preliminaries from the author.

The cancelled anti-Dutch passage on Ee i[v]. This passage was written *c.* 1583–5.[2] Since it would have been tactless any time after the autumn of 1585 when Elizabeth at last decided to assist the Dutch, its cancellation in the press suggests that no complete revision of the *Arte* was made after this date.

One other bibliographical feature of the work may be of some literary significance. In the copies examined (and almost certainly in all) there are two leaves only in the I gathering. Book I of the *Arte* ends on I ij[r]. I ij[v] is blank. Book II begins on K i[r]. The pagination is continuous throughout these pages. The pagination, therefore, shows that when the beginning of Book II was paginated it was known that the end of Book I would cover only four pages. The presence of two leaves only in the I gathering may, therefore, indicate nothing more than that a halt was called when the printing of Book I was finished, but it may equally well shed some light on the date of the final chapter of this book. This, as has been noted above, seems to be of a later date than the rest of Book I and the early chapters

---

1 *V. A Summarie and True Discourse of Sir Frances Drakes West Indian Voyage*, London, 1589, E 2[r] and *Expeditio Francisci Draki*, Leydae, 1588, B 2[v].

2 The reference to the Dutch rebellion against Anjou dates the passage after January 1583.

of Book II. In view of the bibliographical evidence, it is not impossible that Puttenham was at work on this chapter as late as 1589 and that he was still writing while the beginning of Book II was being set up. That there was a break between the printing of the H and I sheets (rather than between the I and K) is, perhaps, indicated by the running title which appears in full on each printed page of the I gathering instead of being divided between the verso and recto of facing pages as in the rest of Book I.

The present text is based on B.M., G. 11548 (Ben Jonson's copy). On doubtful readings B.M., C.21.b.18 has been consulted. Field's text has been rendered as follows. Ornamental pieces have been omitted and some modifications in the running titles have been made. The woodcut portrait of Queen Elizabeth, which (in B.M., G. 11548) at one time faced the beginning of Book I but has been inserted to face the beginning of the dedication, is reproduced as frontispiece to the present text; there is some evidence that this portrait was supplied from another copy. Marginal signatures record the page beginnings of Field's edition and an oblique line marks the page end, save after diagrams, geometrical poems and where a section was terminated by a printer's ornament (*i.e.* after the dedication and at the close of each book). The character of Field's type (ſ, *vv* for *w*, etc.) has been followed except in a few italic ligatures. The distribution of roman and italic type and of upper and lower case letters has been kept; size variations in upper case letters, however, have been ignored and the drop capital (or ornamental initial), followed by an upper case letter at the beginning of the dedication and each chapter, has been replaced by an upper case letter followed by an upper or lower case letter according to the context. Letters from the wrong fount and faulty word-division, except where deliberately made to illustrate a prosodic

(cvi)

point (*e.g.* the verse extracts on p. 126), have been silently corrected. Only obvious compositor's errors have been rectified and all such corrections are noted in Appendix II. Where the text is plainly wrong but where any doubt arises as to the original form Field's reading has been retained. Loose and inexact forms in Greek and the romance languages have not been altered and only such errors in Latin grammatical forms and proper names as are unlikely to have been Puttenham's have been corrected. The punctuation of the original has been adhered to, not only because Elizabethan punctuation, in general, is of interest in itself but because, in this particular text, any tampering with the original pointing entails far-reaching changes and in some places where there was plainly some confusion either in Puttenham's manuscript or in setting up the text (*e.g.* p. 116, l. 11 and p. 147, ll. 11–2) re-punctuation would involve editorial re-writing and would destroy the informality of style and composition which is one of the *Arte*'s most striking features. The only modifications made are the rectification of a misplaced comma, some half-dozen corrections affecting brackets (noted in Appendix II) and the silent bringing into line of italic and roman colons with Field's normal practice (*i.e.* the colon follows the type of the preceding word). Where the chapter numbering of the original is wrong the correct number is given in brackets. For typographical reasons Greek ligatures have been expanded; otherwise contractions have been retained. Much might be said for their expansion, both from an aesthetic point of view and because they were largely (though not invariably) occasioned by the exigencies of the line, but as some spelling variations must be attributed to the same cause the overhauling of the former could not logically be defended without overhauling the latter. In general, our principle has been to present a text with the minimum of editorial handling. To those who may be repelled by its obsolete and uncouth features the encouragement of its open-minded author may be offered: 'to thinke the straungenesse thereof proceedes but of . . . disaquaintance . . . which in processe of tyme . . . will frame very well'.

Description of B.M., G. 11548 with notes on biblio-graphical variations in other copies examined:

Format: Quarto in fours.

Type: Roman and italic.

Preliminaries: [*AB ij^r*], title-page (facsimile on p. 1).
[*AB ij^v*], blank. *AB iij^r–AB iij^v*, dedication. The title-page and dedication leaves in this (and all copies examined) are conjugate. The rest of the preliminary matter consisted of three blank pages and a fourth containing a woodcut portrait of Queen Elizabeth. In Bodl., Art. 4°. P. 21 (the only copy examined still in its original binding and containing intact the whole of the original preliminary matter) [*AB i^r*], [*AB i^v*] and [*AB iiij^r*] are blank. The woodcut portrait appears on [*AB iiij^v*]. In this copy the preliminary matter was printed on a single sheet. In some copies the portrait has been lost; in some it has been mended and shifted from its original position. With the ex-ception of three copies (B.M., C. 21.b.18, B.M., 239.k.7 and U.L.C., SSS.24.24) the portrait now faces or (on the evidence of offsets) at one time faced C i^r. In the U.L.C. copy the portrait has been mended and now faces the title-page. In B.M., 239.k.7 the portrait has been mended and inserted to face the end of the dedication. In B.M., C. 21.b.18 the portrait now faces the title-page; it has been mended and an offset shows that it once faced *AB iij^r*. That this was not its original position is seen from the watermarks,

which show that the title-page and dedication leaves were conjugate. The presence of three watermarks on the three preliminary leaves of this copy suggests that either the preliminaries were printed on two half sheets or that the portrait was supplied from another copy. The portrait in B.M., G. 11548 which (on the evidence of an offset) at one time faced C i^r has been mended and inserted to face *AB iij^r*. From the paper it appears either to have been printed on a half sheet or to have been supplied from another copy. The portrait is reproduced as frontispiece to the present text. Round the head of the original portrait appears the lettering (in blind) ELIZABETH.D.G.REGINA. In B.M., G. 11548 [*AB i*] is missing.

Text and Tables: C—H^4, I^2, K—N^4, i^4, O—Z^4, Aa—Ll^4, Mm^1. Bodl., Art. 4°. P. 21 has [Mm ij] which is blank. In all copies examined there are two leaves only in the I gathering and I ij^v is blank. Fourth leaves are unsigned except C iiij and D iiij. Copies of the A and B types (*v. supra*, p. ciii) are without i^4.

Pagination: The text only (C i^r–Ll iij^v) is paginated—1–51, [52], 53–84, 8 unnumbered pages, 85–92, 101–135, 36 (for 136), 137–232, 235 (for 233), 234–258. In all copies examined p. 52 (I ij^v which is blank) is unnumbered but allowed for; O iiij^v is numbered 92; P i^r is numbered 101; p. 136 appears as 36; p. 233 is misnumbered 235 and p. 252 appears as z52. In some copies p. 258 appears as 25. In copies of the A and B types the eight unnumbered pages do not appear.

Running titles (the norms only are here recorded):
Book I—

verso pages to H iiij^v—OF POETS
recto pages to H iiij^r—AND POESIE. LIB. I.
I i^r—OF POETES AND POESIE. LIB. I.
I i^v—OF POETS AND POESIE. LIB. I.
I ij^r—OF POETS AND POESIE. LIB. I.

Book II—

OF PROPORTION. LIB. II. (on every page).

Book III—

OF ORNAMENT. LIB. III. (on every page).

The Arte of
English Poesie

A colei

Che se stessa rassomiglia
& non altrui.

Facsimile of the woodcut portrait of Queen Elizabeth which, from its
original position (facing the opening of Book I), seems to have con-
stituted Puttenham's dedication to the *Arte*.

Abrahamus Christum Joh 5º

Ut Ceruus Fontem. Psal 42.

THE ARTE
OF ENGLISH
POESIE.

Contriued into three Bookes: The first of Poets
and Poesie, the second of Proportion,
the third of Ornament.

Introite : Nam hic dij sunt. Israelit: Ephes

Ben: Jonson

AT LONDON
Printed by Richard Field, dwelling in the
black-Friers, neere Ludgate.
1589.

Noli timere Abrahame: Ego Protector tuus sum. Genes. 15º.

TO THE RIGHT HONORABLE SIR VVILLIAM
CECILL KNIGHT, LORD OF BVRGHLEY,
LORD HIGH TREASVRER OF ENGLAND,
R. F. Printer wifheth health and profperitie, with the com-
mandement and vfe of his continuall feruice.

This Booke (right Honorable) comming to my handes, with his
bare title without any Authours name or any other ordinarie
addreffe, I doubted how well it might become me to make you a
prefent thereof, feeming by many expreffe paffages in the fame at
large, that it was by the Authour intended to our Soueraigne Lady
the Queene, and for her recreation and feruice chiefly deuifed, in
which cafe to make any other perfon her highnes partener in the
honour of his guift it could not ftãd with my dutie, nor be without
fome preiudice to her Maiefties interest and his merrite. Perceyuing
befides the title to purport fo flender a fubieĉt, as nothing almoft could
be more difcrepant from the grauitie of your yeeres and Honorable
funĉtion, whofe contemplations are euery houre more ferioufly em-
ployed vpon the publicke adminiftration and feruices: I thought it
no condigne gratification, nor fcarce any good fatisfaĉtion for fuch
a perfon as you. Yet when I confidered, that beftowyng vpon your
Lordfhip the firft vewe of this mine impreffion (a feat of mine owne
fimple facultie) it could not fcypher her Maiesties honour or prero-
gatiue in the guift, nor yet the Authour of his thanks: and feeing
the thing it felfe to be a deuice of fome noueltie (which commonly/
giueth euery good thing a fpeciall grace) and a noueltie fo highly
tending to the moft worthy prayfes of her Maiesties moft excellent
name (deerer to you I dare conceiue then any worldly thing befides)
mee thought I could not deuife to haue prefented your Lordfhip any
gift more agreeable to your appetite, or fitter for my vocation and
abilitie to beftow, your Lordfhip beyng learned and a louer of learn-
ing, my prefent a Booke and my felfe a printer alwaies ready and
defirous to be at your Honourable commaundement. And
thus I humbly take my leaue from the Black-friers,
this xxviij. of May. 1589.

Your Honours moft humble
at commaundement,

R. F.

THE FIRST BOOKE,

Of Poets and Poefie.

CHAP. I.

What a Poet and Poefie is, and who may be worthily
fayd the moft excellent Poet of our time.

A Poet is as much to fay as a maker. And our Englifh
name well conformes with the Greeke word: for of ποιεῖν
to make, they call a maker *Poeta*. Such as (by way of
refemblance and reuerently) we may fay of God: who
without any trauell to his diuine imagination, made all
the world of nought, nor alfo by any paterne or mould
as the Platonicks with their Idees do phantaftically fuppofe. Euē fo the very Poet makes and contriues out of
his owne braine, both the verfe and matter of his poeme,
and not by any foreine copie or example, as doth the
tranflator, who therefore may well be fayd a verfifier,
but not a Poet. The premifes confidered, it giueth to
the name and profeffion no fmal dignitie and preheminence, aboue all other artificers, Scientificke or Mechanicall. And neuertheleffe without any repugnancie
at all, a Poet may in fome fort be faid a follower or
imitator, becaufe he can expreffe the true and liuely of
euery thing is fet before him, and which he taketh in
hand to defcribe: and fo in that refpect is both a maker
and a counterfaitor: and Poefie an art not only of making,
but alfo of imitation. And this fcience in his perfection,
can not grow, but by fome diuine inftinct, the Platonicks
call it *furor:* or by excellencie of nature and complexion:
or by great fubtiltie of the fpirits & wit, or by much
experience and obferuation of the world, and courfe of
kinde, or/peraduenture by all or moft part of them.

Otherwife how was it poffible that *Homer* being but a poore priuate man, and as fome fay, in his later age blind, fhould fo exactly fet foorth and defcribe, as if he had bene a moft excellent Captaine or Generall, the order and array of battels, the conduct of whole armies, the fieges and affaults of cities and townes? or as fome great Princes maiordome and perfect Surueyour in Court, the order, fumptuoufneffe and magnificence of royal bankets, feafts, weddings, and enteruewes? or as a Polititian very prudent, and much inured with the priuat and publique affaires, fo grauely examine the lawes and ordinances Ciuill, or fo profoundly difcourfe in matters of eftate, and formes of all politique regiment? Finally how could he fo naturally paint out the fpeeches, countenance and maners of Princely perfons and priuate, to wit, the wrath of *Achilles*, the magnanimitie of *Agamemnon*, the prudence of *Menelaus*, the proweffe of *Hector*, the maieftie of king *Priamus*, the grauitie of *Neftor*, the pollicies and eloquence of *Vlyffes*, the calamities of the diftreffed *Queenes*, and valiance of all the Captaines and aduenturous knights in thofe lamentable warres of Troy? It is therefore of Poets thus to be conceiued, that if they be able to deuife and make all thefe things of them felues, without any fubiect of veritie, that they be (by maner of fpeech) as creating gods. If they do it by inftinct diuine or naturall, then furely much fauoured from aboue. If by their experience, then no doubt very wife men. If by any prefident or paterne layd before them, then truly the moft excellent imitators & counterfaitors of all others. But you (Madame) my moft Honored and Gracious: if I fhould feeme to offer you this my deuife for a difcipline and not a delight, I might well be reputed, of all others the moft arrogant and iniurious: your felfe being alreadie, of any that I know in our time, the moft excellent Poet. Forfooth by your Princely purfe fauours and countenance, making in maner what ye lift, the poore man rich, the lewd well learned, the coward couragious, and vile both noble and valiant. Then for imitation no leſſe, your perſon as a moſt cunning counterfaitor liuely repreſenting *Venus* in countenance, in life *Diana*, *Pallas* for gouernement, and *Iuno* in all honour and regall magnificence./

CHAP. II.

C ijʳ

That there may be an Art of our Engliſh Poeſie, aſwell
as there is of the Latine and Greeke.

Then as there was no art in the world till by experience found out: ſo if Poeſie be now an Art, & of al antiquitie hath bene among the Greeks and Latines, & yet were none, vntill by ſtudious perſons faſhioned and reduced into a method of rules & precepts, then no doubt may there be the like with vs. And if th'art of Poeſie be but a skill appertaining to vtterance, why may not the ſame be with vs aſwel as with them, our language being no leſſe copious pithie and ſignificatiue then theirs, our conceipts the ſame, and our wits no leſſe apt to deuiſe and imitate then theirs were? If againe Art be but a certaine order of rules preſcribed by reaſon, and gathered by experience, why ſhould not Poeſie be a vulgar Art with vs aſwell as with the Greeks and Latines, our language admitting no fewer rules and nice diuerſities then theirs? but peraduenture moe by a peculiar, which our ſpeech hath in many things differing from theirs: and yet in the generall points of that Art, allowed to go in common with them: ſo as if one point perchance which is their feete whereupon their meaſures ſtand, and in deede is all the beautie of their Poeſie, and which feete we haue not, nor as yet neuer went about to frame (the nature of our language and wordes not permitting it) we haue in ſtead thereof twentie other curious points in that skill more then they euer had, by reaſon of our rime and tunable concords or ſimphonie, which they neuer obferued. Poefie therefore may be an Art in our vulgar, and that verie methodicall and commendable.

How Poets were the firft priefts, the firft prophets, the firft Legiflators and polititians in the world.

The profeffion and vfe of Poefie is moft ancient from the beginning, and not as manie errorioufly fuppofe, after, but before any ciuil fociety was among men. For it is written, that Poefie was th'originall caufe and occafion of their firft affemblies, when before the people remained in the woods and mountains, vagarant and difperfed like
C ij^v the wild beafts, lawleffe and naked, or verie ill/clad, and of all good and neceffarie prouifion for harbour or fuftenance vtterly vnfurnifhed: fo as they litle diffred for their maner of life, from the very brute beafts of the field. Whereupon it is fayned that *Amphion* and *Orpheus,* two Poets of the firft ages, one of them, to wit *Amphion,* builded vp cities, and reared walles with the ftones that came in heapes to the found of his harpe, figuring thereby the mollifying of hard and ftonie hearts by his fweete and eloquent perfwafion. And *Orpheus* affembled the wilde beafts to come in heards to harken to his muficke, and by that meanes made them tame, implying thereby, how by his difcreete and wholfome leffons vttered in harmonie and with melodious inftruments, he brought the rude and fauage people to a more ciuill and orderly life, nothing, as it feemeth, more preuailing or fit to redreffe and edifie the cruell and fturdie courage of man then it. And as thefe two Poets and *Linus* before them, and *Mufeus* alfo and *Hefiodus* in Greece and Archadia: fo by all likelihood had mo Poets done in other places, and in other ages before them, though there be no remembrance left of them, by reafon of the Recordes by fome accident of time perifhed and failing. Poets

(6)

therfore are of great antiquitie. Then forafmuch as they were the firſt that entended to the obſeruation of nature and her works, and ſpecially of the Celeſtiall courſes, by reaſon of the continuall motion of the heauens, ſearching after the firſt mouer, and from thence by degrees comming to know and conſider of the ſubſtances ſeparate & abſtract, which we call the diuine intelligences or good Angels (*Demones*) they were the firſt that inſtituted ſacrifices of placation, with inuocations and worſhip to them, as to Gods: and inuented and ſtabliſhed all the reſt of the obſeruances and ceremonies of religion, and ſo were the firſt Prieſts and miniſters of the holy miſteries. And becauſe for the better execution of that high charge and function, it behoued them to liue chaſt, and in all holines of life, and in continuall ſtudie and contemplation: they came by inſtinct diuine, and by deepe meditation, and much abſtinence (the ſame aſſubtiling and refining their ſpirits) to be made apt to receaue viſions, both waking and ſleeping, which made them vtter propheſies, and foretell things to come. So alſo were they the firſt Prophetes or ſeears, *Videntes*, for ſo the Scripture tearmeth them in Latine after/the Hebrue word, and all the oracles and anſwers of the gods were giuen in meeter or verſe, and publiſhed to the people by their direction. And for that they were aged and graue men, and of much wiſedome and experience in th'affaires of the world, they were the firſt lawmakers to the people, and the firſt polititiens, deuiſing all expedient meanes for th'eſtabliſhment of Common wealth, to hold and containe the people in order and duety by force and vertue of good and wholeſome lawes, made for the preſeruation of the publique peace and tranquillitie. The ſame peraduenture not purpoſely intended, but greatly furthered by the aw of their gods, and ſuch ſcruple of conſcience, as the terrors of their late inuented religion had led them into.

C iij^r

(7)

CHAP. IIII.

How the Poets were the firſt Philoſophers, the firſt Aſtronomers and Hiſtoriographers and Oratours and Muſitiens of the world.

Vtterance alſo and language is giuen by nature to man for perſwaſion of others, and aide of them ſelues, I meane the firſt abilite to ſpeake. For ſpeech it ſelfe is artificiall and made by man, and the more pleaſing it is, the more it preuaileth to ſuch purpoſe as it is intended for: but ſpeech by meeter is a kind of vtterance, more cleanly couched and more delicate to the eare then proſe is, becauſe it is more currant and ſlipper vpon the tongue, and withal tunable and melodious, as a kind of Muſicke, and therfore may be tearmed a muſicall ſpeech or vtterance, which cannot but pleaſe the hearer very well. Another cauſe is, for that it is briefer & more compendious, and eaſier to beare away and be retained in memorie, then that which is contained in multitude of words and full of tedious ambage and long periods. It is beſide a maner of vtterance more eloquent and rethoricall then the ordinarie proſe, which we vſe in our daily talke: becauſe it is decked and ſet out with all maner of freſh colours and figures, which maketh that it ſooner inuegleth the iudgement of man, and carieth his opinion this way and that, whither ſoeuer the heart by impreſſion of the eare ſhalbe moſt affectionatly bent and directed. The vtterance in proſe is not of ſo great efficacie, becauſe not only it is dayly vſed, and by that occaſion the eare is ouerglutted with it, but is alſo not ſo voluble/and ſlipper vpon the tong, being wide and loſe, and nothing numerous, nor contriued into meaſures, and ſounded with ſo gallant and harmonical accents, nor in fine alowed that figuratiue conueyance, nor ſo great licence in choiſe of words and phraſes as meeter is. So as the Poets were alſo from the beginning the beſt perſwaders and their eloquence the firſt Rethoricke of the world.

C iij^v

(8)

Euen fo it became that the high myfteries of the gods
fhould be reuealed & taught, by a maner of vtterance
and language of extraordinarie phrafe, and briefe and
compendious, and aboue al others fweet and ciuill as the
Metricall is. The fame alfo was meeteft to regifter the
liues and noble gefts of Princes, and of the great Mon-
arkes of the world, and all other the memorable accidents
of time: fo as the Poet was alfo the firft hiftoriographer.
Then forafmuch as they were the firft obferuers of all
naturall caufes & effects in the things generable and
corruptible, and from thence mounted vp to fearch after
the celeftiall courfes and influences, & yet penetrated
further to know the diuine effences and fubftances fepa-
rate, as is fayd before, they were the firft Aftronomers
and Philofophifts and Metaphificks. Finally, becaufe
they did altogether endeuor thē felues to reduce the life
of man to a certaine method of good maners, and made
the firft differences betweene vertue and vice, and then
tempered all thefe knowledges and skilles with the exercife of a delectable Muficke by melodious inftruments,
which withall ferued them to delight their hearers, & to
call the people together by admiration, to a plaufible
and vertuous conuerfation, therefore were they the firft
Philofophers Ethick, & the firft artificiall Muficiens of
the world. Such was *Linus, Orpheus, Amphiō* & *Mufeus*
the moft ancient Poets and Philofophers, of whom there
is left any memorie by the prophane writers. King
Dauid alfo & *Salomon* his fonne and many other of the
holy Prophets wrate in meeters, and vfed to fing them
to the harpe, although to many of vs ignorant of the
Hebrue language and phrafe, and not obferuing it, the
fame feeme but a profe. It can not bee therefore that
anie fcorne or indignitie fhould iuftly be offred to fo
noble, profitable, ancient and diuine a fcience as Poefie is.

CHAP. V.

*How the wilde and fauage people vfed a naturall Poefie
in verficle and rime as our vulgar is./*

C iiijʳ And the Greeke and Latine Poefie was by verfe numerous
and metricall, running vpon pleafant feete, fometimes
fwift, fometime flow (their words very aptly feruing that
purpofe) but without any rime or tunable concord in
th'end of their verfes, as we and all other nations now
vfe. But the Hebrues & Chaldees who were more ancient then the Greekes, did not only vfe a metricall Poefie,
but alfo with the fame a maner of rime, as hath bene of
late obferued by learned men. Wherby it appeareth, that
our vulgar running Poefie was common to all the nations
of the world befides, whom the Latines and Greekes in
fpeciall called barbarous. So as it was notwithftanding
the firft and moft ancient Poefie, and the moft vniuerfall, which two points do otherwife giue to all humane
inuentions and affaires no fmall credit. This is proued
by certificate of marchants & trauellers, who by late
nauigations haue furueyed the whole world, and difcouered large countries and ftrange peoples wild and
fauage, affirming that the American, the Perufine &
the very Canniball, do fing and alfo fay, their higheft
and holieft matters in certaine riming verficles and not
in profe, which proues alfo that our maner of vulgar
Poefie is more ancient then the artificiall of the Greeks
and Latines, ours comming by inftinct of nature, which
was before Art or obferuation, and vfed with the fauage
and vnciuill, who were before all fcience or ciuilitie,
euen as the naked by prioritie of time is before the
clothed, and the ignorant before the learned. The
naturall Poefie therefore being aided and amended by
Art, and not vtterly altered or obfcured, but fome figne
left of it, (as the Greekes and Latines haue left none)
is no leffe to be allowed and commended then theirs.

CHAP. VI.

*How the riming Poefie came firft to the Grecians and
Latines, and had altered and almoft fpilt
their maner of Poefie.*

But it came to paffe, when fortune fled farre from the
Greekes and Latines, & that their townes florifhed no
more in traficke, nor their Vniuerfities in learning as
they had done continuing thofe Monarchies: the barbarous conquerers inuading them with innumerable
fwarmes of ftrange nations, the Poefie metricall of the
Grecians and Latines came to be much corrupted and
altered,/in fo much as there were times that the very C iiij^v
Greekes and Latines themfelues tooke pleafure in Riming
verfes, and vfed it as a rare and gallant thing: Yea their
Oratours profes nor the Doctors Sermons were acceptable to Princes nor yet to the common people vnleffe
it went in manner of tunable rime or metricall fentences,
as appeares by many of the auncient writers, about that
time and fince. And the great Princes, and Popes, and
Sultans would one falute and greet an other fometime
in frendfhip and fport, fometime in earneft and enmitie
by ryming verfes, & nothing feemed clerkly done, but
muft be done in ryme: Whereof we finde diuers examples
from the time of th'Emperours Gracian & Valentinian
downwardes: For then aboutes began the declination of
the Romain Empire, by the notable inundations of the
Hunnes and *Vandalles* in Europe, vnder the conduct of
Totila & *Atila* and other their generalles. This brought
the ryming Poefie in grace, and made it preuaile in Italie
and Greece (their owne long time caft afide, and almoft
neglected) till after many yeares that the peace of Italie
and of th'Empire Occidentall reuiued new clerkes, who
recouering and perufing the bookes and ftudies of the
ciuiler ages, reftored all maner of arts, and that of the
Greeke and Latine Poefie withall into their former
puritie and netnes. Which neuerthelesse did not fo pre-

uaile, but that the ryming Poefie of the Barbarians remained ftill in his reputation, that one in the fchole, this other in Courts of Princes more ordinary and allowable.

CHAP. VII.

How in the time of Charlemaine and many yeares after him the Latine Poetes wrote in ryme.

And this appeareth euidently by the workes of many learned men, who wrote about the time of *Charlemaines* raigne in the Empire *Occidentall*, where the Chriftian Religion, became through the exceffiue authoritie of Popes, and deepe deuotion of Princes ftrongly fortified and eftablifhed by erection of orders *Monaftical*, in which many fimple clerks for deuotiō fake & fanctitie were receiued more then for any learning, by which occafion & the folitarineffe of their life, waxing ftudious without difcipline or inftruction by any good methode, fome D iᵛ of them grew to be hifto-/riographers, fome Poets, and following either the barbarous rudenes of the time, or els their own idle inuentions, all that they wrote to the fauor or prayfe of Princes, they did it in fuch maner of minftrelfie, and thought themfelues no fmall fooles, when they could make their verfes goe all in ryme as did the fchoole of *Salerne*, dedicating their booke of medicinall rules vnto our king of England, with this beginning.

Anglorum Regi fcripfit tota fchola Salerni
Si vis incolumem, fi vis te reddere fanum
Curas tolle graues, irafci crede prophanum
Nec retine ventrem nec ftringas fortiter anum.

And all the reft that follow throughout the whole booke more curioufly then cleanely, neuertheleffe very well to the purpofe of their arte. In the fame time king *Edward* the iij. him felfe quartering the Armes of England and France, did difcouer his pretence and clayme to the Crowne of Fraunce, in thefe ryming verfes.

Rex ſum regnorum bina ratione duorum
Anglorum regno ſum rex ego iure paterno
Matris iure quidem Francorum nuncupor idem
Hinc eſt armorum variatio faƈta meorum.

Which verſes *Phillip de Valois* then poſſeſſing the Crowne as next heire male by pretexte of the law *Salique*, and holding out *Edward* the third, aunſwered in theſe other of as good ſtuffe.

Prædo regnorum qui diceris eſſe duorum
Regno materno priuaberis atque paterno
Prolis ius nullum vbi matris non fuit vllum
Hinc eſt armorum variatio ſtulta tuorum.

It is found written of Pope *Lucius*, for his great auarice and tyranny vſed ouer the Clergy thus in ryming verſes.

Lucius eſt piſcis rex & tyrannus aquarum
A quo diſcordat Lucius iſte parum
Deuorat hic homines, hic piſcibus inſidiatur
Eſurit hic ſemper hic aliquando ſatur
Amborum vitam ſi laus æquata notaret
Plus rationis habet qui ratione caret.

And as this was vſed in the greateſt and gayeſt matters of Princes and Popes by the idle inuention of Monaſticall men then rai-/gning al in their ſuperlatiue. So did euery D iv ſcholer & ſecular clerke or verſifier, when he wrote any ſhort poeme or matter of good leſſon put it in ryme, whereby it came to paſſe that all your old Prouerbes and common ſayinges, which they would haue plauſible to the reader and eaſie to remember and beare away, were of that ſorte as theſe.

In mundo mira faciunt duo nummus & ira
Mollificant dura peruertunt omnia iura.

And this verſe in diſprayſe of the Courtiers life following the Court of Rome.

Vita palatina dura eſt animæ{que} ruina.

5 (13)

And thefe written by a noble learned man.

> *Ire redire fequi regum fublimia caftra*
> *Eximius ftatus eft, fed non fic itur ad astra.*

And this other which to the great iniurie of all women was written (no doubt by fome forlorne louer, or els fome old malicious Monke) for one womans fake blemifhing the whole fexe.

> *Fallere flere nere mentiri nilᵭ tacere*
> *Hæc quinque vere ftatuit Deus in muliere.*

If I might haue bene his Iudge, I would haue had him for his labour, ferued as *Orpheus* was by the women of Thrace. His eyes to be picket out with pinnes, for his fo deadly belying of them, or worfe handled if worfe could be deuifed. But will ye fee how God raifed a reuenger for the filly innocent women, for about the fame ryming age came an honeft ciuill Courtier fomewhat bookifh, and wrate thefe verfes againft the whole rable of Monkes.

> *O Monachi veftri ftomachi funt amphora Bacchi*
> *Vos eftis Deus eft teftis turpiſſima peftis.*

Anon after came your fecular Prieftes as iolly rymers as the reft, who being fore agreeued with their Pope *Calixtus*, for that he had enioyned them from their wiues, & railed as faft againft him.

> *O bone Calixte totus mundus perodit te*
> *Quondam Presbiteri, poterant vxoribus vti*
> *Hoc deftruxifti, poftquam tu Papa fuifti.*

Thus what in writing of rymes and regiftring of lyes was the Clergy of that fabulous age wholly occupied.

We finde fome but very few of thefe ryming verfes among the/Latines of the ciuiller ages, and thofe rather hapning by chaunce then of any purpofe in the writer, as this *Diftick* among the difportes of *Ouid*.

D ijʳ

> *Quot cælum ftellas tot habet tua Roma puellas*
> *Pafcua quotᵭ hædos tot habet tua Roma Cynædos,*

(14)

The poſteritie taking pleaſure in this manner of *Sim-phonie* had leaſure as it ſeemes to deuiſe many other knackes in their verſifying that the aunciént and ciuill Poets had not vſed before, whereof one was to make euery word of a verſe to begin with the ſame letter, as did *Hugobald* the Monke who made a large poeme to the honour of *Carolus Caluus*, euery word beginning with *C.* which was the firſt letter of the kings name thus.

Carmina clariſonæ Caluis cantate camenæ.

And this was thought no ſmall peece of cunning, being in deed a matter of ſome difficultie to finde out ſo many wordes beginning with one letter as might make a iuſt volume, though in truth it were but a phantaſticall deuiſe and to no purpoſe at all more then to make them harmonicall to the rude eares of thoſe barbarous ages.

Another of their pretie inuentions was to make a verſe of ſuch wordes as by their nature and manner of con-ſtruction and ſituation might be turned backward word by word, and make another perfit verſe, but of quite contrary ſence as the gibing Monke that wrote of Pope *Alexander* theſe two verſes.

Laus tua non tua fraus, virtus non copia rerum,
Scandere te faciunt hoc decus eximium.

Which if ye will turne backward they make two other good verſes, but of a contrary ſence, thus.

Eximium decus hoc faciunt te ſcandere, rerum
Copia, non virtus, fraus tua non tua laus.

And they called it *Verſe Lyon.*

Thus you may ſee the humors and appetites of men how diuers and chaungeable they be in liking new faſhions, though many tymes worſe then the old, and not onely in the manner of their life and vſe of their garments, but alſo in their learninges and arts and ſpecially of their languages./

CHAP. VIII.

In what reputation Poefie and Poets were in old time with Princes and otherwife generally, and hovv they be novv become contemptible and for vvhat caufes.

For the refpectes aforefayd in all former ages and in the moft ciuill countreys and commons wealthes, good Poets and Poefie were highly efteemed and much fauoured of the greateft Princes. For proofe whereof we read how much *Amyntas* king of *Macedonia* made of the Tragicall Poet *Euripides.* And the *Athenians* of *Sophocles.* In what price the noble poemes of *Homer* were holden with *Alexander* the great, in fo much as euery night they were layd vnder his pillow, and by day were carried in the rich iewell cofer of *Darius* lately before vanquifhed by him in battaile. And not onely *Homer* the father and Prince of the Poets was fo honored by him, but for his fake all other meaner Poets, in fo much as *Cherillus* one no very great good Poet had for euery verfe well made a *Phillips* noble of gold, amounting in value to an angell Englifh, and fo for euery hundreth verfes (which a cleanely pen could fpeedely difpatch) he had a hundred angels. And fince *Alexander* the great how *Theocritus* the Greeke Poet was fauored by *Tholomee* king of Egipt & Queene *Berenice* his wife, *Ennius* likewife by *Scipio* Prince of the *Romaines, Virgill* alfo by th'Emperour *Auguftus.* And in later times how much were *Iehan de Mehune* & *Guillaume de Loris* made of by the French kinges, and *Geffrey Chaucer* father of our Englifh Poets by *Richard* the fecond, who as it was fuppofed gaue him the maner of new Holme in Oxfordfhire. And *Govver* to *Henry* the fourth, and *Harding* to *Edvvard* the fourth. Alfo how *Frauncis* the Frenche king made *Sangelais, Salmonius, Macrinus,* and *Clement Marot* of his priuy Chamber for their excellent skill in vulgare and Latine Poefie. And king *Henry* the 8. her *Maiefties* father for a few Pfalmes of *Dauid* turned into Englifh meetre by

(16)

Sternhold, made him groome of his priuy chamber, &
gaue him many other good gifts. And one *Gray* what
good eftimation did he grow vnto with the fame king
Henry, & afterward with the Duke of Sommerfet Pro-
tectour, for making certaine merry Ballades, whereof
one chiefly was, *The hunte is vp, the hunte is vp*. And
Queene *Mary* his daughter for one *Epi-/thalamie* or D iij[r]
nuptiall fong made by *Vargas* a Spanifh Poet at her
mariage with king *Phillip* in Winchefter gaue him
during his life two hundred Crownes penfion: nor this
reputation was giuen them in auncient times altogether
in refpect that Poefie was a delicate arte, and the Poets
them felues cunning Princepleafers, but for that alfo
they were thought for their vniuerfall knowledge to be
very fufficient men for the greateft charges in their common wealthes, were it for counfell or for conduct, whereby no man neede to doubt but that both skilles may very
well concurre and be moft excellent in one perfon. For
we finde that *Iulius Cæfar* the firft Emperour and a moft
noble Captaine, was not onely the moft eloquent Orator
of his time, but alfo a very good Poet, though none of
his doings therein be now extant. And *Quintus Catulus*
a good Poet, and *Cornelius Gallus* treafurer of Egipt,
and *Horace* the moft delicate of all the Romain *Lyrickes*,
was thought meete and by many letters of great inftance
prouoked to be Secretarie of eftate to *Auguftus* th'Emperour, which neuertheleffe he refufed for his vnhealth-
fulneffe fake, and being a quiet mynded man and
nothing ambitious of glory: *non voluit accedere ad Rem-
publicam*, as it is reported. And *Ennius* the Latine Poet
was not as fome perchaunce thinke, onely fauored by
Scipio the *Africane* for his good making of verfes, but
vfed as his familiar and Counfellor in the warres for his
great knowledge and amiable conuerfation. And long
before that*Antimenides* and other Greeke Poets, as *Ariftotle*
reportes in his Politiques, had charge in the warres. And
Tirtæus the Poet being alfo a lame man & halting vpō

(17)

one legge, was chofen by the Oracle of the gods from the *Athenians* to be generall of the *Lacedemonians* armie, not for his Poetrie, but for his wifedome and graue perfwafions, and fubtile Stratagemes whereby he had the victory ouer his enemies. So as the Poets feemed to haue skill not onely in the fubtilties of their arte, but alfo to be meete for all maner of functions ciuill and martiall, euen as they found fauour of the times they liued in, infomuch as their credit and eftimation generally was not fmall. But in thefe dayes (although fome learned Princes may take delight in them) yet vniuerfally it is not fo. For as well Poets as Poefie are defpifed, & the name become, of honorable infamous, fubiect to fcorne and deri-/fion, and rather a reproch than a prayfe to any that vfeth it: for commonly who fo is ftudious in th'Arte or fhewes him felfe excellent in it, they call him in difdayne a *phantafticall:* and a light headed or phantafticall man (by conuerfion) they call a Poet. And this proceedes through the barbarous ignoraunce of the time, and pride of many Gentlemen, and others, whofe groffe heads not being brought vp or acquainted with any excellent Arte, nor able to contriue, or in manner conceiue any matter of fubtiltie in any bufineffe or fcience, they doe deride and fcorne it in all others as fuperfluous knowledges and vayne fciences, and whatfoeuer deuife be of rare inuention they terme it *phantafticall,* conftruing it to the worft fide: and among men fuch as be modeft and graue, & of litle conuerfation, nor delighted in the bufie life and vayne ridiculous actions of the popular, they call him in fcorne a *Philofopher* or *Poet,* as much to fay as a phantafticall man, very iniurioufly (God wot) and to the manifeftation of their own ignoraunce, not making difference betwixt termes. For as the euill and vicious difpofition of the braine hinders the founde iudgement and difcourfe of man with bufie & difordered phantafies, for which caufe the Greekes call him φαντάστικος, fo is that part being well

affected, not onely nothing diforderly or confufed with
any monftruous imaginations or conceits, but very formall,
and in his much multiformitie *vniforme*, that is well pro-
portioned, and fo paffing cleare, that by it as by a glaffe
or mirrour, are reprefented vnto the foule all maner of
bewtifull vifions, whereby the inuentiue parte of the
mynde is fo much holpen, as without it no man could
deuife any new or rare thing: and where it is not
excellent in his kind, there could be no politique Captaine, nor any witty enginer or cunning artificer, nor
yet any law maker or counfellor of deepe difcourfe, yea
the Prince of Philofophers ftickes not to fay *animam nō*
intelligere abfque phantafmate, which text to another purpofe *Alexander Aphrodifeus* well noteth, as learned men
know. And this phantafie may be refembled to a glaffe
as hath bene fayd, whereof there be many tempers and
manner of makinges, as the *perfpectiues* doe acknowledge, for fome be falfe glaffes and fhew thinges otherwife than they be in deede, and others right as they be
in deede, neither fairer nor fouler, nor greater nor
fmaller. There be againe of thefe/glaffes that fhew thinges D iiijʳ
exceeding faire and comely, others that fhew figures
very monftruous & illfauored. Euen fo is the phantafticall part of man (if it be not difordered) a reprefenter
of the beft, moft comely and bewtifull images or ap-
parances of thinges to the foule and according to their
very truth. If otherwife, then doth it breede *Chimeres*
& monfters in mans imaginations, & not onely in his
imaginations, but alfo in all his ordinarie actions and
life which enfues. Wherefore fuch perfons as be illu-
minated with the brighteft irradiations of knowledge
and of the veritie and due proportion of things, they
are called by the learned men not *phantaftici* but *euphan-*
tafiote, and of this forte of phantafie are all good Poets,
notable Captaines ftratagematique, all cunning artificers
and enginers, all Legiflators Polititiens & Counfellours
of eftate, in whofe exercifes the inuentiue part is moft

employed and is to the found & true iudgement of man
moſt needful. This diuerſitie in the termes perchance
euery man hath not noted, & thus much be ſaid in
defence of the Poets honour, to the end no noble and
generous minde be diſcomforted in the ſtudie thereof,
the rather for that worthy & honorable memoriall of
that noble woman twiſe French Queene, Lady *Anne* of
Britaine, wife firſt to king *Charles* the viij. and after to
Lewes the xij. who paſſing one day from her lodging
toward the kinges ſide, ſaw in a gallerie *Maiſter Allaine
Chartier* the kings Secretarie, an excellent maker or
Poet leaning on a tables end a ſleepe, & ſtooped downe
to kiſſe him, ſaying thus in all their hearings, we may
not of Princely courteſie paſſe by and not honor with our
kiſſe the mouth from whence ſo many ſweete ditties &
golden poems haue iſſued. But me thinks at theſe words
I heare ſome ſmilingly ſay, I would be loath to lacke
liuing of my own till the Prince gaue me a maner of new
Elme for my riming. And another to ſay I haue read
that the Lady *Cynthia* came once downe out of her skye
to kiſſe the faire yong lad *Endimion* as he lay a ſleep:
& many noble Queenes that haue beſtowed kiſſes vpon
their Princes paramours, but neuer vpon any Poets.
The third me thinks ſhruggingly ſaith, I kept not to
ſit ſleeping with my Poeſie till a Queene came and kiſſed
me. But what of all this? Princes may giue a good Poet
ſuch conuenient countenaunce and alſo benefite as are
D iiijᵛ due to an excellent artificer, though they nei-/ther kiſſe
nor cokes them, and the diſcret Poet lookes for no ſuch
extraordinarie fauours, and aſwell doth he honour by
his pen the iuſt, liberall, or magnanimous Prince, as the
valiaunt, amiable or bewtifull though they be euery one
of them the good giftes of God. So it ſeemes not altogether the ſcorne and ordinarie diſgrace offered vnto
Poets at theſe dayes, is cauſe why few Gentlemen do
delight in the Art, but for that liberalitie, is come to fayle
in Princes, who for their largeſſe were wont to be ac-

compted th'onely patrons of learning, and firſt founders of all excellent artificers. Beſides it is not perceiued, that Princes them ſelues do take any pleaſure in this ſcience, by whoſe example the ſubieƈt is commonly led, and allured to all delights and exerciſes be they good or bad, according to the graue ſaying of the hiſtorian. *Rex multitudinem religione impleuit, quæ ſemper regenti ſimilis eſt.* And peraduēture in this iron & malitious age of ours, Princes are leſſe delighted in it, being ouer earneſtly bent and affeƈted to the affaires of Empire & ambition, whereby they are as it were inforced to in-deuour them ſelues to armes and praƈtiſes of hoſtilitie, or to entend to the right pollicing of their ſtates, and haue not one houre to beſtow vpon any other ciuill or deleƈtable Art of naturall or morall doƈtrine: nor ſcarce any leiſure to thincke one good thought in perfeƈt and godly contemplation, whereby their troubled mindes might be moderated and brought to tranquillitie. So as, it is hard to find in theſe dayes of noblemē or gentle-men any good *Mathematiciā*, or excellent *Muſitian*, or notable *Philoſopher*, or els a cunning Poet: becauſe we find few great Princes much delighted in the ſame ſtudies. Now alſo of ſuch among the Nobilitie or gentrie as be very well ſeene in many laudable ſciences, and eſpecially in making or Poeſie, it is ſo come to paſſe that they haue no courage to write & if they haue, yet are they loath to be a knowen of their skill. So as I know very many notable Gentlemen in the Court that haue written commendably, and ſuppreſſed it agayne, or els ſuffred it to be publiſht without their owne names to it: as if it were a diſcredit for a Gentleman, to ſeeme learned, and to ſhew him ſelfe amorous of any good Art. In other ages it was not ſo, for we read that Kinges & Princes haue written great volumes and publiſht them vnder their owne regall titles. As to begin with *Salomon* the wiſeſt/of Kings, *Iulius Cæſar* the greateſt of Emperours, *Hermes Triſmegiſtus* the holieſt of Prieſtes E iʳ and Prophetes, *Euax* king of *Arabia* wrote a booke of precious ftones in verfe, Prince *Auicenna* of Phificke and Philofophie, *Alphonfus* king of Spaine his Aftronomicall Tables, *Almanfor* a king of *Marrocco* diuerfe Philofophicall workes, and by their regall example our late foueraigne Lord king *Henry* the eight wrate a booke in defence of his faith, then perfwaded that it was the true and Apoftolicall doctrine, though it hath appeared otherwife fince, yet his honour and learned zeale was nothing leffe to be allowed. Queenes alfo haue bene knowen ftudious, and to write large volumes, as Lady *Margaret* of Fraunce Queene of *Nauarre* in our time. But of all others the Emperour *Nero* was fo well learned in Mufique and Poefie, as when he was taken by order of the Senate and appointed to dye, he offered violence to him felfe and fayd, *O quantus artifex pereo!* as much to fay, as, how is it poffible a man of fuch fcience and learning as my felfe, fhould come to this fhamefull death? Th'emperour *Octauian* being made executor to *Virgill,* who had left by his laft will and teftament, that his bookes of the *Æneidos* fhould be committed to the fire as things not perfited by him, made his excufe for infringing the deads will, by a number of verfes moft excellently written, whereof thefe are part.

> *Frangatur potiùs legum veneranda poteftas,*
> *Quàm tot congeftos noctéfque diéfque labores*
> *Hauferit vna dies.* And put his name to them.

And before him his vncle & father adoptiue *Iulius Cæfar,* was not afhamed to publifh vnder his owne name, his Commentaries of the French and Britaine warres. Since therefore fo many noble Emperours, Kings and Princes haue bene ftudious of Poefie and other ciuill arts, & not afhamed to bewray their skils in the fame, let none other meaner perfon defpife learning, nor (whether it be in profe or in Poefie, if they them felues be able to write, or haue written any thing well

or of rare inuention) be any whit fqueimifh to let it be
publifht vnder their names, for reafon ferues it, and
modeftie doth not repugne./

*How Poefie fhould not be imployed vpon vayne conceits
or vicious or infamous.*

Wherefore the Nobilitie and dignitie of the Art confidered afwell by vniuerfalitie as antiquitie and the
naturall excellence of it felfe, Poefie ought not to be
abafed and imployed vpon any vnworthy matter &
fubiect, nor vfed to vaine purpofes, which neuertheleffe
is dayly feene, and that is to vtter conceits infamous &
vicious or ridiculous and foolifh, or of no good example
& doctrine. Albeit in merry matters (not vnhoneft)
being vfed for mans folace and recreation it may be well
allowed, for as I faid before, Poefie is a pleafant maner
of vtteraunce varying from the ordinarie of purpofe to
refrefh the mynde by the eares delight. Poefie alfo is
not onely laudable, becaufe I faid it was a metricall
fpeach vfed by the firft men, but becaufe it is a metricall
fpeach corrected and reformed by difcreet iudgements,
and with no leffe cunning and curiofitie then the Greeke
and Latine Poefie, and by Art bewtified & adorned, &
brought far from the primitiue rudeneffe of the firft
inuentors, otherwife it might be fayd to me that *Adam*
and *Eues* apernes were the gayeft garmentes, becaufe
they were the firft, and the fhepheardes tente or pauillion,
the beft houfing, becaufe it was the moft auncient &
moft vniuerfall: which I would not haue fo taken, for it
is not my meaning but that Art & cunning concurring
with nature, antiquitie & vniuerfalitie, in things indifferent, and not euill, doe make them more laudable.
And right fo our vulgar riming Poefie, being by good
wittes brought to that perfection we fee, is worthily to
be preferred before any other maner of vtterance in

(23)

profe, for fuch vfe and to fuch purpofe as it is ordained, and fhall hereafter be fet downe more particularly.

CHAP. X.

The fubieſt or matter of Poefie.

Hauing fufficiently fayd of the dignitie of Poets and Poefie, now it is tyme to fpeake of the matter or fubieſt of Poefie, which to myne intent is, what foeuer wittie and delicate conceit of man meet or worthy to be put in written verfe, for any neceffary vfe of the prefent time, or good inftruction of the pofteri-/tie. But the chief and principall is: the laud honour & glory of the immortall gods (I fpeake now in phrafe of the Gentiles.) Secondly the worthy gefts of noble Princes: the memoriall and regiftry of all great fortunes, the praife of vertue & reproofe of vice, the inftruction of morall doctrines, the reuealing of fciences naturall & other profitable Arts, the redreffe of boiftrous & fturdie courages by perfwafion, the confolation and repofe of temperate myndes, finally the common folace of mankind in all his trauails and cares of this tranfitorie life. And in this laft fort being vfed for recreation onely, may allowably beare matter not alwayes of the graueft, or of any great commoditie or profit, but rather in fome fort, vaine, diffolute, or wanton, fo it be not very fcandalous & of euill example. But as our intent is to make this Art vulgar for all Englifh mens vfe, & therefore are of neceffitie to fet downe the principal rules therein to be obferued: fo in mine opinion it is no leffe expedient to touch briefly all the chief points of this auncient Poefie of the Greeks and Latines, fo far forth as it conformeth with ours. So as it may be knowen what we hold of them as borrowed, and what as of our owne peculiar. Wherefore now that we haue faid, what is the matter of Poefie, we will declare the manner and formes of poemes vfed by the auncients.

E ijʳ

CHAP. XI.

Of poemes and their sundry formes and how thereby the auncient Poets receaued surnames.

As the matter of Poesie is diuers, so was the forme of their poemes & maner of writing, for all of them wrote not in one sort, euen as all of them wrote not vpon one matter. Neither was euery Poet alike cunning in all as in some one kinde of Poesie, nor vttered with like felicitie. But wherein any one most excelled, thereof he tooke a surname, as to be called a Poet *Heroick*, *Lyrick*, *Elegiack*, *Epigrāmatist* or otherwise. Such therefore as gaue them selues to write long histories of the noble gests of kings & great Princes entermedling the dealings of the gods, halfe gods or *Heroes* of the gentiles, & the great & waighty consequences of peace and warre, they called Poets *Heroick*, whereof *Homer* was chief and most auncient among the Greeks, *Virgill* among the Latines:/ Others who more delighted to write songs or ballads of pleasure, to be song with the voice, and to the harpe, lute, or citheron & such other musical, instruments, they were called melodious Poets [*melici*] or by a more common name *Lirique* Poets, of which sort was *Pindarus*, *Anacreon* and *Callimachus* with others among the Greeks: *Horace* and *Catullus* among the Latines. There were an other sort, who sought the fauor of faire Ladies, and coueted to bemone their estates at large, & the perplexities of loue in a certain pitious verse called *Elegie*, and thence were called *Eligiack:* such among the Latines were *Ouid*, *Tibullus*, & *Propertius*. There were also Poets that wrote onely for the stage, I meane playes and interludes, to recreate the people with matters of disporte, and to that intent did set forth in shewes pageants, accompanied with speach the common behauiours and maner of life of priuate persons, and such as were the meaner sort of men, and they were called *Comicall* Poets, of whom among the Greekes *Menander* and *Aristophanes*

(25)

were moft excellent, with the Latines *Terence* and *Plautus*.
Befides thofe Poets *Comick* there were other who ferued
alfo the ftage, but medled not with fo bafe matters: For
they fet forth the dolefull falles of infortunate & afflicted
Princes, & were called Poets *Tragicall*. Such were
Euripides and *Sophocles* with the Greeks, *Seneca* among
the Latines. There were yet others who mounted nothing
fo high as any of them both, but in bafe and humble
ftile by maner of Dialogue, vttered the priuate and
familiar talke of the meaneft fort of men, as fhepheards,
heywards and fuch like, fuch was among the Greekes
Theocritus: and *Virgill* among the Latines, their poemes
were named *Eglogues* or fhepheardly talke. There was
yet another kind of Poet, who intended to taxe the common abufes and vice of the people in rough and bitter
fpeaches, and their inuectiues were called *Satyres*, and
them felues *Satyricques*. Such were *Lucilius, Iuuenall*
and *Perfius* among the Latines, & with vs he that wrote
the booke called Piers plowman. Others of a more fine
and pleafant head were giuen wholly to taunting and
fcoffing at vndecent things, and in fhort poemes vttered
pretie merry conceits, and thefe men were called *Epi-
grammatifles*. There were others that for the peoples
good inftruction, and triall of their owne witts vfed in
E iij^r places of great affembly, to/fay by rote nombers of fhort
and fententious meetres, very pithie and of good edification, and thereupon were called Poets *Mimifles:* as who
would fay, imitable and meet to be followed for their
wife and graue leffons. There was another kind of poeme,
inuented onely to make fport, & to refrefh the company
with a maner of buffonry or counterfaiting of merry
fpeaches, conuerting all that which they had hard fpoken
before, to a certaine derifion by a quite contrary fence,
and this was done, when *Comedies* or *Tragedies* were a
playing, & that betweene the actes when the players
went to make ready for another, there was great filence,
and the people waxt weary, then came in thefe maner

of conterfaite vices, they were called *Pantomimi*, and all
that had before bene fayd, or great part of it, they gaue
a croffe conftruction to it very ridiculoufly. Thus haue
you how the names of the Poets were giuen them by
the formes of their poemes and maner of writing.

*In what forme of Poefie the gods of the Gentiles
were prayfed and honored.*

The gods of the Gentiles were honoured by their Poetes
in hymnes, which is an extraordinarie and diuine praife,
extolling and magnifying them for their great powers
and excellencie of nature in the higheft degree of laude,
and yet therein their Poets were after a fort reftrained:
fo as they could not with their credit vntruly praife their
owne gods, or vfe in their lauds any maner of groffe
adulation or vnueritable report. For in any writer vntruth and flatterie are counted moft great reproches.
Wherfore to praife the gods of the Gentiles, for that
by authoritie of their owne fabulous records, they had
fathers and mothers, and kinred and allies, and wiues
and concubines: the Poets firft commended them by their
genealogies or pedegrees, their mariages and aliances,
their notable exploits in the world for the behoofe of
mankind, and yet as I fayd before, none otherwife then
the truth of their owne memorials might beare, and in
fuch fort as it might be well auouched by their old
written reports, though in very deede they were not
from the beginning all hiftorically true, and many of
them verie fictions, and fuch of them as were true, were
grounded vpon fome/part of an hiftorie or matter of E iijᵛ
veritie, the reft altogether figuratiue & mifticall, couertly
applied to fome morall or natural fenfe, as *Cicero* fetteth
it foorth in his bookes *de natura deorum*. For to fay that
Iupiter was fonne to *Saturne*, and that he maried his
owne fifter *Iuno*, might be true, for fuch was the guife

of all great Princes in the Orientall part of the world both at thofe dayes and now is. Againe that he loued *Danae, Europa, Leda, Califto* & other faire Ladies daughters to kings, befides many meaner women, it is likely enough, becaufe he was reported to be a very incontinent perfon, and giuen ouer to his luftes, as are for the moft part all the greateft Princes, but that he fhould be the higheft god in heauen, or that he fhould thunder and lighten, and do manie other things very vnnaturally and abfurdly: alfo that *Saturnus* fhould geld his father *Celius*, to th'intent to make him vnable to get any moe children, and other fuch matters as are reported by them, it feemeth to be fome wittie deuife and fiction made for a purpofe, or a very notable and impudent lye, which could not be reafonably fufpected by the Poets, who were otherwife difcreete and graue men, and teachers of wifedome to others. Therefore either to tranfgreffe the rules of their primitiue records, or to feeke to giue their gods honour by belying them (otherwife then in that fence which I haue alledged) had bene a figne not onely of an vnskilfull Poet, but alfo of a very impudent and leude man. For vntrue praife neuer giueth any true reputation. But with vs Chriftians, who be better difciplined, and do acknowledge but one God Almightie, euerlafting, and in euery refpect felfe fuffizant [*autharcos*] repofed in all perfect reft & foueraigne bliffe, not needing or exacting any forreine helpe or good. To him we can not exhibit ouermuch praife, nor belye him any wayes, vnleffe it be in abafing his excellencie by fcarfitie of praife, or by mifconceauing his diuine nature, weening to praife him, if we impute to him fuch vaine delights and peeuifh affections, as commonly the fraileft men are reproued for. Namely to make him ambitious of honour, iealous and difficult in his worfhips, terrible, angrie, vindicatiue, a louer, a hater, a pitier, and in-digent of mans worfhips: finally fo paffionate as in effect he fhold be altogether *Anthropopathis*. To the gods of

(28)

the Gentiles they might well attribute thefe infirmities, for they were but the chil-/dren of men, great Princes E iiij^r and famous in the world, and not for any other refpect diuine, then by fome refemblance of vertue they had to do good, and to benefite many. So as to the God of the Chriftians, fuch diuine praife might be verified: to th'other gods none, but figuratiuely or in mifticall fenfe as hath bene faid. In which fort the ancient Poets did in deede giue them great honors & praifes, and made to them facrifices, & offred them oblations of fundry fortes, euen as the people were taught and per-fwaded by fuch placations and worfhips to receaue any helpe, comfort or benefite to them felues, their wiues, children, poffeffions or goods. For if that opinion were not, who would acknowledge any God? the verie *Etimologie* of the name with vs of the North partes of the world declaring plainely the nature of the attribute, which is all one as if we fayd good, [*bonus*] or a giuer of good things. Therfore the Gentiles prayed for peace to the goddeffe *Pallas:* for warre (fuch as thriued by it) to the god *Mars:* for honor and empire to the god *Iupiter:* for riches & wealth to *Pluto:* for eloquence and gayne to *Mercurie:* for fafe nauigation to *Neptune:* for faire weather and profperous windes to *Eolus:* for skill in mufick and leechcraft to *Apollo:* for free life & chaftitie to *Diana:* for bewtie and good grace, as alfo for iffue & profperitie in loue to *Venus:* for plenty of crop and corne to *Ceres:* for feafonable vintage to *Bacchus:* and for other things to others. So many things as they could imagine good and defirable, and to fo many gods as they fuppofed to be authors thereof, in fo much as *Fortune* was made a goddeffe, & the feuer quartaine had her aulters, fuch blindnes & ignorance raigned in the harts of men at that time, and whereof it firft proceeded and grew, befides th'opinion hath bene giuen, appeareth more at large in our bookes of *Ierotekni*, the matter being of another confideration then to be

(29)

treated of in this worke. And thefe hymnes to the gods was the firſt forme of Poeſie and the higheſt & the ſtatelieſt, & they were ſong by the Poets as prieſts, and by the people or whole congregation as we ſing in our Churchs the Pſalmes of *Dauid*, but they did it commonly in ſome ſhadie groues of tall tymber trees: In which places they reared aulters of greene turfe, and beſtrewed them all ouer with flowers, and vpon them offred their oblations and made their bloudy ſa-/crifices, (for no kinde of gift can be dearer then life) of ſuch quick cattaille, as euery god was in their conceit moſt delighted in, or in ſome other reſpect moſt fit for the miſterie: temples or churches or other chappels then theſe they had none at thoſe dayes.

E iiijᵛ

CHAP. XIII.

In what forme of Poeſie vice and the common abuſes
of mans life was reprehended.

Some perchance would thinke that next after the praiſe and honoring of their gods, ſhould commence the worſhippings and praiſe of good men, and ſpecially of great Princes and gouernours of the earth in foueraignety and function next vnto the gods. But it is not ſo, for before that came to paſſe, the Poets or holy Prieſts, chiefly ſtudied the rebuke of vice, and to carpe at the common abuſes, ſuch as were moſt offenſiue to the publique and priuate, for as yet for lacke of good ciuility and wholeſome doctrines, there was greater ſtore of lewde lourdaines then of wiſe and learned Lords, or of noble and vertuous Princes and gouernours. So as next after the honours exhibited to their gods, the Poets finding in man generally much to reproue & litle to praiſe, made certaine poems in plaine meetres, more like to ſermons or preachings then otherwiſe, and when the people were aſſembled togither in thoſe hallowed places

(30)

dedicate to their gods, becaufe they had yet no large
halles or places of conuenticle, nor had any other correction of their faults, but fuch as refted onely in rebukes
of wife and graue men, fuch as at thefe dayes make the
people afhamed rather then afeard, the faid auncient
Poets vfed for that purpofe, three kinds of poems reprehenfiue, to wit, the *Satyre*, the *Comedie*, & the *Tragedie*:
and the firft and moft bitter inuectiue againft vice and
vicious men, was the *Satyre*: which to th'intent their
bitterneffe fhould breede none ill will, either to the
Poets, or to the recitours, (which could not haue bene
chofen if they had bene openly knowen) and befides to
make their admonitions and reproofs feeme grauer and
of more efficacie, they made wife as if the gods of the
woods, whom they called *Satyres* or *Siluanes*, fhould
appeare and recite thofe verfes of rebuke, whereas in
deede they were but difguifed perfons vnder the fhape
of *Sa-/tyres* as who would fay, thefe terrene and bafe gods   F ir
being conuerfant with mans affaires, and fpiers out of
all their fecret faults: had fome great care ouer man,
& defired by good admonitions to reforme the euill of
their life, and to bring the bad to amendment by thofe
kinde of preachings, whereupon the Poets inuentours
of the deuife were called *Satyriftes*.

CHAP. XIIII.

*How vice was afterward reproued by two other maner of
poems, better reformed then the Satyre, whereof the
firft was Comedy, the fecond Tragedie.*

But when thefe maner of folitary fpeaches and recitals
of rebuke, vttered by the rurall gods out of bufhes and
briers, feemed not to the finer heads fufficiently per-
fwafiue, nor fo popular as if it were reduced into action
of many perfons, or by many voyces liuely reprefented
to the eare and eye, fo as a man might thinke it were
euen now a doing. The Poets deuifed to haue many

(31)

parts played at once by two or three or foure perfons,
that debated the matters of the world, fometimes of their
owne priuate affaires, fometimes of their neighbours,
but neuer medling with any Princes matters nor fuch
high perfonages, but commonly of marchants, fouldiers,
artificers, good honeft houfholders, and alfo of vnthrifty
youthes, yong damfels, old nurfes, bawds, brokers,
ruffians and parafites, with fuch like, in whofe behauiors,
lyeth in effect the whole courfe and trade of mans life,
and therefore tended altogither to the good amendment
of man by difcipline and example. It was alfo much for
the folace & recreation of the common people by reafon
of the pageants and fhewes. And this kind of poeme
was called *Comedy*, and followed next after the *Satyre*,
& by that occafion was fomwhat fharpe and bitter after
the nature of the *Satyre*, openly & by expreffe names
taxing men more malicioufly and impudently then became, fo as they were enforced for feare of quarell &
blame to difguife their players with ftrange apparell,
and by colouring their faces and carying hatts & capps
of diuerfe fafhions to make them felues leffe knowen.
But as time & experience do reforme euery thing that
is amiffe, fo this bitter poeme called the old *Comedy*,
F iv being difufed and taken away, the/new *Comedy* came in
place, more ciuill and pleafant a great deale and not
touching any man by name, but in a certaine generalitie
glancing at euery abufe, fo as from thenceforth fearing
none illwill or enmitie at any bodies hands, they left
afide their difguifings & played bare face, till one
Rofcius Gallus the moft excellent player among the
Romaines brought vp thefe vizards, which we fee at
this day vfed, partly to fupply the want of players, when
there were moe parts then there were perfons, or that
it was not thought meet to trouble & pefter princes
chambers with too many folkes. Now by the chaunge
of a vizard one man might play the king and the carter,
the old nurfe & the yong damfell, the marchant & the

fouldier or any other part he lifted very conueniently. There be that fay *Rofcius* did it for another purpofe, for being him felfe the beft *Hiftrien* or buffon that was in his dayes to be found, infomuch as *Cicero* faid *Rofcius* contended with him by varietie of liuely geftures, to furmount the copy of his fpeach, yet becaufe he was fquint eyed and had a very vnpleafant countenance, and lookes which made him ridiculous or rather odious to the prefence, he deuifed thefe vizards to hide his owne ilfauored face. And thus much touching the *Comedy*.

CHAP. XV.

In vvhat forme of Poefie the euill and outragious behauiours of Princes vvere reprehended.

But becaufe in thofe dayes when the Poets firft taxed by *Satyre* and *Comedy*, there was no great ftore of Kings or Emperors or fuch high eftats (al men being yet for the moft part rude, & in a maner popularly egall) they could not fay of them or of their behauiours any thing to the purpofe, which cafes of Princes are fithens taken for the higheft and greateft matters of all. But after that fome men among the moe became mighty and famous in the world, foueraignetie and dominion hauing learned them all maner of lufts and licentioufnes of life, by which occafions alfo their high eftates and felicities fell many times into moft lowe and lamentable fortunes: whereas before in their great profperities they were both feared and reuerenced in the higheft degree, after their deathes when the pofteritie ftood no more in dread of them,/their infamous life and tyrannies were layd open F ij^r to all the world, their wickednes reproched, their follies and extreme infolencies derided, and their miferable ends painted out in playes and pageants, to fhew the mutabilitie of fortune, and the iuft punifhment of God in reuenge of a vicious and euill life. Thefe matters were

(33)

alfo handled by the Poets and reprefented by action as that of the *Comedies:* but becaufe the matter was higher then that of the *Comedies* the Poets ftile was alfo higher and more loftie, the prouifion greater, the place more magnificent: for which purpofe alfo the players garments were made more rich & coftly and folemne, and euery other thing apperteining, according to that rate: So as where the *Satyre* was pronounced by rufticall and naked *Syluanes* fpeaking out of a bufh, & the common players of interludes called *Planipedes*, played barefoote vpon the floore: the later *Comedies* vpon fcaffolds, and by men well and cleanely hofed and fhod. Thefe matters of great Princes were played vpon lofty ftages, & the actors thereof ware vpon their legges buskins of leather called *Cothurni*, and other folemne habits, & for a fpeciall preheminence did walke vpon thofe high corked fhoes or pantofles, which now they call in Spaine & Italy *Shoppini*. And becaufe thofe buskins and high fhoes were commonly made of goats skinnes very finely tanned, and dyed into colours: or for that as fome fay the beft players reward, was a goate to be giuen him, or for that as other thinke, a goate was the peculiar facrifice to the god *Pan*, king of all the gods of the woodes: forafmuch as a goate in Greeke is called *Tragos*, therfor thefe ftately playes were called *Tragedies*. And thus haue ye foure fundry formes of Poefie *Drāmatick* reprehenfiue, & put in execution by the feate & dexteritie of mans body, to wit, the *Satyre*, old *Comedie*, new *Comedie*, and *Tragedie*, whereas all other kinde of poems except *Eglogue* whereof fhalbe entreated hereafter, were onely recited by mouth or fong with the voyce to fome melodious inftrument.

CHAP. XVI.

*In what forme of Poeſie the great Princes and dominators
of the world were honored.*

But as the bad and illawdable parts of all eſtates and
degrees were taxed by the Poets in one ſort or an other,
and thoſe of/great Princes by Tragedie in eſpecial, (& F ijʳ
not till after their deaths) as hath bene before remembred, to th'intent that ſuch exemplifying (as it were)
of their blames and aduerſities, being now dead, might
worke for a ſecret reprehenſion to others that were aliue,
liuing in the ſame or like abuſes. So was it great reaſon
that all good and vertuous perſons ſhould for their well
doings be rewarded with commendation, and the great
Princes aboue all others with honors and praiſes, being
for many reſpects of greater moment, to haue them
good & vertuous then any inferior ſort of men. Wherfore the Poets being in deede thc trumpetters of all
praiſe and alſo of ſlaunder (not ſlaunder, but well deſerued reproch) were in conſcience & credit bound next
after the diuine praiſes of the immortall gods, to yeeld
a like ratable honour to all ſuch amongſt men, as moſt
reſembled the gods by excellencie of function, and had
a certaine affinitie with them, by more then humane
and ordinarie vertues ſhewed in their actions here vpon
earth. They were therfore praiſed by a ſecond degree
of laude: ſhewing their high eſtates, their Princely
genealogies and pedegrees, mariages, aliances, and ſuch
noble exploites, as they had done in th'affaires of peace
& of warre to the benefit of their people and countries,
by inuention of any noble ſcience, or profitable Art, or
by making wholſome lawes or enlarging of their dominions by honorable and iuſt conqueſts, and many
other wayes. Such perſonages among the Gentiles were
Bacchus, Ceres, Perſeus, Hercules, Theſeus and many
other, who thereby came to be accompted gods and

(35)

halfe gods or goddeſſes [*Heroes*] & had their cōmēdations giuen by Hymne accordingly or by ſuch other poems as their memorie was therby made famous to the poſteritie for euer after, as ſhal be more at large ſayd in place conuenient. But firſt we will ſpeake ſomewhat of the playing places, and prouiſions which were made for their pageants & pomps repreſentatiue before remembred.

CHAP. XVII.

Of the places where their enterludes or poemes drammaticke vvere repreſented to the people.

As it hath bene declared, the *Satyres* were firſt vttered in their hallowed places within the woods where they honoured their/gods vnder the open heauen, becauſe they had no other houſing fit for great aſſemblies. The old comedies were plaid in the broad ſtreets vpon wagons or carts vncouered, which carts were floored with bords & made for remouable ſtages to paſſe from one ſtreete of their townes to another, where all the people might ſtand at their eaſe to gaze vpō the ſights. Their new comedies or ciuill enterludes were played in open pauilions or tents of linnen cloth or lether, halfe diſplayed that the people might ſee. Afterward when Tragidies came vp they deuiſed to preſent them vpon ſcaffoldes or ſtages of timber, ſhadowed with linen or lether as the other, and theſe ſtages were made in the forme of a *Semicircle*, wherof the bow ſerued for the beholders to ſit in, and the ſtring or forepart was appointed for the floore or place where the players vttered, & had in it ſundry little diuiſions by curteins as trauerſes to ſerue for ſeueral roomes where they might repaire vnto & change their garmēts & come in againe, as their ſpeaches & parts were to be renewed. Alſo there was place appointed for the muſiciens to ſing or to play vpon their inſtrumentes at the end of euery ſcene, to the

F iij ͬ

(36)

intent the people might be refreſhed, and kept occupied. This maner of ſtage in halfe circle, the Greekes called *theatrum*, as much to ſay as a beholding place, which was alſo in ſuch ſort contriued by benches and greeces to ſtand or ſit vpon, as no man ſhould empeach anothers ſight. But as ciuilitie and withall wealth encreaſed, ſo did the minde of man growe dayly more haultie and ſuperfluous in all his deuiſes, ſo as for their *theaters* in halfe circle, they came to be by the great magnificence of the Romain princes and people ſomptuouſly built with marble & ſquare ſtone in forme all round, & were called *Amphitheaters*, wherof as yet appears one amōg the anciēt ruines of Rome, built by *Pompeius Magnus*, for capaſitie able to receiue at eaſe fourſcore thouſand perſons as it is left written, & ſo curiouſly contriued as euery man might depart at his pleaſure, without any annoyance to other. It is alſo to be knowne that in thoſe great *Amphitheaters*, were exhibited all maner of other ſhewes & diſports for the people, as their fence playes, or digladiations of naked men, their wraſtlings, runnings, leapings and other practiſes of actiuitie and ſtrength, alſo their baitings of wild beaſts, as Elephants, Rhinocerōs, Tigers, Leopards/and others, which ſights much delighted the common people, and therefore the places required to be large and of great content. F iij^v

CHAP. XVIII.

Of the Shepheards or paſtorall Poeſie called Eglogue, and to vvhat purpoſe it vvas firſt inuented and vſed.

Some be of opinion, and the chiefe of thoſe who haue written in this Art among the Latines, that the paſtorall Poeſie which we commonly call by the name of *Eglogue* and *Bucolick*, a tearme brought in by the Sicilian Poets, ſhould be the firſt of any other, and before the *Satyre* comedie or tragedie, becauſe, ſay they, the ſhepheards and haywards aſſemblies & meetings when they kept

their cattell and heards in the common fields and forefts, was the firft familiar conuerfation, and their babble and talk vnder bufhes and fhadie trees, the firft difputation and contentious reafoning, and their flefhly heates growing of eafe, the firft idle wooings, and their fongs made to their mates or paramours either vpon forrow or iolity of courage, the firft amorous muficks, fometime alfo they fang and played on their pipes for wagers, ftriuing who fhould get the beft game, and be counted cunningeft. All this I do agree vnto, for no doubt the fhepheards life was the firft example of honeft felowfhip, their trade the firft art of lawfull acquifition or purchafe, for at thofe daies robbery was a manner of purchafe. So faith *Aristotle* in his bookes of the Politiques, and that pafturage was before tillage, or fifhing or fowling, or any other predatory art or cheuifance. And all this may be true, for before there was a fhepheard keeper of his owne, or of fome other bodies flocke, there was none owner in the world, quick cattel being the firft property of any forreine poffeffion. I fay forreine, becaufe alway men claimed property in their apparell and armour, and other like things made by their owne trauel and induftry, nor thereby was there yet any good towne or city or Kings palace, where pageants and pompes might be fhewed by Comedies or Tragedies. But for all this, I do deny that the *Eglogue* fhould be the firft and moft auncient forme of artificiall Poefie, being perfwaded that the Poet deuifed the *Eglogue* long after the other *drammatick* poems, not of purpofe to counterfait
F iiijʳ or reprefent the/rufticall manner of loues and communication: but vnder the vaile of homely perfons, and in rude fpeeches to infinuate and glaunce at greater matters, and fuch as perchance had not bene fafe to haue beene difclofed in any other fort, which may be perceiued by the Eglogues of *Virgill*, in which are treated by figure matters of greater importance then the loues of *Titirus* and *Corydon*. Thefe Eglogues came after

to containe and enforme morall difcipline, for the amendment of mans behauiour, as be thofe of *Mantuan* and
other moderne Poets.

CHAP. XIX.

*Of historicall Poefie, by which the famous acts of Princes
and the vertuous and worthy liues of our forefathers were reported.*

There is nothing in man of all the potential parts of his
mind (reafon and will except) more noble or more
neceffary to the actiue life thē memory: becaufe it
maketh moft to a found iudgement and perfect worldly
wifedome, examining and comparing the times paft with
the prefent, and by them both confidering the time to
come, concludeth with a ftedfaft refolution, what is the
beft courfe to be taken in all his actions and aduices
in this world: it came vpon this reafon, experience to
be fo highly commended in all confultations of importance, and preferred before any learning or fcience,
and yet experience is no more than a maffe of memories
affembled, that is, fuch trials as man hath made in time
before. Right fo no kinde of argument in all the
Oratorie craft, doth better perfwade and more vniuerfally fatisfie then example, which is but the reprefenta-
tion of old memories, and like fucceffes happened in
times paft. For thefe regards the Poefie hiftoricall is of
all other next the diuine moft honorable and worthy,
as well for the common benefit as for the fpeciall comfort euery man receiueth by it. No one thing in the
world with more delectation reuiuing our fpirits then
to behold as it were in a glaffe the liuely image of our
deare forefathers, their noble and vertuous maner of
life, with other things autentike, which becaufe we are
not able otherwife to attaine to the knowledge of, by
any of our fences, we apprehend them by memory,
whereas the prefent time and things/fo fwiftly paffe F iiij^v

away, as they giue vs no leafure almoft to looke into
them, and much leffe to know & confider of them
throughly. The things future, being alfo euents very
vncertaine, and fuch as can not poffibly be knowne
becaufe they be not yet, can not be vfed for example
nor for delight otherwife thē by hope. Though many
promife the contrary, by vaine and deceitfull arts taking
vpon them to reueale the truth of accidents to come,
which if it were fo as they furmife, are yet but fciences
meerely coniecturall, and not of any benefit to man or
to the common wealth, where they be vfed or pro-
feffed. Therefore the good and exemplarie things and
actions of the former ages, were referued only to the
hiftoricall reportes of wife and graue men: thofe of the
prefent time left to the fruition and iudgement of our
fences: the future as hazards and incertaine euentes
vtterly neglected and layd afide for Magicians and
mockers to get their liuings by: fuch manner of men
as by negligence of Magiftrates and remiffes of lawes
euery countrie breedeth great ftore of. Thefe hiftorical
men neuerthleffe vfed not the matter fo precifely to
wifh that al they wrote fhould be accounted true, for
that was not needefull nor expedient to the purpofe,
namely to be vfed either for example or for pleafure:
confidering that many times it is feene a fained matter
or altogether fabulous, befides that it maketh more
mirth than any other, works no leffe good conclufions
for example then the moft true and veritable: but often
times more, becaufe the Poet hath the handling of them
to fafhion at his pleafure, but not fo of th'other which
muft go according to their veritie & none otherwife
without the writers great blame. Againe as ye know
mo and more excellent examples may be fained in one
day by a good wit, then many ages through mans frailtie
are able to put in vre, which made the learned and
wittie men of thofe times to deuife many hiftoricall
matters of no veritie at all, but with purpofe to do good

and no hurt, as vfing them for a maner of difcipline and
prefident of commendable life. Such was the common
wealth of *Plato*, and Sir *Thomas Moores Vtopia*, refting
all in deuife, but neuer put in execution, and eafier to
be wifhed then to be performed. And you fhall perceiue that hiftories were of three fortes, wholly true and
wholly falfe, and a third holding part of either, but for
honeft re-/creation, and good example they were all of G iͬ
them. And this may be apparant to vs not onely by
the Poeticall hiftories, but alfo by thofe that be written
in profe: for as *Homer* wrate a fabulous or mixt report
of the fiege of Troy, and another of *Vliffes* errors or
wandrings, fo did *Mufeus* compile a true treatife of the
life & loues of *Leander* and *Hero*, both of them *Heroick*,
and to none ill edification. Alfo as *Theucidides* wrate a
worthy and veritable hiftorie, of the warres betwixt the
Athenians and the *Peloponefes:* fo did *Zenophon*, a moft
graue Philofopher, and well trained courtier and counfellour make another (but fained and vntrue) of the
childhood of *Cyrus* king of *Perfia*, neuertheles both to
one effeƈt, that is for example and good information
of the pofteritie. Now becaufe the aƈtions of meane &
bafe perfonages, tend in very few cafes to any great
good example: for who paffeth to follow the fteps, and
maner of life of a craftes man, fhepheard or failer,
though he were his father or deareft frend? yea how
almoft is it poffible that fuch maner of men fhould be
of any vertue other then their profeffion requireth?
Therefore was nothing committed to hiftorie, but matters of great and excellent perfons & things that the
fame by irritation of good courages (fuch as emulation
caufeth) might worke more effeƈtually, which occafioned
the ftory writer to chufe an higher ftile fit for his fubieƈt,
the Profaicke in profe, the Poet in meetre, and the Poets
was by verfe exameter for his grauitie and ftatelineffe
moft allowable: neither would they intermingle him
with any other fhorter meafure, vnleffe it were in matters

(41)

of fuch qualitie, as became beft to be fong with the voyce, and to fome muficall inftrument, as were with the Greeks, all your Hymnes & *Encomia* of *Pindarus* & *Callimachus*, not very hiftories but a maner of hiftoricall reportes, in which cafes they made thofe poemes in variable meafures, & coupled a fhort verfe with a long to ferue that purpofe the better, and we our felues who compiled this treatife haue written for pleafure a litle brief *Romance* or hiftoricall ditty in the Englifh tong of the Ifle of great *Britaine* in fhort and long meetres, and by breaches or diuifions to be more commodioufly fong to the harpe in places of affembly, where the company fhalbe defirous to heare of old aduentures & valiaunces of noble knights in times paft, as are thofe

G iv of king *Arthur* and his knights/of the round table, Sir *Beuys* of *Southampton, Guy* of *Warvvicke* and others like. Such as haue not premonition hereof, and confideration of the caufes alledged, would peraduenture reproue and difgrace euery *Romance*, or fhort hiftoricall ditty for that they be not written in long meeters or verfes *Alexandrins*, according to the nature & ftile of large hiftories, wherin they fhould do wrong for they be fundry formes of poems and not all one.

CHAP. XX.

In what forme of Poefie vertue in the inferiour fort vvas commended.

In euerie degree and fort of men vertue is commendable, but not egally: not onely becaufe mens eftates are vnegall, but for that alfo vertue it felfe is not in euery refpeĉt of egall value and eftimation. For continence in a king is of greater merit, then in a carter, th'one hauing all oportunities to allure him to lufts, and abilitie to ferue his appetites, th'other partly, for the bafeneffe of his eftate wanting fuch meanes and occafions, partly by dread of lawes more inhibited, and not fo vehemently

(42)

caried away with vnbridled affections, and therfore
deferue not in th'one and th'other like praife nor equall
reward, by the very ordinarie courfe of diftributiue
iuftice. Euen fo parfimonie and illiberalitie are greater
vices in a Prince then in a priuate perfon, and pufillani-
mitie and iniuftice likewife: for to th'one, fortune hath
fupplied inough to maintaine them in the contrarie
vertues, I meane, fortitude, iuftice, liberalitie, and magnanimitie: the Prince hauing all plentie to vfe largeffe
by, and no want or neede to driue him to do wrong.
Alfo all the aides that may be to lift vp his courage, and
to make him ftout and feareleffe (*augent animos fortunæ*)
faith the *Mimift*, and very truly, for nothing pulleth
downe a mans heart fo much as aduerfitie and lacke.
Againe in a meane man prodigalitie and pride are faultes
more reprehenfible then in Princes, whofe high eftates
do require in their countenance, fpeech & expence, a
certaine extraordinary, and their functions enforce them
fometime to exceede the limites of mediocritie not excufable in a priuat perfon, whofe manner of life and
calling hath no fuch exigence. Befides the good and bad
of Princes is more exemplarie, and thereby of greater
moment then/the priuate perfons. Therfore it is that G ijʳ
the inferiour perfons, with their inferiour vertues haue
a certaine inferiour praife, to guerdon their good with,
& to comfort them to continue a laudable courfe in the
modeft and honeft life and behauiour. But this lyeth
not in written laudes fo much as in ordinary reward and
commendation to be giuen them by the mouth of the
fuperiour magiftrate. For hiftories were not intended to
fo generall and bafe a purpofe, albeit many a meane
fouldier & other obfcure perfons were fpoken of and
made famous in ftories, as we finde of *Irus* the begger,
and *Therfites* the glorious noddie, whom *Homer* maketh
mention of. But that happened (& fo did many like
memories of meane men) by reafon of fome greater
perfonage or matter that it was long of, which there-

(43)

fore could not be an vniuerfall cafe nor chaunce to euery other good and vertuous perfon of the meaner fort. Wherefore the Poet in praifing the maner of life or death of anie meane perfon, did it by fome litle dittie or Epigram or Epitaph in fewe verfes & meane ftile conformable to his fubiect. So haue you how the immortall gods were praifed by hymnes, the great Princes and heroicke perfonages by ballades of praife called *Encomia*, both of them by hiftoricall reports of great grauitie and maieftie, the inferiour perfons by other flight poemes.

CHAP. XXI.

The forme wherein honeft and profitable Artes and fciences were treated.

The profitable fciences were no leffe meete to be imported to the greater number of ciuill men for inftruction of the people and increafe of knowledge, then to be referued and kept for clerkes and great men onely. So as next vnto the things hiftoricall fuch doctrines and arts as the common wealth fared the better by, were efteemed and allowed. And the fame were treated by Poets in verfe *Exameter* fauouring the *Heroicall*, and for the grauitie and comelineffe of the meetre moft vfed with the Greekes and Latines to fad purpofes, Such were the Philofophicall works of *Lucretius Carus* among the Romaines, the Aftronomicall of *Aratus* and *Manilius*, one Greeke th'other Latine, the Medicinall of *Nicander*, and that of *Oppianus* of hunting and fifhes, and many moe that were too long to recite in this place./

CHAP. XXII.

In what forme of Poefie the amorous affections and allurements were vttered.

The firft founder of all good affections is honeft loue, as the mother of all the vicious is hatred. It was not therefore without reafon that fo commendable, yea honourable a thing as loue well meant, were it in Princely eftate or priuate, might in all ciuil common wealths be vttered in good forme and order as other laudable things are. And becaufe loue is of all other humane affeétions the moft puiffant and paffionate, and moft generall to all fortes and ages of men and women, fo as whether it be of the yong or old or wife or holy, or high eftate or low, none euer could truly bragge of any excmptiō in that cafe: it requireth a forme of Poefie variable, inconftant, affeéted, curious and moft witty of any others, whereof the ioyes were to be vttered in one forte, the forrowes in an other, and by the many formes of Poefie, the many moodes and pangs of louers, throughly to be difcouered: the poore foules fometimes praying, befeeching, fometime honouring, auancing, praifing: an other while railing, reuiling, and curfing: then forrowing, weeping, lamenting: in the ende laughing, reioyfing & folacing the beloued againe, with a thoufand delicate deuifes, odes, fongs, elegies, ballads, fonets and other ditties, moouing one way and another to great compaffion.

CHAP. XXIII.

The forme of Poeticall reioyfings.

Pleafure is the chiefe parte of mans felicity in this world, and alfo (as our Theologians fay) in the world to come. Therefore while we may (yea alwaies if it coulde be) to reioyce and take our pleafures in vertuous and honeft fort, it is not only allowable, but alfo neceffary and very naturall to man. And many be the ioyes and confolations of the hart: but none greater, than fuch as he may vtter and difcouer by fome conuenient meanes: euen as to fuppreffe and hide a mans mirth, and not to haue therein a partaker, or at leaft wife a witnes, is no little griefe and infelicity. Therfore nature and ciuility haue ordained (befides the priuate folaces) publike reioifings

G iij^r for the comfort and recreation of many. And/they be of diuerſe ſorts and vpon diuerſe occaſions growne: one & the chiefe was for the publike peace of a countrie the greateſt of any other ciuill good. And wherein your Maieſtie (my moſt gracious Soueraigne) haue ſhewed your ſelfe to all the world for this one and thirty yeares ſpace of your glorious raigne, aboue all other Princes of Chriſtendome, not onely fortunate, but alſo moſt ſufficient vertuous and worthy of Empire. An other is for iuſt & honourable victory atchieued againſt the for-raine enemy. A third at ſolemne feaſts and pompes of coronations and enſtallments of honourable orders. An other for iollity at weddings and marriages. An other at the births of Princes children. An other for priuate entertainements in Court, or other ſecret diſports in chamber, and ſuch ſolitary places. And as theſe reioyſings tend to diuers effects, ſo do they alſo carry diuerſe formes and nominations: for thoſe of victorie and peace are called *Triumphall*, whereof we our ſelues haue hereto-fore giuen ſome example by our *Triumphals* written in honour of her Maieſties long peace. And they were vſed by the auncients in like manner, as we do our generall proceſſions or Letanies with bankets and bone-fires and all manner of ioyes. Thoſe that were to honour the perſons of great Princes or to ſolemniſe the pompes of any inſtallment were called *Encomia*, we may call them carols of honour. Thoſe to celebrate marriages were called ſongs nuptiall or *Epithalamies*, but in a certaine miſticall ſenſe as ſhall be ſaid hereafter. Others for magnificence at the natiuities of Princes children, or by cuſtome vſed yearely vpon the ſame dayes, are called ſongs natall or *Genethliaca*. Others for ſecret recreation and paſtime in chambers with company or alone were the ordinary Muſickes amorous, ſuch as might be ſong with voice or to the Lute, Citheron or Harpe, or daunced by meaſures as the Italian Pauan and galliard are at theſe daies in Princes Courts and other places of honourable or ciuill affembly, and of all thefe we will fpeake in order and very briefly.

The forme of Poeticall lamentations.

Lamenting is altogether contrary to reioifing, euery man faith fo, and yet is it a peece of ioy to be able to lament with eafe,/and freely to poure forth a mans in- G iij^v ward forrowes and the greefs wherewith his minde is furcharged. This was a very neceffary deuife of the Poet and a fine, befides his poetrie to play alfo the Phifitian, and not onely by applying a medicine to the ordinary ficknes of mankind, but by making the very greef it felfe (in part) cure of the difeafe. Nowe are the caufes of mans forrowes many: the death of his parents, frends, allies, and children: (though many of the barbarous nations do reioyce at their burials and forrow at their birthes) the ouerthrowes and difcomforts in battell, the fubuerfions of townes and cities, the defolations of countreis, the loffe of goods and worldly promotions, honour and good renowne: finally the trauails and tor- ments of loue forlorne or ill beftowed, either by difgrace, deniall, delay, and twenty other wayes, that well ex- perienced louers could recite. Such of thefe greefs as might be refrained or holpen by wifedome, and the parties owne good endeuour, the Poet gaue none order to forrow them: for firft as to the good renowne it is loft, for the more part by fome default of the owner, and may be by his well doings recouered againe. And if it be vniuftly taken away, as by vntrue and famous libels, the offenders recantation may fuffife for his amends: fo did the Poet *Stefichorus*, as it is written of him in his *Pallinodie* vpon the difprayfe of *Helena*, and recouered his eye fight. Alfo for worldly goods they come and go, as things not long proprietary to any body, and are not yet fubiect vnto fortunes dominion fo, but that we

our felues are in great part acceffarie to our own loffes
and hinderaunces, by ouerfight & mifguiding of our
felues and our things, therefore why fhould we bewaile
our fuch voluntary detriment? But death the irrecouerable loffe, death the dolefull departure of frendes,
that can neuer be recontinued by any other meeting or
new acquaintance. Befides our vncertaintie and fufpition
of their eftates and welfare in the places of their new
abode, feemeth to carry a reafonable pretext of iuft forrow. Likewife the great ouerthrowes in battell and
defolations of countreys by warres, afwell for the loffe
of many liues and much libertie as for that it toucheth
the whole ftate, and euery priuate man hath his portion
in the damage: Finally for loue, there is no frailtie in
flefh and bloud fo excufable as it, no comfort or dif-
G iiijʳ comfort greater/then the good and bad fucceffe thereof,
nothing more naturall to man, nothing of more force
to vanquifh his will and to inuegle his iudgement.
Therefore of death and burials, of th'aduerfities by
warres, and of true loue loft or ill beftowed, are th'onely
forrowes that the noble Poets fought by their arte to
remoue or appeafe, not with any medicament of a contrary temper, as the *Galeniftes* vfe to cure [*contraria
contrarijs*] but as the *Paracelfians*, who cure [*fimilia
fimilibus*] making one dolour to expell another, and in
this cafe, one fhort forrowing the remedie of a long and
grieuous forrow. And the lamenting of deathes was
chiefly at the very burialls of the dead, alfo at monethes
mindes and longer times, by cuftome continued yearely,
when as they vfed many offices of feruice and loue
towardes the dead, and thereupon are called *Obfequies*
in our vulgare, which was done not onely by cladding
the mourners their friendes and feruauntes in blacke
veftures, of fhape dolefull and fad, but alfo by wofull
countenaunces and voyces, and befides by Poeticall
mournings in verfe. Such funerall fongs were called
Epicedia if they were fong by many, and *Monodia* if they

(48)

were vttered by one alone, and this was vfed at the enterment of Princes and others of great accompt, and it was reckoned a great ciuilitie to vfe fuch ceremonies, as at this day is alfo in fome countrey vfed. In Rome they accuftomed to make orations funerall and commendatorie of the dead parties in the publique place called *Proroftris:* and our *Theologians,* in ftead thereof vfe to make fermons, both teaching the people fome good learning, and alfo faying well of the departed. Thofe fongs of the dolorous difcomfits in battaile, and other defolations in warre, or of townes faccaged and fubuerted, were fong by the remnant of the army ouerthrowen, with great skrikings and outcries, holding the wrong end of their weapon vpwards in figne of forrow and difpaire. The cities alfo made generall mournings & offred facrifices with Poeticall fongs to appeafe the wrath of the martiall gods & goddeffes. The third forrowing was of loues, by long lamentation in *Elegie:* fo was their fong called, and it was in a pitious maner of meetre, placing a limping *Pentameter,* after a lufty *Exameter,* which made it go dolouroufly more then any other meeter./

CHAP. XXV.

Of the folemne reioyfings at the natiuitie of Princes children.

To returne from forrow to reioyfing it is a very good hap and no vnwife part for him that can do it, I fay therefore, that the comfort of iffue and procreation of children is fo naturall and fo great, not onely to all men but fpecially to Princes, as duetie and ciuilitie haue made it a common cuftome to reioyfe at the birth of their noble children, and to keepe thofe dayes hallowed and feftiuall for euer once in the yeare, during the parentes or childrens liues: and that by publique order & confent. Of which reioyfings and mirthes the Poet

miniſtred the firſt occaſion honorable, by preſenting of
ioyfull ſongs and ballades, prayſing the parentes by
proofe, the child by hope, the whole kinred by report,
& the day it ſelfe with wiſhes of all good ſucceſſe, long
life, health & proſperitie for euer to the new borne.
Theſe poemes were called in Greeke *Genetliaca*, with vs
they may be called natall or birth ſongs.

CHAP. XXVI.

The maner of reioyſings at mariages and vveddings.

As the conſolation of children well begotten is great,
no leſſe but rather greater ought to be that which is
occaſion of children, that is honorable matrimonie, a
loue by al lawes allowed, not mutable nor encombred
with ſuch vaine cares & paſſions, as that other loue,
whereof there is no aſſurance, but looſe and fickle affection occaſioned for the moſt part by ſodaine ſights and
acquaintance of no long triall or experience, nor vpon
any other good ground wherein any ſuretie may be
conceiued: wherefore the Ciuill Poet could do no leſſe
in conſcience and credit, then as he had before done
to the ballade of birth: now with much better deuotion
to celebrate by his poeme the chearefull day of mariages
aſwell Princely as others, for that hath alwayes bene
accompted with euery countrey and nation of neuer ſo
barbarous people, the higheſt & holieſt, of any cere-
monie apperteining to man: a match forſooth made for
euer and not for a day, a ſolace prouided for youth, a
comfort for age, a knot of alliance & amitie indiſſoluble:
great reioyſing was therefore due to ſuch a matter and
H iᶜ to ſo glad-/ſome a time. This was done in ballade wiſe
as the natall ſong, and was ſong very ſweetely by
Muſitians at the chamber dore of the Bridegroome and
Bride at ſuch times as ſhalbe hereafter declared and they
were called *Epithalamies* as much to ſay as ballades at
the bedding of the bride: for ſuch as were ſong at the

borde at dinner or fupper were other Muſickes and not
properly *Epithalamies*. Here, if I ſhall ſay that which
apperteineth to th'arte, and diſcloſe the miſterie of the
whole matter, I muſt and doe with all humble reuerence
beſpeake pardon of the chaſte and honorable eares, leaſt
I ſhould either offend them with licentious ſpeach, or
leaue them ignorant of the ancient guiſe in old times
vſed at weddings (in my ſimple opinion) nothing re-
proueable. This *Epithalamie* was deuided by breaches
into three partes to ſerue for three ſeuerall fits or times
to be ſong. The firſt breach was ſong at the firſt parte
of the night when the ſpouſe and her husband were
brought to their bed & at the very chamber dore, where
in a large vtter roome vſed to be (beſides the muſitiēs)
good ſtore of ladies or gētlewomen of their kinſefolkes,
& others who came to honor the mariage, & the tunes
of the ſongs were very loude and ſhrill, to the intent
there might no noiſe be hard out of the bed chāber by
the skreeking & outcry of the`young damoſell feeling
the firſt forces of her ſtiffe & rigorous young man, ſhe
being as all virgins tender & weake, & vnexpert in
thoſe maner of affaires. For which purpoſe alſo they
vſed by old nurſes (appointed to that ſeruice) to ſup-
preſſe the noiſe by caſting of pottes full of nuttes round
about the chamber vpon the hard floore or pauemēt,
for they vſed no mattes nor ruſhes as we doe now. So
as the Ladies and gentlewomen ſhould haue their eares
ſo occupied what with Muſicke, and what with their
handes wantonly ſcambling and catching after the nuttes,
that they could not intend to harken after any other
thing. This was as I ſaid to diminiſh the noiſe of the
laughing lamenting ſpouſe. The tenour of that part of
the ſong was to congratulate the firſt acquaintance and
meeting of the young couple, allowing of their parents
good diſcretions in making the match, thē afterward to
found cherfully to the onſet and firſt encounters of that
amorous battaile, to declare the cōfort of childrē, &

encreafe of loue by that meane cheifly caufed: the bride
H iv fhewing her felf euery waies well difpofed and ftill/fup-
plying occafions of new luftes and loue to her husband,
by her obedience and amorous embracings and all other
allurementes. About midnight or one of the clocke, the
Muficians came again to the chamber dore (all the
Ladies and other women as they were of degree, hauing
taken their leaue, and being gone to their reft.) This
part of the ballade was to refrefh the faint and weried
bodies and fpirits, and to animate new appetites with
cherefull wordes, encoraging thē to the recontinuance
of the fame entertainments, praifing and commēding
(by fuppofall) the good conformities of them both, &
their defire one to vanquifh the other by fuch frēdly
conflictes: alledging that the firft embracementes neuer
bred barnes, by reafon of their ouermuch affection and
heate, but onely made paffage for children and enforced
greater liking to the late made match. That the fecond
affaultes, were leffe rigorous, but more vigorous and apt
to auance the purpofe of procreation, that therefore they
fhould perfift in all good appetite with an inuincible
courage to the end. This was the fecond part of the
Epithalamie. In the morning when it was faire broad
day, & that by liklyhood all tournes were fufficiently
ferued, the laft actes of the enterlude being ended, &
that the bride muft within few hours arife and apparrell
her felfe, no more as a virgine, but as a wife, and about
dinner time muft by order come forth *Sicut fponfa de
thalamo*, very demurely and ftately to be fene and acknowledged of her parents and kinsfolkes whether fhe
were the fame woman or a changeling, or dead or aliue,
or maimed by any accident nocturnall. The fame Muficians came againe with this laft part, and greeted them
both with a Pfalme of new applaufions, for that they
had either of them fo well behaued them felues that
night, the husband to rob his fpoufe of her maidenhead
and faue her life, the bride fo luftely to fatisfie her

(52)

husbandes loue and fcape with fo litle daunger of her
perfon, for which good chaunce that they fhould make
a louely truce and abftinence of that warre till next night
fealing the placard of that louely league, with twentie
maner of fweet kiffes, then by good admonitions en-
formed them to the frugall & thriftie life all the reft
of their dayes. The good man getting and bringing
home, the wife fauing that which her husband fhould
get, therewith to be the better able to keepe good/
hofpitalitie, according to their eftates, and to bring vp H ij^r
their children, (if God fent any) vertuoufly, and the
better by their owne good example. Finally to perfeuer
all the reft of their life in true and inuiolable wedlocke.
This ceremony was omitted when men maried widowes
or fuch as had tafted the frutes of loue before, (we call
them well experienced young women) in whom there
was no feare of daunger to their perfons, or of any outcry at all, at the time of thofe terrible approches. Thus
much touching the vfage of *Epithalamie* or bedding
ballad of the ancient times, in which if there were any
wanton or lafciuious matter more then ordinarie which
they called *Ficenina licētia* it was borne withal for that
time becaufe of the matter no leffe requiring. *Catullus*
hath made of thē one or two very artificiall and ciuil:
but none more excellent then of late yeares a young
noble man of Germanie as I take it *Iohānes fecundus* who
in that and in his poeme *De bafijs,* paffeth any of the
auncient or moderne Poetes in my iudgment.

CHAP. XXVII.

*The manner of Poefie by which they vttered their bitter
taunts, and priuy nips, or witty fcoffes and other
merry conceits.*

But all the world could not keepe, nor any ciuill ordi-
nance to the contrary fo preuaile, but that men would

and muſt needs vtter their ſplenes in all ordinarie matters alſo: or elſe it ſeemed their bowels would burſt, therefore the poet deuiſed a prety faſhioned poeme ſhort and ſweete (as we are wont to ſay) and called it *Epigramma* in which euery mery conceited man might without any long ſtudie or tedious ambage, make his frend ſport, and anger his foe, and giue a prettie nip, or ſhew a ſharpe conceit in few verſes: for this *Epigramme* is but an inſcription or writting made as it were vpon a table, or in a windowe, or vpon the wall or mantell of a chimney in ſome place of common reſort, where it was allowed euery man might come, or be ſitting to chat and prate, as now in our tauernes and common tabling houſes, where many merry heades meete, and ſcrible with ynke with chalke, or with a cole ſuch matters as they would euery mā ſhould know, & deſcant vpō. Afterward the ſame came to be put in paper and in bookes, and vſed

H ijᵛ as ordinarie miſſiues, ſome of frendſhip, ſome/of defiaunce, or as other meſſages of mirth: *Martiall* was the cheife of this ſkil among the Latines, & at theſe days the beſt Epigrāmes we finde, & of the ſharpeſt conceit are thoſe that haue bene gathered among the reliques of the two muet *Satyres* in Rome, *Paſquill* and *Marphorius*, which in time of *Sede vacante*, when merry conceited men liſted to gibe & ieſt at the dead Pope, or any of his Cardinales, they faſtened them vpon thoſe Images which now lie in the open ſtreets, and were tollerated, but after that terme expired they were inhibited againe. Theſe inſcriptions or Epigrammes at their begining had no certaine author that would auouch them, ſome for feare of blame, if they were ouer ſaucy or ſharpe, others for modeſtie of the writer as was that *diſticke* of *Virgil* which he ſet vpon the pallace gate of the emperour *Auguſtus*, which I will recite for the breifnes and quicknes of it, & alſo for another euente that fell out vpon the matter worthy to be remembred. Theſe were the verſes.

Noĉte pluit tota, redeunt ſpeĉtacula mane
Diuiſum imperium cum Ioue Cæſar habet.

Which I haue thus Engliſhed,

It raines all night, early the ſhewes returne
God and Cæſar, do raigne and rule by turne.

As much to ſay, God ſheweth his power by the night
raines. Cæſar his magnificence by the pompes of the day.

Theſe two verſes were very well liked, and brought
to th'Emperours Maieſtie, who tooke great pleaſure in
them, & willed the author ſhould be knowen. A ſauſie
courtier profered him ſelfe to be the man, and had a
good reward giuen him: for the Emperour him ſelf
was not only learned, but of much munificence toward
all learned men: whereupon *Virgill* ſeing him ſelf by his
ouermuch modeſtie defrauded of the reward, that an
impudent had gotten by abuſe of his merit, came the
next night, and faſtened vpon the ſame place this halfe
metre, foure times iterated. Thus.

Sic vos non vobis
Sic vos non vobis
Sic vos non vobis
Sic vos non vobis

And there it remained a great while becauſe no man
wiſt what/it meant, till *Virgill* opened the whole fraude H iijʳ
by this deuiſe. He wrote aboue the ſame halfe metres
this whole verſe *Exameter*.

Hos ego verſiculos feci tulit alter honores.

And then finiſhed the foure half metres, thus.

Sic vos non vobis	*Fertis aratra boues*
Sic vos non vobis	*Vellera fertis oues*
Sic vos non vobis	*Mellificatis apes*
Sic vos non vobis	*Nidificatis aues.*

And put to his name *Publius Virgilius Maro*. This
matter came by and by to Th'emperours eare, who

taking great pleafure in the deuife called for *Virgill*, and gaue him not onely a prefent reward, with a good allowance of dyet a bouche in court as we vfe to call it: but alfo held him for euer after vpon larger triall he had made of his learning and vertue in fo great reputation, as he vouchfafed to giue him the name of a frend (*amicus*) which among the Romanes was fo great an honour and fpeciall fauour, as all fuch perfons were allowed to the Emperours table, or to the Senatours who had receiued them (as frendes) and they were the only men that came ordinarily to their boords, & folaced with them in their chambers, and gardins when none other could be admitted.

CHAP. XXVIII.

Of the poeme called Epitaph vfed for memoriall of the dead.

An Epitaph is but a kind of Epigram only applied to the report of the dead perfons eftate and degree, or of his other good or bad partes, to his commendation or reproch: and is an infcription fuch as a man may commodioufly write or engraue vpon a tombe in few verfes, pithie, quicke and fententious for the paffer by to perufe, and iudge vpon without any long tariaunce: So as if it exceede the meafure of an Epigram, it is then (if the verfe be correfpondent) rather an Elegie then an Epitaph which errour many of thefe baftard rimers commit, becaufe they be not learned, nor (as we are wont to fay) their craftes mafters, for they make long and tedious difcourfes, and write them in large tables to be hanged vp in Churches and chauncells ouer the tombes of great men and others, which be fo exceeding long as one muft H iij haue halfe/a dayes leafure to reade one of them, & muft be called away before he come halfe to the end, or elfe be locked into the Church by the Sexten as I my felfe was once ferued reading an Epitaph in a certain cathe-

(56)

drall Church of England. They be ignorāt of poefie that call fuch lōg tales by the name of Epitaphes, they might better call them Elegies, as I faid before, and then ought neither to be engrauen nor hanged vp in tables. I haue feene them neuertheles vpon many honorable tombes of thefe late times erected, which doe rather difgrace then honour either the matter or maker.

CHAP. XXIX.

A certaine auncient forme of poefie by which men did vfe to reproch their enemies.

As frendes be a rich and ioyfull poffeffion, fo be foes a continuall torment and canker to the minde of man, and yet there is no poffible meane to auoide this incon-uenience, for the beft of vs all, & he that thinketh he liues moft blameleffe, liues not without enemies, that enuy him for his good parts, or hate him for his euill. There be wife men, and of them the great learned man *Plutarch* that tooke vpon them to perfwade the benefite that men receiue by their enemies, which though it may be true in manner of *Paradoxe*, yet I finde mans frailtie to be naturally fuch, and alwayes hath beene, that he cannot conceiue it in his owne cafe, nor fhew that patience and moderation in fuch greifs, as becommeth the man perfite and accomplifht in all vertue: but either in deede or by word, he will feeke reuenge againft them that malice him, or practife his harmes, fpecially fuch foes as oppofe themfelues to a mans loues. This made the auncient Poetes to inuent a meane to rid the gall of all fuch Vindicatiue men: fo as they might be a wrecked of their wrong, & neuer bely their enemie with flaun-derous vntruthes. And this was done by a maner of imprecation, or as we call it by curfing and banning of the parties, and wifhing all euill to a light vpon them, and though it neuer the fooner happened, yet was it great eafment to the boiling ftomacke: They were called

Diræ, fuch as *Virgill* made aginſt *Battarus*, and *Ouide* againſt *Ibis:* we Chriſtians are forbidden to vſe fuch vncharitable faſhions, and willed to referre all our re-uenges to God alone./

CHAP. XXX

Of ſhort Epigrames called Poſies.

There be alſo other like Epigrammes that were ſent vſually for new yeares giftes or to be Printed or put vpon their banketting diſhes of ſuger plate, or of march paines, & ſuch other dainty meates as by the curteſie & cuſtome euery geſt might carry from a common feaſt home with him to his owne houſe, & were made for the nonce, they were called *Nenia* or *apophoreta*, and neuer contained aboue one verſe, or two at the moſt, but the ſhorter the better, we call them Poſies, and do paint them now a dayes vpon the backe ſides of our fruite trenchers of wood, or vſe them as deuiſes in rings and armes and about ſuch courtly purpoſes. So haue we remembred and ſet forth to your Maieſtie very briefly, all the commended fourmes of the auncient Poeſie, which we in our vulgare makings do imitate and vſe vnder theſe common names: enterlude, ſong, ballade, carroll and ditty: borrowing them alſo from the French al ſauing this word (ſong) which is our naturall Saxon Engliſh word. The reſt, ſuch as time and vſurpation by cuſtome haue allowed vs out of the primitiue Greeke & Latine, as Comedie, Tragedie, Ode, Epitaphe, Elegie, Epigramme, and other moe. And we haue purpoſely omitted all nice or ſcholaſticall curioſities not meete for your Maieſties contemplation in this our vulgare arte, and what we haue written of the auncient formes of Poemes, we haue taken from the beſt clerks writing in the ſame arte. The part that next followeth to wit of proportion, becauſe the Greeks nor Latines neuer had it in vſe, nor made any obſeruation, no more then we doe of their feete, we may truly affirme, to haue bene the firſt deuiſers thereof our ſelues, as αὐτοδιδακτοι, and not to haue borrowed it of any other by learning or imitation, and thereby truſting to be holden the more excuſable if any thing in this our labours happen either to miſlike, or to come ſhort of th'authors purpoſe, be-cauſe commonly the firſt attempt in any arte or engine artificiall is amendable, & in time by often experiences reformed. And ſo no doubt may this deuiſe of ours be, by others that ſhall take the penne in hand after vs./

CHAP. XXXI.

H iiijᵛ

Who in any age haue bene the moſt commended writers
in our Engliſh Poeſie, and the Authors
cenſure giuen vpon them.

It appeareth by ſundry records of bookes both printed & written, that many of our countreymen haue pain-fully trauelled in this part: of whoſe works ſome appeare to be but bare tranſlatiōs, other ſome matters of their owne inuention and very commendable, whereof ſome recitall ſhall be made in this place, to th'intent chiefly that their names ſhould not be defrauded of ſuch honour as ſeemeth due to them for hauing by their thankefull ſtudies ſo much beautified our Engliſh tong, as at this day it will be found our nation is in nothing inferiour to the French or Italian for copie of language, ſubtiltie of deuice, good method and proportion in any forme of poeme, but that they may compare with the moſt, and perchance paſſe a great many of them. And I will not reach aboue the time of king *Edward* the third, and *Richard* the ſecond for any that wrote in Engliſh meeter: becauſe before their times by reaſon of the late Nor-mane conqueſt, which had brought into this Realme much alteration both of our langage and lawes, and there withall a certain martiall barbarouſnes, whereby the ſtudy of all good learning was ſo much decayd, as long

time after no man or very few entended to write in any
laudable fcience: fo as beyond that time there is litle or
nothing worth commendation to be founde written in
this arte. And thofe of the firft age were *Chaucer* and
Gower both of them as I fuppofe Knightes. After whom
followed *Iohn Lydgate* the monke of Bury, & that name-
les, who wrote the *Satyre* called Piers Plowman, next
him followed *Harding* the Chronicler, then in king
Henry th'eight times *Skelton*, (I wot not for what great
worthines) furnamed the Poet *Laureat*. In the latter
end of the fame kings raigne fprōg vp a new company
of courtly makers, of whom Sir *Thomas Wyat* th'elder
& *Henry* Earle of Surrey were the two chieftaines, who
hauing trauailed into Italie, and there tafted the fweete
and ftately meafures and ftile of the Italiā Poefie as
nouices newly crept out of the fchooles of *Dante Ariofte*
and *Petrarch*, they greatly pollifhed our rude & homely
maner of vulgar Poefie, from that it had bene before,
and for that caufe may iuftly be fayd the firft reformers
I ᴵ of our Englifh/meetre and ftile. In the fame time or
not long after was the Lord *Nicholas Vaux*, a man of
much facilitie in vulgar makings. Afterward in king
Edward the fixths time came to be in reputation for the
fame facultie *Thomas Sternehold*, who firft tranflated into
Englifh certaine Pfalmes of Dauid, and *Iohn Heywood*
the Epigrammatift who for the myrth and quickneffe
of his conceits more then for any good learning was in
him came to be well benefited by the king. But the
principall man in this profeffion at the fame time was
Maifter *Edward Ferrys* a man of no leffe mirth & felicitie
that way, but of much more skil, & magnificence in his
meeter, and therefore wrate for the moft part to the
ftage, in Tragedie and fometimes in Comedie or Enterlude, wherein he gaue the king fo much good recreation,
as he had thereby many good rewardes. In Queenes
Maries time florifhed aboue any other Doɕtour *Phaer*
one that was well learned & excellently well tranflated

into Englifh verfe Heroicall certaine bookes of *Virgils Æneidos*. Since him followed Maifter *Arthure Golding*, who with no leffe commendation turned into Englifh meetre the Metamorphofis of *Ouide*, and that other Doctour, who made the fupplement to thofe bookes of *Virgils Æneidos*, which Maifter *Phaer* left vndone. And in her Maiefties time that now is are fprong vp an other crew of Courtly makers Noble men and Gentlemen of her Maiefties owne feruauntes, who haue written excellently well as it would appeare if their doings could be found out and made publicke with the reft, of which number is firft that noble Gentleman *Edward* Earle of Oxford. *Thomas* Lord of Bukhurft, when he was young, *Henry* Lord Paget, Sir *Philip Sydney*, Sir *Walter Rawleigh*, Mafter *Edward Dyar*, Maifter *Fulke Greuell*, *Gafcon*, *Britton*, *Turberuille* and a great many other learned Gentlemen, whofe names I do not omit for enuie, but to auoyde tedioufneffe, and who haue deferued no little commendation. But of them all particularly this is myne opinion, that *Chaucer*, with *Gower*, *Lidgat* and *Harding* for their antiquitie ought to haue the firft place, and *Chaucer* as the moft renowmed of them all, for the much learning appeareth to be in him aboue any of the reft. And though many of his bookes be but bare tranflations out of the Latin & French, yet are they wel handled, as his bookes of *Troilus*/and *Creffeid*, and the Romant I iv of the Rofe, whereof he tranflated but one halfe, the deuice was *Iohn de Mehunes* a French Poet, the Canterbury tales were *Chaucers* owne inuention as I fuppofe, and where he fheweth more the naturall of his pleafant wit, then in any other of his workes, his fimilitudes comparifons and all other defcriptions are fuch as can not be amended. His meetre Heroicall of *Troilus* and *Creffeid* is very graue and ftately, keeping the ftaffe of feuen, and the verfe of ten, his other verfes of the Canterbury tales be but riding ryme, neuertheleffe very well becomming the matter of that pleafaunt pilgrimage in which euery

mans part is playd with much decency. *Gower* fauing
for his good and graue moralities, had nothing in him
highly to be commended, for his verfe was homely and
without good meafure, his wordes ftrained much deale
out of the French writers, his ryme wrefted, and in his
inuentions fmall fubtillitie: the applications of his moralities are the beft in him, and yet thofe many times very
groffely beftowed, neither doth the fubftance of his
workes fufficiently aunfwere the fubtilitie of his titles.
Lydgat a tranflatour onely and no deuifer of that which
he wrate, but one that wrate in good verfe. *Harding*
a Poet Epick or Hiftoricall, handled himfelfe well according to the time and maner of his fubiect. He that
wrote the Satyr of Piers Ploughman, feemed to haue
bene a malcontent of that time, and therefore bent himfelfe wholy to taxe the diforders of that age, and fpccially
the pride of the Romane Clergy, of whofe fall he feemeth
to be a very true Prophet, his verfe is but loofe meetre,
and his termes hard and obfcure, fo as in them is litle
pleafure to be taken. *Skelton* a fharpe Satirift, but with
more rayling and fcoffery then became a Poet Lawreat,
fuch among the Greekes were called *Pantomimi*, with
vs Buffons, altogether applying their wits to Scurrillities
& other ridiculous matters. *Henry* Earle of Surrey and
Sir *Thomas Wyat*, betweene whom I finde very litle
differēce, I repute them (as before) for the two chief
lāternes of light to all others that haue fince employed
their pennes vpon Englifh Poefie, their conceits were
loftie, their ftiles ftately, their conueyance cleanely, their
termes proper, their meetre fweete and well propor-
tioned, in all imitating very naturally and ftudioufly their
I ij^r Maifter *Francis Petrarcha.*/The Lord *Vaux* his com-
mendatiō lyeth chiefly in the facillitie of his meetre, and
the aptneffe of his defcriptions fuch as he taketh vpon
him to make, namely in fundry of his Songs, wherein
he fheweth the counterfait actiō very liuely & pleafantly.
Of the later fort I thinke thus. That for Tragedie, the

(62)

Lord of Buckhurſt, & Maiſter *Edward Ferrys* for ſuch doings as I haue ſene of theirs do deſerue the hyeſt price: Th'Earle of Oxford and Maiſter *Edwardes* of her Maieſties Chappell for Comedy and Enterlude. For Eglogue and paſtorall Poeſie, Sir *Philip Sydney* and Maiſter *Challenner*, and that other Gentleman who wrate the late ſhepheardes Callender. For dittie and amourous *Ode* I finde Sir *Walter Rawleyghs* vayne moſt loftie, inſolent, and paſſionate. Maiſter *Edward Dyar*, for Elegie moſt ſweete, ſolempne and of high conceit. *Gaſcon* for a good meeter and for a plentifull vayne. *Phaer* and *Golding* for a learned and well correſted verſe, ſpecially in tranſlation cleare and very faithfully anſwering their authours intent. Others haue alſo written with much facillitie, but more commendably perchance if they had not written ſo much nor ſo popularly. But laſt in recitall and firſt in degree is the Queene our foueraigne Lady, whoſe learned, delicate, noble Muſe, eaſily ſurmounteth all the reſt that haue writtē before her time or ſince, for ſence, ſweetneſſe and ſubtillitie, be it in Ode, Elegie, Epigram, or any other kinde of poeme Heroick or Lyricke, wherein it ſhall pleaſe her Maieſtie to employ her penne, euen by as much oddes as her owne excellent eſtate and degree exceedeth all the reſt of her moſt humble vaſſalls.

THE SECOND BOOKE,
OF PROPORTION POETICAL.

CHAP. I.

Of Proportion Poeticall.

It is faid by fuch as profeffe the Mathematicall fciences, that all things ftand by proportion, and that without it nothing could ftand to be good or beautiful. The Doctors of our Theologie to the fame effect, but in other termes, fay: that God made the world by number, meafure and weight: fome for weight fay tune, and peraduenture better. For weight is a kind of meafure or of much conueniencie with it: and therefore in their defcriptions be always coupled together (*ftatica & metrica*) weight and meafures. Hereupon it feemeth the Philofopher gathers a triple proportion, to wit, the Arithmeticall, the Geometricall, and the Mufical. And by one of thefe three is euery other proportion guided of the things that haue conueniencie by relation, as the vifible by light colour and fhadow: the audible by ftirres, times and accents: the odorable by fmelles of fundry tempera-ments: the taftible by fauours to the rate: the tangible by his obiectes in this or that regard. Of all which we leaue to fpeake, returning to our poeticall proportion, which holdeth of the Mufical, becaufe as we fayd before Poefie is a skill to fpeake & write harmonically: and verfes or rime be a kind of Muficall vtterance, by reafon of a certaine congruitie in founds pleafing the eare, though not perchance fo exquifitely as the harmonicall concents of the artificial Muficke, confifting in ftrained tunes, as is the vocall Mufike, or that of melodious inftruments, as Lutes, Harpes, Regals, Records and

(64)

fuch like. And this our proportion Poeticall/refteth in K iv
fiue points: Staffe, Meafure, Concord, Scituation and
figure all which fhall be fpoken of in their places.

CHAP. II.

Of proportion in Staffe.

Staffe in our vulgare Poefie I know not why it fhould
be fo called, vnleffe it be for that we vnderftand it for
a bearer or fupporter of a fong or ballad, not vnlike the
old weake bodie, that is ftayed vp by his ftaffe, and were
not otherwife able to walke or to ftand vpright. The
Italian called it *Stanza*, as if we fhould fay a refting
place: and if we confider well the forme of this Poeticall
ftaffe, we fhall finde it to be a certaine number of verfes
allowed to go altogether and ioyne without any intermiffion, and doe or fhould finifh vp all the fentēces of
the fame with a full period, vnleffe it be in fom fpecial
cafes, & there to ftay till another ftaffe follow of like
fort: and the fhorteft ftaffe conteineth not vnder foure
verfes, nor the longeft aboue ten, if it paffe that number
it is rather a whole ditty then properly a ftaffe. Alfo
for the more part the ftaues ftand rather vpon the euen
nomber of verfes then the odde, though there be of both
forts. The firft proportion then of a ftaffe is by *quadrien*
or foure verfes. The fecond of fiue verfes, and is feldome
vfed. The third by *fizeine* or fixe verfes, and is not only
moft vfual, but alfo very pleafant to th'eare. The fourth
is in feuē verfes, & is the chiefe of our ancient proportions vfed by any rimer writing any thing of hiftorical
or graue poeme, as ye may fee in *Chaucer* and *Lidgate*
th'one writing the loues of *Troylus* and *Creffeida*, th'other
of the fall of Princes: both by them tranflated not deuifed. The fift proportion is of eight verfes very ftately
and *Heroicke*, and which I like better then that of feuen,
becaufe it receaueth better band. The fixt is of nine
verfes, rare but very graue. The feuenth proportion is

of tenne verfes, very ftately, but in many mens opinion too long: neuertheleffe of very good grace & much grauitie. Of eleuen and twelue I find none ordinary ftaues vfed in any vulgar language, neither doth it ferue well to continue any hiftoricall report or ballade, or other fong: but is a dittie of it felf, and no ftaffe, yet fome moderne writers haue vfed it but very feldome. Then laft of all haue ye a proportion to be vfed in the num-/ber of your ftaues, as to a caroll and a ballade, to a fong, & a round, or virelay. For to an hiftoricall poeme no certain number is limited, but as the matter fals out: alfo a *diftick* or couple of verfes is not to be accompted a ftaffe, but ferues for a continuance as we fee in Elegie, Epitaph, Epigramme or fuch meetres, of plaine concord not harmonically entertangled, as fome other fongs of more delicate mufick be.

K ijr

A ftaffe of foure verfes containeth in it felfe matter fufficient to make a full periode or complement of fence, though it doe not alwayes fo, and therefore may go by diuifions.

A ftaffe of fiue verfes, is not much vfed becaufe he that can not comprehend his periode in foure verfes, will rather driue it into fix then leaue it in fiue, for that the euen number is more agreable to the eare then the odde is.

A ftaffe of fixe verfes, is very pleafant to the eare, and alfo ferueth for a greater complement then the inferiour ftaues, which maketh him more commonly to be vfed.

A ftaffe of feuen verfes, moft vfuall with our auncient makers, alfo the ftaffe of eight, nine and ten of larger complement then the reft, are onely vfed by the later makers, & vnleffe they go with very good bande, do not fo well as the inferiour ftaues. Therefore if ye make your ftaffe of eight, by two fowers not entertangled, it is not a huitaine or a ftaffe of eight, but two quadreins, fo is it in ten verfes, not being entertangled they be but two ftaues of fiue.

CHAP. III.

Of proportion in meafure.

Meeter and meafure is all one, for what the Greekes call μετρον, the Latines call *Menfura*, and is but the quantitie of a verfe, either long or fhort. This quantitie with them confifteth in the number of their feete: & with vs in the number of fillables, which are comprehended in euery verfe, not regarding his feete, otherwife then that we allow in fcanning our verfe, two fillables to make one fhort portiō (fuppofe it a foote) in euery verfe. And after that fort ye may fay, we haue feete in our vulgare rymes, but that is improperly: for a foote by his fence naturall is a mēber of office and function, and ferueth to three purpofes, that is to fay, to go, to/ runne, & to ftand ftill: fo as he muft be fometimes K ijᵛ fwift, fometimes flow, fometime vnegally marching, or peraduēture fteddy. And if our feete Poeticall want thefe qualities it can not be fayd a foote in fence tranflatiue as here. And this commeth to paffe, by reafon of the euident motion and ftirre, which is perceiued in the founding of our wordes not always egall: for fome aske longer, fome fhorter time to be vttered in, & fo by the Philofophers definition, ftirre is the true meafure of time. The Greekes & Latines becaufe their wordes hapned to be of many fillables, and very few of one fillable, it fell out right with them to conceiue and alfo to perceiue, a notable diuerfitie of motion and times in the pronuntiation of their wordes, and therefore to euery *biffillable* they allowed two times, & to a *triffillable* three times, & to euery *polifillable* more, according to his quantitie, & their times were fome long, fome fhort according as their motions were flow or fwift. For the found of fome fillable ftayd the eare a great while, and others flid away fo quickly, as if they had not bene pronounced, then euery fillable being allowed one time,

(67)

either fhort or long, it fell out that euery *tetrafillable* had
foure times, euery *triffillable* three, and the *biffillable* two,
by which obferuation euery word, not vnder that fife,
as he ranne or ftood in a verfe, was called by them a
foote of fuch and fo many times, namely the *biffillable*
was either of two long times as the *fpondeus*, or two
fhort, as the *pirchius*, or of a long & a fhort as the
trocheus, or of a fhort and a long as the *iambus:* the like
rule did they fet vpon the word *triffillable*, calling him
a foote of three times: as the *dactilus* of a long and two
fhort: the *molloffus* of three long, the *tribracchus* of three
fhort, the *amphibracchus* of two long and a fhort, the
amphimacer of two fhort and a long. The word of foure
fillables they called a foote of foure times, fome or all
of them, either long or fhort: and yet not fo content
they mounted higher, and becaufe their wordes ferued
well thereto, they made feete of fixe times: but this
proceeded more of curiofitie, then otherwife: for whatfoeuer foote paffe the *triffillable* is compounded of his
inferiour as euery number Arithmeticall aboue three, is
cōpounded of the inferiour numbers as twife two make
foure, but the three is made of one number, videl. of
two and an vnitie. Now becaufe our naturall & primi-

K iijʳ   tiue language of the *Saxon En-/glifh*, beares not any
wordes (at leaft very few) of moe fillables then one (for
whatfoeuer we fee exceede, commeth to vs by the alterations of our language growen vpon many conqueftes and
otherwife) there could be no fuch obferuation of times
in the found of our wordes, & for that caufe we could
not haue the feete which the Greeks and Latines haue in
their meetres: but of this ftirre & motion of their deuifed
feete, nothing can better fhew the qualitie thē thefe
runners at common games, who fetting forth from the
firft goale, one giueth the ftart fpeedely & perhaps before
he come half way to th'other goale, decayeth his pace,
as a mā weary & fainting: another is flow at the ftart,
but by amending his pace keepes euen with his fellow

or perchance gets before him: another one while gets
ground, another while lofeth it again, either in the beginning, or middle of his race, and fo proceedes vnegally
fometimes fwift fomtimes flow as his breath or forces
ferue him: another fort there be that plod on, & will
neuer change their pace, whether they win or lofe the
game: in this maner doth the Greeke *dactilus* begin
flowly and keepe on fwifter till th'end, for his race being
deuided into three parts, he fpends one, & that is the
firft flowly, the other twaine fwiftly: the *anapeftus* his
two firft parts fwiftly, his laft flowly: the *Moloffus* fpends
all three parts of his race flowly and egally *Bacchius* his
firft part fwiftly, & two laft parts flowly. The *tribrachus*
all his three parts fwiftly: the *antibacchius* his two firft
partes flowly, his laft & third fwiftly: the *amphimacer*,
his firft & laft part flowly & his middle part fwiftly:
the *amphibracus* his firft and laft parts fwiftly but his
midle part flowly, & fo of others by like proportiō. This
was a pretie phantafticall obferuation of them, & yet
brought their meetres to haue a maruelous good grace,
which was in Greeke called ριθμος: whence we haue
deriued this word ryme, but improperly & not wel
becaufe we haue no fuch feete or times or ftirres in our
meeters, by whofe *fimpathie*, or pleafant cōueniēcie with
th'eare, we could take any delight: this *rithmus* of theirs,
is not therfore our rime, but a certaine muficall numerofitie in vtterance, and not a bare number as that of the
Arithmeticall cōputation is, which therfore is not called
rithmus but *arithmus*. Take this away from them, I meane
the running of their feete, there is nothing of curiofitie
among them more then with vs nor yet fo much./

CHAP. III. [IV]

How many forts of meafures we vfe in our vulgar.

To returne from rime to our meafure againe, it hath bene fayd that according to the number of the fillables contained in euery verfe, the fame is fayd a long or fhort meeter, and his fhorteft proportion is of foure fillables, and his longeft of twelue, they that vfe it aboue, paffe the bounds of good proportion. And euery meeter may be afwel in the odde as in the euen fillable, but better in the euen, and one verfe may begin in the euen, & another follow in the odde, and fo keepe a commendable proportion. The verfe that containeth but two filables, which may be in one word, is not vfuall: therefore many do deny him to be a verfe, faying that it is but a foot, and that a meeter can haue no leffe then two feete at the leaft, but I find it otherwife afwell among the beft Italian Poets, as alfo with our vulgar makers, and that two fillables ferue wel for a fhort meafure in the firft place, and midle, and end of a ftaffe: and alfo in diuerfe fcituations and by fundry diftances, and is very paffionate and of good grace, as fhalbe declared more at large in the Chapter of proportion by fcituation.

The next meafure is of two feete or of foure fillables, and then one word *tetrafillable* diuided in the middeft makes vp the whole meeter, as thus

    R̄eūē   r̄entl̄ie

Or a triffillable and one monofillable thus. *Soueraine God*, or two biffillables and that is plefant thus, *Reftore againe*, or with foure monoffillables, and that is beft of all thus, *When I doe thinke*, I finde no fauour in a meetre of three fillables nor in effeƈt in any odde, but they may be vfed for varietie fake, and fpecially being enterlaced with others the meetre of fix fillables is very fweete and dilicate as thus.

O God vvhen I behold
This bright heauen ſo hye
By thine ovvne hands of old
Contriud ſo cunningly.

The meter of ſeuen ſillables is not vſual, no more is
that of nine and eleuen, yet if they be well compoſed,
that is, their *Ceſure* well appointed, and their laſt accent
which makes the concord, they/are cōmendable inough, K iiijʳ
as in this ditty where one verſe is of eight an other is
of ſeuen, and in the one the accent vpon the laſt, in
the other vpon the laſt ſaue on.

The ſmoakie ſighes, the bitter teares
That I in vaine haue waſted
The broken ſleepes, the woe and feares
That long in me haue laſted
Will be my death, all by thy guilt
And not by my deſeruing
Since ſo inconſtantly thou wilt
Not loue but ſtill be ſweruing.

And all the reaſon why theſe meeters in all ſillable
are alowable is, for that the ſharpe accent falles vpon
the *penultima* or laſt ſaue one ſillable of the verſe, which
doth ſo drowne the laſt, as he ſeemeth to paſſe away in
maner vnpronounced, & ſo make the verſe ſeeme euen:
but if the accent fall vpon the laſt and leaue two flat
to finiſh the verſe, it will not ſeeme ſo: for the odnes
will more notoriouſly appeare, as for example in the laſt
verſe before recited *Not loue but ſtill be ſweruing,* ſay
thus *Loue it is a maruelous thing.* Both verſes be of egall
quantitie, vidz. ſeauen ſillables a peece, and yet the firſt
ſeemes ſhorter then the later, who ſhewes a more odneſſe
then the former by reaſon of his ſharpe accent which
is vpō the laſt ſillable, and makes him more audible then
if he had ſlid away with a flat accent, as the word
ſwéruing.

Your ordinarie rimers vſe very much their meaſures

in the odde as nine and eleuen, and the fharpe accent
vpon the laft fillable, which therefore makes him go ill
fauouredly and like a minftrels muficke. Thus fayd one
in a meeter of eleuen very harfhly in mine eare, whether
it be for lacke of good rime or of good reafon, or of
both I wot not.

> *Now fucke childe and fleepe childe, thy mothers owne ioy*
> *Her only fweete comfort, to drowne all annoy*
> *For beauty furpaffing the azured skie*
> *I loue thee my darling, as ball of mine eye.*

This fort of compofition in the odde I like not, vnleffe
it be holpen by the *Cefure* or by the accent as I fayd
before.

The meeter of eight is no leffe pleafant then that of
K iiijᵛ fixe, and/the *Cefure* fals iuft in the middle, as this of the
Earle of Surreyes.

> *When raging loue, with extreme payne.*

The meeter of ten fillables is very ftately and Heroicall, and muft haue his *Cefure* fall vpon the fourth fillable,
and leaue fixe behinde him thus.

> *I ferue at eafe, and gouerne all with woe.*

This meeter of twelue fillables the French man calleth
a verfe *Alexandrine*, and is with our moderne rimers moft
vfuall: with the auncient makers it was not fo. For
before Sir *Thomas Wiats* time they were not vfed in our
vulgar, they be for graue and ftately matters fitter than
for any other ditty of pleafure. Some makers write in
verfes of foureteene fillables, giuing the *Cefure* at the
firft eight, which proportion is tedious, for the length
of the verfe kepeth the eare too long from his delight,
which is to heare the cadence or the tuneable accent in
the ende of the verfe. Neuertheleffe that of twelue if
his *Cefure* be iuft in the middle, and that ye fuffer him
to runne at full length, and do not as the common
rimers do, or their Printer for fparing of paper, cut

(72)

them of in the middeft, wherin they make in two verfes
but halfe rime. They do very wel as wrote the Earle of
Surrey tranflating the booke of the preacher.

Salomon Dauids fonne, king of Ierufalem.

This verfe is a very good *Alexandrine*, but perchaunce
woulde haue founded more mufically, if the firft word
had bene a diffillable, or two monofillables and not a
triffillable: hauing his fharpe accent vppon the *Antepenultima* as it hath, by which occafion it runnes like a
Dactill, and carries the two later fillables away fo fpeedily
as it feemes but one foote in our vulgar meafure, and
by that meanes makes the verfe feeme but of eleuen
fillables, which odneffe is nothing pleafant to the eare.
Iudge fome body whether it would haue done better (if
it might) haue bene fayd thus,

Robóham Dauids fonne king of Ierufalem.

Letting the fharpe accent fall vpon *bo*, or thus

Reftóre king Dáuids fónne vntó Ierúfalém

For now the fharpe accent falles vpon *bo*, and fo doth
it vpon the laft in *reftóre*, which was not in th'other verfe.
But becaufe we haue feemed to make mention of *Cefure*,
and to appoint his place in euery meafure, it fhall not
be amiffe to fay fomewhat more of it,/& alfo of fuch L iͬ
paufes as are vfed in vtterance, & what commoditie or
delectation they bring either to the fpeakers or to the
hearers.

CHAP. IIII. [V]

Of Cefure.

There is no greater difference betwixt a ciuill and brutifh
vtteraunce then cleare diftinction of voices: and the moft
laudable languages are alwaies moft plaine and diftinct,
and the barbarous moft confufe and indiftinct: it is
therefore requifit that leafure be taken in pronuntiation,

(73)

such as may make our wordes plaine & moſt audible
and agreable to the eare: alſo the breath asketh to be
now and then releeued with ſome pauſe or ſtay more or
leſſe: beſides that the very nature of ſpeach (becauſe it
goeth by clauſes of ſeuerall conſtruction & ſence) requireth ſome ſpace betwixt thē with intermiſſiō of ſound,
to th'end they may not huddle one vpon another ſo
rudly & ſo faſt that th'eare may not perceiue their
difference. For theſe reſpectes the auncient reformers
of language, inuented, three maner of pauſes, one of
leſſe leaſure then another, and ſuch ſeuerall intermiſſions
of ſound to ſerue (beſides eaſmēt to the breath) for a
treble diſtinction of ſentēces or parts of ſpeach, as they
happened to be more or leſſe perfect in ſence. The
ſhorteſt pauſe or intermiſſiō they called *comma* as who
would ſay a peece of a ſpeach cut of. The ſecōd they
called *colon*, not a peece but as it were a member for
his larger length, becauſe it occupied twiſe as much time
as the *comma*. The third they called *periodus*, for a cōple-
ment or full pauſe, and as a reſting place and perfection
of ſo much former ſpeach as had bene vttered, and from
whence they needed not to paſſe any further vnles it
were to renew more matter to enlarge the tale. This
cannot be better repreſented then by exāple of theſe
cōmō trauailers by the hie ways, where they ſeeme to
allow thēſelues three maner of ſtaies or eaſements: one a
horſebacke calling perchaunce for a cup of beere or
wine, and hauing dronken it vp rides away and neuer
lights: about noone he commeth to his Inne, & there
baites him ſelfe and his horſe an houre or more: at night
when he can conueniently trauaile no further, he taketh
vp his lodging, and reſts him ſelfe till the morrow: from
whence he followeth the courſe of a further voyage, if
L iv his buſineſſe/be ſuch. Euen ſo our Poet when he hath
made one verſe, hath as it were finiſhed one dayes
iourney, & the while eaſeth him ſelfe with one baite
at the leaſt, which is a *Comma* or *Ceſure* in the mid way,

if the verſe be euen and not odde, otherwiſe in ſome
other place, and not iuſt in the middle. If there be no
Ceſure at all, and the verſe long, the leſſe is the makers
ſkill and hearers delight. Therefore in a verſe of twelue
ſillables the *Ceſure* ought to fall right vpon the ſixt
ſillable: in a verſe of eleuen vpon the ſixt alſo leauing
fiue to follow. In a verſe of ten vpon the fourth, leauing
ſixe to follow. In a verſe of nine vpon the fourth,
leauing fiue to follow. In a verſe of eight iuſt in the
middeſt, that is, vpon the fourth. In a verſe of ſeauen,
either vpon the fourth or none at all, the meeter very
ill brooking any pauſe. In a verſe of ſixe ſillables and
vnder is needefull no *Ceſure* at all, becauſe the breath
asketh no reliefe: yet if ye giue any *Comma*, it is to
make diſtinction of ſenſe more then for any thing elſe:
and ſuch *Ceſure* muſt neuer be made in the middeſt
of any word, if it be well appointed. So may you ſee
that the vſe of theſe pawſes or diſtinctions is not generally
with the vulgar Poet as it is with the Proſe writer becauſe
the Poetes cheife Muſicke lying in his rime or concorde
to heare the Simphonie, he maketh all the haſt he can
to be at an end of his verſe, and delights not in many
ſtayes by the way, and therefore giueth but one *Ceſure*
to any verſe: and thus much for the ſounding of a
meetre. Neuertheleſſe he may vſe in any verſe both his
comma, colon, and *interrogatiue* point, as well as in proſe.
But our auncient rymers, as *Chaucer, Lydgate* & others,
vſed theſe *Ceſures* either very ſeldome, or not at all, or
elſe very licentiouſly, and many times made their meetres
(they called them riding ryme) of ſuch vnſhapely wordes
as would allow no conuenient *Ceſure*, and therefore did
let their rymes runne out at length, and neuer ſtayd
till they came to the end: which maner though it were
not to be miſliked in ſome ſort of meetre, yet in euery
long verſe the *Ceſure* ought to be kept preciſely, if it
were but to ſerue as a law to correct the licentiouſneſſe
of rymers, beſides that it pleaſeth the eare better, &

fheweth more cunning in the maker by following the rule of his reftraint. For a rymer that will be tyed to no rules at all, but range as he lift, may eafily vtter what L ijr he will: but fuch maner of Poefie is called in our/vulgar, ryme dogrell, with which rebuke we will in no cafe our maker fhould be touched. Therfore before all other things let his ryme and concordes be true, cleare and audible with no leffe delight, then almoft the ftrayned note of a Muficians mouth, & not darke or wrenched by wrong writing as many doe to patch vp their meetres, and fo follow in their arte neither rule, reafon, nor ryme. Much more might be fayd for the vfe of your three paufes, *comma, colon,* & *periode,* for perchance it be not all a matter to vfe many *commas,* and few, nor *colons* like-wife, or long or fhort *periodes,* for it is diuerfly vfed, by diuers good writers. But becaufe it apperteineth more to the oratour or writer in profe then in verfe, I will fay no more in it, then thus, that they be vfed for a commodious and fenfible diftinction of claufes in profe, fince euery verfe is as it were a claufe of it felfe, and limited with a *Cefure* howfoeuer the fence beare, perfect or imperfect, which difference is obferuable betwixt the profe and the meeter.

CHAP. V. [VI]

Of Proportion in Concord, called Symphonie or rime.

Becaufe we vfe the word rime (though by maner of abufion) yet to helpe that fault againe we apply it in our vulgar Poefie another way very commendably & curioufly. For wanting the currantneffe of the Greeke and Latine feete, in ftead thereof we make in th' ends of our verfes a certaine tunable found: which anon after with another verfe reafonably diftant we accord together in the laft fall or cadence: the eare taking pleafure to heare the like tune reported, and to feele his returne. And for this purpofe ferue the *monofillables* of our Englifh

(76)

Saxons excellently well, becaufe they do naturally and
indifferently receiue any accent, & in them if they finifh
the verfe, refteth the fhrill accent of neceffitie, and fo
doth it not in the laft of euery *biffillable*, nor of euery
polifillable word: but to the purpofe, *ryme* is a borrowed
word frō the Greeks by the Latines and French, from
them by vs Saxon angles, and by abufion as hath bene
fayd, and therefore it fhall not do amiffe to tell what this
rithmos was with the Greekes, for what is it with vs
hath bene already fayd. There is an accōptable number
which we call *arithmeticall* (*arithmos*) as one, two, three.
There is alfo a mufi-/call or audible number, fafhioned L ijᵛ
by ftirring of tunes & their fundry times in the vtterance
of our wordes, as when the voice goeth high or low,
or fharpe or flat, or fwift or flow: & this is called *rithmos*
or numerofitie, that is to fay, a certaine flowing vtteraunce by flipper words and fillables, fuch as the toung
eafily vtters, and the eare with pleafure receiueth, and
which flowing of wordes with much volubilitie fmoothly
proceeding from the mouth is in fome fort *harmonicall*
and breedeth to th'eare a great compaffion. This point
grew by the fmooth and delicate running of their feete,
which we haue not in our vulgare, though we vfe as
much as may be the moft flowing words & flippery
fillables, that we can picke out: yet do not we call that
by the name of ryme, as the Greekes did: but do giue
the name of ryme onely to our concordes, or tunable
confentes in the latter end of our verfes, and which concordes the Greekes nor Latines neuer vfed in their
Poefie till by the barbarous fouldiers out of the campe,
it was brought into the Court and thence to the fchoole,
as hath bene before remembred: and yet the Greekes
and Latines both vfed a maner of fpeach, by claufes of
like termination, which they called ὁμιοτελητον, and
was the neareft that they approched to our ryme: but is
not our right concord: fo as we in abufing this terme
(*ryme*) be neuertheleffe excufable applying it to another

7 (77)

point in Poefie no leffe curious then their *rithme* or numerofitie which in deede paffed the whole verfe throughout, whereas our concordes keepe but the latter end of euery verfe, or perchaunce the middle and the end in meetres that be long.

CHAP. VI. [VII]

Of accent, time and ftir perceiued euidently in the distinction of mans voice, and which makes the flowing of a meeter.

Nowe becaufe we haue fpoken of accent, time and ftirre or motion in wordes, we will fet you downe more at large what they be. The auncient Greekes and Latines by reafon their fpeech fell out originally to be fafhioned with words of many fillables for the moft part, it was of neceffity that they could not vtter euery fillable with one like and egall founde, nor in like fpace of time, nor with like motion or agility: but that one muft be more fuddenly and quickely forfaken, or longer pawfed vpon/
L iijʳ then another: or founded with a higher note & clearer voyce then another, and of neceffitie this diuerfitie of found, muft fall either vpon the laft fillable, or vpon the laft faue one, or vpon the third and could not reach higher to make any notable difference, it caufed them to giue vnto three different founds, three feuerall names: to that which was higheft lift vp and moft eleuate or fhrilleft in the eare, they gaue the name of the fharpe accent, to the loweft and moft bafe becaufe it feemed to fall downe rather then to rife vp, they gaue the name of the heauy accent, and that other which feemed in part to lift vp and in part to fall downe, they called the circumflex, or compaft accent: and if new termes were not odious, we might very properly call him the (windabout) for fo is the Greek word. Thē bycaufe euerything that by nature fals down is faid heauy, & whatfoeuer naturally mounts vpward is faid light, it

gaue occaſiō to ſay that there were diuerſities in the
motion of the voice, as ſwift & ſlow, which motiō alſo
preſuppoſes time, bycauſe time is *menſura motus*, by the
Philoſopher: ſo haue you the cauſes of their primitiue
inuention and vſe in our arte of Poeſie, all this by good
obſeruatiō we may perceiue in our vulgar wordes if they
be of mo ſillables thē one, but ſpecially if they be
triſſillables, as for example in theſe wordes [*altitude*] and
[*heauineſſe*] the ſharpe accent falles vpō [*al*] & [*he*]
which be the *antepenultimaes:* the other two fall away
ſpeedily as if they were ſcarſe ſounded in this *triſſilable*
[*forſaken*] the ſharp accent fals vpō [*ſa*] which is the
penultima, and in the other two is heauie and obſcure.
Againe in theſe *biſſillables, endúre, vnſúre, demúre: aſpíre,
deſíre, retíre,* your ſharpe accent falles vpon the laſt
ſillable: but in words *monoſillable* which be for the more
part our naturall Saxon Engliſh, the accent is indifferent,
and may be vſed for ſharp or flat and heauy at our
pleaſure. I ſay Saxon Engliſh, for our Normane Engliſh
alloweth vs very many *biſſillables*, and alſo *triſſillables* as,
reuerence, diligence, amorous, deſirous, and ſuch like.

CHAP. VII. [*VIII*]

*Of your Cadences by which your meeter is made
Symphonicall when they be ſweeteſt and moſt
ſolemne in a verſe.*

As the ſmoothneſſe of your words and ſillables running
vpon feete of ſundrie quantities, make with the Greekes
and La-/tines the body of their verſes numerous or L iijᵛ
Rithmicall, ſo in our vulgar Poeſie, and of all other
nations at this day, your verſes anſwering eche other by
couples, or at larger diſtances in good [*cadence*] is it
that maketh your meeter ſymphonicall. This cadence is
the fal of a verſe in euery laſt word with a certaine
tunable ſound which being matched with another of like
ſound, do make a [*concord.*] And the whole cadence is

(79)

contained fometime in one fillable, fometime in two, or
in three at the moft: for aboue the *antepenultima* there
reacheth no accent (which is chiefe caufe of the cadence)
vnleffe it be by vfurpatiō in fome Englifh words, to
which we giue a fharpe accent vpon the fourth as,
Hónorable, mátrimonie, pátrimonie, míferable, and fuch
other as would neither make a fweete cadence, nor eafily
find any word of like quantitie to match them. And
the accented fillable with all the reft vnder him make
the cadence, and no fillable aboue, as in thefe words,
Agíllitie, facíllitie, fubiéction, diréction, and thefe biffilables,
Ténder, flénder, trúftie, lúftie, but alwayes the cadence
which falleth vpon the laft fillable of a verfe is fweeteft
and moft commendable: that vpon the *penultima* more
light, and not fo pleafant: but falling vpon the *antepenultima* is moft vnpleafant of all, becaufe they make
your meeter too light and triuiall, and are fitter for the
Epigrammatift or Comicall Poet then for the Lyrick and
Elegiack, which are accompted the fweeter Muſickes.
But though we haue fayd that (to make good concord)
your feuerall verfes fhould haue their cadences like, yet
muft there be fome difference in their orthographie,
though not in their found, as if one cadence be [*con-
ftraine*] the next [*reftraine*] or one [*aspire*] another [*re-
fpire*] this maketh no good concord, becaufe they are
all one, but if ye will exchange both thefe confonants
of the accented fillable, or voyde but one of them away,
then will your cadences be good and your concord to,
as to fay, *reftraine, refraine, remaine: afpire, defire, retire:*
which rule neuertheleffe is not well obferued by many
makers for lacke of good iudgement and a delicate eare.
And this may fuffife to fhew the vfe and nature of your
cadences, which are in effeƈt all the fweetneffe and cunning in our vulgar Poefie./

How the good maker will not wrench his word to helpe his
rime, either by falfifying his accent, or by vntrue
orthographie.

Now there can not be in a maker a fowler fault, then
to falfifie his accent to ferue his cadence, or by vntrue
orthographie to wrench his words to helpe his rime, for
it is a figne that fuch a maker is not copious in his owne
language, or (as they are wont to fay) not halfe his
crafts maifter: as for example, if one fhould rime to this
word [*Reftore*] he may not match him with [*Doore*] or
[*Poore*] for neither of both are of like terminant, either
by good orthography or in naturall found, therfore fuch
rime is ftrained, fo is it to this word [*Ram*] to fay [*came*]
or to [*Beane* [*Den*] for they found not nor be written
a like, & many other like cadences which were fuperfluous to recite, and are vfuall with rude rimers who
obferue not precifely the rules of [*profodie*] neuertheleffe in all fuch cafes (if neceffitie conftrained) it is fomewhat more tollerable to help the rime by falfe orthographie, then to leaue an vnplefant diffonance to the
eare, by keeping trewe orthographie and loofing the
rime, as for example it is better to rime [*Dore*] with
[*Reftore*] then in his truer orthographie, which is [*Doore*]
and to this word [*Defire*] to fay [*Fier*] then fyre though
it be otherwife better written *fire*. For fince the cheife
grace of our vulgar Poefie confifteth in the Symphonie,
as hath bene already fayd, our maker muft not be too
licentious in his concords, but fee that they go euen,
iuft and melodious in the eare, and right fo in the
numerofitie or currantneffe of the whole body of his
verfe, and in euery other of his proportions. For a
licentious maker is in truth but a bungler and not a
Poet. Such men were in effeƈt the moft part of all your
old rimers and fpecially *Gower*, who to make vp his

(81)

rime would for the moſt part write his terminant ſillable
with falſe orthographie, and many times not ſticke to
put in a plaine French word for an Engliſh, & ſo by
your leaue do many of our common rimers at this day:
as he that by all likelyhood, hauing no word at hand
to rime to this word [*ioy*] he made his other verſe ende
in [*Roy*] ſaying very impudently thus,

L iiijᵛ

> *O mightie Lord of loue, dame Venus onely ioy/*
> *Who art the higheſt God of any heauenly Roy.*

Which word was neuer yet receiued in our lāguage
for an Engliſh word. Such extreme licentiouſneſſe is
vtterly to be baniſhed from our ſchoole, and better it
might haue bene borne with in old riming writers, bycauſe they liued in a barbarous age, & were graue
morall men but very homely Poets, ſuch alſo as made
moſt of their workes by tranſlation out of the Latine
and French toung, & few or none of their owne engine
as may eaſely be knowen to them that liſt to looke
vpon the Poemes of both languages.

Finally as ye may ryme with wordes of all ſortes, be
they of many ſillables or few, ſo neuertheleſſe is there a
choiſe by which to make your cadence (before remembred) moſt commendable, for ſome wordes of exceeding
great length, which haue bene fetched from the Latine
inkhorne or borrowed of ſtrangers, the vſe of them in
ryme is nothing pleaſant, ſauing perchaunce to the
common people, who reioyſe much to be at playes and
enterludes, and beſides their naturall ignoraunce, haue
at all ſuch times their eares ſo attentiue to the matter,
and their eyes vpon the ſhewes of the ſtage, that they
take little heede to the cunning of the rime, and therefore be as well ſatisfied with that which is groſſe, as
with any other finer and more delicate.

CHAP. IX. [X]

*Of concorde in long and ſhort meaſures, and by neare or
farre diſtaunces, and which of them is moſt commendable.*

But this ye muſt obſerue withall, that bycauſe your concordes containe the chief part of Muſicke in your meetre,
their diſtaunces may not be too wide or farre a ſunder,
leſt th'eare ſhould looſe the tune, and be defrauded
of his delight, and whenſoeuer ye ſee any maker vſe
large and extraordinary diſtaunces, ye muſt thinke he
doth intende to ſhew himſelfe more artificiall then
popular, and yet therein is not to be diſcommended, for
reſpeƈts that ſhalbe remembred in ſome other place of
this booke.

    Note alſo that rime or concorde is not commendably
vſed both in the end and middle of a verſe, vnleſſe it
be in toyes and trifling Poeſies, for it ſheweth a certaine
lightneſſe either of the matter or of the makers head,
albeit theſe common rimers vſe it much, for/as I ſayd   M iᵣ
before, like as the Symphonie in a verſe of great length,
is (as it were) loſt by looking after him, and yet may
the meetre be very graue and ſtately: ſo on the other
ſide doth the ouer buſie and too ſpeedy returne of one
maner of tune, too much annoy & as it were glut the
eare, vnleſſe it be in ſmall & popular Muſickes ſong by
theſe *Cantabanqui* vpon benches and barrels heads where
they haue none other audience then boys or countrey
fellowes that paſſe by them in the ſtreete, or elſe by
blind harpers or ſuch like tauerne minſtrels that giue
a fit of mirth for a groat, & their matters being for the
moſt part ſtories of old time, as the tale of Sir *Topas*,
the reportes of *Beuis* of *Southampton*, *Guy* of *Warwicke*,
Adam Bell, and *Clymme* of the *Clough* & ſuch other old
Romances or hiſtoricall rimes, made purpoſely for recreation of the cōmon people at Chriſtmaſſe diners &
brideales, and in tauernes & alehouſes and ſuch other

places of bafe refort, alfo they be vfed in Carols and rounds and fuch light or lafciuious Poemes, which are commonly more commodioufly vttered by thefe buffons or vices in playes then by any other perfon. Such were the rimes of *Skelton* (vfurping the name of a Poet Laureat) being in deede but a rude rayling rimer & all his doings ridiculous, he vfed both fhort diftaunces and fhort meafures pleafing onely the popular eare: in our courtly maker we banifh them vtterly. Now alfo haue ye in euery fong or ditty concorde by compaffe & concorde entertangled and a mixt of both, what that is and how they be vfed fhalbe declared in the chapter of proportion by *fcituation*.

CHAP. X. [XI]

Of proportion by fituation.

This proportion confifteth in placing of euery verfe in a ftaffe or ditty by fuch reafonable diftaunces, as may beft ferue the eare for delight, and alfo to fhew the Poets art and variety of Mufick, and the proportion is double. One by marfhalling the meetres, and limiting their diftaunces hauing regard to the rime or concorde how they go and returne: another by placing euery verfe, hauing a regard to his meafure and quantitie onely, and not to his concorde as to fet one fhort meetre to three long, or foure fhort and two long, or a fhort meafure M iv and a long, or of diuers/lengthes with relation one to another, which maner of *Situation*, euen without refpeÅ¿ of the rime, doth alter the nature of the Poefie, and make it either lighter or grauer, or more merry, or mournfull, and many wayes paffionate to the eare and hart of the hearer, feeming for this point that our maker by his meafures and concordes of fundry proportions doth counterfait the harmonicall tunes of the vocall and inftrumentall Muffickes. As the *Dorien* becaufe his falls, fallyes and compaffe be diuers from thofe of the *Phrigien*,

(84)

the *Phrigien* likewife from the *Lydien*, and all three from
the *Eolien*, *Miolidien* and *Ionien*, mounting and falling
from note to note fuch as be to them peculiar, and with
more or leffe leafure or precipitation. Euen fo by diuerfitie of placing and fcituation of your meafures and concords, a fhort with a long, and by narrow or wide
diftances, or thicker or thinner beftowing of them
your proportions differ, and breedeth a variable and
ftrange harmonie not onely in the eare, but alfo in the
conceit of them that heare it: whereof this may be an
ocular example.

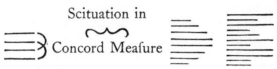

Where ye fee the concord or rime in the third diftance,
and the meafure in the fourth, fixth or fecond diftaunces,
whereof ye may deuife as many other as ye lift, fo the
ftaffe be able to beare it. And I fet you downe an
occular example: becaufe ye may the better conceiue it.
Likewife it fo falleth out moft times your occular proportion doeth declare the nature of the audible: for if
it pleafe the eare well, the fame reprefented by delineation to the view pleafeth the eye well and *è conuerfo:* and
this is by a naturall *fimpathie*, betweene the eare and the
eye, and betweene tunes & colours, euen as there is the
like betweene the other fences and their obiects of which
it apperteineth not here to fpeake. Now for the diftances
vfually obferued in our vulgar Poefie, they be in the
firft fecond third and fourth verfe, or if the verfe be
very fhort in the fift and fixt and in fome maner of
Muſickes farre aboue.

And the firft diftance for the moft part goeth all by
diftick or couples of verfes agreeing in one cadence, and
do paffe fo fpeedily/away and fo often returne agayne, M ijr
as their tunes are neuer loft, nor out of the eare, one

(85)

couple fupplying another fo nye and fo fuddenly, and
this is the moſt vulgar proportion of diſtance or
fituation, fuch as vſed *Chaucer* in his Canterbury
tales, and *Govver* in all his workes.

Second diſtance is, when ye paſſe ouer one verſe, and
ioyne the firſt and the third, and fo continue on
till an other like diſtance fall in, and this is alfo
vſuall and common, as

Third diſtaunce is, when your rime falleth vpon the
firſt and fourth verſe ouerleaping two, this
maner is not fo common but pleaſant and allowable inough.

In which caſe the two verſes ye leaue out are ready
to receiue their concordes by the fame diſtaunce or any
other ye like better. The fourth diſtaunce is by ouer-
skipping three verſes and lighting vpon the fift, this
maner is rare and more artificiall then popular, vnleſſe
it be in fome fpeciall caſe, as when the
meetres be fo little and ſhort as they
make no ſhew of any great delay before
they returne, ye ſhall haue example of
both.

And theſe ten litle meeters make but one *Exameter*
at length.

$$- \; -, \; - \; -, \; - \; -, \; - \; -, \; - \; -, \; - \; -, \; - \; -, \; - \; -, \; - \; -, \; - \; -,$$

There be larger diſtances alfo, as when the
firſt concord falleth vpō the fixt verſe, & is
very pleaſant if they be ioyned with other
diſtances not fo large, as

There be alfo, of the feuenth, eight, tenth, and
twelfth diſtance, but then they may not go thicke, but
two or three fuch diſtāces ſerue to proportiō a whole
fong, and all betweene muſt be of other leſſe diſtances,
and theſe wide diſtaunces ſerue for coupling of ſtaues,
or for to declare high and paſſionate or graue matter,
and alfo for art: *Petrarch* hath giuen vs examples hereof in

his *Canzoni,* and we by lines of fundry lengths & diftances
as followeth,

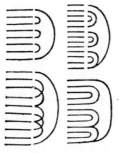

And all that can be obiected againft this wide diftance
is to fay that the eare by loofing his concord is not fatif-
fied. So is in deede the rude and popular eare but not
the learned, and therefore the/Poet muft know to whofe M ij^v
eare he maketh his rime, and accommodate himfelfe
thereto, and not giue fuch muficke to the rude and barbarous, as he would to the learned and delicate eare.

There is another fort of proportion vfed by *Petrarche*
called the *Seizino,* not riming as other fongs do, but
by chufing fixe wordes out of which all the whole dittie
is made, euery of thofe fixe commencing
and ending his verfe by courfe, which reftraint to make the dittie fenfible will try the
makers cunning, as thus.

Befides all this there is in *Situation* of the concords
two other points, one that it go by plaine and cleere
compaffe not intangled: another by enterweauing one
with another by knots, or as it were by band, which is
more or leffe bufie and curious, all as the maker will
double or redouble his rime or concords, and fet his
diftances farre or nigh, of all which I will giue you
ocular examples, as thus.

Concord in

Plaine compaffe 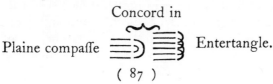 Entertangle.

And firſt in a *Quadreine* there are but two proportions,

for foure verſes in this laſt ſort coupled, are but two
Diſticks, and not a ſtaffe *quadreine* or of foure.

The ſtaffe of fiue hath ſeuen proportions as,

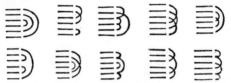

whereof ſome of them be harſher and vnpleaſaunter to
the eare then other ſome be.

The *Sixaine* or ſtaffe of ſixe hath ten proportions,
wherof ſome be vſuall, ſome not vſuall, and not ſo ſweet
one as another.

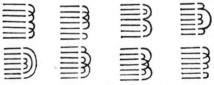

The ſtaffe of ſeuen verſes hath ſeuen proportions,
whereof one onely is the vſuall of our vulgar, and kept
by our old Poets *Chaucer* and other in their hiſtoricall
reports and other ditties: as in the laſt part of them that
follow next.

M iijʳ The *huitain* or ſtaffe of eight verſes, hath eight proportions ſuch as the former ſtaffe, and becauſe he is
longer, he hath one more then the *ſettaine.*

The ſtaffe of nine verſes hath yet moe then the eight,
and the ſtaffe of ten more then the ninth and the twelfth,
if ſuch were allowable in ditties, more then any of them
all, by reaſon of his largeneſſe receiuing moe compaſſes

and enterweauings, alwayes confidered that the very
large diftances be more artificiall, then popularly pleafant, and yet do giue great grace and grauitie, and moue
paffion and affeſtions more vehemently, as it is well to
be obferued by *Petrarcha* his *Canzoni.*

Now ye may perceiue by thefe proportions before
defcribed, that there is a band to be giuen euery verfe
in a ftaffe, fo as none fall out alone or vncoupled, and
this band maketh that the ftaffe is fayd faft and not
loofe: euen as ye fee in buildings of ftone or bricke the
mafon giueth a band, that is a length to two breadths,
& vpon neceffitie diuers other forts of bands to hold
in the worke faft and maintaine the perpendicularitie
of the wall: fo in any ftaffe of feuen or eight or more
verfes, the coupling of the moe meeters by rime or
concord, is the fafter band: the fewer the loofer band,
and therfore in a *huiteine* he that putteth foure verfes
in one concord and foure in another concord, and in a
dizaine fiue, fheweth him felfe more cunning, and alfo
more copious in his owne language. For he that can
find two words of concord, can not find foure or fiue
or fixe, vnleffe he haue his owne language at will. Sometime alfo ye are driuen of neceffitie to clofe and make
band more then ye would, left otherwife the ftaffe fhould
fall afunder and feeme two ftaues: and this is in a ftaffe
of eight and ten verfes: whereas without a band in the
middle, it would feeme two *quadriens* or two *quintaines,*
which is an error that many makers flide away with.
Yet *Chaucer* and others in the ftaffe of feuen and fixe
do almoft as much amiffe, for they fhut vp the ftaffe
with a *diflicke*, concording with none other verfe that
went before, and maketh but a loofe rime, and yet
bycaufe of the double cadence in the laft two verfes
ferue the eare well inough. And as there is in euery
ftaffe, band, giuen to the verfes by concord more or
leffe bufie: fo is there in fome cafes a band giuen to
euery ftaffe,/and that is by one whole verfe running M iij^v

(89)

alone throughout the ditty or ballade, either in the middle or end of euery ftaffe. The Greekes called fuch vncoupled verfe *Epimonie*, the Latines *Verfus intercalaris*. Now touching the fituation of meafures, there are as manie or more proportions of them which I referre to the makers phantafie and choife, contented with two or three ocular examples and no moe.

Which maner of proportion by fituatiō of meafures giueth more efficacie to the matter oftentimes then the concords them felues, and both proportions concurring together as they needes muft, it is of much more beautie and force to the hearers mind.

To finifh the learning of this diuifion, I will fet you downe one example of a dittie written extempore with this deuife, fhewing not onely much promptneffe of wit in the maker, but alfo great arte and a notable memorie. Make me faith this writer to one of the companie, fo many ftrokes or lines with your pen as ye would haue your fong containe verfes: and let euery line beare his feuerall length, euen as ye would haue your verfe of meafure. Suppofe of foure, fiue, fixe or eight or more fillables, and fet a figure of euerie number at th'end of the line, whereby ye may knowe his meafure. Then where you will haue your rime or concord to fall, marke it with a compaft ftroke or femicircle paffing ouer thofe lines, be they farre or neare in diftance, as ye haue feene before defcribed. And bycaufe ye fhall not thinke the maker hath premeditated beforehand any fuch fafhioned ditty, do ye your felfe make one verfe whether it be of perfect or imperfect fenfe, and giue it him for a theame to make all the reft vpon: if ye fhall perceiue

the maker do keepe the meafures and rime as ye haue
appointed him, and befides do make his dittie fenfible
and enfuant to the firft verfe in good reafon, then may
ye fay he is his crafts maifter. For if he were not of a
plentiful difcourfe, he could not vpon the fudden fhape
an entire dittie vpon your imperfeƈt theame or pro-
pofition in one/verfe. And if he were not copious in his M iiijʳ
language, he could not haue fuch ftore of wordes at
commaundement, as fhould fupply your concords. And
if he were not of a maruelous good memory he could
not obferue the rime and meafures after the diftances
of your limitation, keeping with all grauitie and good
fenfe in the whole dittie.

CHAP. XI. [XII]

Of Proportion in figure.

Your laft proportion is that of figure, fo called for that
it yelds an ocular reprefentation, your mceters being
by good fymmetrie reduced into certaine Geometricall
figures, whereby the maker is reftrained to keepe him
within his bounds, and fheweth not onely more art, but
ferueth alfo much better for briefeneffe and fubtiltie of
deuice. And for the fame refpeƈt are alfo fitteft for the
pretie amourets in Court to entertaine their feruants and
the time withall, their delicate wits requiring fome commendable exercife to keepe them from idleneffe. I find
not of this proportion vfed by any of the Greeke or
Latine Poets, or in any vulgar writer, fauing of that
one forme which they cal *Anacreons egge*. But being in
Italie conuerfant with a certaine gentleman, who had
long trauailed the Oriental parts of the world, and feene
the Courts of the great Princes of China and Tartarie.
I being very inquifitiue to know of the fubtillities of
thofe countreyes, and efpecially in matter of learning
and of their vulgar Poefie, he told me that they are in
all their inuentions moft wittie, and haue the vfe of

(91)

Poefie or riming, but do not delight fo much as we do in long tedious defcriptions, and therefore when they will vtter any pretie conceit, they reduce it into metricall feet, and put it in forme of a *Lozange* or fquare, or fuch other figure, and fo engrauen in gold, filuer or iuorie, and fometimes with letters of ametift, rubie, emeralde or topas curioufely cemented and peeced together, they fende them in chaines, bracelets, collars and girdles to their miftreffes to weare for a remembrance. Some fewe meafures compofed in this fort this gentleman gaue me, which I tranflated word for word and as neere as I could followed both the phrafe and the figure, which is fome-what hard to performe, becaufe of the reftraint of the figure from which ye may not digreffe. At the begin-

M iiijᵛ ning they wil feeme/nothing pleafant to an Englifh eare, but time and vfage wil make them acceptable inough, as it doth in all other new guifes, be it for wearing of apparell or otherwife. The formes of your Geometricall figures be hereunder reprefented.

The Lozange called Rombus	The Fuzie or fpindle, called Romboides	The Tri-angle, or Tricquet	The Square or quadrangle

The Pillafter, or Cillinder	The Spire or taper, called piramis	The Rondel or Sphere	The egge or figure ouall

(92)

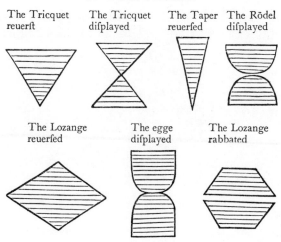

| The Tricquet reuerſt | The Tricquet diſplayed | The Taper reuerſed | The Rõdel diſplayed |

| The Lozange reuerſed | The egge diſplayed | The Lozange rabbated |

Of the Lozange.

The *Lozange* is a moſt beautifull figure, & fit for this purpoſe, being in his kind a quadrangle reuerſt, with his point vpward like to a quarrell of glaſſe the Greekes and Latines both call it *Rombus* which may be the cauſe as I ſuppoſe why they alſo gaue that name to the fiſh commonly called the *Turbot*, who beareth iuſtly that figure, it ought not to contain aboue thirteene or fifteene or one/& twentie meetres, & the longeſt furniſheth the middle angle, the reſt paſſe vpward and downward, ſtill abating their lengthes by one or two ſillables till they come to the point: the Fuzie is of the ſame nature but that he is ſharper and ſlenderer. I will giue you an example or two of thoſe which my Italian friend beſtowed vpon me, which as neare as I could I tranſlated into the ſame figure obſeruing the phraſe of the Orientall ſpeach word for word.

A great Emperor in Tartary whõ they cal *Can*, for his good fortune in the wars & many notable conqueſts he had made, was ſurnamed *Temir Cutzclewe*, this mã loued the Lady *Kermeſine*, who preſented him returning

frō the cōqueſt of *Coraſoon* (a great kingdom adioyning)
with this *Lozange* made in letters of rubies & diamants
entermingled thus

<pre>
                Sound
              O   Harpe
            Shril lie out
          Temir   the   ſtout
        Rider who with sharpe
      Trenching blade of bright ſteele
    Hath made his fierceſt foes to feele
  All ſuch as wrought him shame or harme
 The ſtrength of his braue right arme,
  Cleauing hard downe vnto the eyes
    The raw skulles of his enemies,
      Much honor hath he wonne
        By doughtie deedes done
          In   Cora   ſoon
            And   all   the
                Worlde
                Round.
</pre>

To which Can Temir *anſwered in* Fuzie, *with letters of Emeralds and
Ametiſts artificially cut and entermingled, thus*

<pre>
                Fiue
              Sore batailes
            Manfully fought
          In   blouddy   fielde
        With bright blade in hand
      Hath Temir won & forſt to yeld
    Many a Captaine ſtrong and ſtoute
  And many a king his Crowne to vayle,
 Conquering large countreys and land,
  Yet ne uer wanne I vi ƈto rie,
 I ſpeake it to my greate glo rie,
  So deare and ioy full vn to me,
   As when I did firſt con quere thee
    O Kerme fine, of all myne foes
      The moſt cruell, of all myne woes
        The   ſmarteſt,   the   ſweeteſt
          My   proude   Con   queſt
            My   ri   cheſt   pray
             O   once   a   daye
              Lend me thy fight
               Whoſe only light
                Keepes   me
                 Aliue.
</pre>

Of the Triangle or Triquet.

The Triangle is an halfe ſquare, *Lozange* or *Fuzie*
parted vpon the croſſe angles: and ſo his baſe being
brode and his top narrow, it receaueth meetres of many
ſizes one ſhorter then another: and ye may vſe this
figure ſtanding or reuerſed, as thus.

A certaine great Sultan of Perſia called *Ribuska*, enter-

taynes in loue the Lady *Selamour*, fent her this triquet
reuerft pitioufly bemoning his eftate, all fet in merquetry
with letters of blew Saphire and Topas artificially cut
and entermingled.

Selamour dearer than his owne life,
To thy di ftreffed wretch cap tiue,
Ri buska whome late ly erft
Moft cru el ly thou perft
With thy dead ly dart,
That paire of ftarres
Shi ning a farre
Turne from me, to me
That I may & may not fee
The fmile, the loure
That lead and driue
Me to die to liue
Twife yea thrife
In one
houre.

To which *Selamour* to make the match egall, and the
figure entire, anfwered in a ftanding Triquet richly engrauen with letters of like ftuffe.

Power
Of death
Nor of life
Hath Selamour,
With Gods it is rife
To geue and bereue breath,
I may for pitie perchaunce
Thy loft libertie re ftore,
Vpon thine othe with this penaunce,
That while thou liueft thou neuer loue no more.

This condition feeming to Sultan *Ribuska* very hard
to performe, and cruell to be enioyned him, doeth by
another figure in Taper, fignifying hope, anfwere the
Lady *Selamour*, which dittie for lack of time I tranflated
not.

Of the Spire or Taper called Pyramis.

The Taper is the longeft and fharpeft triangle that is,
& while he mounts vpward he waxeth continually more
flender, taking both his figure and name of the fire,
whofe flame if ye marke it, is alwaies pointed, and
naturally by his forme couets to clymbe: the/Greekes N ijʳ
call him Pyramis of πύρ. The Latines in vfe of Architecture call him *Obelifcus*, it holdeth the altitude of fix

ordinary triangles, and in metrifying his baſe can not well be larger then a meetre of ſix, therefore in his altitude he wil require diuers rabates to hold ſo many ſizes of meetres as ſhall ſerue for his compoſition, for neare the toppe there wilbe roome litle inough for a meetre of two ſillables, and ſometimes of one to finiſh the point. I haue ſet you downe one or two examples to try how ye can diſgeſt the maner of the deuiſe.

Her Maieſtie, for many parts in her moſt noble and vertuous nature to be found, reſembled to the ſpire. Ye muſt begin beneath according to the nature of the deuice

From God the fountaine of all good, are deriued into the world all good things: and vpon her maieſtie all the good fortunes any worldly creature can be furniſht with. Reade down-ward according to the nature of the deuice.

    Skie. 1

    Azurd 2
    in   the
    aſſurde,

    And better,
    And richer,
    Much greter,

    Crown & empir
  After an hier
    For to aſpire 4
    Like flame of fire
    In forme of ſpire

    To mount on hie,
  Con ti nu al ly
    With trauel & teen
    Moſt gratious queen
    Ye haue made a vow 5
    Shews vs plainly how
    Not fained but true,
    To euery mans vew,
    Shining cleere in you
    Of ſo bright an hewe,
    Euen thus vertewe

    Vanish out of our ſight
    Till his fine top be quite
    To Taper in the ayre 6
    Endeuors ſoft and ſaire
    By his kindly nature
    Of tall comely ſtature
    Like as this faire figure

  1 *God*
    On
    Hie
  2 *From*
    Aboue
    Sends loue,
    Wiſedome,
    Iu ſtice
    Cou rage,
    Boun tie,
    And doth geue
    Al that liue,
    Life & breath
    Harts eſe helth
    Childrē, welth
    Beauty ſtrēgth
    Reſtfull age,
    And at length
    A mild death,
  4 *He doeth beſtow*
    All mens fortunes
    Both high & low
    And the beſt things
    That earth cā haue
    Or mankind craue,
    Good queens & kings
    Fi nally is the ſame
    Who gaue you (madā)
    Seyſon of this Crowne
    With poure ſoueraigne
  5 *Impug nable right,*
    Redoubtable might,
    Moſt proſperous raigne
    Eternall re nowme,
    And that your chiefeſt is
    Sure hope of heauens blis.

The Piller, Pillafter or Cillinder.

The Piller is a figure among all the reft of the Geometricall moft beawtifull, in refpeĉt that he is tall and
vpright and of one bigneffe from the bottom to the
toppe. In Architeĉture he is confidered with two acceffarie parts, a pedeftall or bafe, and a chapter or head,
the body is the fhaft. By this figure is fignified ftay,
fupport, reft, ftate and magnificence, your dittie then
being reduced into the forme of a Piller, his bafe will
require to beare the breadth of a meetre of fix or feuen
or eight fillables: the fhaft of foure: the chapter egall
with the bafe, of this proportion I will giue you one or
two examples which may fuffife.

Her Maieftie refembled to the crowned
piller. Ye muft read vpward.

Philo to the Lady Calia, fendeth this
Odolet of her prayfe in forme of a Pil-
ler, which ye muft read downeward.

Is bliſſe with immortalitie.
Her trymeft top of all ye fee,
Garnifh the crowne
Her iuft renowne
Chapter and head,
Parts that maintain
And womanhead
Her mayden raigne
In te gri tie:
In ho nour and
With ve ri tie:
Her roundnes ftand
Strĕgthen the ftate.
By their increafe
With out de bate
Concord and peace
Of her fup port,
They be the bafe
With ftedfaftneſſe
Vertue and grace
Stay and comfort
Of Al bi ons reft,
The founde Pillar
And feene a farre
Is plainely expreft
Tall ftately and ftrayt
By this no ble pour trayt

Thy Princely port and Maieftie
Is my ter rene dei tie,
Thy wit and fence
The ftreame & fource
Of e lo quence
And deepe difcours,
Thy faire eyes are
My bright loadftarre,
Thy fpeache a darte
Percing my harte,
Thy face a las,
My loo king glaſſe,
Thy loue ly lookes
My prayer bookes,
Thy pleafant cheare
My funfhine cleare,
Thy ru full fight
My darke midnight,
Thy will the ftent
Of my con tent,
Thy glo rye flour
Of myne ho nour,
Thy loue doth giue
The lyfe I lyue,
Thy lyfe it is
Mine earthly bliſſe:
But grace & fauour in thine eies
My bodies foule & fouls paradife.

(97)

The Roundell or Spheare.

The moſt excellent of all the figures Geometrical is the round for his many perfeétions. Firſt becauſe he is euen & ſmooth, without any angle, or interruption, moſt voluble and apt to turne, and to continue motion, which is the author of life: he conteyneth in him the commodious deſcription of euery other figure, & for his ample capacitie doth reſemble the world or vniuers, & for his indefiniteneſſe hauing no ſpeciall place of beginning nor end, beareth a ſimilitude with God and eternitie. This figure hath three principall partes in his nature and vſe much conſiderable: the circle, the beame, and the center. The circle is his largeſt compaſſe or circumference: the center is his middle and indiuiſible point: the beame is a line ſtretching direétly from the circle to the center, & contrariwiſe from the center to the circle. By this deſcription our maker may faſhion his meetre in Roundel, either with the circumference, and that is circlewiſe, or from the circūference, that is, like a beame, or by the circumference, and that is ouerthwart and dyametrally from one ſide of the circle to the other.

A generall reſemblance of the Roundell to God, the world and the Queene.

All and whole, and euer, and one,
Single, ſimple, eche where, alone,
Theſe be counted as Clerkes can tell,
True properties, of the Roundell.
His ſtill turning by conſequence
And change, doe breede both life and ſence.
Time, meaſure of ſtirre and rest,
Is alſo by his courſe expreſt.
How ſwift the circle ſtirre aboue,
His center point doeth neuer moue:
All things that euer were or be,
Are cloſde in his concauitie.

(98)

And though he be, ſtill turnde and toſt,
No roome there wants nor none is loſt.
The Roundell hath no bonch or angle,
Which may his courſe ſtay or entangle.
The furtheſt part of all his ſpheare,|
Is equally both farre and neare.   N iij^v
So doth none other figure fare
Where natures chattels cloſed are:
And beyond his wide compaſſe,
There is no body nor no place,
Nor any wit that comprehends,
Where it begins, or where it ends:
And therefore all men doe agree,
That it purports eternitie.
God aboue the heauens ſo hie
Is this Roundell, in world the skie,
Vpon earth ſhe, who beares the bell
Of maydes and Queenes, is this Roundell:
All and whole and euer alone,
Single, ſans peere, ſimple, and one.

A ſpeciall and particular reſemblance of her Maieſtie
to the Roundell.

Firſt her authoritie regall
Is the circle compaſſing all:
The dominion great and large
Which God hath geuen to her charge:
Within which moſt spatious bound
She enuirons her people round,
Retaining them by oth and liegeance.
Within the pale of true obeyſance:
Holding imparked as it were,
Her people like to heards of deere.
Sitting among them in the middes
Where ſhe allowes and bannes and bids
In what faſhion ſhe liſt and when,
The ſeruices of all her men.

(99)

Out of her breaſt as from an eye,
Iſſue the rayes inceſſantly
Of her iuſtice, bountie and might
Spreading abroad their beames ſo bright,
And refleȼt not, till they attaine|
The fardeſt part of her domaine.
And makes eche ſubieȼt clearely ſee,
What he is bounden for to be
To God his Prince and common wealth,
His neighbour, kinred and to himſelfe.
The ſame centre and middle pricke,
Whereto our deedes are dreſt ſo thicke,
From all the parts and outmoſt ſide
Of her Monarchie large and wide,
Alſo fro whence refleȼt theſe rayes,
Twentie hundred maner of wayes
Where her will is them to conuey
Within the circle of her ſuruey.
So is the Queene of Briton ground,
Beame, circle, center of all my round.

N iiijʳ

Of the ſquare or quadrangle equilater.

The ſquare is of all other accompted the figure of
moſt ſolliditie and ſtedfaſtneſſe, and for his owne ſtay
and firmitie requireth none other baſe then himſelfe,
and therefore as the roundell or Spheare is appropriat
to the heauens, the Spire to the element of the fire: the
Triangle to the ayre, and the Lozange to the watèr:
ſo is the ſquare for his inconcuſſable ſteadineſſe likened
to the earth, which perchaunce might be the reaſon that
the Prince of Philoſophers in his firſt booke of the
Ethicks, termeth a conſtant minded man, euen egal and
direȼt on all ſides, and not eaſily ouerthrowne by euery
litle aduerſitie, *hominem quadratū,* a ſquare man. Into
this figure may ye reduce your ditties by vſing no moe
verſes then your verſe is of ſillables, which will make him
fall out ſquare, if ye go aboue it wil grow into the figure

Trapezion, which is fome portion longer then fquare. I neede not giue you any example, bycaufe in good arte all your ditties, Odes & Epigrammes fhould keepe & not exceede the nomber of twelue verfes, and the longeft verfe to be of twelue fillables & not aboue, but vnder that number as much as ye will.

The figure Ouall.

This figure taketh his name of an egge, and alfo as it is thought/his firft origine, and is as it were a baftard or imperfect rounde declining toward a longitude, and yet keeping within one line for his periferie or compaffe as the rounde, and it feemeth that he receiueth this forme not as an imperfection by any impediment vn- naturally hindring his rotunditie, but by the wifedome and prouidence of nature for the commoditie of genera- tion, in fuch of her creatures as bring not forth a liuely body (as do foure footed beafts) but in ftead thereof a certaine quantitie of fhapeleffe matter contained in a veffell, which after it is fequeftred from the dames body receiueth life and perfection, as in the egges of birdes, fifhes, and ferpents: for the matter being of fome quantitie, and to iffue out at a narrow place, for the eafie paffage thereof, it muft of neceffitie beare fuch fhape as might not be fharpe and greeuous to paffe as an angle, nor fo large or obtufe as might not effay fome iffue out with one part moe then other as the rounde, therefore it muft be flenderer in fome part, & yet not without a rotunditie & fmoothneffe to giue the reft an eafie deliuerie. Such is the figure Ouall whom for his antiquitie, dignitie and vfe, I place among the reft of the figures to embellifh our proportions: of this fort are diuers of *Anacreons* ditties, and thofe other of the Grecian Liricks, who wrate wanton amorous deuifes, to folace their witts with all, and many times they would (to giue it right fhape of an egge) deuide a word in the midft, and peece out the next verfe with the other halfe, as ye may fee by perufing their meetres.

N iiijᵛ

*Of the deuice or embleme, and that other which the Greekes
call Anagramma, and we the Poſie tranſpoſed.*

And beſides all the remembred points of Metricall proportiō, ye haue yet two other ſorts of ſome affinitie with
them, which alſo firſt iſſued out of the Poets head, and
whereof the Courtly maker was the principall artificer,
hauing many high conceites and curious imaginations,
with leaſure inough to attend his idle inuentions: and
theſe be the ſhort, quicke and ſententious propoſitions,
ſuch as be at theſe dayes all your deuices of armes and
other amorous inſcriptions which courtiers vſe to giue
and alſo to weare in liuerie for the honour of their ladies,
and commonly containe but two or three words of wittie
ſentence or ſecrete conceit till they be/vnfolded or explaned by ſome interpretatiō. For which cauſe they be
commonly accompanied with a figure or purtraiȼt of
ocular repreſentation, the words ſo aptly correſponding
to the ſubtilitie of the figure, that aſwel the eye is ther-
with recreated as the eare or the mind. The Greekes call
it *Emblema*, the Italiens *Impreſa*, and we, a Deuice, ſuch
as a man may put into letters of gold and ſende to his
miſtreſſes for a token, or cauſe to be embrodered in
ſcutchions of armes, or in any bordure of a rich garment
to giue by his noueltie maruell to the beholder. Such
were the figures and inſcriptions the Romane Emperours
gaue in their money and coignes of largeſſe, and in other
great medailles of ſiluer and gold, as that of the Emperour *Auguſtus*, an arrow entangled by the fiſh *Remora*,
with theſe words, *Feſtina lente*, ſignifying that celeritie
is to be vſed with deliberation: all great enterpriſes being
for the moſt part either ouerthrowen with haſt, or
hindred by delay, in which caſe leaſure in th'aduice,
and ſpeed in th'execution make a very good match for
a glorious ſucceſſe.

Th'Emperour *Heliogabalus* by his name alluding to
the ſunne, which in Greeke is *Helios*, gaue for his deuice,

(102)

the cœleftial funne, with thefe words [*Soli inuicto*] the
fubtilitie lyeth in the word [*foli*] which hath a double
fenfe, viz. to the Sunne, and to him onely.

We our felues attributing that moft excellent figure,
for his incomparable beauty and light, to the perfon of
our Soueraigne lady altring the mot, made it farre paffe
that of Th'Emperour *Heliogabalus* both for fubtilitie
and multiplicitie of fenfe, thus, [*Soli nunquam deficienti*]
to her onely that neuer failes, viz. in bountie and munificence toward all hers that deferue, or elfe thus, To
her onely, whofe glorie and good fortune may neuer
decay or wane. And fo it inureth as a wifh by way of
refemblaunce in [*Simile diffimile*] which is alfo a fubtillitie, likening her Maieftie to the Sunne for his bright-
neffe, but not to him for his paffion, which is ordinarily
to go to glade, and fometime to fuffer eclypfe.

King *Edvvarde* the thirde, her Maiefties moft noble
progenitour, firft founder of the famous order of the
Garter, gaue this pofie with it. *Hony foit qui mal y penfe,*
commonly thus Englifhed, Itl be to him that thinketh
ill, but in mine opinion better thus, Difhonored be he,
who meanes vnho-/norably. There can not be a more j^v
excellent deuife, nor that could containe larger intendment, nor greater fubtilitie, nor (as a mã may fay) more
vertue or Princely generofite. For firft he did by it
mildly & grauely reproue the peruers conftruction of
fuch noble men in his court, as imputed the kings
wearing about his neck the garter of the lady with
whom he danced, to fome amorous alliance betwixt
them, which was not true. He alfo iuftly defended his
owne integritie, faued the noble womans good renowme,
which by licētious fpeeches might haue bene empaired,
and liberally recompenced her iniurie with an honor,
fuch as none could haue bin deuifed greater nor more
glorious or permanent vpon her and all the pofteritie
of her houfe. It inureth alfo as a worthy leffon and
difcipline for all Princely perfonages, whofe actions,

imaginations, coūtenances and fpeeches, fhould euermore correfpond in all trueth and honorable fimplicitie.

Charles the fift Emperour, euen in his yong yeares
fhewing his valour and honorable ambition, gaue for his
new order, the golden Fleece, vfurping it vpon Prince
Iafon & his Argonauts rich fpoile brought from *Cholcos*.
But for his deuice two pillers with this mot *Plus vltra*,
as one not content to be reftrained within the limits
that *Hercules* had fet for an vttermoft bound to all his
trauailes, viz. two pillers in the mouth of the ftraight
Gibraltare, but would go furder: which came fortunately
to paffe, and whereof the good fucceffe gaue great commendation to his deuice: for by the valiancy of his
Captaines before he died he conquered great part of the
weft Indias, neuer knowen to *Hercules* or any of our
world before.

In the fame time (feeming that the heauens and ftarres
had confpired to replenifh the earth with Princes and
gouernours of great courage, and moft famous conquerours) *Selim* Emperour of Turkie gaue for his deuice
a croiffant or new moone, promifing to him felf increafe
of glory and enlargemēt of empire, til he had brought
all Afia vnder his fubieƈtion, which he reafonably well
accomplifhed. For in leffe then eight yeres which he
raigned, he conquered all Syria and Egypt, and layd it
to his dominion. This deuice afterward was vfurped by
Henry the fecond French king, with this mot *Donec
totum compleat orbem*, till he be at his full: meaning it
not fo largely as did *Selim*, but onely that his friendes
ijʳ fhould knowe/how vnable he was to do them good, and
to fhew benificence vntil he attained the crowne of
France vnto which he afpired as next fucceffour.

King *Levvis* the twelfth, a valiant and magnanimous
prince, who becaufe hee was on euery fide enuironed
with mightie neighbours, and moft of them his enemies,
to let them perceiue that they fhould not finde him
vnable or vnfurnifhed (incafe they fhould offer any vn-

lawfull hoftillitie) of fufficient forces of his owne, afwell
to offende as to defend, and to reuenge an iniurie as to
repulfe it. He gaue for his deuice the Porkefpick with
this pofie *pres & loign*, both farre and neare. For the
Purpentines nature is, to fuch as ftand aloofe, to dart
her prickles from her, and if they come neare her, with
the fame as they fticke faft to wound them that hurt her.

But of late yeares in the ranfacke of the Cities of
Cartagena and S. *Dominico* in the Weft Indias, manfully
put in execution by the prowefle of her Maiefties men,
there was found a deuice made peraduenture without
King *Philips* knowledge, wrought al in maffiue copper,
a king fitting on horfebacke vpon a *monde* or world, the
horfe prauncing forward with his forelegges as if he
would leape of, with this infcription, *Non fufficit orbis*,
meaning, as it is to be cōceaued, that one whole world
could not content him. This immeafurable ambition of
the Spaniards, if her Maieftie by Gods prouidence, had
not with her forces, prouidently ftayed and retranched,
no man knoweth what inconuenience might in time
haue infued to all the Princes and common wealthes in
Chriftendome, who haue founde them felues long annoyed with his exceffiue greatneffe.

Atila king of the Huns, inuading Frāce with an army
of 300000. fighting men, as it is reported, thinking
vtterly to abbafe the glory of the Romane Empire, gaue
for his deuice of armes, a fword with a firie point and
thefe words, *Ferro & flamma*, with fword and fire. This
very deuice being as ye fee onely accommodate to a
king or conquerour and not a coillen or any meane
fouldier, a certaine bafe man of England being knowen
euen at that time a bricklayer or mafon by his fcience,
gaue for his creft: whom it had better become to beare
a truell full of morter then a fword and fire, which/is ijᵛ
onely the reuenge of a Prince, and lieth not in any other
mans abilitie to performe, vnleffe ye will allow it to
euery poore knaue that is able to fet fire on a thacht

(105)

houfe. The heraldes ought to vfe great difcretion in fuch matters: for neither any rule of their arte doth warrant fuch abfurdities, nor though fuch a coat or creft were gained by a prifoner taken in the field, or by a flag found in fome ditch & neuer fought for (as many times happens) yet is it no more allowable then it were to beare the deuice of *Tamerlan* an Emperour in Tartary, who gaue the lightning of heauen, with a pofie in that language purporting thefe words, *Ira Dei*, which alfo appeared well to anfwer his fortune. For from a fturdie fhepeheard he became a moft mighty Emperour, and with his innumerable great armies defolated fo many countreyes and people, as he might iuftly be called [*the vvrath of God*.] It appeared alfo by his ftrange ende: for in the midft of his greatneffe and profperitie he died fodainly, & left no child or kinred for a fucceffour to fo large an Empire, nor any memory after him more then of his great puiffance and crueltie.

But that of the king of China in the fardeft part of the Orient, though it be not fo terrible is no leffe admirable, & of much fharpneffe and good implication, worthy for the greateft king and conquerour: and it is, two ftrange ferpents entertangled in their amorous congreffe, the leffer creeping with his head into the greaters mouth, with words purporting [*ama & time*] loue & feare. Which pofie with maruellous much reafon and fubtillity implieth the dutie of euery fubiect to his Prince, and of euery Prince to his fubiect, and that without either of them both, no fubiect could be fayd entirely to performe his liegeance, nor the Prince his part of lawfull gouernement. For without feare and loue the foueraigne authority could not be vpholden, nor without iuftice and mercy the Prince be renowmed and honored of his fubiect. All which parts are difcouered in this figure: loue by the ferpents amorous entertangling: obedience and feare by putting the inferiours head into the others mouth hauing puiffance to deftroy.

On th'other fide, iuftice in the greater to prepare and
manace death and deftruction to offenders. And if he
fpare it, then betokeneth it mercie, and a grateful recompence of the loue and obedience which the foueraigne receaueth./

It is alfo worth the telling, how the king vfeth the iij^r
fame in pollicie, he giueth it in his ordinarie liueries
to be worne in euery vpper garment of all his nobleft
men and greateft Magiftrats & the reft of his officers
and feruants, which are either embrodered vpon the
breaft and the back with filuer or gold or pearle or ftone
more or leffe richly, according to euery mans dignitie
and calling, and they may not prefume to be feene in
publick without them: nor alfo in any place where by
the kings commiffion they vfe to fit in iuftice, or any other
publike affaire, wherby the king is highly both honored
and ferued, the common people retained in dutie and
admiration of his greatneffe: the noblemen, magiftrats
and officers euery one in his degree fo much efteemed
& reuerenced, as in their good and loyall feruice they
want vnto their perfons litle leffe honour for the kings
fake, then can be almoft due or exhibited to the king
him felfe.

I could not forbeare to adde this forraine example to
accōplifh our difcourfe touching deuices. For the beauty
and gallantneffe of it, befides the fubtillitie of the conceit, and princely pollicy in the vfe, more exact then
can be remēbred in any other of any *European* Prince,
whofe deuifes I will not fay but many of them be loftie
and ingenious, many of them louely and beautifull,
many other ambitious and arrogant, and the chiefeft of
them terrible and ful of horror to the nature of man,
but that any of them be comparable with it, for wit,
vertue, grauitie, and if ye lift brauerie, honour and
magnificence, not vfurping vpon the peculiars of the
gods. In my conceipt there is none to be found.

This may fuffice for deuices, a terme which includes

in his generality all thofe other, viz. liueries, cognizãces, emblemes, enfeigns and imprefes. For though the termes be diuers, the vfe and intent is but one whether they reft in colour or figure or both, or in word or in muet fhew, and that is to infinuat fome fecret, wittie, morall and braue purpofe prefented to the beholder, either to recreate his eye, or pleafe his phantafie, or examine his iudgement, or occupie his braine or to manage his will either by hope or by dread, euery of which refpectes be of no litle moment to the intereft and ornament of the ciuill life: and therefore giue them no litle commenda- tion. Then hauing produced fo many worthy and wife iij^v founders/of thefe deuices, and fo many puiffant patrons and protectours of them, I feare no reproch in this difcourfe, which otherwife the venimous appetite of enuie by detraction or fcorne would peraduenture not fticke to offer me.

Of the Anagrame, or pofie tranfpofed.

One other pretie conceit we will impart vnto you and then trouble you with no more, and is alfo borrowed primitiuely of the Poet, or courtly maker, we may terme him, the [*pofie tranfpofed*] or in one word [*a tranfpofe*] a thing if it be done for paftime and exercife of the wit without fuperftition commendable inough and a meete ftudy for Ladies, neither bringing them any great gayne nor any great loffe vnleffe it be of idle time. They that vfe it for pleafure is to breed one word out of another not altering any letter nor the number of them, but onely tranfpofing of the fame, wherupon many times is produced fome grateful newes or matter to them for whofe pleafure and feruice it was intended: and bicaufe there is much difficultie in it, and altogether ftandeth vpon hap hazard, it is compted for a courtly conceit no leffe then the deuice before remembred. *Lycophron* one of the feuen Greeke Lyrickes, who when they met to- gether (as many times they did) for their excellencie and

louely concorde, were called the feuen ftarres [*pleiades*]
this man was very perfit & fortunat in thefe tranfpofes,
& for his delicate wit and other good parts was greatly
fauoured by *Ptolome* king of Egypt and Queene *Arfinoe*
his wife. He after fuch fort called the king ἀπομελῖτος,
which is letter for letter *Ptolomæus* and Queene *Arfinoe*
he called ἴον ἥρας, which is *Arfinoe*, now the fubtillitie
lyeth not in the conuerfion but in the fence in this that
Apomelitos, fignifieth in Greek [*hony fweet*] fo was *Ptolome*
the fweeteft natured man in the world both for countenance and conditions, and *Iôneras*, fignifieth the violet
or flower of *Iuno* a ftile among the Greekes for a woman
endued with all bewtie and magnificence, which conftruction falling out grateful and fo truly, exceedingly
well pleafed the King and the Queene, and got *Lycophron*
no litle thanke and benefite at both their hands./

The French Gentlemen haue very fharpe witts and iiijʳ
withall a delicate language, which may very eafily be
wrefted to any alteration of words fententious, and they
of late yeares haue taken this paftime vp among them
many times gratifying their Ladies, and often times the
Princes of the Realme, with fome fuch thankfull noueltie.
Whereof one made by *François de Vallois*, thus *De façon
fuis Roy*, who in deede was of fafhion countenance and
ftature, befides his regall vertues a very king, for in a
world there could not be feene a goodlier man of perfon.
Another found this by *Henry de Vallois* [*Roy de nulz hay*]
a king hated of no man, and was apparant in his conditions and nature, for there was not a Prince of greater
affabilitie and manfuetude then he.

I my felfe feing this conceit fo well allowed of in
Fraunce and Italie, and being informed that her Maieftie
tooke pleafure fometimes in defciphring of names, and
hearing how diuers Gentlemen of her Court had effayed
but with no great felicitie to make fome delectable tranfpofe of her Maiefties name, I would needs try my luck,
for cunning I know not why I fhould call it, vnleffe it

8 (109)

be for the many and variable applications of fence, which requireth peraduenture fome wit & difcretiō more then of euery vnlearned mā and for the purpofe I tooke me thefe three wordes (of any other in the world) containing in my conceit greateft myfterie, and moft importing good to all them that now be aliue, vnder her noble gouernement.

Eliffabet Anglorum Regina.

Which orthographie (becaufe ye fhall not be abufed) is true & not miftaken, for the letter *zeta*, of the Hebrewes & Greeke and of all other toungs is in truth but a double *ff.* hardly vttered, and *H.* is but a note of afpiration onely and no letter, which therefore is by the Greeks omitted. Vpon the tranfpofition I found this to redound.

Multa regnabis enfe gloria.
By thy fword fhalt thou raigne in great renowne.

Then tranfpofing the word [*enfe*] it came to be

Multa regnabis fene gloria.
Aged and in much glorie fhall ye raigne.

iiij v   Both which refultes falling out vpon the very firft marfhalling of/the letters, without any darkneffe or difficultie, and fo fenfibly and well appropriat to her Maiefties perfon and eftate, and finally fo effectually to mine own wifh (which is a matter of much moment in fuch cafes) I tooke them both for a good boding, and very fatallitie to her Maieftie appointed by Gods prouidence for all our comfortes. Alfo I imputed it for no litle good luck and glorie to my felfe, to haue pronounced to her fo good and profperous a fortune, and fo thankefull newes to all England, which though it cannot be faid by this euent any deftinie or fatal neceffitie, yet furely is it by all probabillitie of reafon, fo likely to come to paffe, as any other worldly euent of things that be vncertaine, her Maieftie continuing the courfe of her moft regal proceedings and vertuous life in all earneft zeale and

godly contemplation of his word, & in the fincere adminiſtration of his terrene iuſtice, aſſigned ouer to her
execution as his Lieutenant vpon earth within the compaſſe of her dominions.

This alſo is worth the noting, and I will aſſure you
of it, that after the firſt ſearch whereupon this tranſpoſe
was faſhioned. The ſame letters being by me, toſſed &
tranlaced fiue hundreth times, I could neuer make any
other, at leaſt of ſome ſence & conformitie to her Maieſties
eſtate and the caſe. If any other man by triall happen
vpon a better omination, or what ſoeuer els ye will call
it, I will reioyſe to be ouermatched in my deuiſe, and
renounce him all the thankes and profite of my trauaile.

When I wrate of theſe deuices, I ſmiled with my
ſelfe, thinking that the readers would do ſo to, and many
of them ſay, that ſuch trifles as theſe might well haue
bene ſpared, conſidering the world is full inough of
them, and that it is pitie mens heades ſhould be fedde
with ſuch vanities as are to none edification nor inſtruc-
tion, either of morall vertue, or otherwiſe behooffull for
the common wealth, to whoſe ſeruice (ſay they) we are
all borne, and not to fill and repleniſh a whole world
full of idle toyes. To which ſort of reprehendours, being
either all holy and mortified to the world, and therefore
eſteeming nothing that fauoureth not of Theologie, or
altogether graue and worldly, and therefore caring for
nothing but matters of pollicie, & diſcourſes of eſtate,
or all giuen to thrift and paſſing for none art that is
not gainefull and lucratiue, as the/ſciences of the Law, O iʳ
Phiſicke and marchaundiſe: to theſe I will giue none
other aunſwere then referre them to the many trifling
poemes of *Homer*, *Ouid*, *Virgill*, *Catullus* and other
notable writers of former ages, which were not of any
grauitie or ſeriouſneſſe, and many of them full of impudicitie and ribaudrie, as are not theſe of ours, nor for
any good in the world ſhould haue bene: and yet thoſe
trifles are come from many former ſiecles vnto our times,

vncontrolled or condemned or fuppreft by any Pope or
Patriarch or other feuere cenfor of the ciuill maners of
men, but haue bene in all ages permitted as the conuenient folaces and recreations of mans wit. And as I
can not denie but thefe conceits of mine be trifles: no
leffe in very deede be all the moft ferious ftudies of man,
if we fhall meafure grauitie and lightneffe by the wife
mans ballance who after he had confidered of all the
profoundeft artes and ftudies among men, in th'ende
cryed out with this Epyphoneme, *Vanitas vanitatum &*
omnia vanitas. Whofe authoritie if it were not fufficient
to make me beleeue fo, I could be content with *Demo-*
critus rather to condemne the vanities of our life by
derifion, then as *Heraclitus* with teares, faying with that
merrie Greeke thus,

> *Omnia funt rifus, funt puluis, & omnia nil funt.*
> *Res hominum cunctæ, nam ratione carent.*

Thus Englifhed,

> *All is but a ieft, all duft, all not vvorth tvvo peafon:*
> *For vvhy in mans matters is neither rime nor reafon.*

Now paffing from thefe courtly trifles, let vs talke of
our fcholaftical toyes, that is of the Grammaticall verfifying of the Greeks and Latines and fee whether it might
be reduced into our Englifh arte or no.

CHAP. XII. [XIII]

How if all maner of fodaine innouations were not very
fcandalous, fpecially in the lawes of any langage or
arte, the vfe of the Greeke and Latine feete
might be brought into our vulgar Poefie,
and with good grace inough.

Now neuertheleffe albeit we haue before alledged that
our vulgar *Saxon Englifh* ftanding moft vpon wordes
monofillable, and little vpon *polyfillables* doth hardly admit
O iv   the vfe of thofe/fine inuented feete of the Greeks &

Latines, and that for the moſt part wiſe and graue men
doe naturally miſlike with all ſodaine innouations ſpecially
of lawes (and this the law of our auncient Engliſh
Poeſie) and therefore lately before we imputed it to a
nice & ſcholaſticall curioſitie in ſuch makers as haue
ſought to bring into our vulgar Poeſie ſome of the
auncient feete, to wit the *Dactile* into verſes *exameters*,
as he that tranſlated certaine bookes of *Virgils Eneydos*
in ſuch meaſures & not vncommendably: if I ſhould
now ſay otherwiſe it would make me ſeeme contra-
dictorie to my ſelfe, yet for the information of our yong
makers, and pleaſure of all others who be delighted in
noueltie, and to th'intent we may not ſeeme by ignorance
or ouerſight to omit any point of ſubtillitie, materiall or
neceſſarie to our vulgar arte, we will in this preſent
chapter & by our own idle obſeruations ſhew how one
may eaſily and commodiouſly lead all thoſe feete of the
aunciens into our vulgar langage. And if mens eares
were not perchaunce to daintie, or their iudgementes
ouer partiall, would peraduenture nothing at all miſ-
become our arte, but make in our meetres a more pleaſant
numeroſitie then now is. Thus farre therefore we will
aduenture and not beyond, to th'intent to ſhew ſome
ſingularitie in our arte that euery man hath not hereto-
fore obſerued, and (her maieſties good liking always had)
whether we make the common readers to laugh or to
lowre, all is a matter, ſince our intent is not ſo exactlie
to proſecute the purpoſe, nor ſo earneſtly, as to thinke
it ſhould by authority of our owne iudgement be generally applauded at to the diſcredit of our forefathers maner
of vulgar Poeſie, or to the alteration or peraduenture
totall deſtruction of the ſame, which could not ſtand
with any good diſcretion or curteſie in vs to attempt,
but thus much I ſay, that by ſome leaſurable trauell it
were no hard matter to induce all their auncient feete
into vſe with vs, and that it ſhould proue very agreable
to the eare and well according with our ordinary times

and pronunciation, which no man could then iuſtly
miſlike, and that is to allow euery word *poliſillable* one
long time of neceſſitie, which ſhould be where his ſharpe
accent falls in our owne *ydiome* moſt aptly and naturally,
wherein we would not follow the licence of the Greeks
and Latines, who made not their ſharpe accent any
O ijʳ neceſſary pro-/longation of their times, but vſed ſuch
ſillable ſometimes long ſometimes ſhort at their pleaſure.
The other ſillables of any word where the ſharpe accent
fell not, to be accompted of ſuch time and quantitie as
his *ortographie* would beſt beare hauing regard to himſelfe, or to his next neighbour, word, bounding him on
either ſide, namely to the ſmoothnes & hardneſſe of the
ſillable in his vtterance, which is occaſioned altogether
by his *ortographie* & ſcituation as in this word [*dáyly*]
the firſt ſillable for his vſuall and ſharpe accentes ſake
to be always long, the ſecond for his flat accents ſake
to be always ſhort, and the rather for his *ortographie*,
bycauſe if he goe before another word commencing with
a vowell not letting him to be eclipſed, his vtterance is
eaſie & currant, in this triſſillable [*daūngĕrŏus*] the firſt
to be long, th'other two ſhort for the ſame cauſes. In
this word [*dāngĕroŭſnēſſe*] the firſt & laſt to be both long,
bycauſe they receiue both of them the ſharpe accent,
and the two middlemoſt to be ſhort, in theſe words
[*remedie*] & [*remedileſſe*] the time to follow alſo the
accent, ſo as if it pleaſe better to ſet the ſharpe accent
vpō [*re*] then vpon [*dye*] that ſillable ſhould be made
long and *è conuerſo*, but in this word [*remedileſſe*] bycauſe many like better to accent the ſillable [*me*] thē
the ſillable [*les*] therfore I leaue him for a cōmon ſillable
to be able to receiue both a long and a ſhort time as
occaſion ſhall ſerue. The like law I ſet in theſe wordes
[*reuocable*] [*recouerable*] [*irreuocable*] [*irrecouerable*] for
ſometime it ſounds better to ſay *rĕuŏ cāblĕ* then *rĕ uōcăblĕ*,
rēcŏuĕr āblĕ thē *rēcōuĕr ăblĕ* for this one thing ye muſt
alwayes marke that if your time fall either by reaſon of

his fharpe accēt or otherwife vpon the *penultima*, ye fhal
finde many other words to rime with him, bycaufe fuch
terminatiōs are not geazon, but if the lōg time fall vpō
the *antepenultima* ye fhall not finde many wordes to
match him in his termination, which is the caufe of his
concord or rime, but if you would let your long time
by his fharpe accent fall aboue the *antepenultima* as to
fay [*cōuĕrăblĕ*] ye fhall feldome or perchance neuer find
one to make vp rime with him vnleffe it be badly and
by abufe, and therefore in all fuch long *polifillables* ye
doe commonly giue two fharpe accents, and thereby
reduce him into two feete as in this word [*rēmŭ nĕrātiŏn*]
which makes a couple of good *Dactils*, and/in this word   o ijᵛ
[*cōntrībūtiŏn*] which makes a good *fpōdeus* & a good
dactill, and in this word [*recāpitŭlātiŏn*] it makes two
dactills and a fillable ouerplus to annexe to the word
precedent to helpe peece vp another foote. But for
wordes *monofillables* (as be moft of ours) becaufe in pro-
nouncing them they do of neceffitie retaine a fharpe
accent, ye may iuftly allow them to be all long if they
will fo beft ferue your turne, and if they be tailed one
to another, or th'one to a *diffillable* or *polyffillable* ye
ought to allow them that time that beft ferues your purpofe and pleafeth your eare moft, and trulieft aunfweres
the nature of the *ortographie* in which I would as neare
as I could obferue and keepe the lawes of the Greeke
and Latine verfifiers, that is to prolong the fillable which
is written with double confonants or by dipthong or
with fingle confonants that run hard and harfhly vpon
the toung: and to fhorten all fillables that ftand vpon
vowels, if there were no caufe of *elifion* and fingle confonants & fuch of them as are moft flowing and flipper
vpon the toung as. *n.r.t.d.l.* and for this purpofe to take
away all afpirations, and many times the laft confonant
of a word as the Latine Poetes vfed to do, fpecially
Lucretius and *Ennius* as to fay [*finibu*] for [*finibus*] and
fo would not I ftick to fay thus [*delite*] for [*delight*]

[*hye*] for [*high*] and fuch like, & doth nothing at all impugne the rule I gaue before againſt the wreſting of wordes by falſe *ortographie* to make vp rime, which may not be falſified. But this omiſſion of letters in the middeſt of a meetre to make him the more ſlipper, helpes the numero-ſitie and hinders not the rime. But generally the ſhort-ning or prolonging of the *monoſillables* dependes much vpō the nature of their *ortographie* which the Latin Grammariens call the rule of poſition, as for example if I ſhall ſay thus.

> *Nōt mănĭe dayēs pāſt.* Twentie dayes after,

This makes a good *Dactill* and a good *ſpondeus*, but if ye turne them backward it would not do ſo, as.

> *Many dayes, not paſt.*

And the *diſtick* made all of *monoſillables*.

> *Bŭt nōne ōf ŭs trūe mēn ānd frēe,*
> *Could finde ſo great good lucke as he.*

Which words ſerue well to make the verfe all *ſpondiacke* or *iambicke*, but not in *dactil*, as other words or the ſame otherwiſe pla-/ced would do, for it were an illfauored *dactil* to ſay.

> *Bŭt nŏne ŏf, ūs ăll trĕwe.*

Therefore whenſoeuer your words will not make a ſmooth *dactil*, ye muſt alter them or their ſituations, or elſe turne them to other feete that may better beare their maner of ſound and orthographie: or if the word be *polyſillable* to deuide him, and to make him ſerue by peeces, that he could not do whole and entierly. And no doubt by like conſideration did the Greeke & Latine verſifiers faſhion all their feete at the firſt to be of ſundry times, and the ſelfe ſame ſillable to be ſometime long and ſometime ſhort for the eares better ſatisfaction as hath bene before remēbred. Now alſo wheras I ſaid before that our old Saxon Engliſh for his many *mono-ſillables* did not naturally admit the vſe of the ancient

O iijʳ

feete in our vulgar meafures fo aptly as in thofe languages which ftood moft vpon *polifillables*, I fayd it in a
fort truly, but now I muft recant and confeffe that our
Normane Englifh which hath growen fince *William* the
Conquerour doth admit any of the auncient feete, by
reafon of the many *polyfillables* euen to fixe and feauen
in one word, which we at this day vfe in our moft
ordinarie language: and which corruption hath bene
occafioned chiefly by the peeuifh affectation not of the
Normans them felues, but of clerks and fcholers or
fecretaries long fince, who not content with the vfual
Normane or Saxon word, would conuert the very Latine
and Greeke word into vulgar French, as to fay innumerable for innombrable, reuocable, irreuocable, ir-
radiation, depopulatiō & fuch like, which are not
naturall Normans nor yet French, but altered Latines,
and without any imitation at all: which therefore were
long time defpifed for inkehorne termes, and now be
reputed the beft & moft delicat of any other. Of which
& many other caufes of corruption of our fpeach we
haue in another place more amply difcourfed, but by
this meane we may at this day very well receiue the
auncient feete *metricall* of the Greeks and Latines fauing
thofe that be fuperflous as be all the feete aboue the
triffillable, which the old Grammarians idly inuented and
diftinguifht by fpeciall names, whereas in deede the fame
do ftand compounded with the inferiour feete, and therefore fome of them were called by the names of *didactilus*,
difpondeus and *difiambus*: all which feete as I fay we may/
be allowed to vfe with good difcretion & precife choife O iij^v
of wordes and with the fauorable approbation of readers,
and fo fhall our plat in this one point be larger and
much furmount that which *Stanihurft* firft tooke in hand
by his *exameters dactilicke* and *fpondaicke* in the tranflation
of *Virgills Eneidos*, and fuch as for a great number of
them my ftomacke can hardly digeft for the ill fhapen
found of many of his wordes *polifillable* and alfo his

copulation of *monofillables* fupplying the quantitie of a *triffillable* to his intent. And right fo in promoting this deuife of ours being (I feare me) much more nyce and affected, and therefore more mifliked then his, we are to befpeake fauour, firft of the delicate eares, then of the rigorous and feuere difpofitions, laftly to craue pardon of the learned & auncient makers in our vulgar, for if we fhould feeke in euery point to egall our fpeach with the Greeke and Latin in their *metricall* obferuations it could not poffible be by vs perfourmed, becaufe their fillables came to be timed fome of them long, fome of them fhort not by reafon of any euident or apparant caufe in writing or founde remaining vpon one more then another, for many times they fhortned the fillable of fharpe accent and made long that of the flat, & therefore we muft needes fay, it was in many of their wordes done by preelection in the firft Poetes, not hauing regard altogether to the *ortographie*, and hardneffe or foftneffe of a fillable, confonant, vowell or dipthong, but at their pleafure, or as it fell out: fo as he that firft put in a verfe this word [*Penelope*] which might be *Homer* or fome other of his antiquitie, where he made [*pē*] in both places long and [*nĕ*] and [*lŏ*] fhort, he might haue made them otherwife and with as good reafon, nothing in the world appearing that might moue them to make fuch (preelection) more in th'one fillable then in the other for *pe. ne.* and *lo.* being fillables vocals be egally fmoth and currant vpon the toung, and might beare afwel the long as the fhort time, but it pleafed the Poet otherwife: fo he that firft fhortned, *ca.* in this word *cano*, and made long *tro*, in *troia*, and *o*, in *oris*, might haue afwell done the contrary, but becaufe he that firft put them into a verfe, found as it is to be fuppofed a more fweetneffe in his owne eare to haue them fo tymed, therefore all other Poets who followed, were fayne to doe the like, O iiijʳ which made that *Virgill* who came many/yeares after the firft reception of wordes in their feuerall times, was

(118)

driuen of neceffitie to accept them in fuch quantities
as they were left him and therefore faid.

> *ārmă uĭ rūmquē că nō trō iē quī*
> *prīmŭs ăb ōrĭs.*

Neither truely doe I fee any other reafon in that lawe
(though in other rules of fhortning and prolonging a
fillable there may be reafon) but that it ftands vpon bare
tradition. Such as the *Cabalifts* auouch in their myfticall
conftructions Theologicall and others, faying that they
receaued the fame from hand to hand from the firft
parent *Adam*, *Abraham* and others, which I will giue
them leaue alone both to fay and beleeue for me, thinking
rather that they haue bene the idle occupations, or perchaunce the malitious and craftie conftructions of the
Talmudifts, and others of the Hebrue clerks to bring the
world into admiration of their lawes and Religion. Now
peraduenture with vs Englifhmen it be fomewhat too
late to admit a new inuention of feete and times that our
forefathers neuer vfed nor neuer obferued till this day,
either in their meafures or in their pronuntiation, and
perchaunce will feeme in vs a prefumptuous part to
attempt, confidering alfo it would be hard to find many
men to like of one mans choife in the limitation of times
and quantities of words, with which not one, but euery
eare is to be pleafed and made a particular iudge, being
moft truly fayd, that a multitude or comminaltie is hard
to pleafe and eafie to offend, and therefore I intend not
to proceed any further in this curiofitie then to fhew
fome fmall fubtillitie that any other hath not yet done,
and not by imitation but by obferuation, nor to th'intent
to haue it put in execution in our vulgar Poefie, but to
be pleafantly fcanned vpon, as are all nouelties fo friuo-
lous and ridiculous as it.

CHAP. XIII. [*XIV*]

*A more particular declaration of the metricall feete of the
ancient Poets Greeke and Latine and chiefly
of the feete of two times.*

Their Grammarians made a great multitude of feete,
I wot not to what huge number, and of fo many fizes
as their wordes/were of length, namely fixe fizes, whereas
in deede, the metricall feete are but twelue in number,
wherof foure only be of two times, and eight of three
times, the reft compounds of the premifed two forts,
euen as the Arithmeticall numbers aboue three are made
of two and three. And if ye will know how many of
thefe feete will be commodioufly receiued with vs, I fay
all the whole twelue, for firft for the foote *fpondeus* of two
long times ye haue thefe Englifh wordes *mōrnīng*, *mīd-
nīght*, *mīfchāunce*, and a number moe whofe ortographie
may direct your iudgement in this point: for your
Trocheus of a long and fhort ye haue thefe wordes *mānĕr*,
brōkĕn, *tākĕn*, *bōdĭe*, *mēmbĕr*, and a great many moe if their
laft fillables abut not vpon the confonant in the beginning of another word, and in thefe whether they do abut
or no *wīttĭe*, *dīttĭe*, *sōrrŏw*, *mōrrŏw*, & fuch like, which
end in a vowell for your *Iambus* of a fhort and a long,
ye haue thefe wordes [*rĕftōre*] [*rĕmōrfe*] [*dĕsīre*] [*ĕndūre*]
and a thoufand befides. For your foote *pirrichius* or of
two fhort filables ye haue thefe words [*mănĭe*] [*mŏnĕy*]
[*pĕnĭe*] [*sĭlĭe*] and others of that conftitution or the like:
for your feete of three times and firft your *dactill*, ye
haue thefe wordes & a number moe *pātĭĕnce*, *tēmpĕrănce*,
vvōmănheăd, *iōlĭtĭe*, *daūngĕrŏus*, *dūetĭfŭll* & others. For
your *moloffus*, of all three long, ye haue a number of
wordes alfo and fpecially moft of your participles actiue,
as *pērsĭftĭng*, *dēfpōilĭng*, *ēndēnīng*, and fuch like in ortographie: for your *anapeftus* of two fhort and a long ye
haue thefe words but not many moe, as *mănĭfōld*, *mŏnĭ-*

O iiij^v

(120)

lēſſe, rĕmănēnt, hŏlĭnēſſe. For your foote *tribracchus* of all
three ſhort, ye haue very few *triſſillables*, becauſe the
ſharpe accent will always make one of them long by
pronunciation, which els would be by ortographie ſhort
as, [*mĕrĭly*] [*minion*] & ſuch like. For your foote *bacchius*
of a ſhort & two long ye haue theſe and the like words
triſſillables [*lămēntīng*] [*rĕquēſtīng*] [*rĕnoūncīng*] [*rĕpēn-
tānce*] [*ĕnūrīng*]. For your foote *antibacchius*, of two
long and a ſhort ye haue theſe wordes [*fŏrsākĕn*] [*īm-
pūgnĕd*] and others many: For your *amphimacer* that is
a long a ſhort and a long ye haue theſe wordes and
many moe [*éxcellént*] [*īmĭnēnt*] and ſpecially ſuch as be
propre names of perſons or townes or other things and
namely Welſh wordes: for your foote *amphibracchus*, of
a ſhort, a long and a ſhort, ye haue theſe wordes and/
many like to theſe [*rĕsīſtĕd*] [*dĕlīghtfŭll*] [*rĕprīſăll*] [*ĭn-   P iᵛ
aūntĕr*] [*ĕnāmĭll*] ſo as for want of Engliſh wordes if
your eare be not to daintie and your rules to preciſe,
ye neede not be without the *metricall* feete of the ancient
Poets ſuch as be moſt pertinent and not ſuperfluous.
This is (ye will perchaunce ſay) my ſingular opinion:
then ye ſhall ſee how well I can maintaine it. Firſt the
quantitie of a word comes either by (preelection) without
reaſon or force as hath bene alledged, and as the auncient
Greekes and Latines did in many wordes, but not in all,
or by (election) with reaſon as they did in ſome, and
not a few. And a ſound is drawen at length either by
the infirmitie of the toung, becauſe the word or ſillable
is of ſuch letters as hangs long in the palate or lippes
ere he will come forth, or becauſe he is accented and
tuned hier and ſharper then another, whereby he ſomewhat obſcureth the other ſillables in the ſame word that
be not accented ſo high, in both theſe caſes we will
eſtabliſh our ſillable long, contrariwiſe the ſhortning of a
ſillable is, when his founde or accent happens to be
heauy and flat, that is to fall away ſpeedily, and as it
were inaudible, or when he is made of ſuch letters as

be by nature flipper & voluble and fmoothly paffe from the mouth. And the vowell is alwayes more eafily de-liuered then the confonant: and of confonants, the liquide more then the mute, & a fingle confonant more then a double, and one more then twayne coupled to-gether: all which points were obferued by the Greekes and Latines, and allowed for *maximes* in verfifying. Now if ye will examine thefe foure *biffillables* [rēmnānt] [rĕmāine] [rēndĕr] [rĕnĕt] for an example by which ye may make a generall rule, and ye fhall finde, that they aunfwere our firft refolution. Firft in [remnant] [rem] bearing the fharpe accent and hauing his confonant abbut vpon another, foundes long. The fillable [nant] being written with two cōfonants muft needs be ac-compted the fame, befides that [nant] by his Latin originall is lōg, viz. [remanēns.] Take this word [re-maine] becaufe the laft fillable beares the fharpe accent, he is long in the eare, and [re] being the firft fillable, paffing obfcurely away with a flat accent is fhort, befides that [re] by his Latine originall and alfo by his orto-graphie is fhort. This word [render] bearing the fharpe accēt vpon [ren] makes it long, the fillable [der] falling/
P iv away fwiftly & being alfo writtē with a fingle cōfonant or liquide is fhort and makes the *trocheus*. This word [rĕnĕt] hauing both fillables fliding and flipper make the foote *Pirrichius*, becaufe if he be truly vttered, he beares in maner no fharper accent vpō the one then the other fillable, but be in effect egall in time and tune, as is alfo the *Spondeus*. And becaufe they be not written with any hard or harfh confonants, I do allow them both for fhort fillables, or to be vfed for common, according as their fituation and place with other words fhall be: and as I haue named to you but onely foure words for an example, fo may ye find out by diligent obferuation foure hundred if ye will. But of all your words *biffillables* the moft part naturally do make the foot *Iambus*, many the *Trocheus*, fewer the *Spondeus*, fewest of all the *Pirri-*

(122)

chius, becaufe in him the fharpe accent (if ye follow the rules of your accent, as we haue prefuppofed) doth make a litle oddes: and ye fhall find verfes made all of *mono-fillables*, and do very well, but lightly they be *Iambickes*, bycaufe for the more part the accent falles fharpe vpon euery fecond word rather then contrariwife, as this of Sir *Thomas Wiats*.

> *I finde nŏ peāce ănd yēt mĭe wārre ĭs dōne,*
> *I feare and hope, and burne and freefe like ife.*

And fome verfes where the fharpe accent falles vpon the firft and third, and fo make the verfe wholly *Tro-chaicke*, as thus,

> *Worke not, no nor, wifh thy friend or foes harme*
> *Try but, truft not, all that fpeake thee fo faire.*

And fome verfes made of *monofillables* and *biffillables* enterlaced as this of th'Earles,

> *When raging loue with extreme paine*

And this

> *A fairer beaft of frefher hue beheld I neuer none.*

And fome verfes made all of *biffillables* and others all of *triffillables*, and others of *polifillables* egally increafing and of diuers quantities, and fundry fituations, as in this of our owne, made to daunt the infolence of a beautifull woman.

> *Brittle beauty bloffome daily fading*
> *Morne, noone, and eue in age and eke in eld*
> *Dangerous difdainefull pleafantly perfwading*
> *Eafie to gripe but combrous to weld|*
> *For flender bottome hard and heauy lading*   P ij^r
> *Gay for a while, but little while durable*
> *Sufpicious, incertaine, irreuocable,*
> *O fince thou art by triall not to truft*
> *Wifedome it is, and it is alfo iust*
> *To found the ftemme before the tree be feld*
> *That is, fince death vvill driue vs all to duft*
> *To leaue thy loue ere that vve be compeld.*

In which ye haue your firſt verſe all of *biſſillables* and of the foot *trocheus*. The ſecond all of *monoſillables*, and all of the foote *Iambus*, the third all of *triſſillables*, and all of the foote *daꝗilus*, your fourth of one *biſſillable*, and two *monoſillables* interlarded, the fift of one *monoſillable* and two *biſſillables* enterlaced, and the reſt of other ſortes and ſcituations, ſome by degrees encreaſing, ſome diminiſhing: which example I haue ſet downe to let you perceiue what pleaſant numeroſity in the meaſure and diſpoſition of your words in a meetre may be contriued by curious wits & theſe with other like were the obſeruations of the Greeke and Latine verſifiers.

CHAP. XIIII. [XV]

Of your feet of three times, and firſt of the Daꝗil.

Your feete of three times by preſcription of the Latine Grammariens are of eight ſundry proportions, for ſome notable difference appearing in euery ſillable of three falling in a word of that ſize: but becauſe aboue the *antepenultima* there was (amõg the Latines) none accent audible in any long word, therfore to deuiſe any foote of lõger meaſure then of three times was to them but ſuperfluous: becauſe all aboue the number of three are but compounded of their inferiours. Omitting therefore to ſpeake of theſe larger feete, we ſay that of all your feete of three times the *Daꝗill* is moſt vſuall and fit for our vulgar meeter, & moſt agreeable to the eare, ſpecially if ye ouerlade not your verſe with too many of them but here and there enterlace a *Iambus* or ſome other foote of two times to giue him grauitie and ſtay, as in this *quadrein Trimeter* or of three meaſures.

> *Rendĕr ăgaīne mĭe lībĕrtĭe*
> *ănd sēt yoŭr cāptĭue frēe|*
> *Glōrĭoŭs īs thĕ vĭꝗŏrĭe*
> *Cōnquĕrŏurs ūſe wĭth lēnĭtĭe*

Where ye ſee euery verſe is all of a meaſure, and yet

vnegall in number of fillables: for the fecond verfe is
but of fixe fillables, where the reft are of eight. But the
reafon is for that in three of the fame verfes are two
Dactils a peece, which abridge two fillables in euery
verfe: and fo maketh the longeft euen with the fhorteft.
Ye may note befides by the firft verfe, how much better
fome *biffillable* becommeth to peece out an other longer
foote then another word doth: for in place of [*render*] if ye
had fayd [*reftore*] it had marred the *Dactil*, and of neceffitie
driuen him out at length to be a verfe *Iambic* of foure feet,
becaufe [*render*] is naturally a *Trocheus* & makes the firft
two times of a *dactil*. [*Reftore*] is naturally a *Iābus*, & in
this place could not poffibly haue made a pleafant *dactil*.

Now againe if ye will fay to me that thefe two words
[*libertie*] and [*conquerours*] be not precife *Dactils* by the
Latine rule. So much will I confeffe to, but fince they
go currant inough vpon the tongue, and be fo vfually
pronounced, they may paffe wel inough for *Dactils* in
our vulgar meeters, & that is inough for me, fecking
but to fafhion an art, & not to finifh it: which time
only & cuftom haue authoritie to do, fpecially in all cafes
of language as the Poet hath wittily remembred in this
verfe   *-fi volet vfus,*
    Quem penes arbitrium est & vis & norma loquendi.

The Earle of Surrey vpon the death of Sir *Thomas
Wiat* made among other this verfe *Pentameter* and of
ten fillables,

    What holy graue (alas) vvhat fepulcher

But if I had had the making of him, he fhould haue
bene of eleuen fillables and kept his meafure of fiue ftill,
and would fo haue runne more pleafantly a great deale:
for as he is now, though he be euen he feemes odde and
defectiue, for not well obferuing the natural accent of
euery word, and this would haue bene foone holpen
by inferting one *monofillable* in the middle of the verfe,
and drawing another fillable in the beginning into a

Dactil, this word [*holy*] being a good [*Pirrichius*] & very well feruing the turne, thus,

Whāt hŏlĭe grāue ă lās whăt fīt sĕpūlchĕr.

Which verfe if ye perufe throughout ye fhall finde him after the firft *dactil* all *Trochaick* & not *Iambic*, nor of P iijʳ any other foot of two/times. But perchance if ye would feeme yet more curious, in place of thefe foure *Trocheus* ye might induce other feete of three times, as to make the three fillables next following the *dactil*, the foote [*amphimacer*] the laft word [*Sepulcher*] the foote [*amphibracus*] leauing the other midle word for a [*Iambus*] thus.

Whāt hŏlĭe grāue ă lās whăt fīt sĕpūlchĕr.

If ye aske me further why I make [*vvhat*] firft long & after fhort in one verfe, to that I fatisfied you before, that it is by reafon of his accent fharpe in one place and flat in another, being a commō *monofillable*, that is, apt to receiue either accent, & fo in the firft place receiuing aptly the fharpe accent he is made long: afterward receiuing the flat accent more aptly thē the fharpe, becaufe the fillable precedent [*las*] vtterly diftaines him, he is made fhort & not long, & that with very good melodie, but to haue giuen him the fharpe accent & plucked it frō the fillable [*las*] it had bene to any mans eare a great difcord: for euermore this word [*alás*] is accēted vpon the laft, & that lowdly & notorioufly as appeareth by all our exclamations vfed vnder that terme. The fame Earle of Surrey & Sir *Thomas Wyat* the firft reformers & polifhers of our vulgar Poefie much affecting the ftile and meafures of the Italian *Petrarcha*, vfed the foote *dactil* very often but not many in one verfe, as in thefe,

Fūll mănĭe that in prefence of thy līuelĭe hĕd,
Shed Cæfars teares vpon Pōmpĕiūs hĕd.
Th'ēnĕmĭe to life deftroi er of all kinde,
If āmŏ rŏus faith in an hart vn fayned,
Myne old deēre ĕnĕ my my froward mafter.
Thē fūrĭ ous gone in his moft ra ging ire.

(126)

And many moe which if ye would not allow for *dactils*
the verfe would halt vnleffe ye would feeme to helpe
it contracting a fillable by vertue of the figure *Syneresis*
which I thinke was neuer their meaning, nor in deede
would haue bred any pleafure to the eare, but hindred
the flowing of the verfe. Howfoeuer ye take it the *dactil*
is commendable inough in our vulgar meetres, but moft
plaufible of all when he is founded vpon the ftage, as in
thefe comicall verfes fhewing how well it becommeth all
noble men and great perfonages to be temperat and
modeft, yea more then any meaner man, thus./

Lēt nŏ nŏbīlĭtĭe rīchĕs ŏr hērĭtăge
Hōnŏur ŏr ēmpĭre ŏr eārthlĭe dŏmīnĭŏn
Brēed ĭn yŏur heād ănĭe pēeuĭfh ŏpīnĭŏn
That yĕ măy sāfĕr ăuōuch ănĭe ōutrāge.

And in this diftique taxing the Prelate fymoniake
ftanding all vpon perfect *dactils*.

Nōvv mānĭe bĭe mōnēy pūruĕy prŏmōtĭŏn
For mony mooues any hart to deuotion.

But this aduertifement I will giue you withall, that
if ye vfe too many *dactils* together ye make your mufike
too light and of no folemne grauitie fuch as the amorous
Elegies in court naturally require, being alwaies either
very dolefull or paffionate as the affections of loue enforce, in which bufines ye muft make your choife of
very few words *dactilique*, or them that ye can not refufe,
to diffolue and breake them into other feete by fuch
meanes as it fhall be taught hereafter: but chiefly in
your courtly ditties take heede ye vfe not thefe maner
of long *polifillables* and fpecially that ye finifh not your
verfe with thē as [*retribution*] *reftitution*] *remuneration*
[*recapitulation*] and fuch like: for they fmatch more the
fchoole of common players than of any delicate Poet
Lyricke or *Elegiacke*.

CHAP. XV. [XVI]

*Of all your other feete of three times and hovv vvell they
vvould fashion a meetre in our vulgar.*

All your other feete of three times I find no vfe of them
in our vulgar meeters nor no fweetenes at all, and yet
words inough to ferue their proportions. So as though
they haue not hitherto bene made artificiall, yet nowe
by more curious obferuation they might be. Since all
artes grew firft by obferuation of natures proceedings
and cuftome. And firft your [*Moloſſus*] being of all three
long is euidently difcouered by this word [*pērmĭttīng*]
The [*Anapeſtus*] of two ſhort and a long by this word
[*fŭrĭōus*] if the next word beginne with a confonant.
The foote [*Bacchius*] of a ſhort and two long by this
word [*rĕsīstāncе*] the foote [*Antibachius*] of two long and
a ſhort by this word [*ēxāmplĕ*] the foote [*Amphimacer*]
of a long a ſhort & a long by this word [*cōnquĕrīng*] the
foote of [*Amphibrachus*] of a ſhort a long and a ſhort by
P iiijʳ this word [*rĕ-/mēmber*] if a vowell follow. The foote
[*Tribrachus*] of three ſhort times is very hard to be made
by any of our *triſſillables* vnles they be cōpounded of the
fmootheft fort of confonants or fillables vocals, or of three
fmooth *monofillables*, or of fome peece of a lōg *polyfillable*
& after that fort we may with wrefting of words ſhape
the foot [*Tribrachus*] rather by vfurpation thē by rule,
which neuertheles is allowed in euery primitiue arte &
inuentiō: & ſo it was by the Greekes and Latines in
their firft verfifying, as if a rule ſhould be fet downe that
from henceforth thefe words ſhould be counted al *Tri-
brachus.* [*ĕnĕmĭe*] *rĕmĕdĭe*] *sĕlĭnĕs*] *mŏnĭlĕs*] *pĕnĭlĕs*] *crŭĕllĭe*]
& fuch like, or a peece of this long word [*rĕcōuĕrāblĕ*]
innŭmĕrāblĕ reădĭlĭe] and others. Of all which manner
of apt wordes to make thefe ftranger feet of three times
which go not fo currant with our eare as the *daƈil*, the
maker ſhould haue a good iudgement to know them by
their manner of orthographie and by their accent which

(128)

ſerue moſt fitly for euery foote, or elſe he ſhoulde haue alwaies a little calender of them apart to vſe readily when he ſhall neede them. But becauſe in very truth I thinke them but vaine & ſuperſtitious obſeruations nothing at all furthering the pleaſant melody of our Engliſh meeter, I leaue to ſpeake any more of them and rather wiſh the continuance of our old maner of Poeſie, ſcanning our verſe by ſillables rather than by feete, and vſing moſt commonly the word *Iambique* & ſometime the *Trochaike* which ye ſhall diſcerne by their accents, and now and then a *daƈill* keeping preciſely our ſymphony or rime without any other mincing meaſures, which an idle inuentiue head could eaſily deuiſe, as the former ex- amples teach.

CHAP. XVI. [XVII]

Of your verſes perfeƈ and defeƈiue, and that which the Græcians called the halfe foote.

The Greekes and Latines vſed verſes in the odde ſillable of two ſortes, which they called *Cataleƈicke* and *Acata- leƈicke*, that is odde vnder and odde ouer the iuſt meaſure of their verſe, & we in our vulgar finde many of the like, and ſpecially in the rimes of Sir Thomas Wiat, ſtrained perchaunce out of their originall, made firſt by *Francis Petrarcha:* as theſe

> *Like vnto theſe, immeaſurable mountaines,/*
> *So is my painefull life the burden of ire:*
> *For hie be they, and hie is my deſire*
> *And I of teares, and they are full of fountaines.*

P iiij

Where in your firſt ſecond and fourth verſe, ye may find a ſillable ſuperfluous, and though in the firſt ye will ſeeme to helpe it, by drawing theſe three ſillables, [*īm mĕ sŭ*] into a *daƈil*, in the reſt it can not be ſo excuſed, where- fore we muſt thinke he did it of purpoſe, by the odde ſillable to giue greater grace to his meetre, and we finde

(129)

in our old rimes, this odde fillable, fometime placed in
the beginning and fometimes in the middle of a verfe,
and is allowed to go alone & to hāg to any other fillable.
But this odde fillable in our meetres is not the halfe
foote as the Greekes and Latines vfed him in their verfes,
and called fuch meafure *pentimimeris* and *eptamimeris*,
but rather is that, which they called the *cataleƈtik* or
maymed verfe. Their *hemimeris* or halfe foote ferued not
by licence Poeticall or neceffitie of words, but to bewtifie
and exornate the verfe by placing one fuch halfe foote
in the middle *Cefure*, & one other in the end of the
verfe, as they vfed all their *pentameters elegiack:* and not
by coupling them together, but by accompt to make
their verfe of a iuſt meafure and not defeƈtiue or fuperflous: our odde fillable is not altogether of that nature,
but is in a maner drownd and fuppreſt by the flat accent,
and fhrinks away as it were inaudible and by that meane
the odde verfe comes almoſt to be an euen in euery
mans hearing. The halfe foote of the aunciens was
referued purpofely to an vfe, and therefore they gaue
fuch odde fillable, wherefoeuer he fell the fharper accent,
and made by him a notorious paufe as in this *pentameter*.

Nīl mĭ hī rēſcrībàs āttămĕn īpsĕ vĕ nì.

Which in all make fiue whole feete, or the verfe
Pentameter. We in our vulgar haue not the vfe of the
like halfe foote.

CHAP. XIII. [XVIII]

*Of the breaking your biffillables and polyfillables and when
it is to be vfed.*

But whether ye fuffer your fillable to receiue his quantitie
by his accent, or by his ortography, or whether ye keepe
your *biffillable* whole or whether ye breake him, all is
Q iʳ one to his quantitie,/ and his time will appeare the felfe

fame ftill and ought not to be altered by our makers, vnleffe it be whē fuch fillable is allowed to be common and to receiue any of both times, as in the *dimeter*, made of two fillables entier.

ēxtrēame dĕsīre

The firft is a good *fpondeus*, the fecond a good *iambus*, and if the fame wordes be broken thus it is not fo pleafant. *ĭn ēx trēame dĕ ſire*

And yet the firft makes a *iambus*, and the fecond a *trocheus* ech fillable retayning ftill his former quantities. And alwaies ye muft haue regard to the fweetenes of the meetre, fo as if your word *polyfillable* would not found pleafantly whole, ye fhould for the nonce breake him, which ye may eafily doo by inferting here and there one *monofillable* among your *polyfillables*, or by chaunging your word into another place then where he foundes vnpleafantly, and by breaking, turne a *trocheus* to a *iambus*, or contrariwife: as thus:

Hōllŏw vāllĕis ūndĕr hīĕſt moūntaĭnes
Crāggĭe clĭffes brĭng foōrth thĕ faīrĕſt foūntaĭnes

Thefe verfes be *trochaik*, and in mine eare not fo fweete and harmonicall as the *iambicque*, thus:

Thĕ hōllŏwſt vāls lĭe ūndĕr hīĕſt mōuntāines
Thĕ crāggĭſt clĭfs brĭng fōrth thĕ faīrĕſt foūntāines.

All which verfes bee now become *iambicque* by breaking the firft *biffillables*, and yet alters not their quantities though the feete be altered: and thus,

Reftleſſe is the heart in his defires
Rauing after that reafon doth denie.

Which being turned thus makes a new harmonie.

The reftleſſe heart, renues his old defires
Ay rauing after that reafon doth it deny.

And following this obferuation your meetres being builded with *polyfillables* will fall diuerfly out, that is fome to be *fpondaick*, fome *iambick*, others *dactilick*, others *trochaick*, and of one mingled with another, as in this verfe.

Hēauĭe ĭs thĕ bŭrdĕn of Prĭncĕs ĭre

The verfe is *trochaick*, but being altered thus, is *iambicque.*/

Fŭll hēauĭe ĭs thĕ pāĭfe ŏf Prīncĕs ĭre

And as Sir *Thomas Wiat* fong in a verfe wholly *trochaick*, becaufe the wordes do beft fhape to that foote by their naturall accent, thus,

Fārewĕll lōue ănd āll thĭe lāwes fŏr ēuĕr

And in this ditty of th'Erle of Surries, paffing fweete and harmonicall: all be *Iambick*.

> *When raging loue with extreme paine*
> *So cruelly doth ftraine my hart,*
> *And that the teares like fluds of raine*
> *Beare witneffe of my wofull fmart.*

Which beyng difpofed otherwife or not broken, would proue all *trochaick*, but nothing pleafant.

Now furthermore ye are to note, that al your *mono-fyllables* may receiue the fharp accent, but not fo aptly one as another, as in this verfe where they ferue well to make him *iambicque*, but not *trochaick*.

Gŏd graūnt thĭs peāce măy lōng ĕndūre

Where the fharpe accent falles more tunably vpon [*graunt*] [*peace*] [*long*] [*dure*] then it would by con-uerfion, as to accent them thus:

Gōd graŭnt-thĭs peāce-māy lŏng-ēndūre,

And yet if ye will afke me the reafon, I can not tell it, but that it fhapes fo to myne eare, and as I thinke to euery other mans. And in this meeter where ye haue

whole words *biſſillable* vnbroken, that maintaine (by
reaſon of their accent) ſundry feete, yet going one with
another be very harmonicall.

Where ye ſee one to be a *trocheus* another the *iambus*,
and ſo entermingled not by election but by conſtraint
of their ſeuerall accents, which ought not to be altred,
yet comes it to paſſe that many times ye muſt of neceſſitie
alter the accent of a ſillable, and put him from his naturall
place, and then one ſillable, of a word *polyſillable*, or one
word *monoſillable*, will abide to be made ſometimes long,
ſometimes ſhort, as in this *quadreyne* of ours playd in
a mery moode.

> *Gèue mé mìne ówne ànd whén I dó dèſíre*
> *Geue others theirs, and nothing that is mine|*
> *Nòr gíue mè thát, wherto all men aspire*
> *Then neither gold, nor faire women nor wine.*

Q ijʳ

Where in your firſt verſe theſe two words [*giue*] and
[*me*] are accented one high th'other low, in the third
verſe the ſame words are accented contrary, and the
reaſon of this exchange is manifeſt, becauſe the maker
playes with theſe two clauſes of ſundry relations [*giue
me*] and [*giue others*] ſo as the *monoſillable* [*me*] being
reſpectiue to the word [*others*] and inferring a ſubtilitie
or wittie implication, ought not to haue the ſame accent,
as when he hath no ſuch reſpect, as in this *diſtik* of ours.

> *Prōue mĕ (Madame) ere ye rēprŏue*
> *Meeke minds ſhould ēxcŭſe not āccŭſe.*

In which verſe ye ſee this word [*reprooue,*] the ſillable
[*prooue*] alters his ſharpe accent into a flat, for naturally
it is long in all his ſingles and compoundes [*reprŏue*]
[*apprŏue*] [*diſprŏue*] & ſo is the ſillable [*cuſe*] in [*excuſe*]
[*accuſe*] [*recuſe*] yet in theſe verſes by reaſon one of them
doth as it were nicke another, and haue a certaine extraordinary ſence with all, it behoueth to remoue the ſharpe
accents from whence they are moſt naturall, to place

(133)

them where the nicke may be more exprefly difcouered, and therefore in this verfe where no fuch implication is, nor no relation it is otherwife, as thus.

*If ye rĕprōue my conſtancie
I will excūfe you curteſly.*

For in this word [repro*ó*ue] becaufe there is no extra-ordinary fence to be inferred, he keepeth his fharpe accent vpon the fillable [pro*ó*ue] but in the former verfes becaufe they feeme to encounter ech other, they do thereby merite an audible and pleafant alteratiō of their accents in thofe fillables that caufe the fubtiltie. Of thefe maner of nicetees ye fhal finde in many places of our booke, but fpecially where we treate of ornament, vnto which we referre you, fauing that we thought good to fet down one example more to folace your mindes with mirth after all thefe fcholafticall preceptes, which can not but bring with them (fpecially to Courtiers) much tedioufneffe, and fo to end. In our Comedie intituled *Ginecocratia:* the king was fuppofed to be a perfon very amorous and effeminate, and therefore moft ruled his

Q ij^v ordinary affaires by the/aduife of women either for the loue he bare to their perfons or liking he had to their pleafant ready witts and vtterance. Comes me to the Court one *Polemon* an honeft plaine man of the country, but rich: and hauing a fuite to the king, met by chaunce with one *Philino*, a louer of wine and a merry companion in Court, and praied him in that he was a ftranger that he would vouchfafe to tell him which way he were beft to worke to get his fuite, and who were moft in credit and fauour about the king, that he might feeke to them to furder his attempt. *Philino* perceyuing the plainneffe of the man, and that there would be fome good done with him, told *Polemon* that if he would well confider him for his labor he would bring him where he fhould know the truth of all his demaundes by the fentence of the Oracle. *Polemon* gaue him twentie crownes, *Philino*

brings him into a place where behind an arras cloth
hee himfelfe fpake in manner of an Oracle in thefe
meeters, for fo did all the Sybils and fothfaiers in old
times giue their anfwers.

> *Your beft way to worke—and marke my words well,*
> *Not money: nor many,*
> *Nor any: but any,*
> *Not weemen, but weemen beare the bell.*

Polemon wift not what to make of this doubtfull
fpeach, & not being lawfull to importune the oracle
more then once in one matter, conceyued in his head
the pleafanter conftruction, and ftacke to it: and hauing
at home a fayre yong damfell of eighteene yeares old
to his daughter, that could very well behaue her felfe
in countenance & alfo in her language, apparelled her
as gay as he could, and brought her to the Court, where
Philino harkning daily after the euent of this matter,
met him, and recommended his daughter to the Lords,
who perceiuing her great beauty and other good parts,
brought her to the King, to whom fhe exhibited her
fathers fupplication, and found fo great fauour in his
eye, as without any long delay fhe obtained her fute
at his hands. *Polemon* by the diligent folliciting of his
daughter, wanne his purpofe: *Philino* gat a good reward
and vfed the matter fo, as howfoeuer the oracle had bene
conftrued, he could not haue receiued blame nor dif-
credit by the fucceffe, for euery waies it would haue
proued true, whether *Polemons* daughter had obtayned
the fute, or not obtained it./And the fubtiltie lay in the   Q iij^r
accent and Ortographie of thefe two wordes [*any*] and
[*weemen*] for [*any*] being deuided founds [*a nie* or neere
perfon to the king: and [*weemen*] being diuided foundes
wee men, and not [*weemen*] and fo by this meane *Philino*
ferued all turnes and fhifted himfelfe from blame, not
vnlike the tale of the Rattlemoufe who in the warres
proclaimed betweene the foure footed beafts, and the

birdes, beyng fent for by the Lyon to be at his mufters, excufed himfelfe for that he was a foule and flew with winges: and beyng fent for by the Eagle to ferue him, fayd that he was a foure footed beaft, and by that craftie cauill efcaped the danger of the warres, and fhunned the feruice of both Princes. And euer fince fate at home by the fires fide, eating vp the poore husbandmans baken, halfe loft for lacke of a good hufwifes looking too.

FINIS.

THE THIRD BOOKE,

OF ORNAMENT.

CHAP. I.

Of Ornament Poeticall.

As no doubt the good proportion of any thing doth greatly adorne and commend it and right fo our late remembred proportions doe to our vulgar Poefie: fo is there yet requifite to the perfection of this arte, another maner of exornation, which refteth in the fafhioning of our makers language and ftile, to fuch purpofe as it may delight and allure as well the mynde as the eare of the hearers with a certaine noueltie and ftrange maner of conueyance, difguifing it no litle from the ordinary and accuftomed: neuerthelefle making it nothing the more vnfeemely or misbecomming, but rather decenter and more agreable to any ciuill eare and vnderftanding. And as we fee in thefe great Madames of honour, be they for perfonage or otherwife neuer fo comely and bewtifull, yet if they want their courtly habillements or at leaftwife fuch other apparell as cuftome and ciuilitie haue ordained to couer their naked bodies, would be halfe afhamed or greatly out of countenaunce to be feen in that fort, and perchance do then thinke themfelues more amiable in euery mans eye, when they be in their richeft attire, fuppofe of filkes or tyffewes & coftly embroderies, then when they go in cloth or in any other plaine and fimple apparell. Euen fo cannot our vulgar Poefie fhew it felfe either gallant or gorgious, if any lymme be left naked and bare and not clad in his kindly clothes and coulours, fuch as may conuey them fomwhat out of fight, that is from the common courfe of ordinary/fpeach and capacitie

of the vulgar iudgement, and yet being artificially handled
muſt needes yeld it much more bewtie and commendation. This ornament we ſpeake of is giuen to it by figures
and figuratiue ſpeaches, which be the flowers as it were
and coulours that a Poet ſetteth vpon his language by
arte, as the embroderer doth his ſtone and perle, or
paſſements of gold vpon the ſtuffe of a Princely garment,
or as th'excellent painter beſtoweth the rich Orient
coulours vpon his table of pourtraite: ſo neuertheleſſe as
if the ſame coulours in our arte of Poeſie (as well as in
thoſe other mechanicall artes) be not well tempered, or
not well layd, or be vſed in exceſſe, or neuer ſo litle
diſordered or miſplaced, they not onely giue it no maner
of grace at all, but rather do disfigure the ſtuffe and ſpill
the whole workmanſhip taking away all bewtie and good
liking from it, no leſſe then if the crimſon tainte, which
ſhould be laid vpon a Ladies lips, or right in the center
of her cheekes ſhould by ſome ouerſight or miſhap be
applied to her forhead or chinne, it would make (ye
would ſay) but a very ridiculous bewtie, wherfore the
chief prayſe and cunning of our Poet is in the diſcreet
vſing of his figures, as the skilfull painters is in the good
conueyance of his coulours and ſhadowing traits of his
penſill, with a delectable varietie, by all meaſure and iuſt
proportion, and in places moſt aptly to be beſtowed.

CHAP, II.

How our writing and ſpeaches publike ought to be figuratiue,
and if they be not doe greatly diſgrace the cauſe and
purpoſe of the ſpeaker and writer.

But as it hath bene alwayes reputed a great fault to vſe
figuratiue ſpeaches fooliſhly and indiſcretly, ſo is it
eſteemed no leſſe an imperfection in mans vtterance, to
haue none vſe of figure at all, ſpecially in our writing
and ſpeaches publike, making them but as our ordinary
talke, then which nothing can be more vnſauourie and

farre from all ciuilitie. I remember in the firſt yeare of
Queenes Maries raigne a Knight of Yorkſhire was choſen
ſpeaker of the Parliament, a good gentleman and wiſe,
in the affaires of his ſhire, and not vnlearned in the lawes
of the Realme, but as well for ſome lack of his teeth, as
for want of language no-/thing well ſpoken, which at Q iiijᵛ
that time and buſineſſe was moſt behooffull for him to
haue bene: this man after he had made his Oration to
the Queene; which ye know is of courſe to be done at
the firſt aſſembly of both houſes; a bencher of the Temple
both well learned and very eloquent, returning from the
Parliament houſe asked another gentleman his frend
how he liked M. Speakers Oration: mary quoth th'other,
me thinks I heard not a better alehouſe tale told this
ſeuen yeares. This happened becauſe the good old
Knight made no difference betweene an Oration or
publike ſpeach to be deliuered to th'eare of a Princes
Maieſtie and ſtate of a Realme, then he would haue
done of an ordinary tale to be told at his table in the
countrey, wherein all men know the oddes is very great.
And though graue and wiſe counſellours in their con-
ſultations doe not vſe much ſuperfluous eloquence, and
alſo in their iudiciall hearings do much miſlike all
ſcholaſticall rhetoricks: yet in ſuch a caſe as it may be
(and as this Parliament was) if the Lord Chancelour of
England or Archbiſhop of Canterbury himſelfe were to
ſpeake, he ought to doe it cunningly and eloquently,
which can not be without the vſe of figures: and neuertheleſſe none impeachment or blemiſh to the grauitie of
their perſons or of the cauſe: wherein I report me to thē
that knew Sir *Nicholas Bacon* Lord keeper of the great
Seale, or the now Lord Treaſorer of England, and haue
bene conuerſant with their ſpeaches made in the Parliament houſe & Starrechamber. From whoſe lippes I haue
ſeene to proceede more graue and naturall eloquence,
then from all the Oratours of Oxford or Cambridge, but
all is as it is handled, and maketh no matter whether

the fame eloquence be naturall to them or artificiall
(though I thinke rather naturall) yet were they knowen
to be learned and not vnskilfull of th'arte, when they
were yonger men: and as learning and arte teacheth a
fchollar to fpeake, fo doth it alfo teach a counfellour, and
afwell an old man as a yong, and a man in authoritie,
afwell as a priuate perfon, and a pleader afwell as a
preacher, euery man after his fort and calling as beft
becommeth: and that fpeach which becommeth one,
doth not become another, for maners of fpeaches, fome
ferue to work in exceffe, fome in mediocritie, fome to
graue purpofes, fome to light, fome to be fhort and/
R iʳ brief, fome to be long, fome to ftirre vp affeƈtions, fome
to pacifie and appeafe them, and thefe common defpifers
of good vtterance, which refteth altogether in figuratiue
fpeaches, being well vfed whether it come by nature or
by arte or by exercife, they be but certaine groffe
ignorants of whom it is truly fpoken *fcientia non habet
inimicum nifi ignorantem.* I haue come to the Lord Keeper
Sir *Nicholas Bacon,* & found him fitting in his gallery
alone with the works of *Quintilian* before him, in deede
he was a moft eloquent man, and of rare learning and
wifedome, as euer I knew England to breed, and one
that ioyed as much in learned men and men of good
witts. A Knight of the Queenes priuie chamber, once
intreated a noble woman of the Court, being in great
fauour about her Maieftie (to th'intent to remoue her
from a certaine difpleafure, which by finifter opinion
fhe had conceiued againft a gentleman his friend) that
it would pleafe her to heare him fpeake in his own caufe,
& not to cōdēne him vpon his aduerfaries report: God
forbid faid fhe, he is to wife for me to talke with, let
him goe and fatisfie fuch a man naming him: why quoth
the Knight againe, had your Ladyfhip rather heare a
man talke like a foole or like a wife man? This was
becaufe the Lady was a litle peruerfe, and not difpofed
to reforme her felfe by hearing reafon, which none other

can fo well beate into the ignorant head, as the well fpoken and eloquent man. And becaufe I am fo farre waded into this difcourfe of eloquence and figuratiue fpeaches, I will tell you what hapned on a time my felfe being prefent when certaine Doctours of the ciuil law were heard in a litigious caufe betwixt a man and his wife: before a great Magiftrat who (as they can tell that knew him) was a man very well learned and graue, but fomewhat fowre, and of no plaufible vtterance: the gentlemans chaunce, was to fay: my Lord the fimple woman is not fo much to blame as her lewde abbettours, who by violent perfwafions haue lead her into this wilful-neffe. Quoth the iudge, what neede fuch eloquent termes in this place, the gentleman replied, doth your Lordfhip miflike the terme, [*violent*] & me thinkes I fpeake it to great purpofe: for I am fure fhe would neuer haue done it, but by force of perfwafion: & if perfwafiōs were not very violent, to the minde of man it could not haue wrought fo ftrāge an effect as we read that it did once in Æ-/gypt, & would haue told the whole tale at large, R iv if the Magiftrate had not paffed it ouer very pleafantly. Now to tell you the whole matter as the gentlemā intēded, thus it was. There came into Ægypt a notable Oratour, whofe name was *Hegefias* who inueyed fo much againft the incōmodities of this tranfitory life, & fo highly commended death the difpatcher of all euils; as a great number of his hearers deftroyed themfelues, fome with weapō, fome with poyfon, others by drowning and hanging themfelues to be rid out of this vale of mifery, in fo much as it was feared leaft many moe of the people would haue mifcaried by occafion of his per-fwafions, if king *Ptolome* had not made a publicke pro-clamation, that the Oratour fhould auoyde the countrey, and no more be allowed to fpeake in any matter. Whether now perfwafions, may not be faid violent and forcible to fimple myndes in fpeciall, I referre it to all mens iudgements that heare the ftory. At leaft waies, I finde

9   (141)

this opinion, confirmed by a pretie deuife or embleme
that *Lucianus* alleageth he faw in the pourtrait of *Hercules*
within the Citie of Marfeills in Prouence: where they
had figured a luftie old man with a long chayne tyed
by one end at his tong, by the other end at the peoples
eares, who ftood a farre of and feemed to be drawen to
him by the force of that chayne faftned to his tong, as
who would fay, by force of his perfwafions. And to
fhew more plainly that eloquence is of great force (and
not as many men thinke amiffe) the propertie and gift
of yong men onely, but rather of old men, and a thing
which better becommeth hory haires then beardleffe
boyes, they feeme to ground it vpon this reafon: age
(fay they and moft truly) brings experience, experience
bringeth wifedome, long life yeldes long vfe and much
exercife of fpeach, exercife and cuftome with wifedome,
make an affured and volluble vtterance: fo is it that old
men more then any other fort fpeake moft grauely, wifely,
affuredly, and plaufibly, which partes are all that can
be required in perfite eloquence, and fo in all delibera-
tions of importance where counfellours are allowed freely
to opyne & fhew their cōceits, good perfwafion is no
leffe requifite then fpeach it felfe: for in great purpofes
to fpeake and not to be able or likely to perfwade, is a
vayne thing: now let vs returne backe to fay more of
this Poeticall ornament./

CHAP. III.

*How ornament Poeticall is of two fortes according to the
double vertue and efficacie of figures.*

This ornament then is of two fortes, one to fatisfie &
delight th'eare onely by a goodly outward fhew fet vpon
the matter with wordes, and fpeaches fmothly and tunably running: another by certaine intendments or fence
of fuch wordes & fpeaches inwardly working a ftirre to

the mynde: that firſt qualitie the Greeks called *Enargia*,
of this word *argos*, becauſe it geueth a glorious luſtre
and light. This latter they called *Energia* of *ergon*, becauſe it wrought with a ſtrong and vertuous operation;
and figure breedeth them both, ſome ſeruing to giue
gloſſe onely to a language, ſome to geue it efficacie by
fence, and ſo by that meanes ſome of them ſerue th'eare
onely, ſome ſerue the conceit onely and not th'eare:
there be of them alſo that ſerue both turnes as commō
ſeruitours appointed for th'one and th'other purpoſe,
which ſhalbe hereafter ſpoken of in place: but becauſe
we haue alleaged before that ornament is but the good
or rather bewtifull habite of language and ſtile, and
figuratiue ſpeaches the inſtrument wherewith we burniſh
our language faſhioning it to this or that meaſure and
proportion, whence finally reſulteth a long and continuall phraſe or maner of writing or ſpeach, which we
call by the name of *ſtile:* we wil firſt ſpeake of language,
then of ſtile, laſtly of figure, and declare their vertue
and differences, and alſo their vſe and beſt application,
& what portion in exornation euery of them bringeth
to the bewtifying of this Arte.

CHAP. IIII.

Of Language.

Speach is not naturall to man ſauing for his onely habilitie
to ſpeake, and that he is by kinde apt to vtter all his conceits with ſounds and voyces diuerſified many maner of
wayes, by meanes of the many & fit inſtruments he hath
by nature to that purpoſe, as a broad and voluble tong,
thinne and mouable lippes, teeth euē and not ſhagged,
thick ranged, a round vaulted pallate, and a long throte,
beſides an excellent capacitie of wit that maketh him
more diſciplinable and imitatiue then any other creature:
then as to the/forme and action of his ſpeach, it com- R ijᵛ

(143)

meth to him by arte & teaching, and by vfe or exercife. But after a fpeach is fully fafhioned to the common vnder-ftanding, & accepted by confent of a whole countrey & natiō, it is called a language, & receaueth none allowed alteration, but by extraordinary occafions by little & little, as it were infenfibly bringing in of many corruptiōs that creepe along with the time: of all which matters, we haue more largely fpoken in our bookes of the originals and pedigree of the Englifh tong. Then when I fay language, I meane the fpeach wherein the Poet or maker writeth be it Greek or Latine, or as our cafe is the vulgar Englifh, & when it is peculiar vnto a countrey it is called the mother fpeach of that people: the Greekes terme it *Idioma:* fo is ours at this day the Norman Englifh. Before the Conqueft of the Normans it was the Anglefaxon, and before that the Britifh, which as fome will, is at this day, the Walfh, or as others affirme the Cornifh: I for my part thinke neither of both, as they be now fpoken and pronounced. This part in our maker or Poet muft be heedyly looked vnto, that it be naturall, pure, and the moft vfuall of all his countrey: and for the fame purpofe rather that which is fpoken in the kings Court, or in the good townes and Cities within the land, then in the marches and frontiers, or in port townes, where ftraungers haunt for traffike fake, or yet in Vniuerfities where Schollers vfe much peeuifh affecta-tion of words out of the primatiue languages, or finally, in any vplandifh village or corner of a Realme, where is no refort but of poore rufticall or vnciuill people: neither fhall he follow the fpeach of a craftes man or carter, or other of the inferiour fort, though he be inhabitant or bred in the beft towne and Citie in this Realme, for fuch perfons doe abufe good fpeaches by ftrange accents or ill fhapen foundes, and falfe ortographie. But he fhall follow generally the better brought vp fort, fuch as the Greekes call [*charientes*] men ciuill and gracioufly behauoured and bred. Our maker therfore at thefe dayes

fhall not follow *Piers plowman* nor *Gower* nor *Lydgate*
nor yet *Chaucer*, for their language is now out of vfe
with vs: neither fhall he take the termes of Northern-
men, fuch as they vfe in dayly talke, whether they be
noble men or gentlemen, or of their beft clarkes all is
a matter: nor in effect any fpeach vfed beyond the/riuer R iij^r
of Trent, though no man can deny but that theirs is
the purer Englifh Saxon at this day, yet it is not fo
Courtly nor fo currant as our Southerne Englifh is, no
more is the far Wefterne mās fpeach: ye fhall therfore
take the vfuall fpeach of the Court, and that of London
and the fhires lying about London within lx. myles, and
not much aboue. I fay not this but that in euery fhyre
of England there be gentlemen and others that fpeake
but fpecially write as good Southerne as we of Middlefex
or Surrey do, but not the common people of eucry fhire,
to whom the gentlemen, and alfo their learned clarkes
do for the moft part condefcend, but herein we are
already ruled by th'Englifh Dictionaries and other
bookes written by learned men, and therefore it needeth
none other direction in that behalfe. Albeit peraduenture fome fmall admonition be not impertinent, for we
finde in our Englifh writers many wordes and fpeaches
amendable, & ye fhall fee in fome many inkhorne termes
fo ill affected brought in by men of learning as preachers
and fchoolemafters: and many ftraunge termes of other
languages by Secretaries and Marchaunts and trauailours, and many darke wordes and not vfuall nor well
founding, though they be dayly fpoken in Court. Wherefore great heed muft be taken by our maker in this point
that his choife be good. And peraduenture the writer
hereof be in that behalfe no leffe faultie then any other,
vfing many ftraunge and vnaccuftomed wordes and borrowed from other languages: and in that refpect him
felfe no meete Magiftrate to reforme the fame errours
in any other perfon, but fince he is not vnwilling to
acknowledge his owne fault, and can the better tell how

to amend it, he may feeme a more excufable correctour of other mens: he intendeth therefore for an indifferent way and vniuerfall benefite to taxe him felfe firft and before any others.

Thefe be words vfed by th'author in this prefent treatife, *ſciētificke*, but with fome reafon, for it anfwereth the word *mechanicall*, which no other word could haue done fo properly, for when hee fpake of all artificers which reft either in fcience or in handy craft, it followed neceffarilie that *ſcientifique* fhould be coupled with *mechanicall:* or els neither of both to haue bene allowed, but in their places: a man of fcience liberall, and a handi-
R iijᵛ crafts man, which/had not bene fo cleanly a fpeech as the other *Maior-domo:* in truth this word is borrowed of the *Spaniard* and *Italian*, and therefore new and not vfuall, but to them that are acquainted with the affaires of Court: and fo for his iolly magnificence (as this cafe is) may be accepted among Courtiers, for whom this is fpecially written. A man might haue faid in fteade of *Maior-domo*, the French word (*maistre d'hoftell*) but il-fauouredly, or the right Englifh word (*Lord Steward.)* But me thinks for my owne opinion this word *Maior-domo* though he be borrowed, is more acceptable thā any of the reft, other men may iudge otherwife. *Politien*, this word alfo is receiued from the Frenchmen, but at this day vfuall in Court and with all good Secretaries: and cannot finde an Englifh word to match him, for to haue faid a man politique, had not bene fo wel: bicaufe in trueth that had bene no more than to haue faid a ciuil perfon. *Politien* is rather a furueyour of ciuilitie than ciuil, & a publique minifter or Counfeller in the ftate. Ye haue alfo this worde *Conduict*, a French word, but well allowed of vs, and long fince vfuall, it foundes fomewhat more than this word (leading) for it is applied onely to the leading of a Captaine, and not as a little boy fhould leade a blinde man, therefore more proper to the cafe when he faide, *conduict* of whole armies: ye

finde alſo this word *Idiome*, taken from the Greekes, yet
ſeruing aptly, when a man wanteth to expreſſe ſo much
vnles it be in two words, which ſurpluſſage to auoide,
we are allowed to draw in other words ſingle, and aſmuch
ſignificatiue: this word *ſignificatiue* is borrowed of the
Latine and French, but to vs brought in firſt by ſome
Noble-mans ˈSecretarie, as I thinke, yet doth ſo well
ſerue the turne, as it could not now be ſpared: and many
more like vſurped Latine and French words: as, *Methode,
methodicall, placation, function, aſſubtiling, refining, compendious, prolixe, figuratiue, inueigle.* A terme borrowed
of our common Lawyers. *impreſſion,* alſo a new terme,
but well expreſſing the matter, and more than our
Engliſh word. Theſe words, *Numerous, numeroſitee, metricall, harmonicall,* but they cannot be refuſed, ſpecially in
this place for deſcription of the arte. Alſo ye finde theſe
words, *penetrate, penetrable, indignitie,* which I cannot
ſee how we may ſpare them, whatſoeuer fault wee finde
with Ink-horne termes: for our ſpeach wanteth wordes
to/ſuch ſence ſo well to be vſed: yet in ſteade of *indignitie,* R iiijʳ
yee haue vnworthineſſe: and for *penetrate,* we may ſay
peerce, and that a French terme alſo, or *broche,* or enter
into with violence, but not ſo well ſounding as *penetrate.*
Item, *ſauage,* for wilde: *obſcure,* for darke. Item theſe
words, *declination, delineation, dimention,* are ſcholaſticall
termes in deede, and yet very proper. But peraduenture
(& I could bring a reaſon for it) many other like words
borrowed out of the Latin and French, were not ſo well
to be allowed by vs, as theſe words, *audacious,* for bold:
facunditie, for eloquence: *egregious,* for great or notable:
implete, for repleniſhed: *attemptat,* for attempt: *compatible,*
for agreeable in nature, and many more. But herein the
noble Poet *Horace* hath ſaid inough to ſatisfie vs all in
theſe few verſes.

> *Multa renaſcentur quæ iam cecidere cadent ⅗*
> *Quæ nunc ſunt in honore vocabula ſi volet vſus*
> *Quem penes arbitrium eſt & vis & norma loquendi.*

Which I haue thus englifhed, but nothing with fo good grace, nor fo briefly as the Poet wrote.

> *Many a word yfalne fhall eft arife*
> *And fuch as now bene held in hieft prife*
> *Will fall as faft, when vfe and cuftome will*
> *Onely vmpiers of fpeach, for force and skill.*

CHAP. V.

Of Stile.

Stile is a conftant & continuall phrafe or tenour of fpeaking and writing, extending to the whole tale or proceffe of the poeme or hiftorie, and not properly to any peece or member of a tale: but is of words fpeeches and fentences together, a certaine contriued forme and qualitie, many times naturall to the writer, many times his peculier by election and arte, and fuch as either he keepeth by skill, or holdeth on by ignorance, and will not or peraduenture cannot eafily alter into any other. So we fay that *Ciceroes* ftile, and *Salufts* were not one, nor *Cefars* and *Liuies*, nor *Homers* and *Hefiodus*, nor *Herodotus* and *Theucidides*, nor *Euripides* & *Ariftophones*, nor *Erafmus* and *Budeus* ftiles. And becaufe this continuall courfe and manner of writing or fpeech fheweth R iiij^v the/matter and difpofition of the writers minde, more than one or few words or fentences can fhew, therefore there be that haue called ftile, the image of man [*mentis character*] for man is but his minde, and as his minde is tempered and qualified, fo are his fpeeches and language at large, and his inward conceits be the mettall of his minde, and his manner of vtterance the very warp & woofe of his conceits, more plaine, or bufie and intricate, or otherwife affected after the rate. Moft men fay that not any one point in all *Phifiognomy* is fo certaine, as to iudge a mans manners by his eye: but more affuredly in mine opinion, by his dayly maner of fpeech

(148)

and ordinary writing. For if the man be graue, his
ſpeech and ſtile is graue: if light-headed, his ſtile and
language alſo light: if the minde be haughtie and hoate,
the ſpeech and ſtile is alſo vehement and ſtirring: if it
be colde and temperate, the ſtile is alſo very modeſt: if
it be humble, or baſe and meeke, ſo is alſo the language
and ſtile. And yet peraduenture not altogether ſo, but
that euery mans ſtile is for the moſt part according to
the matter and ſubiect of the writer, or ſo ought to be,
and conformable thereunto. Thē againe may it be ſaid
as wel, that men doo chuſe their ſubiects according to
the mettal of their minds, & therfore a high minded
man chuſeth him high & lofty matter to write of. The
baſe courage, matter baſe & lowe, the meane & modeſt
mind, meane & moderate matters after the rate. How-
ſoeuer it be, we finde that vnder theſe three principall
cōplexiōs (if I may with leaue ſo terme thē) high,
meane and baſe ſtile, there be contained many other
humors or qualities of ſtile, as the plaine and obſcure,
the rough and ſmoth, the facill and hard, the plentifull
and barraine, the rude and eloquent, the ſtrong and
feeble, the vehement and cold ſtiles, all which in their
euill are to be reformed, and the good to be kept and
vſed. But generally to haue the ſtile decent & comely
it behooueth the maker or Poet to follow the nature of
his ſubiect, that is if his matter be high and loftie that
the ſtile be ſo to, if meane, the ſtile alſo to be meane,
if baſe, the ſtile humble and baſe accordingly: and they
that do otherwiſe vſe it, applying to meane matter, hie
and loftie ſtile, and to hie matters, ſtile eyther meane
or baſe, and to the baſe matters, the meane or hie ſtile,
do vtterly diſgrace their poeſie and ſhew themſelues
nothing skilfull in their arte, nor hauing regard/to the s ir
decencie, which is the chiefe praiſe of any writer. Therefore to ridde all louers of learning from that errour,
I will as neere as I can ſet downe, which matters be hie
and loftie, which be but meane, and which be low and

bafe, to the intent the ftiles may be fafhioned to the matters, and keepe their *decorum* and good proportion in euery refpe&: I am not ignorant that many good clerkes be contrary to mine opinion, and fay that the loftie ftyle may be decently vfed in a meane and bafe fubie& & contrariwife, which I do in parte acknowledge, but with a reafonable qualification. For *Homer* hath fo vfed it in his trifling worke of *Batrachomyomachia:* that is in his treatife of the warre betwixt the frogs and the mice. *Virgill* alfo in his *bucolickes*, and in his *georgicks*, whereof the one is counted meane, the other bafe, that is the husbandmans difcourfes and the fhepheards, but hereunto ferueth a reafon in my fimple conceite: for firft to that trifling poeme of *Homer*, though the frog and the moufe be but litle and ridiculous beafts, yet to treat of warre is an high fubie&, and a thing in euery refpe& terrible and daungerous to them that it alights on: and therefore of learned dutie asketh martiall grandiloquence, if it be fet foorth in his kind and nature of warre, euen betwixt the bafeft creatures that can be imagined: fo alfo is the Ante or pifmire, and they be but little creeping things, not perfe& beafts, but *infe&s*, or wormes: yet in defcribing their nature & inftin&, and their manner of life approching to the forme of a common-welth, and their properties not vnlike to the vertues of moft excel- lent gouernors and captaines, it asketh a more maieftie of fpeach then would the defcription of any other beaftes life or nature, and perchance of many matters perteyning vnto the bafer fort of men, becaufe it refembleth the hiftorie of a ciuill regiment, and of them all the chiefe and moft principall which is *Monarchie:* fo alfo in his *bucolicks*, which are but paftorall fpeaches and the bafeft of any other poeme in their owne proper nature: *Virgill* vfed a fomewhat fwelling ftile when he came to infinuate the birth of *Marcellus* heire apparant to the Emperour *Auguftus*, as child to his fifter, afpiring by hope and greatnes of the houfe, to the fucceffion of the Empire, and eſtabliſhment thereof in that familie: whereupon *Virgill* could do no leſſe then to vſe ſuch manner of ſtile, whatſo-/euer condition the poeme were of and this was ſ iᵛ decent, & no fault or blemiſh, to confound the tennors of the ſtiles for that cauſe. But now when I remember me againe that this *Eglogue*, (for I haue read it ſome-where) was conceiued by *Octauian* th'Emperour to be written to the honour of *Pollio* a citizen of Rome, & of no great nobilitie, the ſame was miſliked againe as an implicatiue, nothing decent nor proportionable to *Pollio* his fortunes and calling, in which reſpect I might ſay likewiſe the ſtile was not to be ſuch as if it had bene for the Emperours owne honour, and thoſe of the bloud imperiall, then which ſubiect there could not be among the *Romane* writers an higher nor grauer to treat vpon: ſo can I not be remoued from mine opinion, but ſtill me thinks that in all decencie the ſtile ought to conforme with the nature of the ſubiect, otherwiſe if a writer will ſeeme to obſerue no *decorum* at all, nor paſſe how he faſhion his tale to his matter, who doubteth but he may in the lighteſt cauſe ſpeake like a Pope, & in the graueſt matters prate like a parrat, & finde wordes & phraſes ynough to ſerue both turnes, and neither of them com-mendably, for neither is all that may be written of Kings and Princes ſuch as ought to keepe a high ſtile, nor all that may be written vpon a ſhepheard to keepe the low, but according to the matter reported, if that be of high or baſe nature: for euery pety pleaſure, and vayne delight of a king are not to be accompted high matter for the height of his eſtate, but meane and perchaunce very baſe and vile: nor ſo a Poet or hiſtoriographer, could decently with a high ſtile reporte the vanities of *Nero*, the ribau-dries of *Caligula*, the idlenes of *Domitian*, & the riots of *Heliogabalus*. But well the magnanimitie and honor-able ambition of *Cæſar*, the proſperities of *Auguſtus*, the grauitie of *Tiberius*, the bountie of *Traiane*, the wiſedome of *Aurelius*, and generally all that which concerned the higheſt honours of Emperours, their birth, alliaunces, gouernement, exploits in warre and peace, and other publike affaires: for they be matter ſtately and high, and require a ſtile to be lift vp and aduaunced by choyſe of wordes, phraſes, ſentences, and figures, high, loftie, eloquent, & magnifik in proportion: ſo be the meane matters, to be caried with all wordes and ſpeaches of ſmothneſſe and pleaſant moderation, & finally the baſe things to be holden with-/in their teder, by a low, myld, and ſimple maner of vtterance, creeping rather then clyming, & marching rather then mounting vpwardes, with the wings of the ſtately ſubieĉts and ſtile.

S ijr

CHAP. VI.

Of the high, low, and meane ſubieĉt.

The matters therefore that concerne the Gods and diuine things are higheſt of all other to be couched in writing, next to them the noble geſts and great fortunes of Princes, and the notable accidēts of time, as the greateſt affaires of war & peace, theſe be all high ſubieĉtes, and therefore are deliuered oüer to the Poets *Hymnick* & hiſtoricall who be occupied either in diuine laudes, or in *heroicall* reports: the meane matters be thoſe that cōcerne meane men, their life and buſines, as lawyers, gentlemen, and marchants, good houſholders and honeſt Citizens, and which ſound neither to matters of ſtate nor of warre, nor leagues, nor great alliances, but ſmatch all the common conuerſation, as of the ciuiller and better ſort of men: the baſe and low matters be the doings of the commō artificer, ſeruingman, yeoman, groome, husbandman, day-labourer, ſailer, ſhepheard, ſwynard, and ſuch like of homely calling, degree and bringing vp: ſo that in euery of the ſayd three degrees, not the ſelfe ſame vertues be egally to be prayſed nor the ſame vices, egally to be diſpraiſed, nor their loues, mariages, quarels, contraĉts and other behauiours, be

(152)

like high nor do require to be fet fourth with the like
ftile: but euery one in his degree and decencie, which
made that all *hymnes* and hiftories, and Tragedies, were
written in the high ftile: all Comedies and Enterludes
and other common Poefies of loues, and fuch like in
the meane ftile, all *Eglogues* and paftorall poemes in the
low and bafe ftile, otherwife they had bene vtterly dif-
proporcioned: likewife for the fame caufe fome phrafes
and figures be onely peculiar to the high ftile, fome to
the bafe or meane, fome common to all three, as fhalbe
declared more at large hereafter when we come to fpeake
of figure and phrafe: alfo fome wordes and fpeaches and
fentences doe become the high ftile, that do not become
th'other two. And contrariwife, as fhalbe faid when we
talke of words and fentences: finally fome kinde of
meafure and concord, doe not befeeme the high ftile,
that well become the meane and low, as we haue faid
fpea-/king of concord and meafure. But generally the S ij^v
high ftile is difgraced and made foolifh and ridiculous
by all wordes affected, counterfait, and puffed vp, as it
were a windball carrying more countenance then matter,
and can not be better refembled then to thefe midfommer
pageants in London, where to make the people wonder
are fet forth great and vglie Gyants marching as if they
were aliue, and armed at all points, but within they are
ftuffed full of browne paper and tow, which the fhrewd
boyes vnderpeering, do guilefully difcouer and turne to
a great derifion: alfo all darke and vnaccuftomed wordes,
or rufticall and homely, and fentences that hold too much
of the mery & light, or infamous & vnfhamefaft are to
be accounted of the fame fort, for fuch fpeaches become
not Princes, nor great eftates, nor them that write of
their doings to vtter or report and intermingle with the
graue and weightie matters.

CHAP. VII.

Of Figures and figuratiue speaches.

As figures be the inftruments of ornament in euery language, fo be they alfo in a forte abufes or rather trefpaffes
in fpeach, becaufe they paffe the ordinary limits of common vtterance, and be occupied of purpofe to deceiue
the eare and alfo the minde, drawing it from plainneffe
and fimplicitie to a certaine doubleneffe, whereby our
talke is the more guilefull & abufing, for what els is
your *Metaphor* but an inuerfion of fence by tranfport;
your *allegorie* by a duplicitie of meaning or diffimulation
vnder couert and darke intendments: one while fpeaking
obfcurely and in riddle called *Ænigma:* another while
by common prouerbe or Adage called *Paremia:* then by
merry fkoffe called *Ironia:* then by bitter tawnt called
Sarcafmus: then by periphrafe or circumlocution when
all might be faid in a word or two: then by incredible
comparifon giuing credit, as by your *Hyperbole*, and
many other waies feeking to inueigle and appaffionate
the mind: which thing made the graue iudges *Areopagites*
(as I find written) to forbid all manner of figuratiue
fpeaches to be vfed before them in their confiftorie of
Iuftice, as meere illufions to the minde, and wrefters
of vpright iudgement, faying that to allow fuch manner
of forraine & coulored talke to make the iudges affec-
S iijr tioned, were/all one as if the carpenter before he began
to fquare his timber would make his fquire crooked: in
fo much as the ftraite and vpright mind of a Iudge is
the very rule of iuftice till it be peruerted by affection.
This no doubt is true and was by them grauely confidered: but in this cafe becaufe our maker or Poet is
appointed not for a iudge, but rather for a pleader, and
that of pleafant & louely caufes and nothing perillous,
fuch as be thofe for the triall of life, limme, or liuely-
hood; and before iudges neither fower nor feuere, but

in the eare of princely dames, yong ladies, gentlewomen and courtiers, beyng all for the moſt part either meeke of nature, or of pleaſant humour, and that all his abuſes tende but to diſpoſe the hearers to mirth and ſollace by pleaſant conueyance and efficacy of ſpeach, they are not in truth to be accompted vices but for vertues in the poetical ſcience very cōmendable. On the other ſide, ſuch treſpaſſes in ſpeach (whereof there be many) as geue dolour and diſliking to the eare & minde, by any foule indecencie or diſproportion of ſound, ſituation, or ſence, they be called and not without cauſe the vicious parts or rather hereſies of language: wherefore the matter reſteth much in the definition and acceptance of this word [*decorum*] for whatſoeuer is ſo, cannot iuſtly be miſliked. In which reſpeƈt it may come to paſſe that what the Grammarian ſetteth downe for a viciofitee in ſpeach may become a vertue and no vice, contrariwiſe his commended figure may fall into a reprochfull fault: the beſt and moſt aſſured remedy whereof is, generally to follow the ſaying of *Bias: ne quid nimis*. So as in keeping meaſure, and not exceeding nor ſhewing any defeƈt in the vſe of his figures, he cannot lightly do amiſſe, if he haue beſides (as that muſt needes be) a ſpeciall regard to all circumſtances of the perſon, place, time, cauſe and purpoſe he hath in hand, which being well obſerued it eaſily auoideth all the recited incon- ueniences, and maketh now and then very vice goe for a formall vertue in the exerciſe of this Arte.

CHAP. VIII.

Sixe points ſet downe by our learned forefathers for a generall regiment of all good vtterance be it by mouth or by writing.

But before there had bene yet any preciſe obſeruation made of figuratiue ſpeeches, the firſt learned artificers of language con-/ſidered that the bewtie and good grace S iijᵛ

(155)

of vtterance refted in no many pointes: and whatfoeuer tranfgreffed thofe lymits, they counted it for vitious; and thereupon did fet downe a manner of regiment in all fpeech generally to be obferued, confifting in fixe pointes. Firft they faid that there ought to be kept a decent proportion in our writings and fpeach, which they termed *Analogia*. Secondly, that it ought to be voluble vpon the tongue, and tunable to the eare, which they called *Tafis*. Thirdly, that it were not tedioufly long, but briefe and compendious, as the matter might beare, which they called *Syntomia*. Fourthly, that it fhould cary an orderly and good conftruction, which they called *Synthefis*. Fiftly, that it fhould be a found, proper and naturall fpeach, which they called *Ciriologia*. Sixtly, that it fhould be liuely & ftirring, which they called *Tropus*. So as it appeareth by this order of theirs, that no vice could be committed in fpeech, keeping within the bounds of that reftraint. But fir, all this being by them very well conceiued, there remayned a greater difficultie to know what this proportion, volubilitie, good conftruction, & the reft were, otherwife we could not be euer the more relieued. It was therefore of neceffitie that a more curious and particular defcription fhould bee made of euery manner of fpeech, either tranfgreffing or agreeing with their faid generall prefcript. Whereupon it came to paffe, that all the commendable parts of fpeech were fet foorth by the name of figures, and all the illaudable partes vnder the name of vices, or viciofities, of both which it fhall bee fpoken in their places.

CHAP. IX.

How the Greeks first, and afterward the Latines, inuented new names for euery figure, which this Author is alfo enforced to doo in his vulgar.

The Greekes were a happy people for the freedome & liberty of their language, becaufe it was allowed thē

to inuēt any new name that they lifted, and to peece
many words together to make of them one entire, much
more fignificatiue than the fingle word. So among other
things did they to their figuratiue fpeeches deuife certaine names. The Latines came fomewhat behind them
in that/point, and for want of conuenient fingle wordes S iiijʳ
to expreffe that which the Greeks could do by cobling
many words together, they were faine to vfe the Greekes
ftill, till after many yeares that the learned Oratours and
good Grammarians among the Romaines, as *Cicero*,
Varro, *Quintilian*, & others ftrained themfelues to giue
the Greeke wordes Latin names, and yet nothing fo apt
and fitty. The fame courfe are we driuen to follow in
this defcription, fince we are enforced to cull out for
the vfe of our Poet or maker all the moft commendable
figures. Now to make them knowen (as behoueth)
either we muft do it by th'originall Greeke name or by
the Latine, or by our owne. But when I confider to
what fort of Readers I write, & how ill faring the Greeke
terme would found in the Englifh eare, then alfo how
fhort the Latines come to expreffe manie of the Greeke
originals. Finally, how well our language ferueth to
fupplie the full fignification of them both, I haue thought
it no leffe lawfull, yea peraduenture vnder licence of the
learned, more laudable to vfe our owne naturall, if they
be well chofen, and of proper fignification, than to borrow theirs. So fhall not our Englifh Poets, though they
be to feeke of the Greeke and Latin languages, lament
for lack of knowledge fufficient to the purpofe of this
arte. And in cafe any of thefe new Englifh names giuen
by me to any figure, fhall happen to offend. I pray that
the learned will beare with me and to thinke the
ftraungeneffe thereof proceedes but of noueltie and dif-
aquaintance with our eares, which in proceffe of tyme,
and by cuftome will frame very well: and fuch others
as are not learned in the primitiue languages, if they
happen to hit vpon any new name of myne (fo ridiculous

(157)

in their opinion) as may moue them to laughter, let
fuch perfons, yet affure themfelues that fuch names go
as neare as may be to their originals, or els ferue better
to the purpofe of the figure then the very originall,
referuing alwayes, that fuch new name fhould not be
vnpleafant in our vulgar nor harfh vpon the tong: and
where it fhall happen otherwife, that it may pleafe the
reader to thinke that hardly any other name in our
Englifh could be found to ferue the turne better. Againe
if to auoid the hazard of this blame I fhould haue kept
the Greek or Latin ftill it would haue appeared a little
too fcholafticall for our makers, and a peece of worke/
S iiij^v more fit for clerkes then for Courtiers for whofe inftruction this trauaile is taken: and if I fhould haue left
out both the Greeke and Latine name, and put in none
of our owne neither: well perchance might the rule of
the figure haue bene fet downe, but no conuenient name
to hold him in memory. It was therfore expedient we
deuifed for euery figure of importance his vulgar name,
and to ioyne the Greeke or Latine originall with them;
after that fort much better fatisfying afwel the vulgar
as the learned learner, and alfo the authors owne purpofe, which is to make of a rude rimer, a learned and
a Courtly Poet.

CHAP. X.

A diuifion of figures, and how they ferue in exornation
of language.

And becaufe our chiefe purpofe herein is for the learning
of Ladies and young Gentlewomen, or idle Courtiers,
defirous to become skilful in their owne mother tongue,
and for their priuate recreation to make now & then
ditties of pleafure, thinking for our parte none other
fcience fo fit for them & the place as that which teacheth
beau femblant, the chiefe profeffiō afwell of Courting as
of poefie: fince to fuch manner of mindes nothing is

more comberfome then tedious doctrines and fchollarly
methodes of difcipline, we haue in our owne conceit
deuifed a new and ftrange modell of this arte, fitter to
pleafe the Court then the fchoole, and yet not vnnecef-
farie for all fuch as be willing themfelues to become good
makers in the vulgar, or to be able to iudge of other
mens makings: wherefore, intending to follow the courfe
which we haue begun, thus we fay: that though the
language of our Poet or maker being pure & clenly,
& not difgraced by fuch vicious parts as haue bene
before remembred in the Chapter of language, be fufficiently pleafing and commendable for the ordinarie vfe
of fpeech; yet is not the fame fo well appointed for all
purpofes of the excellent Poet, as when it is gallātly
arrayed in all his colours which figure can fet vpon it,
therefore we are now further to determine of figures
and figuratiue fpeeches. Figuratiue fpeech is a noueltie
of language euidently (and yet not abfurdly) eftranged
from the ordinarie habite and manner of our dayly talke
and wri-/ting and figure it felfe is a certaine liuely or T i⸳
good grace fet vpon wordes, fpeaches and fentences to
fome purpofe and not in vaine, giuing them ornament
or efficacie by many maner of alterations in fhape, in
founde, and alfo in fence, fometime by way of furplufage,
fometime by defect, fometime by diforder, or mutation,
& alfo by putting into our fpeaches more pithe and
fubftance, fubtilitie, quickneffe, efficacie or moderation,
in this or that fort tuning and tempring them, by amplification, abridgemēt, opening, clofing, enforcing, meek-
ening or otherwife difpofing them to the beft purpofe:
whereupon the learned clerks who haue writtē methodi-
cally of this Arte in the two mafter languages, Greeke
and Latine, haue forted all their figures into three rankes,
and the firft they beftowed vpon the Poet onely: the
fecond vpon the Poet and Oratour indifferently: the
third vpon the Oratour alone. And that firft fort of
figures doth ferue th'eare onely and may be therefore

called *Auricular:* your fecond ferues the conceit onely
and not th'eare, and may be called *fenfable*, not fenfible
nor yet fententious: your third fort ferues as well th'eare
as the conceit and may be called *fententious figures*, becaufe not only they properly apperteine to full fentences,
for bewtifying them with a currant & pleafant numerofitie, but alfo giuing them efficacie, and enlarging the
whole matter befides with copious amplifications. I doubt
not but fome bufie carpers will fcorne at my new deuifed
termes: *auricular* and *fenfable*, faying that I might with
better warrant haue vfed in their fteads thefe words,
orthographicall or *fyntaſticall*, which the learned Grammarians left ready made to our hands, and do importe
as much as th'other that I haue brought, which thing
peraduenture I deny not in part, and neuertheleffe for
fome caufes thought them not fo neceffarie: but with
thefe maner of men I do willingly beare, in refpeſt of
their laudable endeuour to allow antiquitie and flie innouation: with like beneuolence I truſt they will beare
with me writing in the vulgar fpeach and feeking by
my nouelties to fatisfie not the fchoole but the Court:
whereas they know very well all old things foone waxe
ftale & lothfome, and the new deuifes are euer dainty
and delicate, the vulgar inſtruſtion requiring alfo vulgar
and communicable termes, not clerkly or vncouthe as
T iv are all thefe of the Greeke and Latine languages/primi-
tiuely receiued, vnleffe they be qualified or by much vfe
and cuftome allowed and our eares made acquainted
with them. Thus then I fay that *auricular* figures be
thofe which worke alteration in th'eare by found, accent,
time, and flipper volubilitie in vtterance, fuch as for that
refpeſt was called by the auncients numerofitie of fpeach.
And not onely the whole body of a tale in poeme or
hiftorie may be made in fuch fort pleafant and agreable
to the eare, but alfo euery claufe by it felfe, and euery
fingle word carried in a claufe, may haue their pleafant
fweeteneffe apart. And fo long as this qualitie extendeth

(160)

but to the outward tuning of the ſpeach reaching no higher then th'eare and forcing the mynde little or nothing, it is that vertue which the Greeks call *Enargia* and is the office of the *auricular* figures to performe. Therefore as the members of language at large are whole ſentences, and ſentences are compact of clauſes, and clauſes of words, and euery word of letters and ſillables, ſo is the alteration (be it but of a ſillable or letter) much materiall to the ſound and ſweeteneſſe of vtterance. Wherefore beginning firſt at the ſmalleſt alterations which reſt in letters and ſillables, the firſt ſort of our figures *auricular* we do appoint to ſingle words as they lye in language; the ſecond to clauſes of ſpeach; the third to perfit ſentences and to the whole maſſe or body of the tale be it poeme or hiſtorie written or reported.

CHAP. XI.

Of auricular figures apperteining to ſingle wordes and working by their diuers ſoundes and audible tunes alteration to the eare onely and not the mynde.

A word as he lieth in courſe of language is many wayes figured and thereby not a little altered in ſound, which conſequently alters the tune and harmonie of a meeter as to the eare. And this alteration is ſometimes by *adding* ſometimes by *rabbating* of a ſillable or letter to or from a word either in the beginning, middle or ending ioyning or vnioyning of ſillables and letters ſuppreſſing or confounding their ſeuerall ſoundes, or by miſplacing of a letter, or by cleare exchaunge of one letter for another, or by wrong ranging of the accent. And your figures of addition or ſurpluſe be three, videl. In the beginning, as to ſay: *I-doen,*/for *doon, endanger,* for T ijʳ *danger, embolden,* for *bolden.*

In the middle, as to ſay *renuers,* for *reuers, meeterly,* for *meetly, goldylockes,* for *goldlockes.* ·

(161)

In th'end, as to fay [*remembren*] for [*remembre*] [*fpoken*] for [*fpoke*]. And your figures of *rabbate* be as many, videl.

From the beginning, as to fay [*twixt* for *betwixt*] [*gainfay* for *againefay:*] [*ill* for *euill:*]

From the middle, as to fay [*paraunter* for *parauenture*] *poorety* for *pouertie*] *fouraigne* for *foueraigne*] *tane* for *taken*.]

From the end, as to fay [*morne* for *morning*] *bet* for *better*] and fuch like.

Your fwallowing or eating vp one letter by another is when two vowels meete, whereof th'ones found goeth into other, as to fay for *to attaine t'attaine*] for *forrow* and *fmart for'* and *fmart*.]

Your difplacing of a fillable as to fay [*defier* for *defire*.] *fier* for *fire*.]

By cleare exchaunge of one letter or fillable for another, as to fay *euermare* for *euermore, wrang* for *wrong: gould* for *gold: fright* for *fraight* and a hundred moe, which be commonly mifufed and ftrained to make rime.

By wrong ranging the accent of a fillable by which meane a fhort fillable is made long and a long fhort as to fay *fouerdine* for *fouéraine: gratíous* for *grátious: éndure* for *endúre: Salómon* for *Sálomon*.

Thefe many wayes may our maker alter his wordes, and fometimes it is done for pleafure to giue a better found, fometimes vpon neceffitie, and to make vp the rime. But our maker muft take heed that he be not to bold fpecially in exchange of one letter for another, for vnleffe vfuall fpeach and cuftome allow it, it is a fault and no figure, and becaufe thefe be figures of the fmalleft importaunce, I forbeare to giue them any vulgar name.

CHAP. XII.

Of Auricular figures pertaining to claufes of fpeech and by them working no little alteration to the eare.

As your fingle words may be many waies trāsfigured to make the meetre or verfe more tunable and melodious, fo alfo may/your whole and entire claufes be in fuch fort contriued by the order of their conftruction as the eare may receiue a certaine recreation, although the mind for any noueltie of fence be little or nothing affected. And therefore al your figures of *grammaticall* conftruction, I accompt them but merely *auricular* in that they reach no furder then the eare. To which there will appeare fome fweete or vnfauery point to offer you dolour or delight, either by fome euident defect, or furplufage, or diforder, or immutation in the fame fpeaches notably altering either the congruitie *grammaticall*, or the fence, or both. And firft of thofe that worke by defect, if but one word or fome little portion of fpeach be wanting, it may be fupplied by ordinary vnderftanding and vertue of the figure *Eclipfis*, as to fay, *fo early a man*, for [*are ye*] fo early a man: he is to be intreated, for he is [*eafie*] to be intreated: I thanke God I am to liue like a Gentleman, for I am [*able*] to liue, and the Spaniard faid in his deuife of armes *acuerdo oluido*, I remember I forget whereas in right congruitie of fpeach it fhould be. I remember [that I [*doo*] forget. And in a deuife of our owne [*empechement pur a choifon*] a let for a furderance whereas it fhould be faid [*vfe*] a let for a furderance, and a number more like fpeaches defectiue, and fupplied by common vnderftanding.

But if it be to mo claufes then one, that fome fuch word be fupplied to perfit the congruitie or fence of them all, it is by the figure [*Zeugma*] we call him the [*fingle fupplie*] becaufe by one word we ferue many claufes of one congruitie, and may be likened to the man

Eclipfis or the Figure of default.

Zeugma or the Singlefupply.

(163)

that ferues many maifters at once, but all of one country or kinred: as to fay.

Fellowes and friends and kinne forfooke me quite.

Here this word forfooke fatisfieth the congruitie and fence of all three claufes, which would require euery of them afmuch. And as we fetting forth her Maiefties regall petigree, faid in this figure of [*Single fupplie.*]

Her graundfires Father and Brother was a King
Her mother a crowned Queene, her Sifter and her felfe.

Whereas ye fee this one word [*was*] ferues them all in that they require but one congruitie and fence.

Yet hath this figure of [*Single fupply*] another pro-pertie, occa-/fioning him to change now and then his name: by the order of his fupplie, for if it be placed in the forefront of all the feuerall claufes whom he is to ferue as a common feruitour, then is he called by the Greeks *Prozeugma*, by vs the Ringleader: thus

Her beautie perft mine eye, her fpeach mine wofull hart:
Her prefence all the powers of my difcourfe. &c.

Where ye fee this one word [*perft*] placed in the fore-ward, fatisfieth both in fence & congruitie all thofe other claufes that followe him.

And if fuch word of fupplie be placed in the middle of all fuch claufes as he ferues: it is by the Greeks called *Mezozeugma*, by vs the [*Middlemarcher*] thus:

Faire maydes beautie (alack) with yeares it weares away,
And with wether and ficknes, and forrow as they fay.

Where ye fee this word [*weares*] ferues one claufe before him, and two claufes behind him, in one and the fame fence and congruitie. And in this verfe,

Either the troth or talke nothing at all.

Where this word [*talke*] ferues the claufe before and alfo behind. But if fuch fupplie be placed after all the claufes, and not before nor in the middle, then is he

T iij^r

Prozeugma,
or the
Ringleader.

Mezozeugma
or the
Middle mar-
cher.

called by the Greeks *Hypozeugma,* and by vs the [*Rere-*
warder] thus:

> *My mates that vvont, to keepe me companie,*
> *And my neighbours, vvho dvvelt next to my vvall,*
> *The friends that fvvare, they vvould not sticke to die*
> *In my quarrell: they are fled from me all.*

Where ye fee this word [*fled from me*] ferue all the
three claufes requiring but one congruitie & fence. But
if fuch want be in fundrie claufes, and of feuerall con-
gruities or fence, and the fupply be made to ferue them
all, it is by the figure *Sillepfis,* whom for that refpect
we call the [*double fupplie*] conceiuing, and, as it were,
comprehending vnder one, a fupplie of two natures, and
may be likened to the man that ferues many mafters at
once, being of ftrange Countries or kinreds, as in thefe
verfes, where the lamenting widow fhewed the Pilgrim
the graues in which her husband & children lay buried./

> *Here my fweete fonnes and daughters all my bliffe,*
> *Yonder mine owne deere husband buried is.*

Where ye fee one verbe fingular fupplyeth the plurall
and fingular, and thus

> *Iudge ye louers, if it be ftrange or no:*
> *My Ladie laughs for ioy, and I for wo.*

Where ye fee a third perfon fupplie himfelfe and a
firft perfon. And thus,

> *Madame ye neuer fhewed your felfe vntrue,*
> *Nor my deferts would euer fuffer you.*

Viz. to fhow. Where ye fee the moode Indicatiue
fupply him felfe and an Infinitiue. And the like in
thefe other.

> *I neuer yet failde you in conftancie,*
> *Nor neuer doo intend vntill I die.*

Viz. [*to fail.*] Thus much for the congruitie, now for
the fence. One wrote thus of a young man, who flew

(165)

a villaine that had killed his father, and rauifhed his mother.

> *Thus valiantly and with a manly minde,*
> *And by one feate of euerlafting fame,*
> *This luftie lad fully requited kinde,*
> *His fathers death, and eke his mothers fhame.*

Where ye fee this word [*requite*] ferue a double fence: that is to fay, to reuenge, and to fatisfie. For the parents iniurie was reuenged, and the duetie of nature performed or fatisfied by the childe. But if this fupplie be made to fundrie claufes, or to one claufe fundrie times iterated, and by feuerall words, fo as euery claufe hath his owne *Hypozeuxis.* fupplie: then is it called by the Greekes *Hypozeuxis*, we or the call him the fubftitute after his originall, and is a fupplie Subftitute. with iteration, as thus:

> *Vnto the king fhe went, and to the king fhe faid,*
> *Mine owne liege Lord behold thy poore handmaid.*

Here [*went to the king*] and [*faid to the king*] be but one claufe iterated with words of fundrie fupply. Or as in thefe verfes following.

> *My Ladie gaue me, my Lady wift not vvhat,*
> *Geuing me leaue to be her Soueraine:*
> *For by fuch gift my Ladie hath done that,*
> *Which vvhileft fhe liues fhe may not call againe.|*

T iiijʳ Here [*my Ladie gaue*] and [*my Ladie vvift*] be fup- plies with iteration, by vertue of this figure.

Ye haue another *auricular* figure of defect, and is when we begin to fpeake a thing, and breake of in the middle way, as if either it needed no further to be fpoken of, or that we were afhamed, or afraide to fpeake it out. It is alfo fometimes done by way of threatning, and to fhew a moderation of anger. The Greekes call him *Apofiopefis.* *Apofiopefis.* I, the figure of filence, or of interruption, or the Figure indifferently. of filēce

If we doo interrupt our fpeech for feare, this may

(166)

be an example, where as one durſt not make the true
report as it was, but ſtaid halfe way for feare of offence,
thus:

He ſaid you were, I dare not tell you plaine:
For words once out, neuer returne againe.

If it be for ſhame, or that the ſpeaker ſuppoſe it would
be indecent to tell all, then thus: as he that ſaid to his
ſweete hart, whom he checked for ſecretly whiſpering
with a ſuſpeſted perſon.

And did ye not come by his chamber dore?
And tell him that: goe to, I ſay no more.

If it be for anger or by way of manace or to ſhow a
moderatiō of wrath as the graue and diſcreeter ſort of
men do, then thus.

If I take you with ſuch another caſt
I ſweare by God, but let this be the laſt.

Thinking to haue ſaid further viz. I will puniſh you.
If it be for none of all theſe cauſes but vpon ſome
ſodaine occaſion that moues a man to breake of his tale,
then thus.

He told me all at large: lo yonder is the man
Let himſelfe tell the tale that beſt tell can.

This figure is fit for phantaſticall heads and ſuch as
be ſodaine or lacke memorie. I know one of good
learning that greatly blemiſheth his diſcretion with this
maner of ſpeach: for if he be in the graueſt matter of
the world talking, he will vpon the ſodaine for the flying
of a bird ouerthwart the way, or ſome other ſuch ſleight
cauſe, interrupt his tale and neuer returne to it againe.
Ye haue yet another maner of ſpeach purporting at
the firſt bluſh a defeſt which afterward is ſupplied, *Prolepſis.*
the Greekes call him *Prolepſis*, we the Propounder, or or the
the Explaner which ye will: becauſe he workes both Propounder.
effeſtes, as thus, where in certaine verſes we/deſcribe T iiijᵛ

(167)

the triumphant enter-view of two great Princeſſes thus.

> *Theſe two great Queenes, came marching hand in hand,*
> *Vnto the hall, where ſtore of Princes ſtand:*
> *And people of all countreys to behold,*
> *Coronis all clad, in purple cloth of gold:*
> *Celiar in robes, of ſiluer tiſſew vvhite,*
> *With rich rubies, and pearles all bedighte.*

Here ye ſee the firſt propoſition in a ſort defeſtiue and of imperfeſt ſence, till ye come by diuiſion to explane and enlarge it, but if we ſhould follow the originall right, we ought rather to call him the foreſtaller, for like as he that ſtandes in the market way, and takes all vp before it come to the market in groſſe and ſells it by retaile, ſo by this maner of ſpeach our maker ſetts down before all the matter by a brief propoſition, and afterward explanes it by a diuiſion more particularly.

By this other example it appeares alſo.

> *Then deare Lady I pray you let it bee,*
> *That our long loue may lead vs to agree:*
> *Me ſince I may not vved you to my vvife,*
> *To ſerue you as a miſtreſſe all my life:*
> *Ye that may not me for your husband haue,*
> *To clayme me for your ſeruant and your ſlaue.*

CHAP. XII. [XIII]

Of your figures Auricular vvorking by diſorder.

To all their ſpeaches which wrought by diſorder the *Hiperbaton,* Greekes gaue a general name [*Hiperbaton*] as much *or the* to ſay as the [*treſpaſſer*] and becauſe ſuch diſorder may *Treſpaſſer.* be committed many wayes it receiueth ſundry particulars vnder him, whereof ſome are onely proper to the Greekes and Latines and not to vs, other ſome ordinarie in our maner of ſpeaches, but ſo foule and intollerable as I will not ſeeme to place them among the figures, but do

raunge thē as they deſerue among the vicious or faultie
ſpeaches.

Your firſt figure of tollerable diſorder is [*Parentheſis*]
or by an Engliſh name the [*Inſertour*] and is when ye
will ſeeme for larger information or ſome other purpoſe,
to peece or graffe in the middeſt of your tale an vn-
neceſſary parcell of ſpeach, which neuerthe-/leſſe may
be thence without any detriment to the reſt. The figure
is ſo common that it needeth none example, neuertheleſſe becauſe we are to teache Ladies and Gentlewomen
to know their ſchoole points and termes appertaining
to the Art, we may not refuſe to yeeld examples euen
in the plaineſt caſes, as that of maiſter *Diars* very aptly.

Parentheſis.
or the
Inſertour.

V iʳ

> *But novv my Deere (for ſo my loue makes me to call you ſtill)*
> *That loue I ſay, that luckleſſe loue, that vvorks me all this ill.*

Alſo in our Eglogue intituled *Elpine*, which we made
being but eightene yeares old, to king *Edvvard* the ſixt
a Prince of great hope, we ſurmiſed that the Pilot of a
ſhip anſwering the King, being inquiſitiue and deſirous
to know all the parts of the ſhip and tackle, what they
were, & to what vſe they ſerued, vſing this inſertion or
Parentheſis.

> *Soueraigne Lord (for vvhy a greater name*
> *To one on earth no mortall tongue can frame*
> *No ſtatelie ſtile can giue the practiſd penne:*
> *To one on earth conuerſant among men.)*

And ſo proceedes to anſwere the kings queſtion?

> *The ſhippe thou ſeeſt ſayling in ſea ſo large, &c.*

This inſertion is very long and vtterly impertinent
to the principall matter, and makes a great gappe in the
tale, neuertheleſſe is no diſgrace but rather a bewtie and
to very good purpoſe, but you muſt not vſe ſuch inſer-
tions often nor to thick, nor thoſe that bee very long as
this of ours, for it will breede great confuſion to haue
the tale ſo much interrupted.

(169)

Hifteron proteron, or the Prepofterous.

Ye haue another manner of difordered fpeach, when ye mifplace your words or claufes and fet that before which fhould be behind, *& è conuerfo,* we call it in Englifh prouerbe, the cart before the horfe, the Greeks call it *Hifteron proteron,* we name it the Prepofterous, and if it be not too much vfed is tollerable inough, and many times fcarfe perceiueable, vnleffe the fence be thereby made very abfurd: as he that defcribed his manner of departure from his miftreffe, faid thus not much to be mifliked.

I kift her cherry lip and tooke my leaue:

For I tooke my leaue and kift her: And yet I cannot well fay whether a man vfe to kiffe before hee take his leaue, or take his/leaue before he kiffe, or that it be all one bufines. It feemes the taking leaue is by vfing fome fpeach, intreating licence of departure: the kiffe a knitting vp of the farewell, and as it were a teftimoniall of the licence without which here in England one may not prefume of courtefie to depart, let yong Courtiers decide this controuerfie. One defcribing his landing vpon a ftrange coaft, fayd thus prepofteroufly.

When we had climbde the clifs, and were a fhore,

Whereas he fhould haue faid by good order.

When vve vvere come a fhore and clymed had the cliffs

For one muft be on land ere he can clime. And as another faid:

My dame that bred me vp and bare me in her vvombe.

Whereas the bearing is before the bringing vp. All your other figures of diforder becaufe they rather feeme deformities then bewties of language, for fo many of them as be notorioufly vndecent, and make no good harmony, I place them in the Chapter of vices hereafter following.

CHAP. XIIII.

Of your figures Auricular that vvorke by Surplufage.

Your figures *auricular* that worke by furplufage, fuch of them as be materiall and of importaunce to the fence or bewtie of your language, I referre them to the harmonicall fpeaches of oratours among the figures rhetoricall, as be thofe of repetition, and iteration or amplification. All other forts of furplufage, I accompt rather vicious then figuratiue, & therefore not melodious as fhalbe remembred in the chapter of viciofities or faultie fpeaches.

CHAP. XV.

Of auricular figures vvorking by exchange.

Your figures that worke *auricularly* by exchange, were more obferuable to the Greekes and Latines for the braueneffe of their language, ouer that ours is, and for the multiplicitie of their Grammaticall accidents, or verball affects, as I may terme them, that is to fay, their diuers cafes, moodes, tenfes, genders, with variable terminations, by reafon whereof, they changed not the very word, but kept the word, and changed the fhape of him onely, vfing one cafe for another, or tenfe, or perfon, or gender, or number, or moode. We, hauing no fuch varietie of accidents, haue little or/no vfe of this figure. They called it *Enallage*. V ij^r

But another fort of exchange which they had, and very prety, we doe likewife vfe, not changing one word for another, by their accidents or cafes, as the *Enallage:* nor by the places, as the [*Prepofterous*] but changing their true conftruction and application, whereby the fence is quite peruerted and made very abfurd: as, he that fhould fay, for *tell me troth and lie not, lie me troth and tell not.* For *come dine vvith me and ftay not, come ftay vvith me and dine not.*

Enallage.
or the
Figure of ex-
change.

Hipallage.
or the
Changeling.

(171)

A certaine piteous louer, to moue his miſtres to com-
paſſion, wrote among other amorous verſes, this one.

Madame, I ſet your eyes before mine vvoes.

For, mine woes before your eyes, ſpoken to th'intent
to winne fauour in her ſight.

But that was pretie of a certaine ſorrie man of law,
that gaue his Client but bad councell, and yet found fault
with his fee, and ſaid: my fee, good frend, hath deſerued better coūſel. Good maſter, quoth the Client, if
your ſelfe had not ſaid ſo, I would neuer haue beleeued
it: but now I thinke as you doo. The man of law perceiuing his error, I tell thee (quoth he) my coūſel hath
deſerued a better fee. Yet of all others was that a moſt
ridiculous, but very true exchange, which the yeoman
of London vſed with his Sergeant at the Mace, who ſaid
he would goe into the countrie, and make merry a day
or two, while his man plyed his buſines at home: an
example of it you ſhall finde in our Enterlude entituled
Luſtie London: the Sergeant, for ſparing of horſ-hire,
ſaid he would goe with the Carrier on foote. That is not
for your worſhip, ſaide his yeoman, whereunto the
Sergeant replyed.

I vvot vvhat I meane Iohn, it is for to ſtay
And company the knaue Carrier, for looſing my vvay.

The yeoman thinking it good manner to ſoothe his
Sergeant, ſaid againe,

I meane vvhat I vvot Sir, your beſt is to hie,
And carrie a knaue vvith you for companie.

Ye ſee a notorious exchange of the conſtruction, and
application of the words in this: *I vvot vvhat I meane;*
and *I meane vvhat I vvot,* and in the other, *company the
knaue Carrier,* and *carrie a knaue in your company.* The
V ijᵛ Greekes call this figure [*Hipallage*]/the Latins *Sub-
mutatio,* we in our vulgar may call him the [*vnderchange*]

(172)

but I had rather haue him called the [*Changeling*] nothing
at all fweruing from his originall, and much more aptly
to the purpofe, and pleafanter to beare in memory:
fpecially for our Ladies and pretie miftreffes in Court,
for whofe learning I write, becaufe it is a terme often
in their mouthes, and alluding to the opinion of Nurfes,
who are wont to fay, that the Fayries vfe to fteale the
faireft children out of their cradles, and put other ill
fauoured in their places, which they called chāgelings,
or Elfs: fo, if ye mark, doeth our Poet, or maker play
with his wordes, vfing a wrong conftruction for a right,
and an abfurd for a fenfible, by manner of exchange.

CHAP. XVI

*Of fome other figures vvhich becaufe they ferue chiefly to
make the meeters tunable and melodious, and affect
not the minde but very little, be placed
among the auricular.*

The Greekes vfed a manner of fpeech or writing in their
profes, that went by claufes, finifhing in words of like
tune, and might be by vfing like cafes, tenfes, and other
points of confonance, which they called *Omoioteleton*,
and is that wherin they neereft approched to our vulgar
ryme, and may thus be expreffed.

*Omoioteleton,
or the
Like loofe.*

> *Weeping creeping befeeching I vvan,*
> *The loue at length of Lady Lucian.*

Or thus if we fpeake in profe and not in meetre.

> *Mifchaunces ought not to be lamented,*
> *But rather by vvifedome in time preuented:*
> *For fuch mifhappes as be remedileffe,*
> *To forrovv them it is but foolifhneffe:*
> *Yet are vve all fo frayle of nature,*
> *As to be greeued vvith euery difpleafure.*

The craking Scotts as the Cronicle reportes at a certaine time made this bald rime vpon the Englifh-men.

> *Long beards hartleffe,*
> *Painted hoodes vvitleffe:*
> *Gay coates graceleffe,*
> *Make all England thriftleffe.*|

V iij^r Which is no perfit rime in deede, but claufes finifhing
in the felf fame tune: for a rime of good fimphonie
fhould not conclude his concords with one & the fame
terminant fillable, as *leff, leff, leff,* but with diuers and
like terminants, as *les, pref, mef,* as was before declared
in the chapter of your cadences, and your claufes in
profe fhould neither finifh with the fame nor with the
like terminants, but with the contrary as hath bene
fhewed before in the booke of proportions; yet many
vfe it otherwife, neglecting the Poeticall harmonie and
skill. And th'Earle of *Surrey* with Syr *Thomas Wyat*
the moft excellēt makers of their time, more peraduenture refpecting the fitneffe and ponderofitie of their
wordes then the true cadence or fimphonie, were very
licencious in this point. We call this figure following the
originall, the [*like loofe*] alluding to th'Archers terme
who is not faid to finifh the feate of his fhot before he
giue the loofe, and deliuer his arrow from his bow, in
which refpect we vfe to fay marke the loofe of a thing
for marke the end of it.

Parimion,
or the
Figure of like
letter. Ye do by another figure notably affect th'eare when
ye make euery word of the verfe to begin with a like
letter, as for example in this verfe written in an *Epithaphe*
of our making.

> *Time tried his truth his trauailes and his truft,*
> *And time to late tried his integritie.*

It is a figure much vfed by our common rimers, and
doth well if it be not too much vfed, for then it falleth into
the vice which fhalbe hereafter fpoken of called *Tautologia.*
Ye haue another fort of fpeach in a maner defectiue

becaufe it wants good band or coupling, and is the figure [*Afyndeton*] we call him [*loofe language*] and doth not a litle alter th'eare as thus.

> *I favv it, I faid it, I vvill fvveare it.*

Cæfar the Dictator vpon the victorie hee obteined againſt *Pharnax* king of *Bithinia* ſhewing the celeritie of his conqueſt, wrate home to the Senate in this tenour of ſpeach no leſſe ſwift and ſpeedy then his victorie.

> *Veni, vidi, vici,*
> *I came, I favv, I ouercame.*

Meaning thus I was no ſooner come and beheld them but the victorie fell on my ſide./

The Prince of Orenge for his deuiſe of Armes in banner diſplayed againſt the Duke of Alua and the Spaniards in the Low-countrey vſed the like maner of ſpeach.

> *Pro Rege, pro lege, pro grege,*
> *For the king, for the commons, for the countrey lavves.*

It is a figure to be vſed when we will ſeeme to make haſt, or to be earneſt, and theſe examples with a number more be ſpoken by the figure of [*lofe language.*]

Quite contrary to this ye haue another maner of con-ſtruction which they called [*Polifindeton*] we may call him the [*couple claufe*] for that euery clauſe is knit and coupled together with a coniunctiue thus.

> *And I favv it, and I fay it and I*
> *Will fvveare it to be true.*

So might the Poeſie of *Cæfar* haue bene altered thus.

> *I came, and I favv, and I ouercame.*

One wrote theſe verſes after the ſame ſort.

> *For in her mynde no thought there is,*
> *But hovv fhe may be true iwis:*
> *And tenders thee and all thy heale,*
> *And vvifheth both thy health and vveale:*
> *And is thine ovvne, and fo fhe fayes,*
> *And cares for thee ten thoufand vvayes.*

Ye haue another maner of fpeach drawen out at length and going all after one tenure and with an imperfit fence till you come to the laft word or verfe which cōcludes the whole premiffes with a perfit fence & full periode, the Greeks call it *Irmus*, I call him the [*long loofe*] thus appearing in a dittie of Sir *Thomas Wyat* where he defcribes the diuers diftempers of his bed.

Irmus, or the Long loofe.

> *The restleffe ftate renuer of my fmart,*
> *The labours falue increafing my forrow:*
> *The bodies eafe and troubles of my hart,*
> *Quietour of mynde mine vnquiet foe:*
> *Forgetter of paine remembrer of my woe,*
> *The place of fleepe wherein I do but wake:*
> *Befprent with teares my bed I thee forfake.*

Ye fee here how ye can gather no perfection of fence in all this/dittie till ye come to the laft verfe in thefe wordes *my bed I thee forfake.* And in another Sonet of *Petrarcha* which was thus Englifhed by the fame Sir *Thomas Wyat.*

V iiijʳ

> *If weaker care if fodaine pale collour,*
> *If many fighes with little fpeach to plaine:*
> *Now ioy now woe, if they my ioyes distaine,*
> *For hope of fmall, if much to feare therefore,*
> *Be figne of loue then do I loue againe.*

Here all the whole fence of the dittie is fufpended till ye come to the laft three wordes, *then do I loue againe,* which finifheth the fong with a full and perfit fence.

When ye will fpeake giuing euery perfon or thing befides his proper name a qualitie by way of addition whether it be of good or of bad it is a figuratiue fpeach of audible alteration, fo is it alfo of fence as to fay.

Epitheton, or the Qualifier.

> *Fierce Achilles, wife Neftor wilie Vlyffes,*
> *Diana the chaft and thou louely Venus:*
> *With thy blind boy that almoft neuer miffes,*
> *But hits our hartes when he leuels at vs.*

(176)

Or thus commending the Ifle of great Brittaine.

> *Albion hugefl of Wefterne Ilands all,*
> *Soyle of fweete ayre and of good ftore:*
> *God fend we fee thy glory neuer fall,*
> *But rather dayly to grow more and more.*

Or as we fang of our Soueraigne Lady giuing her
thefe Attributes befides her proper name.

> *Elizabeth regent of the great Brittaine Ile,*
> *Honour of all regents and of Queenes.*

But if we fpeake thus not expreffing her proper name
Elizabeth, videl.

> *The Englifh Diana, the great Britton mayde.*

Then is it not by *Epitheton* or figure of Attribution
but by the figures *Antonomafia,* or *Periphrafis.*

Ye haue yet another manner of fpeach when ye will *Endiadis,*
feeme to make two of one not thereunto conftrained, or the
which therefore we call the figure of Twynnes, the Twinnes.
Greekes *Endiadis* thus.

> *Not you coy dame your lowrs nor your lookes.*/

For [*your lowring lookes.*] And as one of our ordinary V iiij˅
rimers faid.

> *Of fortune nor her frowning face,*
> *I am nothing agaft.*

In ftead, of [*fortunes frowning face.*] One prayfing
the Neapolitans for good men at armes, faid by the
figure of Twynnes thus.

> *A proud people and wife and valiant,*
> *Fiercely fighting with horfes and with barbes:*
> *By whofe provves the Romain Prince did daunt,*
> *Wild Affricanes and the lavvleffe Alarbes:*
> *The Nubiens marching vvith their armed cartes,*
> *And fleaing a farre vvith venim and vvith dartes.*

Where ye fee this figure of Twynnes twife vfed, once when he faid *horfes and barbes* for barbd horfes: againe when he faith with *venim* and with *dartes* for venimous dartes.

CHAP. XVI. [*XVII*]

Of the figures which we call Senfable, becaufe they alter and affect the minde by alteration of fence, and firft in fingle wordes.

The eare hauing receiued his due fatisfaction by the *auricular* figures, now muft the minde alfo be ferued, with his naturall delight by figures *fenfible* fuch as by alteration of intendmentes affect the courage, and geue a good liking to the conceit. And firft, fingle words haue their fence and vnderftanding altered and figured many wayes, to wit, by tranfport, abufe, croffe-naming, new naming, change of name. This will feeme very darke to you, vnleffe it be otherwife explaned more par-
Metaphora, ticularly: and firft of *Tranfport*. There is a kinde of
or the wrefting of a fingle word from his owne right fignifica-
Figure of
tranfporte. tion, to another not fo naturall, but yet of fome affinitie or conueniencie with it, as to fay, *I cannot digeft your vnkinde words*, for I cannot take them in good part: or as the man of law faid, *I feele you not*, for I vnderftand not your cafe, becaufe he had not his fee in his hand. Or as another faid to a mouthy Aduocate, *why barkeft thou at me fo fore?* Or to call the top of a tree, or of a hill, the crowne of a tree or of a hill: for in deede *crowne* is the higheft ornament of a Princes head, made like a clofe garland, or els the top of a mans head, where the haire windes about, and becaufe fuch terme is not ap-
X i[r] plyed naturally to a tree, or to a hill, but/is tranfported from a mans head to a hill or tree, therefore it is called by *metaphore*, or the figure of *tranfport*. And three caufes moues vs to vfe this figure, one for neceffitie or want of a better word, thus:

(178)

As the drie ground that thirstes after a showr
Seemes to reioyce when it is well iwet,
And speedely brings foorth both grasse and flowr,
If lacke of sunne or seafon doo not let.

Here for want of an apter and more naturall word
to declare the drie temper of the earth, it is faid to
thirst & to reioyce, which is onely proper to liuing
creatures, and yet being fo inuerted, doth not fo much
fwerue from the true fence, but that euery man can
eafilie conceiue the meaning thereof.

Againe, we vfe it for pleafure and ornament of our
fpeach, as thus in an Epitaph of our owne making, to
the honourable memorie of a deere friend, Sir *Iohn
Throgmorton*, knight, Iuftice of Chefter, and a man of
many commendable vertues.

Whom vertue rerde, enuy hath ouerthrowen
And lodged full low, vnder this marble stone:
Ne neuer were his values fo well knowen,
Whilest he liued here, as now that he is gone.

Here thefe words, *rered*, *ouerthrowen*, and *lodged*, are
inuerted, & *metaphorically* applyed, not vpon neceffitie,
but for ornament onely, afterward againe in thefe verfes.

No sunne by day that euer faw him rest
Free from the toyles of his fo busie charge,
No night that harbourd rankor in his breast,
Nor merry moode, made reafon runne at large.

In thefe verfes the inuerfion or metaphore, lyeth in
thefe words, *faw*, *harbourd*, *run*: which naturally are
applyed to liuing things, & not to infenfible: as, the
funne, or the *night*: & yet they approch fo neere, & fo cō-
ueniently, as the fpeech is thereby made more commendable. Againe, in moe verfes of the fame Epitaph, thus.

His head a fource of grauitie and fence,
His memory a shop of ciuill arte:
His tongue a streame of fugred eloquence,
Wifdome and meekenes lay mingled in his harte,|

(179)

X iv In which verſes ye ſee that theſe words, *ſource, ſhop,*
flud, ſugred, are inuerted from their owne ſignification
to another, not altogether ſo naturall, but of much
affinitie with it.

Then alſo do we it ſometimes to enforce a ſence and
make the word more ſignificatiue: as thus,

> *I burne in loue, I freeſe in deadly hate*
> *I ſwimme in hope, and ſinke in deepe diſpaire.*

Theſe examples I haue the willinger giuē you to ſet
foorth the nature and vſe of your figure metaphore,
which of any other being choiſly made, is the moſt commendable and moſt common.

Catachreſis,
or the
Figure of
abuſe

But if for lacke of naturall and proper terme or worde
we take another, neither naturall nor proper and do
vntruly applie it to the thing which we would ſeeme
to expreſſe, and without any iuſt inconuenience, it is not
then ſpoken by this figure *Metaphore* or of *inuerſion* as
before, but by plaine abuſe, as he that bad his man go
into his library and fet him his bowe and arrowes, for
in deede there was neuer a booke there to be found,
or as one ſhould in reproch ſay to a poore man, thou
raskall knaue, where *raskall* is properly the hunters
terme giuen to young deere, leane & out of ſeaſon, and
not to people: or as one ſaid very pretily in this verſe.

> *I lent my loue to loſſe, and gaged my life in vaine.*

Whereas this worde *lent* is properly of mony or ſome
ſuch other thing, as men do commonly borrow, for vſe
to be repayed againe, and being applied to loue is vtterly
abuſed, and yet very commendably ſpoken by vertue
of this figure. For he that loueth and is not beloued
againe, hath no leſſe wrong, than he that lendeth and
is neuer repayde.

Metonimia,
or the
Miſnamer.

Now doth this vnderſtanding or ſecret conceyt reach
many times to the only nomination of perſons or things
in their names, as of men, or mountaines, ſeas, countries
and ſuch like, in which reſpect the wrōg naming, or

otherwife naming of them then is due, carieth not onely
an alteration of fence but a neceffitie of intendment
figuratiuely, as when we cal loue by the name of *Venus*,
flefhly luft by the name of *Cupid*, bicaufe they were fuppofed by the auncient poets to be authors and kindlers
of loue and luft: *Vulcane* for fire, *Ceres* for bread: *Bacchus*
for wine by the fame reafon; alfo if one fhould fay to a
skilfull craftesman knowen for a/glutton or common X ij^r
drunkard, that had fpent all his goods on riot and delicate fare.

Thy hands they made thee rich, thy pallat made thee poore.

It is ment, his trauaile and arte made him wealthie,
his riotous life had made him a beggar: and as one that
boafted of his houfekeeping, faid that neuer a yeare
paffed ouer his head, that he drank not in his houfe
euery moneth foure tonnes of beere, & one hogfhead
of wine, meaning not the caskes or veffels, but that
quantitie which they conteyned. Thefe and fuch other
fpeaches, where ye take the name of the Author for the
thing it felfe; or the thing cōteining, for that which is
contained, & in many other cafes do as it were wrong
name the perfon or the thing. So neuertheleffe as it may
be vnderftood, it is by the figure *metonymia*, or mifnamer.

And if this manner of naming of perfons or things be   *Antonomafia,*
not by way of mifnaming as before, but by a conuenient   *or the*
difference, and fuch as is true or efteemed and likely to   *Surnamer.*
be true, it is then called not *metonimia*, but *antonomafia*,
or the Surnamer, (not the mifnamer, which might ex-
tend to any other thing afwell as to a perfon) as he that
would fay: not king Philip of Spaine, but the Wefterne
king, becaufe his dominiō lieth the furdeft Weft of any
Chriften prince: and the French king the great *Vallois*,
becaufe fo is the name of his houfe, or the Queene of
England, *The maiden Queene*, for that is her hieft peculiar
among all the Queenes of the world, or as we faid in

(181)

one of our *Partheniades*, the *Bryton mayde*, becaufe fhe is the moft great and famous mayden of all Brittayne: thus,

> *But in chaste ftile, am borne as I weene*
> *To blazon foorth the Brytton mayden Queene.*

So did our forefathers call *Henry the first, Beauclerke, Edmund Ironfide, Richard cœur de lion: Edward the Confeffor*, and we of her Maieftie *Elifabeth* the peafible.

Onomatopeia, or the New namer. Then alfo is the fence figuratiue when we deuife a new name to any thing confonant, as neere as we can to the nature thereof, as to fay: *flafhing of lightning, clafhing of blades, clinking of fetters, chinking of mony:* & as the poet *Virgil* faid of the founding a trumpet, *ta-ra-tant, taratantara*, or as we giue fpecial names to the voices of dombe beafts, as to fay, a horfe neigheth, a lyō

X ijᵛ brayes, a fwine/grunts, a hen cackleth, a dogge howles, and a hundreth mo fuch new names as any man hath libertie to deuife, fo it be fittie for the thing which he couets to expreffe.

Epitheton. or the Quallifier otherwife the figure of Attribution. Your *Epitheton* or *qualifier*, whereof we fpake before, placing him among the figures *auricular*, now becaufe he ferues alfo to alter and enforce the fence, we will fay fomewhat more of him in this place, and do conclude that he muft be apt and proper for the thing he is added vnto, & not difagreable or repugnant, as one that faid: *darke difdaine*, and *miferable pride*, very abfurdly, for difdaine or difdained things cannot be faid darke, but rather bright and cleere, becaufe they be beholden and much looked vpon, and pride is rather enuied then pitied or miferable, vnleffe it be in Chriftian charitie, which helpeth not the terme in this cafe. Some of our vulgar writers take great pleafure in giuing Epithets and do it almoft to euery word which may receiue them, and fhould not be fo, yea though they were neuer fo propre and apt, for fometimes wordes fuffered to go fingle, do giue greater fence and grace than words quallified by attributions do.

(182)

But the fence is much altered & the hearers conceit *Metalepfis.* ftrangly entangled by the figure *Metalepfis*, which I call *or the Farrefet.* the *farfet*, as when we had rather fetch a word a great way off thē to vfe one nerer hād to expreffe the matter afwel & plainer. And it feemeth the deuifer of this figure, had a defire to pleafe women rather then men: for we vfe to fay by manner of Prouerbe: things farrefet and deare bought are good for Ladies: fo in this manner of fpeach we vfe it, leaping ouer the heads of a great many words, we take one that is furdeft off, to vtter our matter by: as *Medea* curfing hir firft acquaintance with prince *Iafon*, who had very vnkindly forfaken her, faid:

> *Woe worth the mountaine that the mafte bare*
> *Which was the firft caufer of all my care.*

Where fhe might afwell haue faid, woe worth our firft meeting, or woe worth the time that *Iafon* arriued with his fhip at my fathers cittie in *Colchos*, when he tooke me away with him, & not fo farre off as to curfe the mountaine that bare the pinetree, that made the maft, that bare the failes, that the fhip failed with, which caried her away. A pleafant Gentleman came into a Ladies nur-/fery, and faw her for her owne pleafure X iijʳ rocking of her young child in the cradle, and fayd to her:

> *I fpeake it Madame without any mocke,*
> *Many a fuch cradell may I fee you rocke.*

Gods paffion hourfon faid fhe, would thou haue me beare mo children yet, no *Madame* quoth the Gentle-man, but I would haue you liue long, that ye might the better pleafure your friends, for his meaning was that as euery cradle fignified a new borne childe, & euery child the leafure of one yeares birth, & many yeares a lōg life: fo by wifhing her to rocke many cradels of her owne, he wifhed her long life. *Virgill* faid:

> *Poft multas mea regna videns mirabor ariftas*

Thus in Englifh.

After many a ftubble fhall I come
And wonder at the fight of my kingdome.

By ftubble the Poet vnderftoode yeares, for haruefts come but once euery yeare, at leaft wayes with vs in Europe. This is fpoken by the figure of farre-fet. *Meta-lepfis.*

Emphafis. And one notable meane to affeĉt the minde, is to
or the inforce the fence of any thing by a word of more than
Renforcer. ordinary efficacie, and neuertheles is not apparant, but as it were, fecretly implyed, as he that faid thus of a faire Lady. *O rare beautie, ô grace, and curtefie.*

And by a very euill man thus.

O finne it felfe, not wretch, but wretchednes.

Whereas if he had faid thus, *O gratious, courteous and beautifull woman:* and, *O finfull and wretched man*, it had bene all to one effeĉt, yet not with fuch force and efficacie, to fpeake by the denominatiue, as by the thing it felfe.

As by the former figure we vfe to enforce our fence, fo by another we temper our fence with wordes of fuch moderation, as in appearaunce it abateth it but not in
Liptote. deede, and is by the figure *Liptote*, which therefore I call
or the the *Moderator*, and becomes vs many times better to fpeake
Moderatour. in that fort quallified, than if we fpake it by more forcible termes, and neuertheles is equipolent in fence, thus.

I know you hate me not, nor wifh me any ill.|

X iij^v Meaning in deede that he loued him very well and dearely, and yet the words doe not expreffe fo much, though they purport fo much. Or if you would fay, I am not ignorant, for I know well inough. Such a man is no foole, meaning in deede that he is a very wife man.

Paradiaftole, But if fuch moderation of words tend to flattery, or
or the foothing, or excufing, it is by the figure *Paradiaftole*,
Curry fauell. which therfore nothing improperly we call the *Curry-fauell*, as when we make the beft of a bad thing, or turne

(184)

a fignification to the more plaufible fence: as, to call an
vnthrift, a liberall Gentleman: the foolifh-hardy, valiant
or couragious: the niggard, thriftie: a great riot, or
outrage, an youthfull pranke, and fuch like termes:
moderating and abating the force of the matter by craft,
and for a pleafing purpofe, as appeareth by thefe verfes
of ours, teaching in what cafes it may commendably
be vfed by Courtiers.

But if you diminifh and abbafe a thing by way of *Meiofis,*
fpight or mallice, as it were to depraue it, fuch fpeach or the
is by the figure *Meiofis* or the *difabler* fpoken of hereafter Difabler.
in the place of *fententious* figures.

> *A great mountaine as bigge as a molehill,*
> *A heauy burthen perdy, as a pound of fethers.*

But if ye abafe your thing or matter by ignorance or *Tapinofis,*
errour in the choife of your word, then is it by vicious or the
maner of fpeach called *Tapinofis,* whereof ye fhall haue Abbafer.
examples in the chapter of vices hereafter folowing.

Then againe if we vfe fuch a word (as many times *Synecdoche,*
we doe) by which we driue the hearer to conceiue more or the
or leffe or beyond or otherwife then the letter expreffeth, Figure of
and it be not by vertue of the former figures *Metaphore* quick con-
and *Abafe* and the reft, the Greeks then call it *Synecdoche,* ceite.
the Latines *fub intellectio* or vnderftanding, for by part
we are enforced to vnderftand the whole, by the whole
part, by many things one thing, by one, many, by a
thing precedent, a thing confequent, and generally one
thing out of another by maner of contrariety to the
word which is fpoken, *aliud ex alio,* which becaufe it
feemeth to aske a good, quick, and pregnant capacitie,
and is not for an ordinarie or dull wit fo to do, I chofe
to call him the figure not onely of conceit after the
Greeke originall, but alfo of quick conceite. As for
example we will giue none becaufe we/will fpeake of X iiij^r
him againe in another place, where he is ranged among
the figures *fenfable* apperteining to claufes.

CHAP. XVIII.

Of senfable figures altering and affecting the mynde by alteration of fence or intendements in whole claufes or fpeaches.

As by the laft remembred figures the fence of fingle wordes is altered, fo by thefe that follow is that of whole and entier fpeach: and firft by the Courtly figure *Allegoria*, which is when we fpeake one thing and thinke another, and that our wordes and our meanings meete not. The vfe of this figure is fo large, and his vertue of fo great efficacie as it is fuppofed no man can pleafantly vtter and perfwade without it, but in effect is fure neuer or very feldome to thriue and profper in the world, that cannot fkilfully put in vre, in fomuch as not onely euery common Courtier, but alfo the graueft Counfellour, yea and the moft noble and wifeft Prince of them all are many times enforced to vfe it, by example (fay they) of the great Emperour who had it vfually in his mouth to fay, *Qui nefcit diffimulare nefcit regnare*. Of this figure therefore which for his duplicitie we call the figure of [*falfe femblant or diffimulation*] we will fpeake firft as of the chief ringleader and captaine of all other figures, either in the Poeticall or oratorie fcience.

Allegoria, or the Figure of falfe femblant. And ye fhall know that we may diffemble, I meane fpeake otherwife then we thinke, in earneft afwell as in fport, vnder couert and darke termes, and in learned and apparant fpeaches, in fhort fentences, and by long ambage and circumftance of wordes, and finally afwell when we lye as when we tell truth. To be fhort euery fpeach wrefted from his owne naturall fignification to another not altogether fo naturall is a kinde of diffimulation, becaufe the wordes beare contrary countenaunce to th'intent. But properly & in his principall vertue *Allegoria* is when we do fpeake in fence tranflatiue and wrefted from the owne fignification, neuertheleffe applied to another not altogether contrary, but hauing much cōueniencie with it as before we ſaid of the metaphore: as for example if we ſhould call the common wealth, a ſhippe; the Prince a Pilot, the Counſellours mariners, the ſtormes warres, the calme/and [*hauen*] x iiijᵛ peace, this is ſpoken all in allegorie: and becauſe ſuch inuerſion of ſence in one ſingle worde is by the figure *Metaphore*, of whom we ſpake before, and this manner of inuerſion extending to whole and large ſpeaches, it maketh the figure *allegorie* to be called a long and perpetuall Metaphore. A noble man after a whole yeares abſence from his ladie, ſent to know how ſhe did, and whether ſhe remayned affeſted toward him as ſhe was when he left her.

Louely Lady I long full ſore to heare,
If ye remaine the ſame, I left you the laſt yeare.

To whom ſhe anſwered in *allegorie* other two verſes:

My louing Lorde I will well that ye wiſt,
The thred is ſpon, that neuer ſhall vntwiſt.

Meaning, that her loue was ſo ſtedfaſt and cōſtant toward him as no time or occaſion could alter it. *Virgill* in his ſhepeherdly poemes called *Eglogues* vſed as ruſticall but fit *allegorie* for the purpoſe thus:

Claudite iam riuos pueri ſat prata biberunt.

Which I Engliſh thus:

Stop vp your ſtreámes (my lads) the medes haue
drunk ther fill.

As much to ſay, leaue of now, yee haue talked of the matter inough: for the ſhepheards guiſe in many places is by opening certaine ſluces to water their paſtures, ſo as when they are wet inough they ſhut them againe: this application is full Allegoricke.

Ye haue another manner of Allegorie not full, but mixt, as he that wrate thus:

The cloudes of care haue coured all my coste,
The ſtormes of ſtrife, do threaten to appeare:
The waues of woe, wherein my ſhip is toste.
Haue broke the banks, where lay my life ſo deere.
Chippes of ill chance, are fallen amidſt my choiſe,
To marre the minde that ment for to reioyce.

I call him not a full Allegorie, but mixt, bicauſe he diſcouers withall what the *cloud, ſtorme, waue,* and the reſt are, which in a full allegorie ſhould not be diſcouered, but left at large to the readers iudgement and conieċture.

We diſſemble againe vnder couert and darke ſpeaches, when/we ſpeake by way of riddle (*Enigma*) of which the ſence can hardly be picked out, but by the parties owne aſſoile, as he that ſaid:

It is my mother well I wot,
And yet the daughter that I begot.

Meaning it by the iſe which is made of frozen water, the ſame being molten by the ſunne or fire, makes water againe.

My mother had an old womā in her nurſerie, who in the winter nights would put vs forth many prety ridles, whereof this is one:

I haue a thing and rough it is
And in the midſt a hole Iwis:
There came a yong man with his ginne,
And he put it a handfull in.

The good old Gentlewoman would tell vs that were children how it was meant by a furd glooue. Some other naughtie body would peraduenture haue conſtrued it not halfe ſo mannerly. The riddle is pretie but that it holdes too much of the *Cachemphaton* or foule ſpeach and may be drawen to a reprobate ſence.

(188)

We diſſemble after a ſort, when we ſpeake by cōmon prouerbs, or, as we vſe to call them, old ſaid ſawes, as thus:

Parimia, or Prouerb.

> *As the olde cocke crowes ſo doeth the chick:*
> *A bad Cooke that cannot his owne fingers lick.*

Meaning by the firſt, that the young learne by the olde, either to be good or euill in their behauiours: by the ſecond, that he is not to be counted a wiſe man, who being in authority, and hauing the adminiſtration of many good and great things, will not ſerue his owne turne and his friends whileſt he may, & many ſuch prouerbiall ſpeeches: as, *Totneſſe is turned French*, for a ſtrange alteration: *Skarborow warning*, for a ſodaine commandement, allowing no reſpeſt or delay to be-thinke a man of his buſines. Note neuertheleſſe a diuer-ſitie, for the two laſt examples be prouerbs, the two firſt prouerbiall ſpeeches.

Ye doe likewiſe diſſemble, when ye ſpeake in deriſion or mockerie, & that may be many waies: as ſometime in ſport, ſometime in earneſt, and priuily, and apertly, and pleaſantly, and bitterly: but firſt by the figure *Ironia*, which we call the *drye mock:* as he that ſaid to a bragging Ruffian, that threatened he would kill and ſlay, no doubt you are a good man of your hands: or, as it was ſaid by/a French king, to one that praide his reward, ſhewing how he had bene cut in the face at a certain battell fought in his ſeruice: ye may ſee, quoth the king, what it is to runne away & looke backwards. And as *Alphonſo* king of Naples, ſaid to one that profered to take his ring when he waſht before dinner, this wil ſerue another well: meaning that the Gentlemā had another time takē thē, & becauſe the king forgot to aske for them, neuer reſtored his ring againe.

Ironia, or the Drie mock

Y iv

Or when we deride with a certaine ſeueritie, we may call it the bitter taunt [*Sarcaſmus*] as *Charles* the fift Emperour aunſwered the Duke of Arskot, beſeeching

Sarcaſmus. or the Bitter taunt.

(189)

him recompence of feruice done at the fiege of **Renty**, againft *Henry* the French king, where the Duke was taken prifoner, and afterward efcaped clad like a Colliar. Thou wert taken, quoth the Emperour, like a coward, and fcapedft like a Colliar, wherefore get thee home and liue vpon thine owne. Or as king *Henry* the eight faid to one of his priuy chamber, who fued for Sir *Anthony Rowfe*, a knight of Norfolke that his Maieftie would be good vnto him, for that he was an ill begger. Quoth the king againe, if he be afhamed to beg, we are afhamed to geue. Or as *Charles* the fift Emperour, hauing taken in battaile *Iohn Frederike* Duke of Saxon, with the Lant-graue of Heffen and others: this Duke being a man of monftrous bigneffe and corpulence, after the Emperor had feene the prifoners, faid to thofe that were about him, I haue gone a hunting many times, yet neuer tooke I fuch a fwine before.

Afteifmus. or the Merry fcoffe. otherwife The ciuill ieft. Or when we fpeake by manner of pleafantery, or mery skoffe, that is, by a kinde of mock, whereof the fence is farre fet, & without any gall or offence. The Greekes call it [*Afteifmus*] we may terme it the ciuill ieft, becaufe it is a mirth very full of ciuilitie, and fuch as the moft ciuill men doo vfe. As *Cato* faid to one that had geuen him a good knock on the head with a long peece of timber he bare on his fhoulder, and then bad him beware: what (quoth *Cato*) wilt thou ftrike me againe? for ye know, a warning fhould be geuen before a man haue receiued harme, and not after. And as king *Edward* the fixt, being of young yeres, but olde in wit, faide to one of his priuie chamber, who fued for a pardon for one that was condemned for a robberie, telling the king that it was but a fmall trifle, not paft fixteene fhillings Yij^r matter which he had taken:/quoth the king againe, but I warrant you the fellow was forrie it had not bene fixteene pound: meaning how the malefactors intent was as euill in that trifle, as if it had bene a greater fumme of money. In thefe examples if ye marke there is no

griefe or offence miniſtred as in thoſe other before, and
yet are very wittie, and ſpoken in plaine deriſion.

The Emperor *Charles* the fift was a man of very few
words, and delighted little in talke. His brother king
Ferdinando being a man of more pleaſant diſcourſe,
ſitting at the table with him, ſaid, I pray your Maieſtie
be not ſo ſilent, but let vs talke a little. What neede that
brother, quoth the Emperor, ſince you haue words
enough for vs both.

Or when we giue a mocke with a ſcornefull countenance as in ſome ſmiling ſort looking aſide or by drawing
the lippe awry, or ſhrinking vp the noſe; the Greeks
called it *Micteriſmus*, we may terme it a fleering frumpe,
as he that ſaid to one whoſe wordes he beleued not, no
doubt Sir of that. This fleering frumpe is one of the
Courtly graces of *hicke the ſcorner*.

Or when we deride by plaine and flat contradiction,
as he that ſaw a dwarfe go in the ſtreete ſaid to his companion that walked with him: See yonder gyant: and
to a Negro or woman blackemoore, in good ſooth ye
are a faire one, we may call it the broad floute.

Or when ye giue a mocke vnder ſmooth and lowly
wordes as he that hard one call him all to nought and
ſay, thou art ſure to be hanged ere thou dye: quoth
th'other very ſoberly. Sir I know your maiſterſhip
ſpeakes but in ieſt, the Greeks call it (*charientiſmus*) we
may call it the priuy nippe, or a myld and appeaſing
mockery: all theſe be ſouldiers to the figure *allegoria*
and fight vnder the banner of diſſimulation.

Neuertheleſſe ye haue yet two or three other figures
that ſmatch a ſpice of the ſame *falſe ſemblant*, but in
another ſort and maner of phraſe, whereof one is when
we ſpeake in the ſuperlatiue and beyond the limites of
credit, that is by the figure which the Greeks call
Hiperbole, the Latines *Dementiens* or the lying figure.
I for his immoderate exceſſe cal him the ouer reacher
right with his originall or [*lowd lyar*] & me thinks not

Micteriſmus.
or the
Fleering
frūpe.

Antiphraſis.
or the
Broad floute.

Chariētiſmus.
or the
Priuy nippe.

Hiperbole.
or the
Ouer reacher,
otherwiſe
called the loud
lyer.

(191)

Y ijᵛ amiffe: now whē I fpeake that/which neither I my felfe thinke to be true, nor would haue any other body beleeue, it muft needs be a great diffimulation, becaufe I meane nothing leffe then that I fpeake, and this maner of fpeach is vfed, when either we would greatly aduaunce or greatly abafe the reputation of any thing or perfon, and muft be vfed very difcreetly, or els it will feeme odious, for although a prayfe or other report may be allowed beyōd credit, it may not be beyōd all meafure, fpecially in the profeman, as he that was fpeaker in a Parliament of king *Henry* the eights raigne, in his Oration which ye know is of ordinary to be made before the Prince at the firft affembly of both houfes, would feeme to prayfe his Maieftie thus. What fhould I go about to recite your Maiefties innumerable vertues, euen as much as if I tooke vpon me to number the ftarres of the skie, or to tell the fands of the fea. This *Hyperbole* was both *vltra fidem* and alfo *vltra modum*, and therefore of a graue and wife Counfellour made the fpeaker to be accompted a groffe flattering foole: peraduenture if he had vfed it thus, it had bene better and neuertheleffe a lye too, but a more moderate lye and no leffe to the purpofe of the kings commendation, thus. I am not able with any wordes fufficiently to expreffe your Maiefties regall vertues, your kingly merites alfo towardes vs your people and realme are fo exceeding many, as your prayfes therefore are infinite, your honour and renowne euerlafting: And yet all this if we fhall meafure it by the rule of exaȼt veritie, is but an vntruth, yet a more cleanely commendation then was maifter Speakers. Neuertheleffe as I faid before if we fall a prayfing, fpecially of our miftreffes vertue, bewtie, or other good parts, we be allowed now and then to ouer-reach a little by way of comparifon as he that faid thus in prayfe of his Lady.

> *Giue place ye louers here before,*
> *That fpent your boafts and braggs in vaine:*

My Ladies bewtie paſſeth more,
The beſt of your I dare well ſayne:
Then doth the ſunne the candle light,
Or brighteſt day the darkeſt night.

And as a certaine noble Gentlewoman laměting at the vnkindneſſe of her louer ſaid very pretily in this figure./

Y iijʳ

But ſince it will no better be,
My teares ſhall neuer blin:
To moiſt the earth in ſuch degree,
That I may drowne therein:
That by my death all men may ſay,
Lo weemen are as true as they.

Then haue ye the figure *Periphraſis*, holding ſome-what of the diſsěbler, by reaſon of a ſecret intent not appearing by the words, as when we go about the buſh, and will not in one or a few words expreſſe that thing which we deſire to haue knowen, but do choſe rather to do it by many words, as we our ſelues wrote of our Soueraigne Lady thus:

Periphraſis, or the Figure of ambage.

Whom Princes ſerue, and Realmes obay,
And greateſt of Bryton kings begot:
She came abroade euen yeſterday,
When ſuch as ſaw her, knew her not.

And the reſt that followeth, meaning her Maieſties perſon, which we would ſeeme to hide leauing her name vnſpoken, to the intent the reader ſhould geſſe at it: neuertheleſſe vpon the matter did ſo manifeſtly diſcloſe it, as any ſimple iudgement might eaſily perceiue by whom it was ment, that is by Lady *Elizabeth, Queene of England and daughter to king Henry the eight,* and therein reſteth the diſſimulation. It is one of the gal-lanteſt figures among the poetes ſo it be vſed diſcretely and in his right kinde, but many of theſe makers that be not halfe their craftes maiſters, do very often abuſe it and alſo many waies. For if the thing or perſon they

(193)

go about to defcribe by circumftance, be by the writers improuidence otherwife bewrayed, it loofeth the grace of a figure, as he that faid:

> *The tenth of March when Aries receiued,*
> *Dan Phœbus raies into his horned hed.*

Intending to defcribe the fpring of the yeare, which euery man knoweth of himfelfe, hearing the day of March named: the verfes be very good the figure nought worth, if it were meant in Periphrafe for the matter, that is the feafon of the yeare which fhould haue bene couertly difclofed by ambage, was by and by blabbed out by naming the day of the moneth, & fo the purpofe of the figure difapointed, peraduenture it had bin better to haue faid thus:/

Y iij^v
> *The month and daie when Aries receiud,*
> *Dan Phœbus raies into his horned head.*

For now there remaineth for the Reader fomewhat to ftudie and geffe vpon, and yet the fpring time to the learned iudgement fufficiently expreffed.

The Noble Earle of Surrey wrote thus:

> *In winters iuft returne, when Boreas gan his raigne,*
> *And euery tree vnclothed him faft as nature taught*
> *thē plaine.*

I would faine learne of fome good maker, whether the Earle fpake this in figure of *Periphrafe* or not, for mine owne opinion I thinke that if he ment to defcribe the winter feafon, he would not haue difclofed it fo broadly, as to fay winter at the firft worde, for that had bene againft the rules of arte, and without any good iudgement: which in fo learned & excellent a perfonage we ought not to fufpect, we fay therefore that for winter it is no *Periphrafe* but language at large: we fay for all that, hauing regard to the fecond verfe that followeth it is a *Periphrafe*, feeming that thereby he intended to fhew in what part of the winter his loues gaue him anguiſh, that is in the time which we call the fall of the leafe, which begins in the moneth of October, and ſtands very well with the figure to be vttered in that ſort notwithſtanding winter be named before, for winter hath many parts: ſuch namely as do not ſhake of the leafe, nor vncloth the trees as here is mencioned: thus may ye iudge as I do, that this noble Erle wrate excellently well and to purpoſe. Moreouer, when a maker will ſeeme to vſe circumlocution to ſet forth any thing pleaſantly and figuratiuely, yet no leſſe plaine to a ripe reader, then if it were named expreſly, and when all is done, no man can perceyue it to be the thing intended. This is a foule ouerſight in any writer as did a good fellow, who weening to ſhew his cunning, would needs by periphraſe expreſſe the realme of Scotland in no leſſe then eight verſes, and when he had ſaid all, no man could imagine it to be ſpoken of Scotland: and did beſides many other faults in his verſe, ſo deadly belie the matter by his deſcriptiō, as it would pitie any good maker to heare it.

Now for the ſhutting vp of this Chapter, will I remember you farther of that manner of ſpeech which the Greekes call *Synecdoche,* and we the figure of [*quicke conceite*] who for the reaſons be-/fore alledged, may be put vnder the ſpeeches *allegoricall,* becauſe of the darkenes and duplicitie of his ſence: as when one would tell me how the French king was ouerthrowen at Saint Quintans, I am enforced to think that it was not the king himſelfe in perſon, but the Conſtable of Fraunce with the French kings power. Or if one would ſay, the towne of Andwerpe were famiſhed, it is not ſo to be taken, but of the people of the towne of Andwerp, and this conceit being drawen aſide, and (as it were) from one thing to another, it encombers the minde with a certaine imagination what it may be that is meant, and not expreſſed: as he that ſaid to a young gentlewoman, who was in her chamber making her ſelfe vnready. Miſtreſſe will ye

Synechdoche.
or Y iiij^r the
Figure of
quick con-
ceite.

(195)

geue me leaue to vnlace your peticote, meaning (perchance) the other thing that might follow fuch vnlafing.
In the olde time, whofoeuer was allowed to vndoe his
Ladies girdle, he might lie with her all night: wherfore,
the taking of a womans maydenhead away, was faid to
vndoo her girdle. *Virgineam diffoluit zonam,* faith the
Poet, conceiuing out of a thing precedent, a thing fub-
fequent. This may fuffice for the knowledge of this
figure [*quicke conceit.*]

CHAP. XIX.

Of Figures fententious, otherwife called Rhetoricall.

Now if our prefuppofall be true, that the Poet is of all
other the moft auncient Orator, as he that by good &
pleafant perfwafions firft reduced the wilde and beaftly
people into publicke focieties and ciuilitie of life, infinuating vnto them, vnder fictions with fweete and
coloured fpeeches, many wholefome leffons and doctrines, then no doubt there is nothing fo fitte for him,
as to be furnifhed with all the figures that be *Rhetoricall,*
and fuch as do moft beautifie language with eloquence
& fententioufnes. Therfore, fince we haue already allowed to our maker his *auricular* figures, and alfo his
fenfable, by which all the words and claufes of his
meeters are made as well tunable to the eare, as ftirring
to the minde, we are now by order to beftow vpon him
thofe other figures which may execute both offices, and
all at once to beautifie and geue fence and fententioufnes
to the whole language at large. So as if we fhould in-
Y iiijᵛ treate our maker to play alfo the Orator, and/whether
it be to pleade, or to praife, or to aduife, that in all three
cafes he may vtter, and alfo perfwade both copioufly and
vehemently.

And your figures rhethoricall, befides their remembred ordinarie vertues, that is, fentētioufnes, & copious
amplification, or enlargement of language, doe alfo con-

(196)

teine a certaine fweet and melodious manner of fpeech, in which refpeᶜt, they may, after a fort, be faid *auricular:* becaufe the eare is no leffe rauifhed with their currant tune, than the mind is with their fententioufnes. For the eare is properly but an inftrument of conueyance for the minde, to apprehend the fence by the found. And our fpeech is made melodious or harmonicall, not onely by ftrayned tunes, as thofe of *Muſick*, but alfo by choife of fmoothe words: and thus, or thus, marfhalling them in their comelieft conftruᶜtion and order, and afwell by fometimes fparing, fometimes fpending them more or leffe liberally, and carrying or tranfporting of them farther off or neerer, fetting them with fundry relations, and variable formes, in the miniftery and vfe of words, doe breede no little alteration in man. For to fay truely, what els is man but his minde? which, whofoeuer haue skil to compaffe, and make yeelding and flexible, what may not he commaund the body to perfourme? He therefore that hath vanquifhed the minde of man, hath made the greateft and moft glorious conqueft. But the minde is not affailable vnleffe it be by fenfible approches, whereof the audible is of greateft force for inftruᶜtion or difcipline: the vifible, for apprehenfion of exterior knowledges as the Philofopher faith. Therefore the well tuning of your words and claufes to the delight of the eare, maketh your information no leffe plaufible to the minde than to the eare: no though you filled them with neuer fo much fence and fententioufnes. Then alfo muft the whole tale (if it tende to perfwafion) beare his iuft and reafonable meafure, being rather with the largeft, than with the fcarceft. For like as one or two drops of water perce not the flint ftone, but many and often droppings doo: fo cannot a few words (be they neuer fo pithie or fententious) in all cafes and to all manner of mindes, make fo deepe an impreffion, as a more multitude of words to the purpofe difcreetely, and without fuperfluitie vttered: the minde being no leffe vanqui-/fhed Z iʳ with large loade of fpeech, than the limmes are with heauie burden. Sweetenes of fpeech, fentence, and ampli-fication, are therfore neceffarie to an excellent Orator and Poet, ne may in no wife be fpared from any of them.

And firft of all others your figure that worketh by iteration or repetition of one word or claufe doth much alter and affect the eare and alfo the mynde of the hearer, and therefore is counted a very braue figure both with the Poets and rhetoriciens, and this repetition may be in feuen fortes.

Anaphora, or the Figure of Report. Repetition in the firft degree we call the figure of *Report* according to the Greeke originall, and is when we make one word begin, and as they are wont to fay, lead the daunce to many verfes in fute, as thus.

> *To thinke on death it is a miferie,*
> *To thinke on life it is a vanitie:*
> *To thinke on the world verily it is,*
> *To thinke that heare man hath no perfit bliffe.*

And this writtē by Sir *Walter Raleigh* of his greateft miftreffe in moft excellent verfes.

> *In vayne mine eyes in vaine you waft your teares,*
> *In vayne my fighs the fmokes of my defpaires:*
> *In vayne you fearch th'earth and heauens aboue,*
> *In vayne ye feeke, for fortune keeps my loue.*

Or as the buffon in our enterlude called *Luftie London* faid very knauifhly and like himfelfe.

> *Many a faire laffe in London towne,*
> *Many a bavvdie basket borne vp and downe:*
> *Many a broker in a thridbare gowne.*
> *Many a bankrowte fcarce worth a crowne.*
> > *In London.*

Antiftrophe, or the Counter turne. Ye haue another fort of repetition quite contrary to the former when ye make one word finifh many verfes in fute, and that which is harder, to finifh many claufes in the middeft of your verfes or dittie (for to make them

finiſh the verſe in our vulgar it ſhould hinder the rime)
and becauſe I do finde few of our Engliſh makers vſe
this figure, I haue ſet you down two litle ditties which
our ſelues in our yonger yeares played vpon the *Anti-*
ſtrophe, for ſo/is the figures name in Greeke: one vpon z iv
the mutable loue of a Lady, another vpon the meritorious
loue of Chriſt our Sauiour, thus.

> *Her lowly lookes, that gaue life to my loue,*
> *With spitefull ſpeach, curſtneſſe and crueltie:*
> *She kild my loue, let her rigour remoue,*
> *Her cherefull lights and ſpeaches of pitie*
> *Reuiue my loue: anone with great diſdaine,*
> *She ſhunnes my loue, and after by a traine*
> *She ſeekes my loue, and ſaith ſhe loues me moſt,*
> *But ſeing her loue, ſo lightly wonne and loſt:*
> *I longd not for her loue, for well I thought,*
> *Firme is the loue, if it be as it ought.*

The ſecond vpon the merites of Chriſtes paſſion toward mankind, thus,

> *Our Chriſt the ſonne of God, chief authour of all good,*
> *Was he by his allmight, that firſt created man:*
> *And vvith the coſtly price, of his moſt precious bloud,*
> *He that redeemed man: and by his instance vvan*
> *Grace in the ſight of God, his onely father deare,*
> *And reconciled man: and to make man his peere*
> *Made himſelfe very man: brief to conclude the caſe,*
> *This Chriſt both God and man, he all and onely is:*
> *The man brings man to God and to all heauens bliſſe.*

The Greekes call this figure *Antiſtrophe,* the Latines,
conuerſio, I following the originall call him the *counter-*
turne, becauſe he turnes counter in the middeſt of euery
meetre.

Take me the two former figures and put them into
one, and it is that which the Greekes call *ſymploche,* the   *Symploche,*
Latines *complexio,* or *conduplicatio,* and is a maner of   or the
repetition, when one and the ſelfe word doth begin and   figure of
                                                            replie.

(199)

end many verſes in ſute & ſo wrappes vp both the former figures in one, as he that ſportingly complained of his vntruſtie miſtreſſe, thus.

> *Who made me ſhent for her loues ſake?*
> *Myne owne miſtreſſe.*
> *Who would not ſeeme my part to take,*
> *Myne owne miſtreſſe.|*
> *What made me firſt ſo well content*
> *Her curteſie.*
> *What makes me now ſo ſore repent*
> *Her crueltie.*

Z ij^r

The Greekes name this figure *Symploche*, the Latins *Complexio*, perchaunce for that he ſeemes to hold in and to wrap vp the verſes by reduplication, ſo as nothing can fall out. I had rather call him the figure of replie.

Anadiploſis, or the Redouble. Ye haue another ſort of repetition when with the worde by which you finiſh your verſe, ye beginne the next verſe with the ſame, as thus:

> *Comforte it is for man to haue a wife,*
> *Wife chaſt, and wiſe, and lowly all her life.*

Or thus:

> *Your beutie was the cauſe of my firſt loue,*
> *Looue while I liue, that I may ſore repent.*

The Greeks call this figure *Anadiploſis*, I call him the *Redouble* as the originall beares.

Epanalepſis, or the Eccho ſound. otherwiſe, the ſlow return. Ye haue an other ſorte of repetition, when ye make one worde both beginne and end your verſe, which therefore I call the ſlow retourne, otherwiſe the Eccho ſound, as thus:

> *Much muſt he be beloued, that loueth much,*
> *Feare many muſt he needs, whom many feare.*

Vnleſſe I called him the *eccho ſound*, I could not tell what name to giue him, vnleſſe it were the ſlow returne.

(200)

Ye haue another fort of repetition when in one verfe or claufe of a verfe, ye iterate one word without any intermiffion, as thus:

> *It was Maryne, Maryne that wrought mine woe.*

And this bemoaning the departure of a deere friend.

> *The chiefeft ftaffe of mine affured ftay,*
> *With no fmall griefe, is gon, is gon away.*

And that of Sir *Walter Raleighs* very fweet.

> *With wifdomes eyes had but blind fortune feene,*
> *Than had my looue, my looue for euer beene.*

The Greeks call him *Epizeuxis*, the Latines *Subiunctio*, we may call him the *vnderlay*, me thinks if we regard his manner of iteration, & would depart from the originall, we might very properly,/in our vulgar and for pleafure call him the *cuckowfpell*, for right as the cuckow repeats his lay, which is but one manner of note, and doth not infert any other tune betwixt, and fometimes for haft ftammers out two or three of them one immediatly after another, as *cuck, cuck, cuckow*, fo doth the figure *Epizeuxis* in the former verfes, *Maryne, Maryne*, without any intermiffion at all.

Z ij^v

Yet haue ye one forte of repetition, which we call the *doubler*, and is as the next before, a fpeedie iteration of one word, but with fome little intermiffiō by inferting one or two words betweene, as in a moft excellent dittie written by Sir *Walter Raleigh* thefe two clofing verfes:

> *Yet vvhen I favve my felfe to you vvas true,*
> *I loued my felfe, bycaufe my felfe loued you.*

And this fpoken in common Prouerbe.

> *An ape vvilbe an ape, by kinde as they fay,*
> *Though that ye clad him all in purple array.*

Or as we once fported vpon a fellowes name who was

called *Woodcock*, and for an ill part he had plaid entreated
fauour by his friend.

> *I praie you intreate no more for the man,*
> *Woodcocke vvilbe a vvoodcocke do vvhat ye can.*

Now alfo be there many other fortes of repetition if
a man would vfe them, but are nothing commendable,
and therefore are not obferued in good poefie, as a
vulgar rimer who doubled one word in the end of euery
verfe, thus:

> *adieu, adieu,*
> *my face, my face.*

And an other that did the like in the beginning of his
verfe, thus:

> *To loue him and loue him, as finners fhould doo.*

Thefe repetitiōs be not figuratiue but phantaftical,
for a figure is euer vfed to a purpofe, either of beautie
or of efficacie: and thefe laft recited be to no purpofe,
for neither can ye fay that it vrges affeҫion, nor that
it beautifieth or enforceth the fence, nor hath any other
fubtilitie in it, and therfore is a very foolifh impertinency
of fpeech, and not a figure.

Ye haue a figure by which ye play with a couple of
Profonomafia, words or names much refembling, and becaufe the one
or Z iijʳ feemes to anfwere/th'other by manner of illufion, and
the
Nicknamer. doth, as it were, nick him, I call him the *Nicknamer.*
If any other man can geue him a fitter Englifh name,
I will not be angrie, but I am fure mine is very neere
the originall fence of *Profonomafia,* and is rather a by-
name geuen in fport, than a furname geuen of any
earneft purpofe. As, *Tiberius* the Emperor, becaufe he
was a great drinker of wine, they called him by way
of derifion to his owne name, *Caldius Biberius Mero,* in
fteade of *Claudius Tiberius Nero:* and fo a iefting frier that
wrate againft *Erafmus,* called him by refemblance to his
own name, *Errans mus,* and are mainteined by this figure
Profonomafia, or the Nicknamer. But euery name geuen

in ieſt or by way of a ſurname, if it do not reſemble
the true, is not by this figure, as, the Emperor of Greece,
who was ſurnamed *Conſtantinus Copronimus*, becauſe he
beſhit the foont at the time he was chriſtened: and ſo ye
may ſee the difference betwixt the figures *Antonomaſia
& Proſonomatia.* Now when ſuch reſemblance happens
betweene words of another nature, and not vpon mens
names, yet doeth the Poet or maker finde pretty ſport
to play with them in his verſe, ſpecially the Comicall
Poet and the Epigrammatiſt. Sir *Philip Sidney* in a dittie
plaide very pretily with theſe two words, *Loue and liue*,
thus.

> *And all my life I will confeſſe,*
> *The leſſe I loue, I liue the leſſe.*

And we in our Enterlude called the woer, plaid with
theſe two words, *lubber* and *louer*, thus, the countrey
clowne came & woed a young maide of the Citie, and
being agreeued to come ſo oft, and not to haue his
anſwere, ſaid to the old nurſe very impatiently.

> *Iche pray you good mother tell our young dame,*   Woer.
> *Whence I am come and what is my name,*
> *I cannot come a woing euery day.*

Quoth the nurſe.

> *They be lubbers not louers that ſo vſe to ſay.*   Nurſe.

Or as one replyed to his miſtreſſe charging him with
ſome diſloyaltie towards her.

> *Proue me madame ere ye fall to reproue,*
> *Meeke mindes ſhould rather excuſe than accuſe.*

Here the words proue and reproue, excuſe and accuſe,
do plea-/ſantly encounter, and (as it were) mock one   Z iijᵛ
another by their much reſemblance: and this is by the
figure *Proſonomatia*, as wel as if they were mens proper
names, alluding to each other.

Then haue ye a figure which the Latines call *Traductio*,   *Traductio,*
and I the tranlacer: which is when ye turne and tranlace   or the
a word into many ſundry ſhapes as the Tailor doth his   *Tranlacer.*

garment, & after that fort do play with him in your dittie: as thus,

> *Who liues in loue his life is full of feares,*
> *To lofe his loue, liuelode or libertie*
> *But liuely fprites that young and reckleffe be,*
> *Thinke that there is no liuing like to theirs.*

Or as one who much gloried in his owne wit, whom *Perfius* taxed in a verfe very pithily and pleafantly, thus.

> *Scire tuum nihil eft nifi te fcire, hoc fciat alter.*

Which I haue turned into Englifh, not fo briefly, but more at large of purpofe the better to declare the nature of the figure: as thus,

> *Thou vveeneft thy vvit nought vvorth if other vveet*
> *it not*
> *As vvel as thou thy felfe, but o thing vvell I vvot,*
> *Who fo in earneft vveenes, he doth in mine aduife,*
> *Shevv himfelfe vvitleffe, or more vvittie than vvife.*

Here ye fee how in the former rime this word life is tranlaced into liue, liuing, liuely, liuelode: & in the latter rime this word wit is tranflated into weete, weene, wotte, witleffe, witty & wife: which come all from one originall.

Ye haue a figuratiue fpeach which the Greeks cal *Antipophora*, I name him the *Refponce*, and is when we will feeme to aske a queftion to th'intent we will aunfwere it our felues, and is a figure of argument and alfo of amplification. Of argument, becaufe proponing fuch matter as our aduerfarie might obiect and then to anfwere it our felues, we do vnfurnifh and preuent him of fuch helpe as he would otherwife haue vfed for himfelfe: then becaufe fuch obiection and anfwere fpend much language it ferues as well to amplifie and enlarge our tale. Thus for example.

Antipophora,
or Figure of
refponce.

> *Wylie vvorldling come tell me I thee pray,*
> *Wherein hopeft thou, that makes thee fo to fvvell?*

Riches? alack it taries not a day,|
But vvhere fortune the fickle lift to dvvell: Z iiij^r
In thy children? hovv hardlie fhalt thou finde,
Them all at once, good and thriftie and kinde:
Thy vvife? ô faire but fraile mettall to truft,
Seruants? what theeues? what treachours and iniuft?
Honour perchance? it reftes in other men:
Glorie? a fmoake: but wherein hopeft thou then?
In Gods iuftice? and by what merite tell?
In his mercy? ô now thou speakeft vvel,
But thy lewd life hath loft his loue and grace,   .
Daunting all hope to put difpaire in place.

We read that *Crates* the Philofopher Cinicke in refpect
of the manifold difcommodities of mans life, held opinion
that it was beft for man neuer to haue bene borne or
foone after to dye, [*Optimum non nafci vel citò mori*] of
whom certaine verfes are left written in Greeke which
I haue Englifhed, thus.

What life is the liefeft? the needy is full of woe and awe,
The wealthie full of brawle and brabbles of the law:
To be a maried man? how much art thou beguild,
Seeking thy reft by carke, for houfhold wife and child:
To till it is a toyle, to grafe fome honeft gaine,
But fuch as gotten is with great hazard and paine:
The fayler of his fhippe, the marchant of his ware,
The fouldier in armes, how full of dread and care?
A fhrewd wife brings thee bate, wiue not and neuer thriue,
Children a charge, childleffe the greatest lacke aliue:
Youth witleffe is and fraile, age ficklie and forlorne,
Then better to dye foone, or neuer to be borne.

Metrodorus the Philofopher *Stoick* was of a contrary
opinion reuerfing all the former fuppofitions againft
Crates, thus.

What life lift ye to lead? in good Citie and towne
Is wonne both wit and wealth, Court gets vs great renowne:

11   (205)

Countrey keepes vs in heale, and quietneſſe of mynd,
Where holeſome aires and exerciſe and pretie ſports we find:
Traffick it turnes to gaine, by land and eke by ſeas,
The land-borne liues ſafe, the forreine at his eaſe:
Houſholder hath his home, the roge romes with delight,|
And makes moe merry meales, then doth the Lordly wight:
Wed and thou haſt a bed, of ſolace and of ioy,
Wed not and haue a bed, of rest without annoy:
The ſetled loue is ſafe, ſweete is the loue at large,
Children they are a ſtore, no children are no charge,
Luſtie and gay is youth, old age honourd and wiſe:
Then not to dye or be vnborne, is beſt in myne aduiſe.

Z iiijᵛ

Edvvard Earle of Oxford a moſt noble & learned
Gentleman made in this figure of reſponce an emblē
of deſire otherwiſe called *Cupide* which for his excellencie and wit, I ſet downe ſome part of the verſes, for
example.

When wert thou borne deſire?
In pompe and pryme of May,
By whom ſweete boy wert thou begot?
By good conceit men ſay,
Tell me who was thy nurſe?
Freſh youth in ſugred ioy.
What was thy meate and dayly foode?
Sad ſighes with great annoy.
What hadſt thou then to drinke?
Vnfayned louers teares.
What cradle wert thou rocked in?
In hope deuoyde of feares.

Synecioſis,
or the
Croſſe
copling.

Ye haue another figure which me thinkes may well
be called (not much ſweruing from his originall in ſence)
the *Croſſe-couple,* becauſe it takes me two contrary words,
and tieth them as it were in a paire of couples, and ſo
makes them agree like good fellowes, as I ſaw once in
Fraunce a wolfe coupled with a maſtiffe, and a foxe with
a hounde. Thus it is.

(206)

The niggards fault and the vnthrifts is all one,
For neither of them both knoweth how to vfe his owne.

Or thus.

The couetous mifer, of all his goods ill got,
Afwell wants that he hath, as that he hath not.

In this figure of the *Croffe-couple* we wrate for a forlorne louer complaining of his miftreffe crueltie thefe
verfes among other.

Thus for your fake I dayly dye,|
And do but feeme to liue in deede: Aa iʳ
Thus is my bliffe but miferie,
My lucre loffe without your meede.

Ye haue another figure which by his nature we may   *Atanaclasis.*
call the *Rebound*, alluding to the tennis ball which being   or the
fmitten with the racket reboundes backe againe, and   Rebounde.
where the laft figure before played with two wordes
fomewhat like, this playeth with one word written all
alike but carrying diuers fences as thus.

The maide that foone married is, foone marred is.

Or thus better becaufe *married* & *marred* be differēt
in one letter.

To pray for you euer I cannot refufe,
To pray vpon you I fhould you much abufe.

Or as we once fported vpon a countrey fellow who
came to runne for the beft game, and was by his occupation a dyer and had very bigge fwelling legges.

He is but courfe to runne a courfe,
Whofe fhankes are bigger then his thye:
Yet is his lucke a little worfe,
That often dyes before he dye.

Where ye fee this word *courfe* and *dye*, vfed in diuers
fences, one giuing the *Rebounde* vpon th'other.

Ye haue a figure which as well by his Greeke and
Latine originals, & alfo by allufion to the maner of a

mans gate or going may be called the *marching figure*,
for after the firſt ſteppe all the reſt proceede by double
the ſpace, and ſo in our ſpeach one word proceedes
double to the firſt that was ſpoken, and goeth as it were
by ſtrides or paces: it may aſwell be called the *clyming*
figure, for *Clymax* is as much to ſay as a ladder, as in
one of our Epitaphes ſhewing how a very meane man
by his wiſedome and good fortune came to great eſtate
and dignitie.

Clymax.
or the
Marching
figure.

> *His vertue made him wiſe, his wiſedome brought him*
> > *wealth,*
> *His wealth wan many friends, his friends made much*
> > *ſupply:*
> *Of aides in weale and woe in ſickneſſe and in health,*
> *Thus came he from a low, to ſit in ſeate ſo hye.*

Or as *Ihean de Mehune* the French Poet.

> *Peace makes plentie, plentie makes pride,*
> *Pride breeds quarrell, and quarrell brings warre:|*
> *Warre brings ſpoile, and ſpoile pouertie,*
> *Pouertie pacience, and pacience peace:*
> *So peace brings warre, and warre brings peace.*

Aa iv

Antimetauole
or the
Counter-
chāge.

Ye haue a figure which takes a couple of words to
play with in a verſe, and by making them to chaunge
and ſhift one into others place they do very pretily exchange and ſhift the ſence, as thus.

> *We dwell not here to build vs boures,*
> *And halles for pleaſure and good cheare:*
> *But halles we build for vs and ours,*
> *To dwell in them whileſt we are here.*

Meaning that we dwell not here to build, but we
build to dwel, as we liue not to eate, but eate to liue,
or thus.

> *We wiſh not peace to maintaine cruell warre,*
> *But vve make vvarre to maintaine vs in peace.*

Or thus.

> *If Poefie be, as fome haue faid,*
> *A fpeaking picture to the eye:*
> *Then is a picture not denaid,*
> *To be a muet Poefie.*

Or as the Philofopher *Mufonius* vvrote.

> *With pleafure if vve vvorke vnhonestly and ill,*
> *The pleafure paffeth, the bad it bideth ftill:*
> *Well if vve vvorke vvith trauaile and vvith paines,*
> *The paine paffeth and still the good remaines.*

A wittie fellow in Rome wrate vnder the Image of *Cæfar* the Dictator thefe two verfes in Latine, which becaufe they are fpokē by this figure of *Counterchaunge* I haue turned into a couple of Englifh verfes very well keeping the grace of the figure.

> *Brutus for cafting out of kings, was firft of Confuls past,*
> *Cæfar for cafting Confuls out, is of our kings the last.*

Cato of any Senatour not onely the graueft but alfo the prompteft and wittieft in any ciuill fcoffe, mifliking greatly the engroffing of offices in Rome that one man fhould haue many at once, and a great number goe without that were as able men, faid thus by *Counterchaunge.*

> *It feemes your offices are very litle worth,*
> *Or very few of you worthy of offices.*

Againe:/

> *In trifles earnest as any man can bee,*
> *In earnest matters no fuch trifler as hee.*

Aa ij^r

Yee haue another figure much like to the *Sarcafmus*, or bitter taunt wee fpake of before: and is when with proud and infolent words, we do vpbraid a man, or ride him as we terme it: for which caufe the Latines alfo call it *Infultatio*, I choofe to name him the *Reprochfull*

Infultatio, or the Difdainefull.

(209)

or *fcorner*, as when Queene *Dido* faw, that for all her great loue and entertainements beftowed vpon *Æneas*, he would needs depart, and follow the *Oracle* of his deftinies, fhe brake out in a great rage and faid very difdainefully.

> *Hye thee, and by the wild waues and the wind,*
> *Seeke Italie and Realmes for thee to raigne,*
> *If piteous Gods haue power amidst the mayne,*
> *On ragged rocks thy penaunce thou maift find.*

Or as the poet *Iuuenall* reproched the couetous Merchant, who for lucres fake paffed on no perill either by land or fea, thus:

> *Goe now and giue thy life vnto the winde,*
> *Trusting vnto a piece of bruckle wood,*
> *Foure inches from thy death or feauen good*
> *The thickeft planke for fhipboord that we finde.*

Antitheton, or the renconter. Ye haue another figure very pleafant and fit for amplification, which to anfwer the Greeke terme, we may call the encounter, but following the Latine name by reafon of his contentious nature, we may call him the Quarreller, for fo be al fuch perfons as delight in taking the contrary part of whatfoeuer fhalbe fpoken: when I was a fcholler in Oxford they called euery fuch one *Iohannes ad oppofitum.*

> *Good haue I doone you, much, harme did I neuer none,*
> *Ready to ioy your gaines, your loffes to bemone,*
> *Why therefore fhould you grutch fo fore at my welfare:*
> *Who onely bred your bliffe, and neuer caufd your care.*

Or as it is in thefe two verfes where one fpeaking of *Cupids* bowe, deciphered thereby the nature of fenfual loue, whofe beginning is more pleafant than the end, thus allegorically and by *antitheton*.

> *His bent is fweete, his loofe is fomewhat fowre,*
> *In ioy begunne, ends oft in wofull howre.|*

Maiſter *Diar* in this quarelling figure.

Nor loue hath now the force, on me which it ones had,
Your frownes can neither make me mourne, nor fauors
make me glad.

Iſocrates the Greek Oratour was a litle too full of this
figure, & ſo was the Spaniard that wrote the life of
Marcus Aurelius, & many of our moderne writers in
vulgar, vſe it in exceſſe & incurre the vice of fond
affeƈtation: otherwiſe the figure is very cōmendable.

In this quarrelling figure we once plaid this merry
Epigrame of an importune and ſhrewd wife, thus:

My neighbour hath a wife, not fit to make him thriue,
But good to kill a quicke man, or make a dead reuiue.
So ſhrewd ſhe is for God, ſo cunning and ſo wiſe,
To counter vvith her goodman, and all by contraries.
For vvhen he is merry, ſhe lurcheth and ſhe loures,
When he is ſad ſhe ſinges, or laughes it out by houres.
Bid her be ſtill her tongue to talke ſhall neuer ceaſe,
When ſhe ſhould ſpeake and pleaſe, for ſpight ſhe holds
her peace,
Bid ſpare and ſhe vvill ſpend, bid ſpend ſhe ſpares as
faſt,
What firſt ye vvould haue done, be ſure it ſhalbe laſt.
Say go, ſhe comes, ſay come, ſhe goes, and leaues him
all alone,
Her husband (as I thinke) calles her ouerthvvart
Ione.

There is a kinde of figuratiue ſpeach when we aske   *Erotema.*
many queſtions and looke for none anſwere, ſpeaking   or the
indeed by interrogation, which we might as well ſay by   Queſtioner.
affirmation. This figure I call the *Queſtioner* or inquiſitiue,
as whan *Medea* excuſing her great crueltie vſed in the
murder of her owne children which ſhe had by *Iaſon*,
ſaid: *Was I able to make them I praie you tell,*
And am I not able to marre them all aſvvell?

Or as another wrote very commendably.

Why striue I vvith the streame, or hoppe against the hill,
Or search that neuer can be found, and loose my labour still?

Cato vnderstãding that the Senate had appointed three citizens of Rome for embassadours to the king of *Bithinia*, whereof one had the Gowte, another the Meigrim, the third very little courage or discretion to be employd in any such businesse, said by way of skoffe in this figure./

Aa iij^r *Must not (trovve ye) this message be vvell sped,*
That hath neither heart, nor heeles, nor hed?

And as a great Princesse aunswered her seruitour, who distrusting in her fauours toward him, praised his owne constancie in these verses.

No fortune base or frayle can alter me:

To whome she in this figure repeting his words:

No fortune base or frayle can alter thee.
And can so blind a vvitch so conquere mee?

Ecphonisis.
or the
Outcry. The figure of exclamation, I call him [*the outcrie*] becaufe it vtters our minde by all such words as do shew any extreme passion, whether it be by way of exclamation or crying out, admiration or wondering, imprecation or cursing, obtestation or taking God and the world to witnes, or any such like as declare an impotent affection, as *Chaucer* of the Lady *Cresseida* by exclamation.

O soppe of sorrow soonken into care,
O caytife Cresseid, for now and euermare.

Or as *Gascoine* wrote very passionatly and well to purpose.

Ay me the dayes that I in dole consume,
Alas the nights which vvitnesse vvell mine vvoe:
O vvrongfull vvorld vvhich makest my fancie fume,
Fie fickle fortune, fie, fie thou art my foe:
Out and alas so frovvard is my chance,
No nights nor daies, nor vvorldes can me auance.

Petrarche in a fonet which Sir *Thomas Wiat* Englifhed
excellently well, faid in this figure by way of imprecation
and obteftation: thus,

> *Perdie I faid it not,*
> *Nor neuer thought to doo:*
> *Afwell as I ye wot,*
> *I haue no power thereto:*
> " *And if I did the lot*
> *That firft did me enchaine,*
> *May neuer flake the knot*
> *But ftraite it to my paine.|*
> " *And if I did each thing,*
> *That may do harme or woe:*
> *Continually may wring,*
> *My harte where fo I goe.*
> " *Report may alwaies ring:*
> *Of fhame on me for aye,*
> *If in my hart did fpring,*
> *The wordes that you doo fay.*
> " *And if I did each ftarre,*
> *That is in heauen aboue.*

Aa iij^v

And fo forth, &c.

We vfe fometimes to proceede all by fingle words,
without any clofe or coupling, fauing that a little paufe
or comma is geuen to euery word. This figure for
pleafure may be called in our vulgar the cutted comma,
for that there cannot be a fhorter diuifion then at euery
words end. The Greekes in their language call it fhort
language, as thus. *Brachiologa,*
or the
Cutted
comma

> *Enuy, malice, flattery, difdaine,*
> *Auarice, deceit, falfhed, filthy gaine.*

If this loofe language be vfed, not in fingle words,
but in long claufes, it is called *Afindeton*, and in both
cafes we vtter in that fafhion, when either we be earneft,
or would feeme to make haft.

Ye haue another figure which we may call the figure

Parifon,
or the
Figure of
euen.

of euen, becaufe it goeth by claufes of egall quantitie, and not very long, but yet not fo fhort as the cutted comma: and they geue good grace to a dittie, but fpecially to a profe. In this figure we once wrote in a melancholike humor thefe verfes.

> *The good is geafon, and fhort is his abode,*
> *The bad bides long, and eafie to be found:*
> *Our life is loathfome, our finnes a heauy lode,*
> *Confcience a curst iudge, remorfe a priuie goade.*
> *Difeafe, age and death ftill in our eare they round,*
> *That hence we muft the fickly and the found:*
> *Treading the fteps that our forefathers troad,*
> *Rich, poore, holy, wife, all flefh it goes to ground.*

In a profe there fhould not be vfed at once of fuch euen claufes paft three or foure at the moft./

Aa iiij^r

Sinonimia,
or the
Figure of
ftore.

When fo euer we multiply our fpeech by many words or claufes of one fence, the Greekes call it *Sinonimia,* as who would fay, like or confenting names: the Latines hauing no fitte terme to giue him, called it by a name of euent, for (faid they) many words of one nature and fence, one of them doth expound another. And therefore they called this figure the [*Interpreter*] I for my part had rather call him the figure of [*ftore*] becaufe plenty of one manner of thing in our vulgar we call fo. *Æneas* asking whether his Captaine *Orontes* were dead or aliue, vfed this ftore of fpeeches all to one purpofe.

> *Is he aliue,*
> *Is he as I left him queauing and quick,*
> *And hath he not yet geuen vp the ghost,*
> *Among the reft of thofe that I haue lost?*

Or if it be in fingle words, then thus.

> *What is become of that beautifull face,*
> *Thofe louely lookes, that fauour amiable,*
> *Thofe fweete features, and vifage full of grace,*
> *That countenance which is alonly able*
> *To kill and cure?*

Ye fee that all thefe words, face, lookes, fauour, features, vifage, countenance, are in fence but all one. Which ftore, neuertheleffe, doeth much beautifie and inlarge the matter. So faid another.

> *My faith, my hope, my truft, my God and eke my guide,*
> *Stretch forth thy hand to faue the foule, vvhat ere the*
> *body bide.*

Here faith, hope and truft be words of one effect, allowed to vs by this figure of ftore.

Otherwhiles we fpeake and be forry for it, as if we had not wel fpoken, fo that we feeme to call in our word againe, and to put in another fitter for the purpofe: for which refpects the Greekes called this manner of fpeech the figure of repentance: then for that vpon repentance commonly followes amendment, the Latins called it the figure of correction, in that the fpeaker feemeth to re-forme that which was faid amiffe. I following the Greeke originall, choofe to call him the penitent, or repentant: and finging in honor of the mayden Queen, meaning to praife her for her greatneffe of courage, ouerfhooting my felfe, called it firft by the name/of pride: then fearing leaft fault might be found with that terme, by & by turned this word pride to praife: refembling her Maiefty to the Lion, being her owne noble armory, which by a flie conftruction purporteth magnanimitie. Thus in the latter end of a Partheniade. *(Metanoia, or the Penitent.)* *(Aa iiijv)*

> *O peereles you, or els no one aliue,*
> " *Your pride ferues you to feaze them all alone:*
> " *Not pride madame, but praife of the lion,*
> *To conquer all and be conquerd by none.*

And in another Partheniade thus infinuating her Maiefties great conftancy in refufall of all marriages offred her, thus:

> " *Her heart is hid none may it fee,*
> " *Marble or flinte folke vveene it be.*

Which may imploy rigour and cruelty, than cor-
rečteth it thus.

> *Not flinte I trovve I am a lier,*
> *But Siderite that feeles no fire.*

By which is intended, that it proceeded of a cold and
chaſt complexion not eaſily allured to loue.

Antenagoge.
or the
Recom-
pencer.

We haue another manner of ſpeech much like to the
repentant, but doth not as the ſame recant or vnſay a
word that hath bene ſaid before, putting another fitter
in his place, but hauing ſpoken any thing to depraue
the matter or partie, he denieth it not, but as it were
helpeth it againe by another more fauourable ſpeach:
and ſo ſeemeth to make amends, for which cauſe it is
called by the originall name in both languages, the
Recompencer, as he that was merily asked the queſtion,
whether his wife were not a ſhrewe as well as others of
his neighbours wiues, anſwered in this figure as pleaſantly, for he could not well denie it.

> *I muſt needs ſay, that my wife is a ſhrevve,*
> *But ſuch a huſvvife as I knovv but a fevve.*

Another in his firſt prepoſition giuing a very faint
cōmendation to the Courtiers life, weaning to make him
amends, made it worſe by a ſecond propoſition, thus:

> *The Courtiers life full delicate it is,*
> *But vvhere no vviſe man vvill euer ſet his blis.*

And an other ſpeaking to the incoragement of youth
in ſtudie and to become excellent in letters and armes,
ſaid thus:/

Bb i^r

> *Many are the paines and perils to be paſt,*
> *But great is the gaine and glory at the laſt.*

Epithonema.
or the
Surcloſe.

Our poet in his ſhort ditties, but ſpecially playing the
Epigrammatiſt will vſe to conclude and ſhut vp his
Epigram with a verſe or two, ſpoken in ſuch ſort, as
it may ſeeme a manner of allowance to all the premiſſes,
and that with a ioyfull approbation, which the Latines

call *Acclamatio,* we therefore call this figure the *furcloze* or *confenting clofe,* as *Virgill* when he had largely fpoken of Prince *Eneas* his fucceffe and fortunes concluded with this clofe.

> *Tantæ molis erat Romanam condere gentem.*

In Englifh thus:

> *So huge a peece of vvorke it vvas and fo hie,*
> *To reare the houfe of Romane progenie.*

Sir *Philip Sidney* very pretily clofed vp a dittie in this fort.

> *What medcine then, can fuch difeafe remoue,*
> *Where loue breedes hate, and hate engenders loue.*

And we in a *Partheniade* written of her Maieftie, declaring to what perils vertue is generally fubiect, and applying that fortune to her felfe, clofed it vp with this *Epiphoneme.*

> *Than if there bee,*
> *Any fo cancard hart to grutch,*
> *At your glories: my Queene: in vaine,*
> *Repining at your fatall raigne:*
> *It is for that they feele too much,*
> *Of your bountee.*

As who would fay her owne ouermuch lenitie and good-neffe, made her ill willers the more bold and prefumptuous.

Lucretius Carus the philofopher and poet inueighing fore againft the abufes of the fuperftitious religion of the Gentils, and recompting the wicked fact of king *Agamemnon* in facrificing his only daughter *Iphigenia,* being a yoong damfell of excellent bewtie, to th'intent to pleafe the wrathfull gods, hinderers of his nauigation, after he had faid all, clofed it vp in this one verfe, fpoken in *Epiphonema.*

> *Tantum relligio potuit fuadere malorum.*

In Englifh thus:/

> *Lo what an outrage, could caufe to be done,*
> *The peeuifh fcruple of blinde religion.*

Auxefis,
or the
Auancer.

It happens many times that to vrge and enforce the matter we fpeake of, we go ftill mounting by degrees and encreafing our fpeech with wordes or with fentences of more waight one then another, & is a figure of great both efficacie & ornament, as he that declaring the great calamitie of an infortunate prince, faid thus:

> *He loft befides his children and his vvife,*
> *His realme, ronovvne, liege, libertie and life.*

By which it appeareth that to any noble Prince the loffe of his eftate ought not to be fo greeuous, as of his honour, nor any of them both like to the lacke of his libertie, but that life is the deareft detriment of any other. We call this figure by the Greeke originall the *Auancer* or figure of encreafe becaufe euery word that is fpoken is one of more weight then another.
And as we lamented the crueltie of an inexorable and vnfaithfull miftreffe.

> *If by the lavves of loue it be a falt,*
> *The faithfull friend, in abfence to forget:*
> *But if it be (once do thy heart but halt,)*
> *A fecret finne: vvhat forfet is fo great:*
> *As by defpite in view of euery eye,*
> *The folemne vovves oft fvvorne vvith teares fo falt,*
> *And holy Leagues faft feald vvith hand and hart:*
> *For to repeale and breake fo vvilfully?*
> *But novv (alas) vvithout all iuft defart,*
> *My lot is for my troth and much good vvill,*
> *To reape difdaine, hatred and rude refufe,*
> *Or if ye vvould vvorke me fome greater ill:*
> *And of myne earned ioyes to feele no part,*
> *What els is this (ô cruell) but to vfe,*
> *Thy murdring knife the guiltleffe bloud to fpill.*

Where ye fee how fhe is charged firft with a fault, then with a fecret finne, afterward with a foule forfet, laft of all with a moft cruell & bloudy deede. And thus

(218)

againe in a certaine louers complaint made to the like
effect.

> *They fay it is a ruth to fee thy louer neede,|*
> *But you can fee me vveepe, but you can fee me bleede:*
> *And neuer fhrinke nor fhame, ne fhed no teare at all,*
> *You make my wounds your felfe, and fill them vp with gall:*
> *Yea you can fee me found, and faint for want of breath,*
> *And gafpe and grone for life, and ftruggle still with death,*
> *What can you now do more, fweare by your maydenhead,*
> *Then for to flea me quicke, or ftrip me being dead.*

In thefe verfes you fee how one crueltie furmounts
another by degrees till it come to very flaughter and
beyond, for it is thought a defpite done to a dead carkas
to be an euidence of greater crueltie then to haue killed
him.

After the Auancer followeth the abbafer working by   *Meiofis.*
wordes and fentences of extenuation or diminution.   *or the*
Whereupon we call him the *Difabler* or figure of *Extenua-*   *Difabler.*
tion: and this extenuation is vfed to diuers purpofes,
fometimes for modefties fake, and to auoide the opinion
of arrogancie, fpeaking of our felues or of ours, as he
that difabled himfelfe to his miftreffe, thus.

> *Not all the skill I haue to fpeake or do,*
> *Which litle is God wot (fet loue apart:)*
> *Liueload nor life, and put them both thereto,*
> *Can counterpeife the due of your defart.*

It may be alfo done for defpite to bring our aduerfaries in contempt, as he that fayd by one (commended
for a very braue fouldier) difabling him fcornefully, thus.

> *A iollie man (forfooth) and fit for the warre,*
> *Good at hand grippes, better to fight a farre:*
> *Whom bright weapon in fhevv as it is faid,*
> *Yea his ovvne fhade, hath often made afraide.*

The fubtilitie of the fcoffe lieth in thefe Latin wordes
[*eminus & cominus pugnare.*] Alfo we vfe this kind of

Extenuation when we take in hand to comfort or cheare any perillous enterprife, making a great matter feeme fmall, and of litle difficultie, & is much vfed by captaines in the warre, when they (to giue courage to their fouldiers) will feeme to difable the perfons of their enemies, and abafe their forces, and make light of euery thing that might be a difcouragement to the attempt, as *Hanniball* did in his Oration to his fouldiers, when they fhould come to paffe the Alpes to en-/ter Italie, and for fharpneffe of the weather, and fteepneffe of the mountaines their hearts began to faile them.

Bb ij^v

We vfe it againe to excufe a fault, & to make an offence feeme leffe then it is, by giuing a terme more fauorable and of leffe vehemencie then the troth requires, as to fay of a great robbery, that it was but a pilfry matter: of an arrant ruffian that he is a tall fellow of his hands: of a prodigall foole, that he is a kind hearted man: of a notorious vnthrift, a luftie youth, and fuch like phrafes of extenuation, which fall more aptly to the office of the figure *Curry fauell* before remembred.

And we vfe the like termes by way of pleafant familiaritie, and as it were for a Courtly maner of fpeach with our egalls or inferiours, as to call a young Gentlewoman *Mall* for *Mary*, *Nell* for *Elner: Iack* for *Iohn*, *Robin* for *Robert:* or any other like affected termes fpoken of pleafure, as in our triumphals calling familiarly vpon our *Mufe*, I called her *Moppe*.

> But vvill you vveet,
> My litle mufe, my prettie moppe:
> If vve fhall algates change our ftoppe,
> Chofe me a fvveet.

Vnderftanding by this word [*Moppe*] a litle prety Lady, or tender young thing. For fo we call litle fifhes, that be not come to their full growth [*moppes*,] as whiting moppes, gurnard moppes.

Alfo fuch termes are vfed to be giuen in derifion and

(220)

for a kind of contempt, as when we fay Lording for Lord, & as the Spaniard that calleth an Earle of fmall reuenue *Contadilio:* the Italian calleth the poore man, by contempt *pouerachio,* or *pouerino,* the little beaſt *animalculo* or *animaluchio,* and fuch like *diminutiues* apperteining to this figure, the [*Difabler*] more ordinary in other languages than in our vulgar.

This figure of retire holds part with the propounder of which we fpake before (*prolepfis*) becaufe of the refumption of a former propofition vttered in generalitie to explane the fame better by a particular diuifion. But their difference is, in that the propounder refumes but the matter only. This [*retire*] refumes both the matter and the termes, and is therefore accompted one of the figures of repetition, and in that refpeɕ may be called by his originall/Greeke name the [*Refounde*] or the [*retire*] for this word [ὸδος] ſerues both fences refound and retire. The vfe of this figure, is feen in this dittie following,

Epanodis, or the figure of Retire.

Bb iijʳ

> *Loue hope and death, do ſtirre in me much ſtrife,*
> *As neuer man but I lead fuch a life:*
> *For burning loue doth vvound my heart to death:*
> *And vvhen death comes at call of invvard grief,*
> *Cold lingring hope doth feede my fainting breath:*
> *Againſt my vvill, and yeelds my vvound relief,*
> *So that I liue, but yet my life is fuch:*
> *As neuer death could greeue me halfe fo much.*

Then haue ye a maner of fpeach, not fo figuratiue as fit for argumentation, and worketh not vnlike the *dilemma* of the Logicians, becaufe he propones two or moe matters entierly, and doth as it were fet downe the whole tale or rekoning of an argument and then cleare euery part by it felfe, as thus.

Dialifis, or the Dif-membrer.

> *It can not be but nigardſhip or neede,*
> *Made him attempt this foule and vvicked deede:*
> *Nigardſhip not, for alvvayes he vvas free,*
> *Nor neede, for vvho doth not his richeſſe fee?*

(221)

Or as one that entreated for a faire young maide who was taken by the watch in London and carried to Bride-well to be punifhed.

> *Novv gentill Sirs let this young maide alone,*
> *For either fhe hath grace or els fhe hath none:*
> *If fhe haue grace, fhe may in time repent,*
> *If fhe haue none vvhat bootes her punifhment.*

Or as another pleaded his deferts with his miftreffe.

> *Were it for grace, or els in hope of gaine,*
> *To fay of my deferts, it is but vaine:*
> *For vvell in minde, in cafe ye do them beare,*
> *To tell them oft, it fhould but irke your eare:*
> *Be they forgot: as likely fhould I faile,*
> *To vvinne vvith vvordes, vvhere deedes can not preuaile.*

Merifmus.
or the
Diftributer.

Bb iijᵛ

Then haue ye a figure very meete for Orators or eloquent perfwaders fuch as our maker or Poet muft in fome cafes fhew him felfe to be, and is when we may conueniently vtter a matter in one/entier fpeach or pro-pofition and will rather do it peecemeale and by diftributiō of euery part for amplification fake, as for exāple he that might fay, a houfe was outragioufly plucked downe: will not be fatisfied fo to fay, but rather will fpeake it in this fort: they firft vndermined the groundfills, they beate downe the walles, they vnfloored the loftes, they vntiled it and pulled downe the roofe. For fo in deede is a houfe pulled downe by circūftances, which this figure of diftri-bution doth fet forth euery one apart, and therefore I name him the *diftributor* according to his originall, as wrate the *Tufcane* Poet in a Sonet which Sir *Thomas Wyat* tranflated with very good grace, thus.

> *Set me vvhereas the funne doth parch the greene,*
> *Or vvhere his beames do not diffolue the yce:*
> *In temperate heate vvhere he is felt and feene,*
> *In prefence preft of people mad or vvife:*
> *Set me in hye or yet in low degree,*
> *In longeft night or in the fhorteft day:*

(222)

In cleareſt skie, or where clouds thickeſt bee,
In luſtie youth or when my heares are gray:
Set me in heauen, in earth or els in hell,
In hill or dale or in the foming flood:
Thrall or at large, aliue where ſo I dwell,
Sicke or in health, in euill fame or good:
Hers will I be, and onely with this thought,
Content my ſelfe, although my chaunce be naught.

All which might haue bene ſaid in theſe two verſes.

Set me whereſoeuer ye vvill,
I am and vvilbe yours ſtill.

The zealous Poet writing in prayſe of the maiden
Queene would not ſeeme to wrap vp all her moſt excellent parts in a few words them entierly comprehending,
but did it by a diſtributor or *meriſmus* in the negatiue
for the better grace, thus.

Not your bewtie, moſt gracious foueraine,
Nor maidenly lookes, mainteind vvith maieſtie:
Your ſtately port, vvhich doth not match but ſtaine,
For your preſence, your pallace and your traine,
All Princes Courts, mine eye could euer ſee:|
Not your quicke vvits, your ſober gouernaunce: Bb iiij^r
Your cleare forſight, your faithfull memorie,
So ſweete features, in ſo ſtaid countenaunce:
Nor languages, with plentuous vtterance,
So able to diſcourſe, and entertaine:
Not noble race, farre beyond Cæſars raigne,
Runne in right line, and bloud of nointed kings:
Not large empire, armies, treaſurs, domaine,
Luſtie liueries, of fortunes dearſt darlings:
Not all the skilles, fit for a Princely dame,
Your learned Muſe, vvith vſe and ſtudie brings.
Not true honour, ne that immortall fame
Of mayden raigne, your only owne renowne
And no Queenes els, yet ſuch as yeeldes your name
Greater glory than doeth your treble crowne.

(223)

And then concludes thus.

> *Not any one of all thefe honord parts*
> *Your Princely happes, and habites that do moue,*
> *And as it were, enforcell all the hearts*
> *Of Chriften kings to quarrell for your loue,*
> *But to poffeffe, at once and all the good*
> *Arte and engine, and euery ftarre aboue*
> *Fortune or kinde, could farce in flefh and bloud,*
> *Was force inough to make fo many ftriue*
> *For your perfon, which in our world ftoode*
> *By all confents the minionft mayde to wiue.*

Where ye fee that all the parts of her commendation which were particularly remembred in twenty verfes before, are wrapt vp in the two verfes of this laft part, videl.

> *Not any one of all your honord parts,*
> *Thofe Princely haps and habites, &c.*

This figure ferues for amplification, and alfo for ornament, and to enforce perfwafion mightely. Sir *Geffrey Chaucer,* father of our Englifh Poets, hath thefe verfes following in the diftributor.

> *When faith failes in Prieftes fawes,*
> *And Lords heftes are holden for lawes,*
> *And robberie is tane for purchafe,/*
> *And lechery for folace*
> *Then fhall the Realme of Albion*
> *Be brought to great confufion.*

Bb iiij^v

Where he might haue faid as much in thefe words: when vice abounds, and vertue decayeth in Albion, then &c. And as another faid,

> *When Prince for his people is wakefull and wife,*
> *Peeres ayding with armes, Counfellors with aduife,*
> *Magiftrate fincerely vfing his charge,*
> *People preft to obey, nor let to runne at large,*

Prelate of holy life, and with deuotion
Preferring pietie before promotion,
Priest ſtill preaching, and praying for our heale:
Then bleſſed is the ſtate of a common-weale.

All which might haue bene ſaid in theſe few words, when euery man in charge and authoritie doeth his duety, & executeth his funćtion well, then is the common-wealth happy.

The Greeke Poets who made muſicall ditties to be ſong to the lute or harpe, did vſe to linke their ſtaues together with one verſe running throughout the whole ſong by equall diſtance, and was, for the moſt part, the firſt verſe of the ſtaffe, which kept ſo good ſence and conformitie with the whole, as his often repetition did geue it greater grace. They called ſuch linking verſe *Epimone*, the Latines *verſus intercalaris*, and we may terme him the Loue-burden, following the originall, or if it pleaſe you, the long repeate: in one reſpećt becauſe that one verſe alone beareth the whole burden of the ſong according to the originall: in another reſpećt, for that it comes by large diſtances to be often repeated, as in this ditty made by the noble knight Sir *Philip Sidney*, *Epimone, or the Loue-burden.*

My true loue hath my heart and I haue his,
By iuſt exchange one for another geuen:
I holde his deare, and mine he cannot miſſe,
There neuer was a better bargaine driuen.
　　My true loue hath my heart and I haue his.

His heart in me keepes him and me in one,
My heart in him his thoughts and ſences guides:
He loues my heart, for once it was his owne,/
I cheriſh his becauſe in me it bides. Cc iʳ
　　My true loue hath my heart, and I haue his.

Many times our Poet is caried by ſome occaſion to report of a thing that is maruelous, and then he will

Paradoxon, feeme not to fpeake it fimply but with fome figne of
or the admiration, as in our enterlude called the *Woer.*
Wondrer.

> *I woonder much to fee fo many husbands thriue,*
> *That haue but little wit, before they come to wiue:*
> *For one would eafily weene who fo hath little wit,*
> *His wife to teach it him, vvere a thing much vnfit.*

Or as *Cato* the Romane Senatour faid one day merily
to his companion that walked with him, pointing his
finger to a yong vnthrift in the ftreete who lately before
had fold his patrimonie, of a goodly quātitie of falt
marfhes, lying neere vnto *Capua* fhore.

> *Now is it not, a wonder to behold,*
> *Yonder gallant skarce twenty winter old,*
> *By might (marke ye) able to doo more?*
> *Than the mayne fea that batters on his fhore?*
> *For what the waues could neuer wafh away,*
> *This proper youth hath wafted in a day.*

Aporia, Not much vnlike the *vvondrer* haue ye another figure
or the called the *doubtfull,* becaufe oftentimes we will feeme to
Doubtfull. caft perils, and make doubt of things when by a plaine
manner of fpeech wee might affirme or deny him, as thus
of a cruell mother who murdred her owne child.

> *Whether the cruell mother were more to blame,*
> *Or the fhrevvd childe come of fo curft a dame:*
> *Or vvhether fome fmatch of the fathers blood,*
> *Whofe kinne vvere neuer kinde, nor neuer good.*
> *Mooued her thereto, &c.*

Epitropis, This manner of fpeech is vfed when we will not feeme,
or the either for manner fake or to auoid tedioufneffe, to trouble
Figure of the iudge or hearer with all that we could fay, but
Reference. hauing faid inough already, we referre the reft to their
confideration, as he that faid thus:

> *Me thinkes that I haue faid, vvhat may vvell fuffife,*
> *Referring all the reft, to your better aduife.*

The fine and fubtill perfwader when his intent is to
fting his/aduerfary, or els to declare his mind in broad
and liberal fpeeches, which might breede offence or
fcandall, he will feeme to befpeake pardon before hand,
whereby his licentioufnes may be the better borne withall, as he that faid:

Cc iv

Parifia,
or the
Licentious.

> *If my fpeech hap t'offend you any vvay,*
> *Thinke it their fault, that force me fo to fay.*

Not much vnlike to the figure of *reference*, is there
another with fome little diuerfitie which we call the *im-*
partener, becaufe many times in pleading and perfwading,
we thinke it a very good pollicie to acquaint our iudge
or hearer or very aduerfarie with fome part of our
Counfell and aduice, and to aske their opinion, as who
would fay they could not otherwife thinke of the matter
then we do. As he that had tolde a long tale before
certaine noble women, of a matter fomewhat in honour
touching the Sex.

Anachinofis.
or the
Impartener

> *Tell me faire Ladies, if the cafe were your owne,*
> *So foule a fault would you haue it be knowen?*

Maifter *Gorge* in this figure, faid very fweetly.

> *All you who read thefe lines and skanne of my defart,*
> *Iudge whether was more good, my hap or els my*
> *hart.*

The good Orator vfeth a manner of fpeach in his
perfwafion and is when all that fhould feeme to make
againft him being fpoken by th'otherfide, he will firft
admit it, and in th'end auoid all for his better aduantage,
and this figure is much vfed by our Englifh pleaders
in the Starchamber and Chancery, which they call to
confeffe and auoid, if it be in cafe of crime or iniury,
and is a very good way. For when the matter is fo
plaine that it cannot be denied or trauerfed, it is good

Paramologia,
or the
figure of Ad-
mittance.

(227)

that it be iuſtified by confeſſall and auoidance. I call it
the figure of *admittance*. As we once wrate to the reproofe of a Ladies faire but crueltie.

> *I know your witte, I know your pleaſant tongue,*
> *Your ſome ſweete ſmiles, your ſome, but louely lowrs:*
> *A beautie to enamour olde and yong.*
> *Thoſe chaſt deſires, that noble minde of yours,*
> *And that chiefe part whence all your honor ſprings,*
> *A grace to entertaine the greatest kings.*
> *All this I know: but ſinne it is to ſee,*
> *So faire partes ſpilt by too much crueltie.*|

Cc ijʳ In many caſes we are driuen for better perſwaſion to
Etiologia, tell the cauſe that mooues vs to ſay thus or thus: or els
or the when we would fortifie our allegations by rendring
Reaſon reaſons to euery one, this aſſignation of cauſe the Greekes
rendrer called *Etiologia*, which if we might without ſcorne of a
or the new inuented terme call [*Tellcauſe*] it were right ac-
Tell cauſe. cording to the Greeke originall: & I pray you why
ſhould we not? and with as good authoritie as the
Greekes? Sir *Thomas Smith*, her Maieſties principall
Secretary, and a man of great learning and grauitie,
ſeeking to geue an Engliſh word to this Greeke word
ἄγαμος called it Spitewed, or wedſpite. Maſter Secretary
Wilſon geuing an Engliſh name to his arte of Logicke,
called it *Witcraft*, me thinke I may be bolde with like
liberty to call the figure *Etiologia* [*Tell cauſe.*] And this
manner of ſpeech is alwayes contemned, with theſe
words, for, becauſe, and ſuch other confirmatiues. The
Latines hauing no fitte name to geue it in one ſingle
word, gaue it no name at all, but by circumlocution.
We alſo call him the reaſon-rendrer, and leaue the right
Engliſh word [*Tel cauſe*] much better anſwering the
Greeke originall. *Ariſtotle* was moſt excellent in vſe of
this figure, for he neuer propones any allegation, or
makes any ſurmiſe, but he yeelds a reaſon or cauſe to
fortifie and proue it, which geues it great credit. For

(228)

example ye may take thefe verfes, firft pointing, than confirming by fimilitudes.

> *When fortune fhall haue spit out all her gall,*
> *I truft good luck fhall be to me allowde,*
> *For I haue feene a fhippe in hauen fall,*
> *After the ftorme had broke both mafte and fhrowde.*

And this.

> *Good is the thing that moues vs to defire,*
> *That is to ioy the beauty we behold:*
> *Els were we louers as in an endleffe fire,*
> *Alwaies burning and euer chill a colde.*

And in thefe verfes.

> *Accufed though I be without defart,*
> *Sith none can proue beleeue it not for true:*
> *For neuer yet fince firft ye had my hart,*
> *Entended I to falfe or be vntrue.|*

And in this Difticque.

> *And for her beauties praife, no wight that with her*
> *warres:*
> *For where fhe comes fhe fhewes her felfe like fun among*
> *the ftars.*

And in this other dittie of ours where the louer complaines of his Ladies crueltie, rendring for euery furmife a reafon, and by telling the caufe, feeketh (as it were) to get credit, thus.

> *Cruel you be who can fay nay,*
> *Since ye delight in others wo:*
> *Vnwife am I, ye may well fay,*
> *For that I haue, honourd you fo.*
> *But blameleffe I, who could not chufe,*
> *To be enchaunted by your eye:*
> *But ye to blame, thus to refufe*
> *My feruice, and to let me die.*

(229)

Dichologia,
or the
Figure of
excufe.

Sometimes our error is fo manifeft, or we be fo hardly preft with our aduerfaries, as we cannot deny the fault layd vnto our charge: in which cafe it is good pollicie to excufe it by fome allowable pretext, as did one whom his miftreffe burdened with fome vnkinde fpeeches which he had paft of her, thus.

> *I faid it: but by lapfe of lying tongue,*
> *When furie and iuft griefe my heart oppreft:*
> *I fayd it: as ye fee, both fraile and young,*
> *When your rigor hadranckled in my breft.*
> *The cruell wound that fmarted me fo fore,*
> *Pardon therefore (fweete forrow) or at leaft*
> *Beare with mine youth that neuer fell before,*
> *Leaft your offence encreafe my griefe the more.*

And againe in thefe,

> *I fpake amyffe I cannot it deny*
> *But caufed by your great difcourtefie:*
> *And if I faid that which I now repent,*
> *And faid it not, but by mifgouernment*
> *Of youthfull yeres, your felfe that are fo young*
> *Pardon for once this error of my tongue,*
> *And thinke amends can neuer come to late:*
> *Loue may be curft, but loue can neuer hate.*

Speaking before of the figure [*Synecdoche*] wee called him/[*Quicke conceit*] becaufe he inured in a fingle word onely by way of intendment or large meaning, but fuch as was fpeedily difcouered by euery quicke wit, as by the halfe to vnderftand the whole, and many other waies appearing by the examples. But by this figure [*Noema*] the obfcurity of the fence lieth not in a fingle word, but in an entier fpeech, whereof we do not fo eafily conceiue the meaning, but as it were by conie&ture, becaufe it is wittie and fubtile or darke, which makes me therefore call him in our vulgar the [*Clofe conceit*] as he that faid by himfelfe and his wife, I thanke God in fortie winters that we haue liued together, neuer any of our neigh-

Cc iij^r
Noema,
or the
Figure of
clofe cōceit.

bours fet vs at one, meaning that they neuer fell out
in all that fpace, which had bene the directer fpeech
and more apert, and yet by intendment amounts all to
one, being neuertheleffe diffemblable and in effect contrary. *Pawlet* Lord Treaforer of England, and firft
Marques of Winchefter, with the like fubtill fpeech gaue
a quippe to Sir *William Gyfford*, who had married the
Marques fifter, and all her life time could neuer loue
her nor like of her company, but when fhe was dead
made the greateft moane for her in the world, and with
teares and much lamentation vttered his griefe to the
L. Treaforer, ô good brother quoth the Marques, I am
right fory to fee you now loue my fifter fo well, meaning
that he fhewed his loue too late, and fhould haue done
it while fhe was a liue.

A great counfellour fomewhat forgetting his modeftie,
vfed thefe words: Gods lady I reckon my felfe as good
a man as he he you talke of, and yet I am not able to do fo.
Yea fir quoth the party, your L. is too good to be a
man, I would ye were a Saint, meaning he would he were
dead, for none are fhrined for Saints before they be dead.

The Logician vfeth a definition to expreffe the truth
or nature of euery thing by his true kinde and difference,
as to fay wifedome is a prudent and wittie forefight and
confideration of humane or worldly actions with their
euentes. This definition is Logicall. The Oratour vfeth
another maner of definition, thus: Is this wifedome?
no it is a certaine fubtill knauifh craftie wit, it is no
induftrie as ye call it, but a certaine bufie brainfickneffe,
for induftrie is a liuely and vnweried fearch and occupation in honeft/things, egerneffe is an appetite in bafe and
fmall matters.

Orifmus,
or the
Definer of
difference.

Cc iijᵛ

It ferueth many times to great purpofe to preuent
our aduerfaries arguments, and take vpon vs to know
before what our iudge or aduerfary or hearer thinketh,
and that we will feeme to vtter it before it be fpoken
or alleaged by them, in refpect of which boldneffe to

(231)

enter fo deeply into another mans conceit or confcience, and to be fo priuie of another mans mynde, gaue caufe *Procatalepfis,* that this figure was called the [*prefumptuous*] I will alfo or the call him the figure of *prefuppofall* or the *preuenter,* for prefump- by reafon we fuppofe before what may be faid, or per- wife the chaunce would be faid by our aduerfary or any other, figure of we do preuent them of their aduantage, and do catch Prefuppofall. the ball (as they are wont to fay) before it come to the ground.

Paralepfis, It is alfo very many times vfed for a good pollicie or the in pleading or perfwafion to make wife as if we fet but Paffager. light of the matter, and that therefore we do paffe it ouer flightly when in deede we do then intend moft effectually and defpightfully if it be inuectiue to re- member it: it is alfo when we will not feeme to know a thing, and yet we know it well inough, and may be likened to the maner of women, who as the cōmon faying is, will fay nay and take it.

> *I hold my peace and will not fay for fhame,*
> *The much vntruth of that vnciuill dame:*
> *For if I fhould her coullours kindly blaze,*
> *It would fo make the chaft eares amaze. &c.*

Commoratio, It is faid by maner of a prouerbiall fpeach that he or the who findes himfelfe well fhould not wagge, euen fo the figure of perfwader finding a fubftantiall point in his matter to abode ferue his purpofe, fhould dwell vpon that point longer then vpon any other leffe affured, and vfe all endeuour to maintaine that one, & as it were to make his chief aboad thereupon, for which caufe I name him the figure of aboad, according to the Latine name: Some take it not but for a courfe of argument & therefore hardly may one giue any examples therof.

Metaftafis, Now as arte and good pollicy in perfwafion bids vs or the to abide & not to ftirre from the point of our moft flitting figure. or the aduantage, but the fame to enforce and tarry vpon with Remoue. all poffible argument, fo doth difcretion will vs fome-

(232)

times to flit from one matter to another, as a thing meete to be forſaken, and another entred vpon, I call him therefore the *flitting* figure, or figure of *remoue*, like as the other/before was called the figure of *aboade*.

Euen ſo againe, as it is wiſdome for a perſwader to tarrie and make his aboad as long as he may conueniently without tediouſnes to the hearer, vpon his chiefe proofes or points of the cauſe tending to his aduantage, and like-wiſe to depart againe when time ſerues, and goe to a new matter ſeruing the purpoſe aſwell. So is it requiſite many times for him to talke farre from the principall matter, and as it were to range aſide, to th'intent by ſuch extraordinary meane to induce or inferre other matter, aſwell or better ſeruing the principal purpoſe, and neuertheles in ſeaſon to returne home where he firſt ſtrayed out. This maner of ſpeech is termed the figure of digreſſion by the Latines, following the Greeke originall, we alſo call him the *ſtraggler* by alluſiõ to the ſouldier that marches out of his array, or by thoſe that keepe no order in their marche, as the battailes well ranged do: of this figure there need be geuen no example.

Parecnaſis, or the Stragler.

Occaſion offers many times that our maker as an oratour, or perſwader, or pleader ſhould go roundly to worke, and by a quick and ſwift argument diſpatch his perſwaſion, & as they are woont to ſay not to ſtand all day trifling to no purpoſe, but to rid it out of the way quickly. This is done by a manner of ſpeech, both figuratiue and argumentatiue, when we do briefly ſet downe all our beſt reaſons ſeruing the purpoſe, and reieçt all of them ſauing one, which we accept to ſatisfie the cauſe: as he that in a litigious caſe for land would prooue it not the aduerſaries, but his clients.

Expeditio, or the ſpeedie diſ-patcher.

No man can ſay its his by heritage,
Nor by Legacie, or Teſtatours deuice:
Nor that it came by purchaſe or engage,
Nor from his Prince for any good ſeruice.

(233)

Then needs muſt it be his by very vvrong,
Which he hath offred this poore plaintife ſo long.

Though we might call this figure very well and properly the [*Paragon*] yet dare I not ſo to doe for feare of the Courtiers enuy, who will haue no man vſe that terme but after a courtly manner, that is, in prayſing of horſes, haukes, hounds, pearles, diamonds, rubies, emerodes, and other precious ſtones: ſpecially of faire women whoſe excellencie is diſcouered by paragonizing Cc iiijᵛ or ſetting one to/another, which moued the zealous Poet, ſpeaking of the mayden Queene, to call her the paragon of Queenes. This conſidered, I will let our figure enioy his beſt beknowen name, and call him ſtil in all ordinarie caſes the figure of compariſon: as when a man wil ſeeme to make things appeare good or bad, or better or worſe, or more or leſſe excellent, either vpon ſpite or for pleaſure, or any other good affectiō, then he ſets the leſſe by the greater, or the greater to the leſſe, the equall to his equall, and by ſuch confronting of them together, driues out the true ods that is betwixt them, and makes it better appeare, as when we ſang of our Soueraigne Lady thus, in the twentieth Partheniade.

As falcon fares to buſſards flight,
As egles eyes to owlates ſight,
As fierce ſaker to coward kite,
As brighteſt noone to darkeſt night:
As ſummer ſunne exceedeth farre,
The moone and euery other ſtarre:
So farre my Princeſſe praiſe doeth paſſe,
The famouſt Queene that euer was.

And in the eighteene Partheniade thus.

Set rich rubie to red eſmayle,
The rauens plume to peacocks tayle,
Lay me the larkes to lizards eye,
The duskie cloude to azure skie,

(234)

Set ſhallow brookes to ſurging ſeas,
An orient pearle to a white peaſe:

&c. Concluding.

There ſhall no leſſe an ods be ſeene
In mine from euery other Queene.

We are ſometimes occaſioned in our tale to report *Dialogiſmus,*
ſome ſpeech from another mans mouth, as what a king or the right
ſaid to his priuy counſell or ſubiect, a captaine to his reaſoner.
ſouldier, a ſouldiar to his captaine, a man to a woman,
and contrariwiſe: in which report we muſt alwaies geue
to euery perſon his fit and naturall, & that which beſt
becommeth him. For that ſpeech becommeth a king
which doth not a carter, and a young man that doeth
not an old: and ſo in euery ſort and degree. *Virgil*
ſpeaking in the perſon of *Eneas, Tur-/nus* and many other Dd iʳ
great Princes, and ſometimes of meaner men, ye ſhall ſee
what decencie euery of their ſpeeches holdeth with the
qualitie, degree and yeares of the ſpeaker. To which
examples I will for this time referre you.

So if by way of fiction we will ſeem to ſpeake in
another mans perſon, as if king *Henry* the eight were
aliue, and ſhould ſay of the towne of Bulleyn, what we
by warre to the hazard of our perſon hardly obteined,
our young ſonne without any peril at all, for litle mony
deliuered vp againe. Or if we ſhould faine king *Edward*
the thirde, vnderſtanding how his ſucceſſour Queene
Marie had loſt the towne of Calays by negligence, ſhould
ſay: That which the ſword wanne, the diſtaffe hath loſt.
This manner of ſpeech is by the figure *Dialogiſmus*, or
the right reaſoner.

In waightie cauſes and for great purpoſes, wiſe per- *Gnome,*
ſwaders vſe graue & weighty ſpeaches, ſpecially in or the
matter of aduiſe or counſel, for which purpoſe there is Director.
a maner of ſpeach to alleage textes or authorities of
wittie ſentence, ſuch as ſmatch morall doctrine and teach
wiſedome and good behauiour, by the Greeke originall

(235)

we call him the *directour*, by the Latin he is called *fententia:* we may call him the *fage fayer*, thus.

Sententia.
or the
Sage fayer.

"*Nature bids vs as a louing mother,*
"*To loue our felues firft and next to loue another.*
"*The Prince that couets all to know and fee,*
"*Had neede full milde and patient to bee.*
"*Nothing ftickes fafter by vs as appeares,*
"*Then that which we learne in our tender yeares.*

And that which our foueraigne Lady wrate in defiance of fortune.

Neuer thinke you fortune can beare the fwvay,
Where vertues force, can caufe her to obay.

Heede muft be taken that fuch rules or fentences be choifly made and not often vfed leaft exceffe breed loth-fomneffe.

Sinathrifmus.
or the
Heaping
figure

Arte and good pollicie moues vs many times to be earneft in our fpeach, and then we lay on fuch load and fo go to it by heapes as if we would winne the game by multitude of words & fpeaches, not all of one but Dd iv of diuers matter and fence, for which caufe the/Latines called it *Congeries* and we the *heaping figure,* as he that faid

To mufe in minde how faire, hovv vvife, hovv good,
Hovv braue, hovv free, hovv curteous and hovv true,
My Lady is doth but inflame my blood.

Or thus.

I deeme, I dreame, I do, I taft, I touch,
Nothing at all but fmells of perfit bliffe.

And thus by maifter *Edvvard Diar,* vehement fwift & paffionatly.

But if my faith my hope, my loue my true intent,
My libertie, my feruice vowed, my time and all be fpent,
In vaine, &c.

But if fuch earneft and haftie heaping vp of fpeaches be made by way of recapitulation, which commonly is

(236)

in the end of euery long tale and Oration, becaufe the
fpeaker feemes to make a collection of all the former
materiall points, to binde them as it were in a bundle
and lay them forth to enforce the caufe and renew the
hearers memory, then ye may geue him more properly
the name of the [*collectour*] or recapitulatour, and ferueth
to very great purpofe as in an hympne written by vs to
the Queenes Maieftie entitled (*Minerua*) wherein fpeaking of the mutabilitie of fortune in the cafe of all Princes
generally, wee feemed to exempt her Maieftie of all
fuch cafualtie, by reafon fhe was by her deftinie and
many diuine partes in her, ordained to a moft long and
conftant profperitie in this world, concluding with this
recapitulation.

> *But thou art free, but were thou not in deede,*
> *But were thou not, come of immortall feede:*
> *Neuer yborne, and thy minde made to bliffe,*
> *Heauens mettall that euerlafting is:*
> *Were not thy vvit, and that thy vertues fhall,*
> *Be deemd diuine thy fauour face and all:*
> *And that thy loze, ne name may neuer dye,*
> *Nor thy ftate turne, ftayd by deftinie:*
> *Dread were least once thy noble hart may feele,*
> *Some rufull turne, of her vnfteady vvheele.*

Many times when we haue runne a long race in our
tale fpoken to the hearers, we do fodainly flye out &
either fpeake or ex-/claime at fome other perfon or thing,
and therefore the Greekes call fuch figure (as we do)
the turnway or turnetale, & breedeth by fuch exchaunge
a certaine recreation to the hearers minds, as this vfed
by a louer to his vnkind miftreffe.

Apoftrophe,
or the
turne tale.
Dd ij[r]

> *And as for you (faire one) fay now by proofe ye finde,*
> *That rigour and ingratitude foone kill a gentle minde.*

And as we in our triumphals, fpeaking long to the
Queenes Maieftie, vpō the fodaine we burft out in an

exclamation to *Phebus*, feeming to draw in a new matter, thus.

> *But O Phebus,*
> *All gliftering in thy gorgious gowne,*
> *Wouldft thou vvitfafe to flide a dovvne:*
> *And dvvell with vs,*
>
> *But for a day,*
> *I could tell thee clofe in thine eare,*
> *A tale that thou hadft leuer heare*
> *I dare vvell fay:*
>
> *Then ere thou vvert,*
> *To kiffe that vnkind runneavvay,*
> *Who vvas transformed to boughs of bay:*
> *For her curft hert. &c.*

And fo returned againe to the firft matter.

Hypotipofis, or the counterfait reprefenta-tion. The matter and occafion leadeth vs many times to defcribe and fet foorth many things, in fuch fort as it fhould appeare they were truly before our eyes though they were not prefent, which to do it requireth cunning: for nothing can be kindly counterfait or reprefented in his abfence, but by great difcretion in the doer. And if the things we couet to defcribe be not naturall or not veritable, than yet the fame axeth more cunning to do it, becaufe to faine a thing that neuer was nor is like to be, proceedeth of a greater wit and fharper inuention than to defcribe things that be true.

Profopo-graphia. And thefe be things that a poet or maker is woont to defcribe fometimes as true or naturall, and fometimes to faine as artificiall and not true. *viz.* The vifage, fpeach and countenance of any perfon abfent or dead: and this kinde of reprefentation is called the Counterfait counte-

Dd ij^v nance: as *Homer* doth in his *Iliades*, diuerfe/perfonages: namely *Achilles* and *Therfites*, according to the truth and not by fiction. And as our poet *Chaucer* doth in his Canterbury tales fet forth the Sumner, Pardoner, Manciple, and the reſt of the pilgrims, moſt naturally and pleaſantly.

But if ye wil faine any perſon with ſuch features, qualities & cōditiōs, or if ye wil attribute any humane quality, as reaſon or ſpeech to dōbe creatures or other infenſible things, & do ſtudy (as one may ſay) to giue thē a humane perſon, it is not *Proſopographia*, but *Proſopopeia*, becauſe it is by way of fictiō, & no prettier examples can be giuen to you thereof, than in the Romant of the roſe tranſlated out of French by *Chaucer*, deſcribing the perſons of auarice, enuie, old age, and many others, whereby much moralitie is taught. *Proſopopeia.* or the Counterfait in perſonation.

So if we deſcribe the time or ſeaſon of the yeare, as winter, ſummer, harueſt, day, midnight, noone, euening, or ſuch like: we call ſuch deſcription the counterfait time. *Cronographia* examples are euery where to be found. *Cronographia.* or the Counterfait time.

And if this deſcriptiō be of any true place, citie, caſtell, hill, valley or ſea, & ſuch like: we call it the counterfait place *Topographia*, or if ye fayne places vntrue, as heauen, hell, paradiſe, the houſe of fame, the pallace of the ſunne, the denne of ſleepe, and ſuch like which ye ſhall ſee in Poetes: ſo did *Chaucer* very well deſcribe the country of *Saluces* in *Italie*, which ye may ſee, in his report of the Lady *Gryſyll*. *Topographia.* or the Counterfait place.

But if ſuch deſcription be made to repreſent the handling of any buſines with the circumſtances belonging thereunto as the manner of a battell, a feaſt, a marriage, a buriall or any other matter that lieth in feat and actiuitie: we call it then the counterfait action [*Pragmatographia.*] *Pragmatographia.* or the Counterfait action.

In this figure the Lord *Nicholas Vaux* a noble gentleman, and much delighted in vulgar making, & a man otherwiſe of no great learning but hauing herein a maruelous facillitie, made a dittie repreſenting the battayle and aſſault of *Cupide*, ſo excellently well, as for the gallant and propre application of his fiction in euery part,

I cannot choofe but fet downe the greateft part of his ditty, for in truth it can not be amended.

When Cupid fcaled firft the fort,
Wherein my hart lay wounded fore|
Dd iij^r *The battrie was of fuch a fort,*
That I muft yeeld or die therefore.
There faw I loue vpon the wall,
How he his banner did difplay,
Alarme alarme he gan to call,
And bad his fouldiers keepe aray.

The armes the vvhich that Cupid bare,
Were pearced harts vvith teares befprent:
In filuer and fable to declare
The ftedfast loue he alvvaies meant.

There might you fee his band all drest
In colours like to vvhite and blacke,
With pouder and vvith pellets preft,
To bring them forth to fpoile and facke,
Good vvill the maifter of the fhot,
Stood in the Rampire braue and proude,
For expence of pouder he fpared not,
Affault affault to crie aloude.

There might you heare the Canons rore,
Eche peece difcharging a louers looke, &c.

Omiofis.
or Refem-
blance. As well to a good maker and Poet as to an excellent perfwader in profe, the figure of *Similitude* is very necef- fary, by which we not onely bewtifie our tale, but alfo very much inforce & inlarge it. I fay inforce becaufe no one thing more preuaileth with all ordinary iudgements than perfwafion by *fimilitude*. Now becaufe there are fundry forts of them, which alfo do worke after diuerfe fafhions in the hearers conceits, I will fet them all foorth by a triple diuifion, exempting the generall *Similitude* as their common Aunceftour, and I will cal him by the name of *Refemblance* without any addition, from which I deriue three other forts: and giue euery one his particular

name, as *Refemblance* by Pourtrait or Imagery, which the
Greeks call *Icon, Refemblance* morall or mifticall, which
they call *Parabola, & Refemblance* by example, which
they call *Paradigma,* and firft we will fpeake of the
generall *refemblance,* or bare *fimilitude,* which may be
thus fpoken.

> *But as the watrie fhowres delay the raging wind,*
> *So doeth good hope cleane put away difpaire out of my mind.|*

And in this other likening the forlorne louer to a Dd iijᵛ
ftriken deere.

> *Then as the ftriken deere, withdrawes himfelfe alone,*
> *So do I feeke fome fecret place, where I may make my mone.*

And in this of ours where we liken glory to a fhadow.

> *As the fhadow (his nature beyng fuch,)*
> *Followeth the body, vvhether it vvill or no,*
> *So doeth glory, refufe it nere fo much,*
> *Wait on vertue, be it in vveale or vvo.*
> *And euen as the fhadow in his kind,*
> *What time it beares the carkas company,*
> *Goth oft before, and often comes behind:*
> *So doth renowme, that raifeth vs fo hye,*
> *Come to vs quicke, fometime not till vve dye.*
> *But the glory, that growth not ouer faft,*
> *Is euer great, and likelieft long to laft.*

Againe in a ditty to a miftreffe of ours, where we
likened the cure of Loue to *Achilles* launce.

> *The launce fo bright, that made Telephus vvound,*
> *The fame rufty, falued the fore againe,*
> *So may my meede (Madame) of you redownd,*
> *Whofe rigour vvas first authour of my paine.*

The *Tuskan* poet vfeth this *Refemblance,* inuring as
well by *Diffimilitude* as *Similitude,* likening himfelfe (by
Implication) to the flie, and neither to the eagle nor to
the owle: very well Englifhed by Sir *Thomas Wiat* after
his fafhion, and by my felfe thus:

(241)

There be fome fowles of fight fo prowd and ftarke,
As can behold the funne, and neuer fhrinke,
Some fo feeble, as they are faine to vvinke,
Or neuer come abroad till it be darke:
Others there be fo fimple, as they thinke,
Becaufe it fhines, to fport them in the fire,
And feele vnware, the vvrong of their defire,
Fluttring amidft the flame that doth them burne,
Of this laft ranke (alas) am I aright,
For in my ladies lookes to ftand or turne
I haue no povver, ne find place to retire,
Where any darke may fhade me from her fight|
Dd iiij^r *But to her beames fo bright whilst I afpire,*
I perifh by the bane of my delight.

Againe in thefe likening a wife man to the true louer.

As true loue is content with his enioy,
And asketh no witneffe nor no record,
And as faint loue is euermore moft coy,
To boaft and brag his troth at euery vvord:
Euen fo the vvife vvithouten other meede:
Contents him vvith the guilt of his good deede.

And in this refembling the learning of an euill man
to the feedes fowen in barren ground.

As the good feedes fowen in fruitfull foyle,
Bring foorth foyfon when barren doeth them fpoile:
So doeth it fare when much good learning hits,
Vpon fhrewde willes and ill difpofed wits.

And in thefe likening the wife man to an idiot.

A fage man faid, many of thofe that come
To Athens fchoole for vvifdome, ere they went
They first feem'd wife, then louers of wifdome,
Then Orators, then idiots, which is meant
That in wifdome all fuch as profite moft,
Are least furlie, and little apt to boast.

(242)

Againe, for a louer, whofe credit vpon fome report
had bene fhaken, he prayeth better opinion by fimilitude.

After ill crop the foyle muft eft be fowen,
And fro fhipwracke we fayle to feas againe,
Then God forbid whofe fault hath once bene knowen,
Should for euer a fpotted wight remaine.

And in this working by refemblance in a kinde of
diffimilitude betweene a father and a mafter.

It fares not by fathers as by masters it doeth fare,
For a foolifh father may get a wife fonne,
But of a foolifh mafter it haps very rare
Is bread a wife feruant where euer he wonne.

And in thefe, likening the wife man to the Giant, the
foole to the Dwarfe.

Set the Giant deepe in a dale, the dwarfe vpon an hill,|
Yet will the one be but a dwarfe, th'other a giant ftill.
So will the wife be great and high, euen in the lowest place:
The foole when he is moft aloft, will feeme but low and bafe.

Dd iiij▼

But when we liken an humane perfon to another in
countenaunce, ftature, fpeach or other qualitie, it is not
called bare refemblance, but refemblaunce by imagerie
or pourtrait, alluding to the painters terme, who yeldeth
to th'eye a vifible reprefentatiō of the thing he defcribes
and painteth in his table. So we commending her
Maieftie for wifedome bewtie and magnanimitie likened
her to the Serpent, the Lion and the Angell, becaufe by
common vfurpation, nothing is wifer then the Serpent,
more couragious then the Lion, more bewtifull then the
Angell. Thefe are our verfes in the end of the feuenth
Partheniade.

Icon.
or Refem-
blance by
imagerie.

Nature that feldome vvorkes amiffe,
In vvomans breft by paffing art:
Hath lodged fafe the Lyons hart,
And feately fixt vvith all good grace,
To Serpents head an Angels face.

(243)

And this maner of refemblaunce is not onely performed by likening of liuely creatures one to another, but alfo of any other naturall thing, bearing a proportion of fimilitude, as to liken yealow to gold, white to filuer, red to the rofe, foft to filke, hard to the ftone and fuch like. Sir *Philip Sidney* in the defcription of his miftreffe excellently well handled this figure of refemblaunce by imagerie, as ye may fee in his booke of *Archadia:* and ye may fee the like, of our doings, in a *Partheniade* written of our foueraigne Lady, wherein we refemble euery part of her body to fome naturall thing of excellent perfection in his kind, as of her forehead, browes and haire, thus.

> *Of filuer vvas her forehead hye,*
> *Her browes two bowes of hebenie,*
> *Her treffes trust vvere to behold*
> *Frizled and fine as fringe of gold.*

And of her lips.

> *Two lips vvrought out of rubie rocke,*
> *Like leaues to fhut and to vnlock.*
> *As portall dore in Princes chamber:*
> *A golden tongue in mouth of amber.|*

Ee iʳ And of her eyes.

> *Her eyes God wot vvhat ftuffe they are,*
> *I durft be fworne each is a ftarre:*
> *As cleere and bright as woont to guide*
> *The Pylot in his vvinter tide.*

And of her breafts.

> *Her bofome fleake as Paris plaster,*
> *Helde vp two balles of alabafter,*
> *Eche byas was a little cherrie:*
> *Or els I thinke a strawberie.*

And all the reft that followeth, which may fuffice to exemplifie your figure of *Icon,* or refemblance by imagerie and portrait.

(244)

But whenfoeuer by your fimilitude ye will feeme to teach any moralitie or good leffon by fpeeches mifticall and darke, or farre fette, vnder a fence metaphoricall applying one naturall thing to another, or one cafe to another, inferring by them a like confequence in other cafes the Greekes call it *Parabola*, which terme is alfo by cuftome accepted of vs: neuertheleffe we may call him in Englifh the refemblance mifticall: as when we liken a young childe to a greene twigge which ye may eafilie bende euery way ye lift: or an old man who laboureth with continuall infirmities, to a drie and drickfie oke. Such parables were all the preachings of Chrift in the Gofpell, as thofe of the wife and foolifh virgins, of the euil fteward, of the labourers in the vine-yard, and a number more. And they may be fayned afwell as true: as thofe fables of *Æfope*, and other apologies inuented for doctrine fake by wife and graue men. *Parabola. or Refemblance mifticall.*

Finally, if in matter of counfell or perfwafion we will feeme to liken one cafe to another, fuch as paffe ordinarily in mans affaires, and doe compare the paft with the prefent, gathering probabilitie of like fucceffe to come in the things wee haue prefently in hand: or if ye will draw the iudgements precedent and authorized by antiquitie as veritable, and peraduenture fayned and imagined for fome purpofe, into fimilitude or diffimilitude with our prefent actions and affaires, it is called refemblance by example: as if one fhould fay thus, *Alexander* the great in his expedition to Afia did thus, fo did *Hanniball* comming into Spaine, fo did *Cæfar*/in Egypt, therfore all great Captains & Generals ought to doe it. *Paradigma, or a refemblance by example.*

And thus againe, It hath bene alwayes vfuall among great and magnanimous princes in all ages, not only to repulfe any iniury & inuafion from their owne realmes and dominions, but alfo with a charitable & Princely compaffion to defend their good neighbors Princes and Potentats, from all oppreffion of tyrants & vfurpers. So did the Romaines by their armes reftore many Kings

Ee iv

(245)

of Aſia and Affricke expulſed out of their kingdoms.
So did K. *Edward* 1. reſtabliſh *Baliol* rightfull owner
of the crowne of Scotlād againſt *Robert le brus* no lawfull
King. So did king *Edward* the third aide *Dampeeter*
king of Spaine againſt *Henry* baſtard and vſurper. So
haue many Engliſh Princes holpen with their forces the
poore Dukes of Britaine their ancient friends and allies,
againſt the outrages of the French kings: and why may
not the Queene our ſoueraine Lady with like honor and
godly zele yeld protection to the people of the Low
countries, her neereſt neighbours to reſcue them a free
people from the Spaniſh ſeruitude.

And as this reſemblance is of one mans action to
another, ſo may it be made by examples of bruite
beaſtes, aptly correſponding in qualitie or euent, as one
that wrote certaine prety verſes of the Emperor *Maximinus*, to warne him that he ſhould not glory too much
in his owne ſtrength, for ſo he did in very deede, and
would take any common ſouldier to taske at wraſtling,
or weapon, or in any other actiuitie and feates of armes,
which was by the wiſer ſort miſliked, theſe were the
verſes.

> *The Elephant is ſtrong, yet death doeth it ſubdue,*
> *The bull is ſtrong, yet cannot death eſchue.*
> *The Lion ſtrong, and ſlaine for all his ſtrength:*
> *The Tygar ſtrong, yet kilde is at the length.*
> *Dread thou many, that dreadest not any one,*
> *Many can kill, that cannot kill alone.*

And ſo it fell out, for *Maximinus* was ſlaine in a
mutinie of his ſouldiers, taking no warning by theſe
examples written for his admonition.

CHAP. XX.

The last and principall figure of our poeticall Ornament.

For the glorious luftre it fetteth vpon our fpeech and language, the Greeks call it [*Exargafia*] the Latine [*Expolitio*] a terme/transferred from thefe polifhers of marble or porphirite, who after it is rough hewen & reduced to that fafhiō they will, do fet vpon it a goodly glaffe, fo fmoth and cleere as ye may fee your face in it, or otherwife as it fareth by the bare and naked body, which being attired in rich and gorgious apparell, feemeth to the common vfage of th'eye much more comely & bewtifull then the naturall. So doth this figure (which therefore I call the *Gorgious*) polifh our fpeech & as it were attire it with copious & pleafant amplifications and much varietie of fentences all running vpon one point & to one intēt: fo as I doubt whether I may terme it a figure, or rather a maffe of many figuratiue fpeaches, applied to the bewtifying of our tale or argu-mēt. In a worke of ours intituled *Philocalia* we haue ftrained to fhew the vfe & application of this figure and all others mentioned in this booke, to which we referre you. I finde none example in Englifh meetre, fo well maintayning this figure as that dittie of her Maiefties owne making paffing fweete and harmonicall, which figure beyng as his very originall name purporteth the moft bewtifull and gorgious of all others, it asketh in reafon to be referued for a laft complement, and def-ciphred by the arte of a Ladies penne, her felfe beyng the moft bewtifull, or rather bewtie of Queenes. And this was the occafion: our foueraigne Lady perceiuing how by the Sc. Q. refidence within this Realme at fo great libertie and eafe (as were skarce meete for fo great and daungerous a pryfoner) bred fecret factions among her people, and made many of the nobilitie incline to fauour her partie: fome of them defirous of innouation

Exargafia. or The Gorgious.

Ee ij^r

(247)

in the ſtate: others aſpiring to greater fortunes by her libertie and life. The Queene our ſoueraigne Lady to declare that ſhe was nothing ignorāt of thoſe ſecret practizes, though ſhe had long with great wiſdome and pacience diſſembled it, writeth this ditty moſt ſweet and ſententious, not hiding from all ſuch aſpiring minds the daunger of their ambition and diſloyaltie: which afterward fell out moſt truly by th'exemplary chaſtiſement of ſundry perſons, who in fauour of the ſayd Sc. Q. declining from her Maieſtie, ſought to interrupt the quiet of the Realme by many euill and vndutifull practizes. The ditty is as followeth./

Ee ij^v

The doubt of future foes, exiles my preſent ioy,
And wit me warnes to ſhun ſuch ſnares as threaten mine annoy.
For falſhood novv doth flow, and ſubiect faith doth ebbe,
Which would not be, if reaſon rul'd or wiſdome weu'd the webbe.
But clowdes of tois vntried, do cloake aſpiring mindes,
Which turne to raigne of late repent, by courſe of changed vvindes.
The toppe of hope ſuppoſed, the roote of ruth vvil be,
And fruteleſſe all their graffed guiles, as ſhortly ye ſhall ſee.
Then dazeld eyes vvith pride, vvhich great ambition blinds,
Shalbe vnſeeld by vvorthy wights, vvhoſe foreſight falſhood finds.
The daughter of debate, that eke diſcord doth ſovve
Shal reap no gaine where formor rule hath taught ſtil peace to growe.
No forreine banniſht vvight ſhall ancre in this port,
Our realme it brookes no ſtrangers force, let them elſvvhere reſort.
Our ruſty ſvvorde vvith rest, ſhall firſt his edge employ,
To polle their toppes that ſeeke, ſuch change and gape for ioy.

In a worke of ours entituled [*Philo Calia*] where we

(248)

entreat of the loues betwene prince *Philo* and Lady
Calia, in their mutual letters, meſſages, and ſpeeches:
we haue ſtrained our muſe to ſhew the vſe and application of this figure, and of all others.

CHAP. XXI.

*Of the vices or deformities in ſpeach and vvriting
principally noted by auncient Poets.*

It hath bene ſaid before how by ignorance of the maker
a good figure may become a vice, and by his good
diſcretion, a vicious ſpeach go for a vertue in the Poeticall
ſcience. This ſaying is to be explaned and qualified, for
ſome maner of ſpeaches are alwayes intollerable and
ſuch as cannot be vſed with any decencie, but are euer
vndecent namely barbarouſneſſe, incongruitie, ill diſpoſition, fond affectation, ruſticitie, and all extreme
darkneſſe, ſuch as it is not poſſible for a man to vnder-
ſtand the matter without an interpretour, all which
partes are generally to be baniſhed out of euery language, vnleſſe it may appeare that the maker or Poet
do it for the nonce, as it was reported by the Philoſopher
Heraclitus that he wrote in obſcure and darke termes of
purpoſe not to be vnderſtood, whence he merited the
nickname *Scotinus*, otherwiſe I ſee not but the reſt of
the common faultes may be borne with/ſometimes, or Ee iijʳ
paſſe without any great reproofe, not being vſed ouermuch or out of ſeaſon as I ſaid before: ſo as euery
ſurpluſage or prepoſterous placing or vndue iteration or
darke word, or doubtfull ſpeach are not ſo narrowly to
be looked vpon in a large poeme, nor ſpecially in the
pretie Poeſies and deuiſes of Ladies, and Gentlewomen
makers, whom we would not haue too preciſe Poets leaſt
with their ſhrewd wits, when they were maried they
might become a little too phantaſticall wiues, neuertheleſſe becauſe we ſeem to promiſe an arte, which doth

(249)

not iuſtly admit any wilful errour in the teacher, and
to th'end we may not be carped at by theſe methodicall
men, that we haue omitted any neceſſary point in this
buſineſſe to be regarded, I will ſpeake ſomewhat touching
theſe vicioſities of language particularly and briefly,
leauing no little to the Grammarians for maintenaunce
of the ſcholaſticall warre, and altercations: we for our
part condeſcending in this deuiſe of ours, to the appetite
of Princely perſonages & other ſo tender & queſie
complexions in Court, as are annoyed with nothing more
then long leſſons and ouermuch good order.

CHAP. XXII.

Some vices in ſpeaches and vvriting are alwayes intoller-
able, ſome others now and then borne vvithall by
licence of approued authors and cuſtome.

Barbariſmus.
or Forrein
ſpeech

The fouleſt vice in language is to ſpeake barbarouſly:
this terme grew by the great pride of the Greekes and
Latines, whē they were dominatours of the world reck-
oning no language ſo ſweete and ciuill as their owne, and
that all nations beſide them ſelues were rude and vnciuill, which they called barbarous: So as when any
ſtraunge word not of the naturall Greeke or Latin was
ſpoken, in the old time they called it *barbariſme*, or
when any of their owne naturall wordes were ſounded
and pronounced with ſtraunge and ill ſhapen accents,
or written by wrong ortographie, as he that would ſay
with vs in England, a douſand for a thouſand, iſterday,
for yeſterday, as commonly the Dutch and French people
do, they ſaid it was barbarouſly ſpoken. The Italian
at this day by like arrogance calleth the Frenchman,
Spaniard, Dutch, Engliſh, and all other breed behither
their mountaines *Appennines,*/*Tramontani*, as who would
ſay Barbarous. This terme being then ſo vſed by the
auncient Greekes, there haue bene ſince, notwithſtanding
who haue digged for the Etimologie ſomewhat deeper,

Ee iij^v

and many of them haue faid that it was fpoken by the rude and barking language of the Affricans now called Barbarians, who had great trafficke with the Greekes and Romanes, but that can not be fo, for that part of Affricke hath but of late receiued the name of Barbarie, and fome others rather thinke that of this word Barbarous, that countrey came to be called *Barbaria* and but few yeares in refpect agone. Others among whom is *Ihan Leon* a Moore of *Granada*, will feeme to deriue *Barbaria*, from this word *Bar*, twife iterated thus *Barbar*, as much to fay as flye, flye, which chaunced in a perfecution of the Arabians by fome feditious Mahometanes in the time of their Pontif. *Habdul mumi*, when they were had in the chafe, & driuen out of Arabia Weftward into the countreys of *Mauritania*, & during the purfuite cried one vpon another flye away, flye away, or paffe paffe, by which occafiō they fay, when the Arabians which were had in chafe came to ftay and fettle themfelues in that part of Affrica, they called it *Barbar*, as much to fay, the region of their flight or purfuite. Thus much for the terme, though not greatly pertinent to the matter, yet not vnpleafant to know for them that delight in fuch niceties.

Your next intollerable vice is *folecifmus* or incongruitie, as whē we fpeake falfe Englifh, that is by mifufing the *Grammaticall* rules to be obferued in cafes, genders, tenfes and fuch like, euery poore fcholler knowes the fault, & cals it the breaking of *Prifcians* head, for he was among the Latines a principall Grammarian.

Solecifmus. or Incongruitie.

Ye haue another intollerable ill maner of fpeach, which by the Greekes originall we may call *fonde affectation*, and is when we affect new words and phrafes other then the good fpeakers and writers in any language, or then cuftome hath allowed, & is the common fault of young fchollers not halfe well ftudied before they come from the Vniuerfitie or fchooles, and when they come to their friends, or happen to get fome benefice or other

Cacozelia. or Fonde affectation.

(251)

promotion in their countreys, will feeme to coigne fine wordes out of the Latin, and to vfe new fangled fpeaches, thereby to fhew themfelues among the ignorant the better learned./

Another of your intollerable vices is that which the Greekes call *Soraifmus*, & we may call the [*mingle mangle*] as whē we make our fpeach or writinges of fundry languages vfing fome Italian word, or French, or Spanifh, or Dutch, or Scottifh, not for the nonce or for any purpofe (which were in part excufable) but ignorantly and affectedly as one that faid vfing this French word *Roy*, to make ryme with another verfe, thus.

O mightie Lord of loue, dame Venus onely ioy,
Whofe Princely povver exceedes ech other heauenly roy.

The verfe is good but the terme peeuifhly affected.

Another of reafonable good facilitie in tranflation finding certaine of the hymnes of *Pyndarus* and of *Anacreons odes*, and other *Lirickes* among the Greekes very well tranflated by *Rounfard* the French Poet, & applied to the honour of a great Prince in France, comes our minion and tranflates the fame out of French into Englifh, and applieth them to the honour of a great noble man in England (wherein I commend his reuerent minde and duetie) but doth fo impudently robbe the French Poet both of his prayfe and alfo of his French termes, that I cannot fo much pitie him as be angry with him for his iniurious dealing, our fayd maker not being afhamed to vfe thefe French wordes *freddon, egar, fuperbous, filanding, celeft, calabrois, thebanois* and a number of others, for Englifh wordes, which haue no maner of conformitie with our language either by cuftome or deriuation which may make them tollerable. And in the end (which is worft of all) makes his vaunt that neuer Englifh finger but his hath toucht *Pindars* ftring which was neuerthelefle word by word

(252)

as *Rounfard* had faid before by like braggery. Thefe be his verfes.

> *And of an ingenious inuention, infanted with pleafant*
> *trauaile.*

Whereas the French word is *enfante* as much to fay borne as a child, in another verfe he faith.

> *I vvill freddon in thine honour.*

For I will fhake or quiuer my fingers, for fo in French is *freddon*, and in another verfe.

> *But if I vvill thus like pindar,*
> *In many difcourfes egar.*

This word *egar* is as much to fay as to wander or ftray out of/the way, which in our Englifh is not re- Ee iiij^v ceiued, nor thefe wordes *calabrois, thebanois*, but rather *calabrian, thebā* [*filanding fifters*] for the fpinning fifters: this man deferues to be endited of pety *larceny* for pilfring other mens deuifes from them & conuerting them to his owne vfe, for in deede as I would wifh euery inuētour which is the very Poet to receaue the prayfes of his inuention, fo would I not haue a trāflatour be afhamed to be acknowen of his tranflation.

Another of your intollerable vices is ill difpofition *Cacofintheton* or placing of your words in a claufe or fentence: as when or the you will place your adiectiue after your fubftantiue, Mifplacer. thus: *Mayde faire, vvidovv riche, prieft holy*, and fuch like, which though the Latines did admit, yet our Englifh did not, as one that faid ridiculoufly.

> *In my yeares luftie, many a deed doughtie did I.*

All thefe remembred faults be intollerable and euer vndecent.

Now haue ye other vicious manners of fpeech, but *Cacemphaton.* fometimes and in fome cafes tollerable, and chiefly to or the the intent to mooue laughter, and to make fport, or to foule fpeech. giue it fome pretty ftrange grace, and is when we vfe fuch wordes as may be drawen to a foule and vnfhamefaft fence, as one that would fay to a young woman, *I pray you let me iape vvith you,* which in deed is no more but let me fport with you. Yea and though it were not altogether fo directly fpoken, the very founding of the word were not commendable, as he that in the prefence of Ladies would vfe this common Prouerbe,

> *Iape vvith me but hurt me not,*
> *Bourde vvith me but fhame me not.*

For it may be taken in another peruerfer fence by that forte of perfons that heare it, in whofe eares no fuch matter ought almoft to be called in memory, this vice is called by the Greekes *Cacemphaton,* we call it the vnfhamefaft or figure of foule fpeech, which our courtly maker fhall in any cafe fhunne, leaft of a Poet he become a Buffon or rayling companion, the Latines called him *Scurra.* There is alfo another fort of il-fauoured fpeech fubiect to this vice, but refting more in the manner of the ilfhapen found and accent, than for the matter it felfe, which may eafily be auoyded in choofing your wordes thofe that bee of the pleafanteft orthography, and not to rime too many like founding words together./

Ff i^r

Tautologia, or the figure of felfe faying.

Ye haue another manner of compofing your metre nothing commendable, fpecially if it be too much vfed, and is whē our maker takes too much delight to fill his verfe with wordes beginning all with a letter, as an Englifh rimer that faid:

> *The deadly droppes of darke difdaine,*
> *Do daily drench my due defartes.*

And as the Monke we fpake of before, wrote a whole Poeme to the honor of *Carolus Caluus,* euery word in his verfe beginning with C, thus:

> *Carmina clarifonæ Caluis cantcte camenæ.*

Many of our Englifh makers vfe it too much, yet we confeffe it doth not ill but pretily becomes the

(254)

meetre, if ye paſſe not two or three words in one verſe, and vſe it not very much, as he that ſaid by way of *Epithete.*

The ſmoakie ſighes: the trickling teares.

And ſuch like, for ſuch compoſition makes the meetre runne away ſmoother, and paſſeth from the lippes with more facilitie by iteration of a letter then by alteration, which alteration of a letter requires an exchange of miniſtery and office in the lippes, teeth or palate, and ſo doth not the iteration.

Your miſplacing and prepoſterous placing is not all one in behauiour of language, for the miſplacing is alwaies intollerable, but the prepoſterous is a pardonable fault, and many times giues a pretie grace vnto the ſpeech. We call it by a common ſaying to *ſet the carte before the horſe*, and it may be done, eyther by a ſingle word or by a clauſe of ſpeech: by a ſingle word thus:

And if I not performe, God let me neuer thriue.

For performe not: and this vice is ſometime tollerable inough, but if the word carry any notable fence, it is a vice not tollerable, as he that ſaid praiſing a woman for her red lippes, thus:

A corrall lippe of hew.

Which is no good ſpeech, becauſe either he ſhould haue ſayd no more but a corrall lip, which had bene inough to declare the redneſſe, or els he ſhould haue ſaid, a lip of corrall hew, and not a corrall lip of hew. Now if this diſorder be in a whole clauſe which carieth more ſentence then a word, it is then worſt of all.

Ye haue another vicious ſpeech which the Greeks call *Acyron,/*we call it the *vncouthe,* and is when we vſe an obſcure and darke word, and vtterly repugnant to that we would expreſſe, if it be not by vertue of the figures *metaphore, allegorie, abuſion,* or ſuch other laudable figure before remembred, as he that ſaid by way of *Epithete.*

A dongeon deepe, a dampe as darke as hell.

Hiſteron, proteron.
or the
Prepoſterous.

Acyron,
Ff iv   or the
Vncouthe.

Where it is euident that a dampe being but a breath or vapour, and not to be difcerned by the eye, ought not to haue this *epithete* (*darke,*) no more then another that prayfing his miftreffe for her bewtifull haire, faid very improperly and with an vncouth terme.

> *Her haire furmounts Apollos pride,*
> *In it fuch bewty raignes.*

Whereas this word *raigne* is ill applied to the bewtie of a womans haire, and might better haue bene fpoken of her whole perfon, in which bewtie, fauour, and good grace, may perhaps in fome fort be faid to raigne as our felues wrate, in a *Partheniade* praifing her Maiefties countenance, thus:

> *A cheare vvhere loue and Maieflie do raigne,*
> *Both milde and flerne, &c.*

Becaufe this word Maieftie is a word expreffing a certaine Soueraigne dignitie, as well as a quallitie of countenance, and therefore may properly be faid to *raigne*, & requires no meaner a word to fet him foorth by. So it is not of the bewtie that remaines in a womans haire, or in her hand or any other member: therfore when ye fee all thefe improper or harde Epithets vfed, ye may put them in the number of [*vncouths*] as one that faid, *the flouds of graces:* I haue heard of *the flouds of teares,* and *the flouds of eloquence,* or of any thing that may refemble the nature of a water-courfe, and in that refpect we fay alfo, *the ftreames of teares,* and *the ftreames of vtterance,* but not *the ftreames of graces,* or of *beautie.* Such manner of vncouth fpeech did the Tanner of Tamworth vfe to king *Edward* the fourth, which Tāner hauing a great while miftaken him, and vfed very broad talke with him, at length perceiuing by his traine that it was the king, was afraide he fhould be punifhed for it, faid thus with a certaine rude repentance.

> *I hope I fhall be hanged to morrow.*

For [*I feare me*] *I fhall be hanged,* whereat the king

laughed a/good, not only to fee the Tanners vaine feare, but alfo to heare his ill fhapen terme, and gaue him for recōpence of his good fport, the inheritance of Plumton parke, I am afraid the Poets of our time that fpeake more finely and correctedly will come too fhort of fuch a reward.

Alfo the Poet or makers fpeech becomes vicious and vnpleafant by nothing more than by vfing too much furplufage: and this lieth not only in a word or two more than ordinary, but in whole claufes, and peraduenture large fentences impertinently fpoken, or with more labour and curiofitie than is requifite. The firft furplufage the Greekes call *Pleonafmus*, I call him [*too full fpeech*] and is no great fault, as if one fhould fay, *I heard it with mine eares, and faw it vvith mine eyes*, as if a man could heare with his heeles, or fee with his nofe. We our felues vfed this fuperfluous fpeech in a verfe written of our miftreffe, neuertheles, not much to be mifliked, for euen a vice fometime being feafonably vfed, hath a pretie grace, The vice of Surplufage.

> *For euer may my true loue liue and neuer die*
> *And that mine eyes may fee her crownde a Queene.*

Pleonafmus, or Too ful fpeech

As, if fhe liued euer. fhe could euer die, or that one might fee her crowned without his eyes.

Another part of furplufage is called *Macrologia*, or long language, when we vfe large claufes or fentences more than is requifite to the matter: it is alfo named by the Greeks *Periffologia*, as he that faid, the Ambaffadours after they had receiued this anfwere at the kings hands, they tooke their leaue and returned home into their countrey from whence they came. *Macrologia,* or Long language

So faid another of our rimers, meaning to fhew the great annoy and difficultie of thofe warres of Troy, caufed for *Helenas* fake.

> *Nor Menelaus vvas vnwife,*
> *Or troupe of Troians mad,*
> *When he vvith them and they vvith him,*
> *For her fuch combat had.*

Thefe claufes (*he vvith them and they vvith him*) are furplufage, and one of them very impertinent, becaufe it could not otherwife be intended, but that *Menelaus*, Ff ij^v fighting with the Troians, the/Troians muft of neceffitie fight with him.

Another point of furplufage lieth not fo much in fuperfluitie of your words, as of your trauaile to defcribe the matter which yee take in hand, and that ye ouer-labour your felfe in your bufineffe. And therefore the *Periergia*, Greekes call it *Periergia*, we call it ouer-labor, iumpe or with the originall: or rather [*the curious*] for his ouer-Ouerlabour, much curiofitie and ftudie to fhew himfelfe fine in a light otherwife matter, as one of our late makers, who in moft of his called the things wrote very well, in this (to mine opinion) more curious. curioufly than needed, the matter being ripely confidered: yet is his verfe very good, and his meetre cleanly. His intent was to declare how vpon the tenth day of March he croffed the riuer of Thames, to walke in Saint *Georges* field, the matter was not great as ye may fuppofe.

> *The tenth of March vvhen Aries receiued*
> *Dan Phœbus raies into his horned head,*
> *And I my felfe by learned lore perceiued*
> *That Ver approcht and frofty vvinter fled*
> *I croft the Thames to take the cheerefull aire,*
> *In open fields, the vveather was fo faire.*

Firft, the whole matter is not worth all this folemne circumftance to defcribe the tenth day of March, but if he had left at the two firft verfes, it had bene inough. But when he comes with two other verfes to enlarge his defcription, it is not only more than needes, but alfo very ridiculous, for he makes wife, as if he had not bene a mā learned in fome of the mathematickes (by learned lore) that he could not haue told that the x. of March had fallen in the fpring of the yeare: which euery carter, and alfo euery child knoweth without any learning. Then alfo, whē he faith [*Ver approcht, and frosty winter fled*] though it were a surplusage (becaufe one feafon muft needes geue place to the other) yet doeth it well inough passe without blame in the maker. Thefe, and a hundred more of fuch faultie and impertinent fpeeches may yee finde amongft vs vulgar Poets, when we be careleffe of our doings.

It is no fmall fault in a maker to vfe fuch wordes *Tapinofis,* and termes as do diminifh and abbafe the matter he *or the Abbafer.* would feeme to fet forth, by imparing the dignitie, height vigour or maieftie of the caufe he takes in hand, as one that would fay king *Philip* fhrewdly harmed/the Ff iij^r towne of *S. Quintaines,* when in deede he wanne it and put it to the facke, and that king *Henry* the eight made fpoiles in *Turwin,* when as in deede he did more then fpoile it, for he caufed it to be defaced and razed flat to the earth, and made it inhabitable. Therefore the hiftoriographer that fhould by fuch wordes report of thefe two kings geftes in that behalfe, fhould greatly blemifh the honour of their doings and almoft fpeake vntruly and iniurioufly by way of abbafement, as another of our bad rymers that very indecently faid.

A mifers mynde thou haft, thou haft a Princes pelfe.

A lewd terme to be giuen to a Princes treafure (*pelfe*) and was a little more manerly fpoken by *Seriant Bend-lowes,* when in a progreffe time comming to falute the Queene in Huntingtonfhire he faid to her Cochman, ftay thy cart good fellow, ftay thy cart, that I may fpeake to the Queene, whereat her Maieftie laughed as fhe had bene tickled, and all the reft of the company although very gracioufly (as her manner is) fhe gaue him great thankes and her hand to kiffe. Thefe and fuch other bafe wordes do greatly difgrace the thing & the fpeaker or writer: the Greekes call it [*Tapinofis*] we the [*abbafer.*]

Others there be that fall into the contrary vice by *Bomphiologia,* vfing fuch bombafted wordes, as feeme altogether farced *or* full of winde, being a great deale to high and loftie for *Pompious fpeech.*

the matter, whereof ye may finde too many in all popular rymers.

Amphibologia or the Ambiguous. Then haue ye one other vicious fpeach with which we will finifh this Chapter, and is when we fpeake or write doubtfully and that the fence may be taken two wayes, fuch ambiguous termes they call *Amphibologia*, we call it the *ambiguous*, or figure of fence incertaine, as if one fhould fay *Thomas Tayler* faw *William Tyler* dronke, it is indifferent to thinke either th'one or th'other dronke. Thus faid a gentleman in our vulgar pretily notwithftanding becaufe he did it not ignorantly, but for the nonce.

I fat by my Lady foundly fleeping,
My miftreffe lay by me bitterly weeping.

No man can tell by this, whether the miftreffe or the man, flept or wept: thefe doubtfull fpeaches were vfed much in the old times by their falfe Prophets as ap-peareth by the Oracles of *Delphos* and/of the *Sybilles* prophecies deuifed by the religious perfons of thofe dayes to abufe the fuperftitious people, and to encomber their bufie braynes with vaine hope or vaine feare.

Lucianus the merry Greeke reciteth a great number of them, deuifed by a coofening companion one *Alexander*, to get himfelfe the name and reputation of the God *Æfculapius*, and in effect all our old Brittifh and Saxon prophefies be of the fame fort, that turne them on which fide ye will, the matter of them may be verified, neuer-theleffe carryeth generally fuch force in the heades of fonde people, that by the comfort of thofe blind pro-phecies many infurrections and rebellions haue bene ftirred vp in this Realme, as that of *Iacke Straw*, & *Iacke Cade* in *Richard* the feconds time, and in our time by a feditious fellow in Norffolke calling himfelf Captaine Ket and others in other places of the Realme lead altogether by certaine propheticall rymes, which might be conftred two or three wayes as well as to that one

Ff iijᵛ

whereunto the rebelles applied it, our maker ſhall therefore auoyde all ſuch ambiguous ſpeaches vnleſſe it be
when he doth it for the nonce and for ſome purpoſe.

CHAP. XXIII.

*What it is that generally makes our ſpeach well pleaſing
& commendable, and of that which the Latines
call Decorum.*

In all things to vſe decencie, is it onely that giueth euery
thing his good grace & without which nothing in mans
ſpeach could ſeeme good or gracious, in ſo much as
many times it makes a bewtifull figure fall into a de-
formitie, and on th'other ſide a vicious ſpeach ſeeme
pleaſaunt and bewtifull: this decencie is therfore the
line & leuell for al good makers to do their buſines by.
But herein reſteth the difficultie, to know what this good
grace is, & wherein it conſiſteth, for peraduenture it be
eaſier to conceaue then to expreſſe, we wil therfore
examine it to the bottome & ſay: that euery thing which
pleaſeth the mind or ſences, & the mind by the ſences
as by means inſtrumētall, doth it for ſome amiable point
or qualitie that is in it, which draweth them to a good
liking and contentment with their proper obiects. But
that cannot be if they diſcouer any illfauoredneſſe or
diſproportion to the partes apprehen-/ſiue, as for example, Ff iiijr
when a ſound is either too loude or too low or otherwiſe confuſe, the eare is ill affected: ſo is th'eye if the
coulour be ſad or not liminous and recreatiue, or the
ſhape of a membred body without his due meaſures
and ſimmetry, and the like of euery other ſence in his
proper function. Theſe exceſſes or defectes or confuſions
and diſorders in the ſenſible obiectes are deformities and
vnſeemely to the ſence. In like ſort the mynde for the
things that be his mentall obiectes hath his good graces
and his bad, whereof th'one contents him wonderous

(261)

well, th'other difpleafeth him continually, no more nor
no leffe then ye fee the difcordes of muficke do to a well
tuned eare. The Greekes call this good grace of euery
thing in his kinde, το πρεπον, the Latines [*decorum*] we in
our vulgar call it by a fcholafticall terme [*decencie*] our
owne Saxon Englifh terme is [*feemelyneffe*] that is to
fay, for his good fhape and vtter appearance well pleafing
the eye, we call it alfo [*comelyneffe*] for the delight it
bringeth comming towardes vs, and to that purpofe may
be called [*pleafant approche*] fo as euery way feeking to
expreffe this πρεπον of the Greekes and *decorum* of the
Latines, we are faine in our vulgar toung to borrow the
terme which our eye onely for his noble prerogatiue
ouer all the reft of the fences doth vfurpe, and to apply
the fame to all good, comely, pleafant and honeft things,
euen to the fpirituall obiectes of the mynde, which
ftand no leffe in the due proportion of reafon and difcourfe than any other materiall thing doth in his fenfible
bewtie, proportion and comelyneffe.

Now becaufe this comelyneffe refteth in the good conformitie of many things and their fundry circumftances,
with refpect one to another, fo as there be found a iuft
correfpondencie betweene them by this or that relation,
the Greekes call it *Analogie* or a conuenient proportion.
This louely conformitie, or proportion, or conueniencie
betweene the fence and the fenfible hath nature her
felfe firft moft carefully obferued in all her owne workes,
then alfo by kinde graft it in the appetites of euery
creature working by intelligence to couet and defire:
and in their actions to imitate & performe: and of man
chiefly before any other creature afwell in his fpeaches
as in euery other part of his behauiour. And this in
generalitie and by an vfuall terme is that which the
Latines call/[*decorum*.] So albeit we before alleaged that
all our figures be but tranfgreffions of our dayly fpeach,
yet if they fall out decently to the good liking of the
mynde or eare and to the bewtifying of the matter or

Ff iiijᵛ

(262)

language, all is well, if indecently, and to the eares and
myndes misliking (be the figure of it selfe neuer so commendable) all is amisse, the election is the writers, the
iudgemēt is the worlds, as theirs to whom the reading
apperteineth. But since the actions of man with their
circumstances be infinite, and the world likewise re-
plenished with many iudgements, it may be a question
who shal haue the determination of such controuersie as
may arise whether this or that action or speach be decent
or indecent: and verely it seemes to go all by discretion,
not perchaunce of euery one, but by a learned and experienced discretion, for otherwise seemes the *decorum*
to a weake and ignorant iudgement, then it doth to
one of better knowledge and experience: which sheweth
that it resteth in the discerning part of the minde, so as
he who can make the best and most differences of things
by reasonable and wittie distinction is to be the fittest
iudge or sentencer of [*decencie.*] Such generally is the
discreetest man, particularly in any art the most skilfull
and discreetest, and in all other things for the more part
those that be of much obseruation and greatest experience.
The case then standing that discretion must chiefly guide
all those businesse, since there be sundry sortes of discretion all vnlike, euen as there be men of action or art,
I see no way so fit to enable a man truly to estimate of
[*decencie*] as example, by whose veritie we may deeme
the differences of things and their proportions, and by
particular discussions come at length to sentence of it
generally, and also in our behauiours the more easily to
put it in execution. But by reason of the sundry circumstances, that mans affaires are as it were wrapt in, this
[*decencie*] comes to be very much alterable and subiect
to varietie, in so much as our speach asketh one maner
of *decencie*, in respect of the person who speakes: another
of his to whom it is spoken: another of whom we speake:
another of what we speake, and in what place and time
and to what purpose. And as it is of speach, so of al

(263)

other our behauiours. We wil therefore fet you down fome few examples of euery circumftance how it alters
Gg iͬ the decencie of fpeach or action. And/by thefe few fhal ye be able to gather a number more to confirme and eftablifh your iudgement by a perfit difcretion.

This decencie, fo farfoorth as apperteineth to the confideration of our art, refteth in writing, fpeech and behauiour. But becaufe writing is no more then the image or character of fpeech, they fhall goe together in thefe our obferuations. And firft wee wil fort you out diuers points, in which the wife and learned men of times paft haue noted much decency or vndecencie, euery man according to his difcretion, as it hath bene faid afore: but wherein for the moft part all difcreete men doe generally agree, and varie not in opinion, whereof the examples I will geue you be worthie of remembrance: & though they brought with them no doctrine or inftitution at all, yet for the folace they may geue the readers, after fuch a rable of fcholaftical precepts which be tedious, thefe reports being of the nature of matters hiftoricall, they are to be embraced: but olde memories are very profitable to the mind, and ferue as a glaffe to looke vpon and behold the euents of time, and more exactly to skan the trueth of euery cafe that fhall happen in the affaires of man, and many there be that haply doe not obferue euery particularitie in matters of decencie or vndecencie: and yet when the cafe is tolde them by another man, they commonly geue the fame fentence vpon it. But yet whofoeuer obferueth much, fhalbe counted the wifeft and difcreeteft man, and whofoeuer fpends all his life in his owne vaine actions and con-ceits, and obferues no mans elfe, he fhal in the ende prooue but a fimple man. In which refpect it is alwaies faid, one man of experience is wifer than tenne learned men, becaufe of his long and ftudious obferuation and often triall.

And your decencies are of fundrie forts, according to

the many circumſtances accompanying our writing,
ſpeech or behauiour, ſo as in the very ſound or voice
of him that ſpeaketh, there is a decencie that becommeth,
and an vndecencie that misbecōmeth vs, which th'Emperor *Anthonine* marked well in the Orator *Philiſcus*,
who ſpake before him with ſo ſmall and ſhrill a voice
as the Emperor was greatly annoyed therewith, and to
make him ſhorten his tale, ſaid, by thy beard thou
ſhouldſt be a man, but by thy voice a woman./

Phauorinus the Philoſopher was counted very wiſe Gg iv
and well learned, but a little too talkatiue and full of
words: for the which *Timocrates* reprooued him in the
hearing of one *Polemon*. That is no wonder quoth
Polemon, for ſo be all women. And beſides, *Phauorinus*
being knowen for an Eunuke or gelded man, came by
the ſame nippe to be noted as an effeminate and de-
generate perſon.

And there is a meaſure to be vſed in a mans ſpeech
or tale, ſo as it be neither for ſhortneſſe too darke, nor
for length too tedious. Which made *Cleomenes* king of
the Lacedemonians geue this vnpleaſant anſwere to the
Ambaſſadors of the Samiens, who had tolde him a long
meſſage from their Citie, and deſired to know his pleaſure
in it. My maiſters (ſaith he) the firſt part of your tale
was ſo long, that I remember it not, which made that
the ſecond I vnderſtoode not, and as for the third part
I doe nothing well allow of. Great princes and graue
counſellers who haue little ſpare leiſure to hearken,
would haue ſpeeches vſed to them ſuch as be ſhort and
ſweete.

And if they be ſpoken by a man of account, or one
who for his yeares, profeſſion or dignitie ſhould be
thought wiſe & reuerend, his ſpeeches & words ſhould
alſo be graue, pithie & ſententious, which was well noted
by king *Antiochus*, who likened *Hermogenes* the famous
Orator of Greece, vnto theſe fowles in their moulting
time, when their feathers be ſick, and be ſo loaſe in the

(265)

fleſh that at any little rowſe they can eaſilie ſhake them off: ſo ſaith he, can *Hermogenes* of all the men that euer I knew, as eaſilie deliuer from him his vaine and impertinent ſpeeches and words.

And there is a decencie, that euery ſpeech ſhould be to the appetite and delight, or dignitie of the hearer & not for any reſpect arrogant or vndutifull, as was that of *Alexander* ſent Embaſſadour from the *Athenians* to th'Emperour *Marcus*, this man ſeing th'emperour not ſo attentiue to his tale, as he would haue had him, ſaid by way of interruption, *Cæſar* I pray thee giue me better eare, it ſeemeſt thou knoweſt me not, nor from whom I came: the Emperour nothing well liking his bold malapert ſpeech, ſaid: thou art deceyued, for I heare thee and know well inough, that thou art that fine, fooliſh, curious, ſawcie *Alexāder* that tendeſt to nothing/but to combe & cury thy haire, to pare thy nailes, to pick thy teeth, and to perfume thy ſelfe with ſweet oyles, that no man may abide the ſent of thee. Prowde ſpeeches, and too much fineſſe and curioſitie is not commendable in an Embaſſadour. And I haue knowen in my time ſuch of them, as ſtudied more vpon what apparell they ſhould weare, and what countenaunces they ſhould keepe at the times of their audience, then they did vpon th'effect of their errant or commiſſion.

And there is decēcy in that euery mā ſhould talke of the things they haue beſt ſkill of, and not in that, their knowledge and learning ſerueth them not to do, as we are wont to ſay, he ſpeaketh of Robin hood that neuer ſhot in his bow: there came a great Oratour before *Cleomenes* king of *Lacedemonia*, and vttered much matter to him touching fortitude and valiancie in the warres: the king laughed: why laugheſt thou quoth the learned mā, ſince thou art a king thy ſelfe, and one whom fortitude beſt becommeth? why ſaid *Cleomenes* would it not make any body laugh, to heare the ſwallow who feeds onely vpon flies, to boaſt of his great pray, and

Gg ij^r

fee the eagle ftand by and fay nothing? if thou wert a
man of warre or euer hadft bene day of thy life, I would
not laugh to here thee fpeake of valiancie, but neuer
being fo, & fpeaking before an old captaine I can not
choofe but laugh.

And fome things and fpeaches are decent or indecent
in refpect of the time they be fpoken or done in. As
when a great clerk prefented king *Antiochus* with a booke
treating all of iuftice, the king that time lying at the
fiege of a towne, who lookt vpon the title of the booke,
and caft it to him againe: faying, what a diuell telleft
thou to me of iuftice, now thou feeft me vfe force and
do the beft I can to bereeue mine enimie of his towne?
euery thing hath his feafon which is called Oportunitie,
and the vnfitneffe or vndecency of the time is called
Importunitie.

Sometime the vndecency arifeth by the indignitie of
the word in refpect of the fpeaker himfelfe, as whan a
daughter of Fraunce and next heyre generall to the
crowne (if the law *Salique* had not barred her) being
fet in a great chaufe by fome harde words giuen her
by another prince of the bloud, faid in her anger, thou
durft not haue faid thus much to me if God had giuē
me a paire of, &c./and told all out, meaning if God Gg ij^v
had made her a man and not a woman fhe had bene
king of Fraunce. The word became not the greatneffe
of her perfon, and much leffe her fex, whofe chiefe
vertue is fhamefaftneffe, which the Latines call *Vere-
cundia*, that is a naturall feare to be noted with any
impudicitie: fo as when they heare or fee any thing
tending that way they commonly blufh, & is a part
greatly praifed in all women.

Yet will ye fee in many cafes how pleafant fpeeches
and fauouring fome skurrillity and vnfhamefaftnes haue
now and then a certaine decencie, and well become both
the fpeaker to fay, and the hearer to abide, but that is
by reafon of fome other circumftance, as when the

(267)

ſpeaker himſelfe is knowne to be a common ieſter or buffon, ſuch as take vpon them to make princes merry, or when ſome occaſion is giuen by the hearer to induce ſuch a pleaſaunt ſpeach, and in many other caſes whereof no generall rule can be giuen, but are beſt knowen by example: as when Sir *Andrew Flamock* king *Henry* the eights ſtanderdbearer, a merry conceyted man and apt to ſkoffe, waiting one day at the kings heeles when he entred the parke at Greenewich, the king blew his horne, *Flamock* hauing his belly full, and his tayle at commaundement, gaue out a rappe nothing faintly, that the king turned him about and ſaid how now ſirra? *Flamock* not well knowing how to excuſe his vnmanerly aćt, if it pleaſe you Sir quoth he, your Maieſty blew one blaſt for the keeper and I another for his man. The king laughed hartily and tooke it nothing offenſiuely: for indeed as the caſe fell out it was not vndecently ſpoken by Sir *Andrew Flamock*, for it was the cleanelieſt excuſe he could make, and a merry implicatiue in termes nothing odious, and therefore a ſporting ſatisfaćtion to the kings mind, in a matter which without ſome ſuch merry anſwere could not haue bene well taken. So was *Flamocks* aćtion moſt vncomely, but his ſpeech excellently well becōming the occaſion.

But at another time and in another like caſe, the ſame ſkurrillitie of *Flamock* was more offenſiue, becauſe it was more indecent. As when the king hauing *Flamock* with him in his barge, paſſing from Weſtminſter to Greenewich to viſite a fayre Lady whom the king loued and was lodged in the tower of the Parke: the/king comming within ſight of the tower, and being diſpoſed to be merry, ſaid, *Flamock* let vs rime: as well as I can ſaid *Flamock* if it pleaſe your grace. The king began thus:

Gg iijʳ

> *Within this towre,*
> *There lieth a flowre,*
> *That hath my hart.*

Flamock for aunfwer: *Within this hower, fhe will, &c.*
with the reft in fo vncleanly termes, as might not now
become me by the rule of *Decorum* to vtter writing to
fo great a Maieftie, but the king tooke them in fo euill
part, as he bid *Flamock* auant varlet, and that he fhould
no more be fo neere vnto him. And wherein I would
faine learne, lay this vndecencie? in the fkurrill and
filthy termes not meete for a kings eare? perchance fo.
For the king was a wife and graue man, and though
he hated not a faire woman, yet liked he nothing well
to heare fpeeches of ribaudrie: as they report of th'emperour *Octauian: Licet fuerit ipfe incontinentiffimus, fuit
tamen incontinentiæ feueriffimus vltor.* But the very caufe
in deed was for that *Flamocks* reply anfwered not the
kings expectation, for the kings rime commencing with
a pleafant and amorous propofitiō: Sir *Andrew Flamock*
to finifh it not with loue but with lothfomneffe, by termes
very rude and vnciuill, and feing the king greatly fauour
that Ladie for her much beauty by like or fome other
good partes, by his faftidious aunfwer to make her feeme
odious to him, it helde a great difproportion to the kings
appetite, for nothing is fo vnpleafant to a man, as to
be encountred in his chiefe affection, & fpecially in his
loues, & whom we honour we fhould alfo reuerence
their appetites, or at the leaft beare with them (not being
wicked and vtterly euill) and whatfoeuer they do affect,
we do not as becōmeth vs if we make it feeme to them
horrible. This in mine opinion was the chiefe caufe of
the vndecencie and alfo of the kings offence. *Ariftotle*
the great philofopher knowing this very well, what time
he put *Califtenes* to king *Alexāder* the greats feruice gaue
him this leffon. Sirra quoth he, ye go now from a
fcholler to be a courtier, fee ye fpeake to the king your
maifter, either nothing at all, or elfe that which pleafeth
him, which rule if *Calistenes* had followed and forborne
to croffe the kings appetite in diuerfe fpeeches, it had
not coft him fo/deepely as afterward it did. A like Gg iijᵛ

13 (269)

matter of offence fell out betweene th'Emperour *Charles* the fifth, & an Embaſſadour of king *Henry* the eight, whō I could name but will not for the great opinion the world had of his wiſdome and ſufficiency in that behalfe, and all for miſuſing of a terme. The king in the matter of controuerſie betwixt him and Ladie *Catherine* of *Caſtill* the Emperours awnt, found himſelfe grieued that the Emperour ſhould take her part and worke vnder hand with the Pope to hinder the diuorce: and gaue his Embaſſadour commiſſion in good termes to open his griefes to the Emperour, and to expoſtulat with his Maieſtie, for that he ſeemed to forget the kings great kindneſſe and friendſhip before times vſed with th'Emperour, aſwell by disburſing for him ſundry great ſummes of monie which were not all yet repayd: as alſo by furniſhing him at his neede with ſtore of men and munition to his warres, and now to be thus vſed he thought it a very euill requitall. The Embaſſadour for too much animoſitie and more then needed in the caſe, or perchance by ignorance of the proprietie of the Spaniſh tongue, told the Emperour among other words, that he was *Hombre el mas ingrato enel mondo*, the ingrateſt perſon in the world to vſe his maiſter ſo. The Emperour tooke him ſuddainly with the word, and ſaid: calleſt thou me *ingrato?* I tell thee learne better termes, or elſe I will teach them thee. Th'Embaſſadour excuſed it by his com-miſſion, and ſaid: they were the king his maiſters words, and not his owne. Nay quoth th'Emperour, thy maiſter durſt not haue ſent me theſe words, were it not for that broad ditch betweene him & me, meaning the ſea, which is hard to paſſe with an army of reuenge. The Embaſ-ſadour was cōmanded away & no more hard by the Emperor, til by ſome other means afterward the grief was either pacified or forgotten, & all this inconueniēce grew by miſuſe of one word, which being otherwiſe ſpoken & in ſome ſort qualified, had eaſily holpen all, & yet th'Embaſſadour might ſufficiently haue ſatisfied

his commiſſion & much better aduaunced his purpoſe,
as to haue ſaid for this word [*ye are ingrate,*] ye haue not
vſed ſuch gratitude towards him as he hath deſerued:
ſo ye may ſee how a word ſpokē vndecently, not knowing
the phraſe or proprietie of a language, maketh a whole
matter many times miſcarrie. In which reſpect it/is to   Gg iiijʳ
be wiſhed, that none Ambaſſadour ſpeake his principall
cōmandements but in his own language, or in another
as naturall to him as his owne, and ſo it is vſed in all
places of the world ſauing in England. The Princes and
their commiſſioners fearing leaſt otherwiſe they might
vtter any thing to their diſaduantage, or els to their
diſgrace: and I my ſelfe hauing ſeene the Courts of
Fraunce, Spaine, Italie, and that of the Empire, with
many inferior Courts, could neuer perceiue that the moſt
noble perſonages, though they knew very well how to
ſpeake many forraine languages, would at any times
that they had bene ſpoken vnto, anſwere but in their
owne, the Frenchman in French, the Spaniard in Spaniſh,
the Italian in Italian, and the very Dutch Prince in the
Dutch language: whether it were more for pride, or for
feare of any lapſe, I cannot tell. And *Henrie* Earle of
Arundel being an old Courtier and a very princely man
in all his actions, kept that rule alwaies. For on a time
paſſing from England towards Italie by her maieſties
licence, he was very honorably enterteined at the Court
of Bruſſels, by the Lady Duches of Parma, Regent there:
and ſitting at a banquet with her, where alſo was the
Prince of Orange, with all the greateſt Princes of the
ſtate, the Earle, though he could reaſonably well ſpeake
French, would not ſpeake one French word, but all
Engliſh, whether he asked any queſtion, or anſwered it,
but all was done by Truchemen. In ſo much as the
Prince of Orange maruelling at it, looked a ſide on that
part where I ſtoode a beholder of the feaſt, and ſayd,
I maruell your Noblemen of England doe not deſire to
be better languaged in the forraine languages. This word

(271)

was by and by reported to the Earle. Quoth the Earle againe, tell my Lord the Prince, that I loue to fpeake in that language, in which I can beft vtter my mind and not miftake.

Another Ambaffadour vfed the like ouerfight by ouerweening himfelfe that he could naturally fpeake the French tongue, whereas in troth he was not fkilfull in their termes. This Ambaffadour being a Bohemian, fent from the Emperour to the French Court, where after his firft audience, he was highly feafted and banquetted. On a time, among other, a great Princeffe fitting at the table, by way of talke asked the Ambaffador whether the

Gg iiij^v Empreffe his/miftreffe when fhe went a hunting, or otherwife trauailed abroad for her folace, did ride a horfback or goe in her coach. To which the Ambaffadour anfwered vnwares and not knowing the French terme, *Par ma foy elle cheuauche fort bien, & fi en prend grand plaifir.* She rides (faith he) very well, and takes great pleafure in it. There was good fmiling one vpon another of the Ladies and Lords, the Ambaffador wift not whereat, but laughed himfelfe for companie. This word *Cheuaucher* in the French tongue hath a reprobate fence, fpecially being fpoken of a womans riding.

And as rude and vnciuill fpeaches carry a marueilous great indecencie, fo doe fometimes thofe that be ouermuch affeƈted and nice: or that doe fauour of ignorance or adulation, and be in the eare of graue and wife perfons no leffe offenfiue than the other: as when a futor in Rome came to *Tiberius* the Emperor and faid, I would open my cafe to your Maieftie, if it were not to trouble your facred bufineffe, *facras veftras occupationes* as the Hiftoriographer reporteth. What meaneft thou by that terme quoth the Emperor, fay *laboriofas* I pray thee, & fo thou maift truely fay, and bid him leaue off fuch affeƈted flattering termes.

The like vndecencie vfed a Herald at armes fent by *Charles* the fifth Emperor, to *Fraunces* the firft French

king, bringing him a meſſage of defiance, and thinking
to qualifie the bitterneſſe of his meſſage with words
pompous and magnificent for the kings honor, vſed
much this terme (ſacred Maieſtie) which was not vſually
geuen to the French king, but to ſay for the moſt part
[*Sire*] The French king neither liking of his errant, nor
yet of his pompous ſpeech, ſaid ſomewhat ſharply, I pray
thee good fellow clawe me not where I itch not with
thy ſacred maieſtie, but goe to thy buſineſſe, and tell
thine errand in ſuch termes as are decent betwixt enemies,
for thy maſter is not my frend, and turned him to a
Prince of the bloud who ſtoode by, ſaying, me thinks
this fellow ſpeakes like Biſhop *Nicholas*, for on Saint
Nicholas night commonly the Scholars of the Countrey
make them a Biſhop, who like a fooliſh boy, goeth about
bleſſing and preaching with ſo childiſh termes, as maketh
the people laugh at his fooliſh counterfaite ſpeeches.

And yet in ſpeaking or writing of a Princes affaires
& fortunes there is a certaine *Decorum*, that we may not
vſe the ſame termes/in their buſines, as we might very Hh iʳ
wel doe in a meaner perſons, the caſe being all one, ſuch
reuerence is due to their eſtates. As for example, if an
Hiſtoriographer ſhal write of an Emperor or King, how
ſuch a day hee ioyned battel with his enemie, and being
ouer-laide ranne out of the fielde, and tooke his heeles,
or put ſpurre to his horſe and fled as faſt as hee could:
the termes be not decent, but of a meane ſouldier or
captaine, it were not vndecently ſpoken. And as one,
who tranſlating certaine bookes of *Virgils Æneidos* into
Engliſh meetre, ſaid that *Æneas* was fayne to trudge
out of Troy: which terme became better to be ſpoken
of a beggar, or of a rogue, or a lackey: for ſo wee vſe
to ſay to ſuch maner of people, be trudging hence.

Another Engliſhing this word of *Virgill* [*fato profugus*]
called *Æneas* [*by fate a fugitiue*] which was vndecently
ſpoken, and not to the Authours intent in the ſame
word: for whom he ſtudied by all means to auaunce

(273)

aboue all other men of the world for vertue and magnanimitie, he meant not to make him a fugitiue. But
by occafion of his great diftreffes, and of the hardneffe
of his deftinies, he would haue it appeare that *Æneas*
was enforced to flie out of *Troy*, and for many yeeres
to be a romer and a wandrer about the world both by
land and fea [*fato profugus*] and neuer to find any
refting place till he came into *Italy*, fo as ye may euidētly
perceiue in this terme [*fugitiue*] a notable indignity
offred to that princely perfon, and by th'other word
(a wanderer) none indignitie at all, but rather a terme
of much loue and commiferation. The fame tranflatour
when he came to thefe wordes: *Infignem pietate virum,*
tot voluere cafus tot adire labores compulit. Hee turned it
thus, what moued *Iuno* to tugge fo great a captaine as
Æneas, which word tugge fpoken in this cafe is fo
vndecent as none other coulde haue bene deuifed, and
tooke his firft originall from the cart, becaufe it fignifieth
the pull or draught of the oxen or horfes, and therefore
the leathers that beare the chiefe ftreffe of the draught,
the cartars call them tugges, and fo wee vfe to fay that
fhrewd boyes tugge each other by the eares, for pull.

Another of our vulgar makers, fpake as illfaringly in
this verfe written to the difpraife of a rich man and
couetous. Thou haft a/mifers minde (thou haft a princes
pelfe) a lewde terme to be fpoken of a princes treafure,
which in no refpeᵈ nor for any caufe is to be called
pelfe, though it were neuer fo meane, for pelfe is properly the fcrappes or fhreds of taylors and of skinners,
which are accompted of fo vile price as they be commonly caft out of dores, or otherwife beftowed vpon
bafe purpofes: and carrieth not the like reafon or decencie, as when we fay in reproch of a niggard or vferer,
or worldly couetous man, that he fetteth more by a little
pelfe of the world, than by his credit or health, or
confcience. For in comparifon of thefe treafours, all the
gold or filuer in the world may by a skornefull terme

Hh iᵛ

(274)

be called pelfe, & fo ye fee that the reafon of the
decencie holdeth not alike in both cafes. Now let vs
paffe from thefe examples, to treate of thofe that concerne the comelineffe and decencie of mans behauiour.

And fome fpeech may be whan it is fpoken very vndecent, and yet the fame hauing afterward fomewhat
added to it may become prety and decent, as was the
ftowte worde vfed by a captaine in Fraunce, who fitting
at the lower end of the Duke of *Guyfes* table among
many, the day after there had bene a great battaile
foughten, the Duke finding that this captaine was not
feene that day to do any thing in the field, taxed him
priuily thus in al the hearings. Where were you Sir
the day of the battaile, for I faw ye not? the captaine
anfwered promptly: where ye durft not haue bene: and
the Duke began to kindle with the worde, which the
Gentleman perceiuing, faid fpedily: I was that day
among the carriages, where your excellencie would not
for a thoufand crownes haue bene feene. Thus from vndecent it came by a wittie reformation to be made decent
againe.

The like hapned on a time at the Duke of North-
umberlandes bourd, where merry *Iohn Heywood* was
allowed to fit at the tables end. The Duke had a very
noble and honorable mynde alwayes to pay his debts
well, and when he lacked money, would not ftick to fell
the greateft part of his plate: fo had he done few dayes
before. *Heywood* being loth to call for his drinke fo oft
as he was dry, turned his eye toward the cupbord and
fayd I finde great miffe of your graces ftanding cups:
the Duke thinking he had fpoken it of fome knowledge
that his plate was lately fold, faid fomewhat/fharpely, Hh ij^r
why Sir will not thofe cuppes ferue as good a man as
your felfe. *Heywood* readily replied. Yes if it pleafe
your grace, but I would haue one of them ftand ftill
at myne elbow full of drinke that I might not be driuen
to trouble your men fo often to call for it. This pleafant

(275)

and fpeedy reuers of the former wordes holpe all the matter againe, whereupon the Duke became very plea- faunt and dranke a bolle of wine to *Heywood*, and bid a cup fhould alwayes be ftanding by him.

It were to bufie a peece of worke for me to tell you of all the partes of decencie and indecency which haue bene obferued in the fpeaches of man & in his writings, and this that I tell you is rather to folace your eares with pretie conceits after a fort of long fcholafticall preceptes which may happen haue doubled them, rather then for any other purpofe of inftitutiō or doɔctrine, which to any Courtier of experience, is not neceffarie in this behalfe. And as they appeare by the former examples to reft in our fpeach and writing: fo do the fame by like propor- tion confift in the whole behauiour of man, and that which he doth well and commendably is euer decent, and the contrary vndecent, not in euery mans iudgement alwayes one, but after their feuerall difcretion and by circumftance diuerfly, as by the next Chapter fhalbe fhewed.

CHAP. XXIIII.

Of decencie in behauiour which alfo belongs to the confideration of the Poet or maker.

And there is a decēcy to be obferued in euery mans actiō & behauiour afwell as in his fpeach & writing which fome peraduēture would thinke impertinent to be treated of in this booke, where we do but informe the cōmendable fafhions of language & ftile: but that is otherwife, for the good maker or poet who is in decēt fpeach & good termes to defcribe all things and with prayfe or difpraife to report euery mās behauiour, ought to know the comelineffe of an actiō afwell as of a word & thereby to direct himfelfe both in praife & perfwafiō or any other point that perteines to the Oratours arte. Wherefore fome exāples we will fet downe of this

(276)

maner of decēcy in behauiour leauing you for the reſt to our booke which we haue written *de Decoro*, where ye ſhall ſee both partes/handled more exactly. And this decencie of mans behauiour aſwell as of his ſpeach muſt alſo be deemed by diſcretion, in which regard the thing that may well become one man to do may not become another, and that which is ſeemely to be done in this place is not ſo ſeemely in that, and at ſuch a time decent, but at another time vndecent, and in ſuch a caſe and for ſuch a purpoſe, and to this and that end and by this and that euent, peruſing all the circumſtances with like cōſideration. Therefore we ſay that it might become king *Alexander* to giue a hundreth talentes to *Anaxagoras* the Philoſopher, but not for a beggerly Philoſopher to accept ſo great a gift, for ſuch a Prince could not be impoueriſhed by that expence, but the Philoſopher was by it exceſſiuely to be enriched, ſo was the kings action proportionable to his eſtate and therefore decent, the Philoſophers, diſproportionable both to his profeſſion and calling and therefore indecent.

And yet if we ſhall examine the ſame point with a clearer diſcretion, it may be ſaid that whatſoeuer it might become king *Alexander* of his regal largeſſe to beſtow vpon a poore Philoſopher vnasked, that might aſwell become the Philoſopher to receiue at his hands without refuſal, and had otherwiſe bene ſome empeachement of the kings abilitie or wiſedome, which had not bene decent in the Philoſopher, nor the immoderatneſſe of the kinges gift in reſpect of the Philoſophers meane eſtate made his acceptance the leſſe decent, ſince Princes liberalities are not meaſured by merite nor by other mens eſtimations, but by their owne appetits and according to their greatneſſe. So ſaid king *Alexander* very like himſelfe to one *Perillus* to whom he had geuen a very great gift, which he made curteſy to accept, ſaying it was too much for ſuch a mean perſon, what quoth the king if it be too much for thy ſelfe, haſt thou neuer a friend or kinſman that may fare the better by it? But peraduenture if any ſuch immoderat gift had bene craued by the Philoſopher and not voluntarily offred by the king it had bene vndecent to haue taken it. Euen ſo if one that ſtandeth vpon his merite, and ſpares to craue the Princes liberalitie in that which is moderate and fit for him, doth as vndecently. For men ſhould not expect till the Prince remembred it of himſelfe and Hh iijʳ began as it were the gratification, but ought to be/put in remembraunce by humble ſolicitations, and that is duetifull & decent, which made king *Henry* th'eight her Maieſties moſt noble father, and for liberality nothing inferiour to king *Alexander* the great, aunſwere one of his priuie chamber, who prayd him to be good & gracious to a certaine old Knight being his ſeruant, for that he was but an ill begger, if he be aſhamed to begge we wil thinke ſcorne to giue. And yet peraduenture in both theſe caſes, the vndecencie for too much crauing or ſparing to craue, might be eaſily holpen by a decent magnificence in the Prince, as *Amazis* king of Ægypt very honorably conſidered, who asking one day for one *Diopithus* a noble man of his Court, what was become of him for that he had not ſene him wait of long time, one about the king told him that he heard ſay he was ſicke and of ſome conceit he had taken that his Maieſtie had but ſlenderly looked to him, vſing many others very bountifully. I beſhrew his fooles head quoth the king, why had he not ſued vnto vs and made vs priuie of his want, then added, but in truth we are moſt to blame our ſelues, who by a mindeful beneficence without ſute ſhould haue ſupplied his baſhfulneſſe, and forthwith commaunded a great reward in money & penſion to be ſent vnto him, but it hapned that when the kings meſ-fengers entred the chamber of *Diopithus*, he had newly giuen vp the ghoſt: the meſſengers ſorrowed the caſe, and *Diopithus* friends ſate by and wept, not ſo much for *Diopithus* death, as for pitie that he ouerliued not

the comming of the kings reward. Therupon it came
euer after to be vfed for a prouerbe that when any good
turne commeth too late to be vfed, to cal it *Diopithus*
reward.

In Italy and Fraunce I haue knowen it vfed for common pollicie, the Princes to differre the beftowing of
their great liberalities as Cardinalfhips and other high
dignities & offices of gayne, till the parties whom they
fhould feeme to gratifie be fo old or fo ficke as it is not
likely they fhould long enioy them.

In the time of *Charles* the ninth French king, I being
at the Spaw waters, there lay a Marfhall of Fraunce
called *Monfieur de Sipier*, to vfe thofe waters for his
health, but when the Phifitions had all giuen him vp,
and that there was no hope of life in him, came frō
the king to him a letters patents of fix thoufand crownes/
yearely penfion during his life with many comfortable   Hh iij^v
wordes: the man was not fo much paft remembraunce,
but he could fay to the meffenger *trop tard, trop tard*,
it fhould haue come before, for in deede it had bene
promifed long and came not till now that he could not
fare the better by it.

And it became king *Antiochus*, better to beftow the
faire Lady *Stratonica* his wife vpon his fonne *Demetrius*
who lay ficke for her loue and would elfe haue perifhed,
as the Phyfitions cunningly difcouered by the beating of
his pulfe, then it could become *Demetrius* to be inamored
with his fathers wife, or to enioy her of his guift, becaufe the fathers act was led by difcretion and of a
fatherly compaffion, not grutching to depart from his
deereft poffeffion to faue his childes life, where as the
fonne in his appetite had no reafon to lead him to loue
vnlawfully, for whom it had rather bene decent to die,
then to haue violated his fathers bed with fafetie of
his life.

No more would it be feemely for an aged man to
play the wanton like a child, for it ftands not with the

(279)

conueniency of nature, yet when king *Agefilaus* hauing
a great fort of little children, was one day difpofed to
folace himfelf among them in a gallery where they
plaied, and tooke a little hobby horfe of wood and beftrid
it to keepe them in play, one of his friends feemed
to miflike his lightnes, ô good friend quoth *Agefilaus*,
rebuke me not for this fault till thou haue children of
thine owne, fhewing in deede that it came not of vanitie
but of a fatherly affectiõ, ioying in the fport and company of his little children, in which refpect and as that
place and time ferued, it was difpenceable in him &
not indecent.

And in the choife of a mans delights & maner of his
life, there is a decencie, and fo we fay th'old man generally
is no fit companion for the young man, nor the rich
for the poore, nor the wife for the foolifh. Yet in fome
refpects and by difcretion it may be otherwife, as when
the old man hath the gouernment of the young, the
wife teaches the foolifh, the rich is wayted on by the
poore for their reliefe, in which regard the conuerfation
is not indecent.

And *Proclus* the Philofopher knowing how euery indecencie is vnpleafant to nature, and namely, how vncomely a thing it is for young men to doe as old men
Hh iiij^r doe (at leaftwife as young men/for the moft part doe
take it) applyed it very wittily to his purpofe: for hauing
his fonne and heire a notable vnthrift, & delighting in
nothing but in haukes and hounds, and gay apparrell,
and fuch like vanities, which neither by gentle nor
fharpe admonitions of his father, could make him leaue.
Proclus himfelfe not onely bare with his fonne, but alfo
vfed it himfelfe for company, which fome of his frends
greatly rebuked him for, faying, ô *Proclus*, an olde man
and a Philofopher to play the foole and lafciuious more
than the fonne. Mary, quoth *Proclus*, & therefore I do
it, for it is the next way to make my fonne change his
life, when he fhall fee how vndecent it is in me to leade

fuch a life, and for him being a yong man, to keepe
companie with me being an old man, and to doe that
which I doe.

So is it not vnfeemely for any ordinarie Captaine to
winne the victory or any other auantage in warre by
fraud & breach of faith: as *Hanniball* with the Romans,
but it could not well become the Romaines managing
fo great an Empire, by examples of honour and iuftice
to doe as *Hanniball* did. And when *Parmenio* in a like
cafe perfwaded king *Alexander* to breake the day of his
appointment, and to fet vpon *Darius* at the fodaine,
which *Alexander* refufed to doe, *Parmenio* faying, I would
doe it if I were *Alexander*, and I too quoth *Alexander*
if I were *Parmenio:* but it behooueth me in honour to
fight liberally with mine enemies, and iuftly to ouer-
come. And thus ye fee that was decent in *Parmenios*
action, which was not in the king his mafters.

A great nobleman and Counfeller in this Realme was
fecretlie aduifed by his friend, not to vfe fo much writing
his letters in fauour of euery man that asked them,
fpecially to the Iudges of the Realme in cafes of iuftice.
To whom the noble man anfwered, it becomes vs
Councellors better to vfe inftance for our friend, then
for the Iudges to fentence at inftance: for whatfoeuer
we doe require them, it is in their choife to refufe to
doe, but for all that the example was ill and dangerous.

And there is a decencie in chufing the times of a mans
bufines, and as the Spaniard fayes, *es tiempo de negotiar*,
there is a fitte time for euery man to performe his bufineffe in, & to attēd his affaires, which out of that time
would be vndecent: as to fleepe al day and/wake al
night, and to goe a hunting by torch-light, as an old
Earle of Arundel vfed to doe, or for any occafion of little
importance, to wake a man out of his fleepe, or to make
him rife from his dinner to talke with him, or fuch like
importunities, for fo we call euery vnfeafonable action,
and the vndecencie of the time.

Hh iiij^v

(281)

Callicratides being fent Ambaffador by the Lacedemonians, to *Cirus* the young king of Perfia to contract
with him for money and men toward their warres againft
the Athenians, came to the Court at fuch vnfeafonable
time as the king was yet in the midft of his dinner, and
went away againe faying, it is now no time to interrupt
the kings mirth. He came againe another day in the
after noone, and finding the king at a rere-banquet, and
to haue taken the wine fomewhat plentifully, turned
back againe, faying, I thinke there is no houre fitte to
deale with *Cirus*, for he is euer in his banquets: I will
rather leaue all the bufines vndone, then doe any thing
that fhall not become the Lacedemonians: meaning to
offer conference of fo great importaunce to his Countrey,
with a man fo diftempered by furfet, as hee was not
likely to geue him any reafonable refolution in the
caufe.

One *Eudamonia* brother to king *Agis* of *Lacedemonia*,
cōming by *Zenocrates* fchoole and looking in, faw him
fit in his chaire, difputing with a long hoare beard,
asked who it was, one anfwered, Sir it is a wife man
and one of them that fearches after vertue, and if he
haue not yet found it quoth *Eudamidas* when will he
vfe it, that now at this yeares is feeking after it, as who
would fay it is not time to talke of matters when they
fhould be put in execution, nor for an old man to be to
feeke what vertue is, which all his youth he fhould haue
had in exercife.

Another time comming to heare a notable Philofopher difpute, it happened, that all was ended euen as
he came, and one of his familiers would haue had him
requefted the Philofopher to beginne againe, that were
indecent and nothing ciuill quoth *Eudamidas*, for if he
fhould come to me fupperleffe when I had fupped before,
were it feemely for him to pray me to fuppe againe for
his companie?

And the place makes a thing decent or indecent, in

which confideration one *Euboidas* being fent Embaffadour into a forraine/realme, fome of his familiars tooke Ii iʳ
occafion at the table to praife the wiues and women of
that country in prefence of their owne husbands, which
th'embaffadour mifliked, and when fupper was ended
and the gueftes departed, tooke his familiars afide, and
told them that it was nothing decent in a ftrange country
to praife the women, nor fpecially a wife before her
husbands face, for inconueniencie that might rife thereby, afwell to the prayfer as to the woman, and that the
chiefe commendation of a chaft matrone, was to be
knowen onely to her husband, and not to be obferued
by ftraungers and gueftes.

And in the vfe of apparell there is no litle decency
and vndecencie to be perceiued, as well for the fafhion
as the ftuffe, for it is comely that euery eftate and vocation fhould be knowen by the differences of their habit:
a clarke from a lay man: a gentleman from a yeoman:
a fouldier from a citizen, and the chiefe of euery degree
frō their inferiours, becaufe in confufion and diforder
there is no manner of decencie.

The Romaines of any other people moft feuere cēfurers
of decencie, thought no vpper garment fo comely for
a ciuill man as a long playted gowne, becaufe it fheweth
much grauitie & alfo pudicitie, hiding euery member
of the body which had not bin pleafant to behold. In
fomuch as a certain *Proconfull* or Legat of theirs dealing
one day with *Ptolome* king of Egipt, feeing him clad in
a ftraite narrow garment very lafciuioufly, difcouering
euery part of his body, gaue him a great checke for it:
and faid, that vnleffe he vfed more fad and comely garments, the Romaines would take no pleafure to hold
amitie with him, for by the wantonnes of his garment
they would iudge the vanitie of his mind, not to be
worthy of their conftant friendfhip. A pleafant old
courtier wearing one day in the fight of a great councel-
lour, after the new guife, a french cloake fkarce reaching

to the waſt, a long beaked doublet hanging downe to his thies, & an high paire of ſilke netherſtocks that couered all his buttockes and loignes, the Councellor marueled to ſee him in that ſort diſguiſed, and otherwiſe than he had bin woont to be. Sir quoth the Gentleman to excuſe it: if I ſhould not be able whan I had need to piſſe out of my doublet, and to do the reſt in my netherſtocks (vſing the plaine terme) all men would/ Ii iv ſay I were but a lowte, the Councellor laughed hartily at the abſurditie of the ſpeech, but what would thoſe ſower fellowes of Rome haue ſaid trowe ye? truely in mine opinion, that all ſuch perſons as take pleaſure to ſhew their limbes, ſpecially thoſe that nature hath cō-manded out of ſight, ſhould be inioyned either to go ſtarke naked, or elſe to reſort backe to the comely and modeſt faſhion of their owne countrie apparell, vſed by their old honorable aunceſtors.

And there is a decēcy of apparrel in reſpect of the place where it is to be vſed: as, in the Court to be richly apparrelled: in the countrey to weare more plain & homely garmēts. For who would not thinke it a ridiculous thing to ſee a Lady in her milke-houſe with a veluet gowne, and at a bridall in her caſſock of mockado: a Gentleman of the Countrey among the buſhes and briers, goe in a pounced dublet and a paire of embrodered hoſen, in the Citie to weare a friſe Ierkin and a paire of leather breeches? yet ſome ſuch phantaſticals haue I knowen, and one a certaine knight, of all other the moſt vaine, who commonly would come to the Seſſions, and other ordinarie meetings and Commiſſions in the Countrey, ſo bedect with buttons and aglets of gold and ſuch coſtly embroderies, as the poore plaine men of the Countrey called him (for his gayneſſe) the golden knight. Another for the like cauſe was called Saint Sunday: I thinke at this day they be ſo farre ſpent, as either of thē would be content with a good cloath cloake: and this came by want of diſcretion, to diſcerne and deeme

(284)

right of decencie, which many Gentlemen doe wholly
limite by the perſon or degree, where reaſon doeth it
by the place and preſence: which may be ſuch as it might
very well become a great Prince to weare courſer apparrell than in another place or preſence a meaner
perſon.

Neuertheleſſe in the vſe of a garment many occaſions alter the decencie, ſometimes the qualitie of the
perſon, ſometimes of the caſe, otherwhiles the countrie
cuſtome, and often the conſtitution of lawes, and the
very nature of vſe it ſelfe. As for example a king and
prince may vſe rich and gorgious apparell decently, ſo
cannot a meane perſon doo, yet if an herald of armes
to whom a king giueth his gowne of cloth of gold, or
to whom it was incident as a fee of his office, do were
the ſame, he doth it decently, becauſe ſuch/hath alwaies Ii ij^r
bene th'allowances of heraldes: but if ſuch herald haue
worne out, or ſold, or loſt that gowne, to buy him a
new of the like ſtuffe with his owne mony and to weare
it, is not decent in the eye and iudgement of them that
know it.

And the country cuſtome maketh things decent in
vſe, as in Aſia for all men to weare long gownes both
a foot and horſebacke: in Europa ſhort gaberdins, or
clokes, or iackets, euen for their vpper garments. The
Turke and Perſian to weare great tolibants of ten,
fifteene, and twentie elles of linnen a peece vpon their
heads, which can not be remooued: in Europe to were
caps or hats, which vpon euery occaſion of ſalutation
we vſe to put of, as a ſigne of reuerence. In th'Eaſt
partes the men to make water couring like women, with
vs ſtanding at a wall. With them to congratulat and
ſalute by giuing a becke with the head, or a bende of
the bodie, with vs here in England, and in Germany,
and all other Northerne parts of the world to ſhake
handes. In France, Italie, and Spaine to embrace ouer
the ſhoulder, vnder the armes, at the very knees, ac-

cording to the fuperiors degree. With vs the wemen giue
their mouth to be kiffed, in other places their cheek,
in many places their hand, or in fteed of an offer to the
hand, to fay thefe words *Bezo los manos*. And yet fome
others furmounting in all courtly ciuilitie will fay, *Los
manos & los piedes*. And aboue that reach too, there be
that will fay to the Ladies, *Lombra de fus pifadas*, the
fhadow of your fteps. Which I recite vnto you to fhew
the phrafe of thofe courtly feruitours in yeelding the
miftreffes honour and reuerence.

And it is feen that very particular vfe of it felfe makes
a matter of much decencie and vndecencie, without any
countrey cuftome or allowance, as if one that hath many
yeares worne a gowne fhall come to be feen weare a
iakquet or ierkin, or he that hath many yeares worne
a beard or long haire among thofe that had done the
contrary, and come fodainly to be pold or fhauen, it
will feeme not onely to himfelfe, a defpight and very vndecent, but alfo to all others that neuer vfed to go fo,
vntill the time and cuftome haue abrogated that miflike.

So was it here in England till her Maiefties moft
noble father for diuers good refpects, caufed his owne
head and all his Courtiers to be polled and his beard
Ii ij^v to be cut fhort. Before that time it/was thought more
decent both for old men and young to be all fhauen
and to weare long haire either rounded or fquare. Now
againe at this time, the young Gentlemen of the Court
haue taken vp the long haire trayling on their fhoulders,
and thinke it more decent: for what refpect I would be
glad to know.

The Lacedemonians bearing long bufhes of haire,
finely kept & curled vp, vfed this ciuill argument to
maintaine that cuftome. Haire (fay they) is the very
ornament of nature appointed for the head, which therfore to vfe in his moft fumptuous degree is comely,
fpecially for them that be Lordes, Maifters of men, and
of a free life, hauing abilitie & leafure inough to keepe

it cleane, and fo for a figne of feignorie, riches and libertie,
the mafters of the Lacedemonians vfed long haire. But
their vaffals, feruaunts and flaues vfed it fhort or fhauen
in figne of feruitude and becaufe they had no meane
nor leafure to kembe and keepe it cleanely. It was befides
comberfome to them hauing many bufineffe to attende,
in fome feruices there might no maner of filth be falling
from their heads. And to all fouldiers it is very noyfome
and a daungerous difauantage in the warres or in any
particular combat, which being the moft comely profeffion of euery noble young Gentleman, it ought to
perfwade them greatly from wearing long haire. If there
be any that feeke by long haire to helpe or to hide an
ill featured face, it is in them allowable fo to do, becaufe
euery man may decently reforme by arte, the faultes and
imperfections that nature hath wrought in them.

And all fingularities or affected parts of a mās behauiour feeme vndecēt, as for one man to march or iet
in the ftreet more ftately, or to looke more folēpnely,
or to go more gayly & in other coulours or fafhioned
garmēts then another of the fame degree and eftate.

Yet fuch fingularities haue had many times both good
liking and good fucceffe, otherwife then many would
haue looked for. As when *Dinocrates* the famous architect, defirous to be knowen to king *Alexander* the great,
and hauing none acquaintance to bring him to the kings
fpeech, he came one day to the Court very ftrangely
apparelled in long skarlet robes, his head compaft with
a garland of Laurell, and his face all to be flicked with
fweet oyle, and ftoode in the kings chamber, motioning
nothing to any man:/newes of this ftranger came to the Ii iijʳ
king, who caufed him to be brought to his prefence, and
asked his name, and the caufe of his repaire to the Court.
He aunfwered, his name was *Dinocrates* the Architect,
who came to prefent his Maieftie with a platforme of his
owne deuifing, how his Maieftie might buylde a Citie
vpon the mountaine Athos in Macedonia, which fhould

beare the figure of a mans body, and tolde him all how. Forſooth the breaſt and bulke of his body ſhould reſt vpon ſuch a flat: that hil ſhould be his head, all ſet with foregrowen woods like haire: his right arme ſhould ſtretch out to ſuch a hollow bottome as might be like his hand: holding a diſh conteyning al the waters that ſhould ſerue that Citie: the left arme with his hand ſhould hold a valley of all the orchards and gardens of pleaſure pertaining thereunto: and either legge ſhould lie vpon a ridge of rocke, very gallantly to behold, and ſo ſhould accompliſh the full figure of a man. The king asked him what commoditie of ſoyle, or ſea, or nauigable riuer lay neere vnto it, to be able to ſuſtaine ſo great a number of inhabitants. Truely Sir (quoth *Dinocrates*) I haue not yet conſidered thereof: for in trueth it is the bareſt part of all the Countrey of Macedonia. The king ſmiled at it, and ſaid very honourably, we like your deuice well, and meane to vſe your ſeruice in the building of a Citie, but we wil chuſe out a more commodious ſcituation: and made him attend in that voyage in which he conquered Aſia and Egypt, and there made him chiefe Surueyour of his new Citie of Alexandria. Thus did *Dinocrates* ſingularitie in attire greatly further him to his aduancement.

Yet are generally all rare things and ſuch as breede maruell & admiration ſomewhat holding of the vn-decent, as when a man is bigger & exceeding the ordinary ſtature of a man like a Giaunt, or farre vnder the reaſonable and common ſize of men, as a dwarfe, and ſuch vndecencies do not angre vs, but either we pittie them or ſcorne at them.

But at all inſolent and vnwoonted partes of a mans behauiour, we find many times cauſe to miſlike or to be miſtruſtfull, which proceedeth of ſome vndecency that is in it, as when a man that hath alwaies bene ſtrange & vnacquainted with vs, will ſuddenly become our familiar and domeſtick: and another that hath bene/

alwaies fterne and churlifh, wilbe vpon the fuddaine Ii iijᵛ
affable and curteous, it is neyther a comely fight, nor
a figne of any good towardes vs. Which the fubtill
Italian well obferued by the fucceffes thereof, faying in
Prouerbe.

Chi me fa meglio che non fuole,
Tradito me ha o tradir me vuole.

He that fpeakes me fairer, than his woont was too
Hath done me harme, or meanes for to doo.

Now againe all maner of conceites that ftirre vp any
vehement paffion in a man, doo it by fome turpitude
or euill and vndecency that is in them, as to make a
man angry there muft be fome iniury or contempt offered,
to make him enuy there muft proceede fome vndeferued
profperitie of his egall or inferiour, to make him pitie
fome miferable fortune or fpectakle to behold.

And yet in euery of thefe paffions being as it were
vndecencies, there is a comelineffe to be difcerned, which
fome men can keepe and fome men can not, as to be
angry, or to enuy, or to hate, or to pitie, or to be
afhamed decently, that is none otherwife then reafon
requireth. This furmife appeareth to be true, for *Homer*
the father of Poets writing that famous and moft honourable poeme called the *Illiades* or warres of Troy: made
his commēcement the magnanimous wrath and anger
of *Achilles* in his firft verfe thus: μενην αιδε θεα πιλιαδεοῦ
ἀχιλλείους. Sing foorth my mufe the wrath of *Achilles*
Peleus fonne: which the Poet would neuer haue done
if the wrath of a prince had not beene in fome fort
comely & allowable. But when *Arrianus* and *Curtius*
hiftoriographers that wrote the noble geftes of king
Alexander the great, came to prayfe him for many things,
yet for his wrath and anger they reproched him, becaufe
it proceeded not of any magnanimitie, but vpon furfet
& diftemper in his diet, nor growing of any iuft caufes,
was exercifed to the deftruction of his deareft friends and

(289)

familiers, and not of his enemies, nor any other waies
fo honorably as th'others was, and fo could not be
reputed a decent and comely anger.

So may al your other paffions be vfed decently though
the very matter of their originall be grounded vpon
fome vndecencie, as it is written by a certaine king of
Ii iiij^r Egypt, who looking out of his/window, and feing his
owne fonne for fome grieuous offence, carried by the
officers of his iuftice to the place of execution: he neuer
once changed his countenance at the matter, though the
fight were neuer fo full of ruth and atrocitie. And it
was thought a decent countenance and conftant ani-
mofitie in the king to be fo affeted, the cafe concerning
fo high and rare a peece of his owne iuftice. But within
few daies after when he beheld out of the fame window
an old friend and familiar of his, ftand begging an almes
in the ftreete, he wept tenderly, remembring their old
familiarity and confidering how by the mutabilitie of
fortune and frailtie of mās eftate, it might one day come
to paffe that he himfelfe fhould fall into the like miferable
eftate. He therfore had a remorfe very comely for a
king in that behalfe, which alfo caufed him to giue order
for his poore friends plentiful reliefe.

But generally to weepe for any forrow (as one may
doe for pitie) is not fo decent in a man: and therefore all
high minded perfons, when they cannot chufe but fhed
teares, wil turne away their face as a countenance vndecent for a man to fhew, and fo will the ftanders by till
they haue fuppreft fuch paffiō, thinking it nothing decent
to behold fuch an vncomely countenance. But for
Ladies and women to weepe and fhed teares at euery
little greefe, it is nothing vncomely, but rather a figne
of much good nature & meeknes of minde, a moft decent
propertie for that fexe; and therefore they be for the
more part more deuout and charitable, and greater geuers
of almes than men, and zealous relieuers of prifoners,
and befeechers of pardons, and fuch like parts of com-

miſeration. Yea they be more than ſo too: for by the common prouerbe, a woman will weepe for pitie to ſee a goſling goe barefoote.

But moſt certainly all things that moue a man to laughter, as doe theſe ſcurrilities & other ridiculous behauiours, it is for ſome vndecencie that is foūd in them: which maketh it decent for euery man to laugh at them. And therefore when we ſee or heare a natural foole and idiot doe or ſay any thing fooliſhly, we laugh not at him: but when he doeth or ſpeaketh wiſely, becauſe that is vnlike him ſelfe: and a buffonne or counterfet foole, to heare him ſpeake wiſely which is like himſelfe, it is no ſport at all, but for ſuch a counterfait to talke and looke fooliſhly it maketh vs laugh,/becauſe Ii iiijᵛ it is no part of his naturall, for in euery vncomlineſſe there muſt be a certaine abſurditie and diſproportion to nature, and the opinion of the hearer or beholder to make the thing ridiculous. But for a foole to talke fooliſhly or a wiſeman wiſely, there is no ſuch abſurditie or diſproportion.

And though at all abſurdities we may decently laugh, & when they be no abſurdities not decently, yet in laughing is there an vndecencie for other reſpectes ſometime, than of the matter it ſelfe, Which made *Philippus* ſonne to the firſt Chriſten Emperour, *Philippus Arabicus* ſitting with his father one day in the theatre to behold the ſports, giue his father a great rebuke becauſe he laughed, ſaying that it was no comely coun-tenance for an Emperour to bewray in ſuch a publicke place, nor ſpecially to laugh at euery fooliſh toy: the poſteritie gaue the ſonne for that cauſe the name of *Philippus Agelaſtos* or without laughter.

I haue ſeene forraine Embaſſadours in the Queenes preſence laugh ſo diſſolutely at ſome rare paſtime or ſport that hath beene made there, that nothing in the world could worſe haue becomen them, and others very wiſe men, whether it haue ben of ſome pleaſant humour

(291)

and complexion, or for other default in the fpleene, or for ill education or cuftome, that could not vtter any graue and earneft fpeech without laughter, which part was greatly difcommended in them.

And *Cicero* the wifeft of any Romane writers, thought it vncomely for a man to daunce: faying, *Saltantem fobrium vidi neminem.* I neuer faw any man daunce that was fober and in his right wits, but there by your leaue he failed, nor our young Courtiers will allow it, befides that it is the moft decent and comely demeanour of all exultations and reioycements of the hart, which is no leffe naturall to man then to be wife or well learned, or fober.

To tell you the decencies of a number of other be-hauiours, one might do it to pleafe you with pretie reportes, but to the skilfull Courtiers it fhalbe nothing neceffary, for they know all by experience without learning. Yet fome few remembraunces wee will make you of the moft materiall, which our felues haue ob-ferued, and fo make an end.

It is decent to be affable and curteous at meales & Kk iʳ meetings, in/open affemblies more folemne and ftraunge, in place of authoritie and iudgement not familiar nor pleafant, in counfell fecret and fad, in ordinary con-ferences eafie and apert, in conuerfation fimple, in capitulation fubtill and miftruftfull, at mournings and burials fad and forrowfull, in feafts and bankets merry & ioyfull, in houfhold expence pinching and fparing, in publicke entertainement fpending and pompous. The Prince to be fumptuous and magnificent, the priuate man liberall with moderation, a man to be in giuing free, in asking fpare, in promife flow, in performance fpeedy, in contract circumfpect but iuft, in amitie fincere, in ennimitie wily and cautelous [*dolus an virtus quis in hofte requirit*, faith the Poet] and after the fame rate euery fort and maner of bufineffe or affaire or action hath his decencie and vndecencie, either for the time or place or perſon or ſome other circumſtaunce, as Prieſts to be ſober and ſad, a Preacher by his life to giue good example, a Iudge to be incorrupted, ſolitarie and vnacquainted with Courtiers or Courtly entertainements, & as the Philoſopher ſaith *Oportet iudicē eſſe rudem & ſimplicem*, without plaite or wrinkle, ſower in looke and churliſh in ſpeach, contrariwiſe a Courtly Gentleman to be loftie and curious in countenaunce, yet ſometimes a creeper, and a curry fauell with his ſuperiours.

And touching the perſon, we ſay it is comely for a man to be a lambe in the houſe, and a Lyon in the field, appointing the decencie of his qualitie by the place, by which reaſon alſo we limit the comely parts of a woman to conſiſt in foure points, that is to be a ſhrewe in the kitchin, a ſaint in the Church, an Angell at the bourd, and an Ape in the bed, as the Chronicle reportes by Miſtreſſe *Shore* paramour to king *Edward* the fourth.

Then alſo there is a decency in reſpect of the perſons with whō we do negotiate, as with the great perſonages his egals to be ſolemne and ſurly, with meaner men pleaſant and popular, ſtoute with the ſturdie and milde with the meek, which is a moſt decent conuerſation and not reprochfull or vnſeemely, as the prouerbe goeth, by thoſe that vſe the contrary, a Lyon among ſheepe and a ſheepe among Lyons.

Right ſo in negotiating with Princes we ought to ſeeke their fauour by humilitie & not by ſternneſſe, nor to trafficke with thē/by way of indent or condition, but Kk iv
frankly and by manner of ſubmiſſion to their wils, for Princes may be lead but not driuen, nor they are to be vanquiſht by allegation, but muſt be ſuffred to haue the victorie and be relented vnto: nor they are not to be chalenged for right or iuſtice, for that is a maner of accuſation: nor to be charged with their promiſes, for that is a kinde of condemnation: and at their requeſt we ought not to be hardly entreated but eaſily, for that is a ſigne of deffidence and miſtruſt in their bountie and

gratitude: nor to recite the good feruices which they haue receiued at our hāds, for that is but a kind of exprobratiō, but in crauing their bountie or largeffe to remember vnto them all their former beneficences, making no mētion of our owne merites, & fo it is thankfull, and in prayfing them to their faces to do it very modeftly: and in their commendations not to be exceffiue for that is tedious, and alwayes fauours of futtelty more then of fincere loue.

And in fpeaking to a Prince the voyce ought to be lowe and not lowde nor fhrill, for th'one is a figne of humilitie th'other of too much audacitie and prefumption. Nor in looking on them feeme to ouerlooke them, nor yet behold them too ftedfaftly, for that is a figne of impudence or litle reuerence, and therefore to the great Princes Orientall their feruitours fpeaking or being fpoken vnto abbafe their eyes in token of lowlines, which behauiour we do not obferue to our Princes with fo good a difcretion as they do: & fuch as retire from the Princes prefence, do not by & by turne tayle to them as we do, but go backward or fideling for a reafonable fpace, til they be at the wal or chāber doore paffing out of fight, and is thought a moft decent behauiour to their foueraignes. I haue heard that king *Henry* th'eight her Maiefties father, though otherwife the moft gentle and affable Prince of the world, could not abide to haue any man ftare in his face or to fix his eye too fteedily vpon him when he talked with them: nor for a common futer to exclame or cry out for iuftice, for that is offenfiue and as it were a fecret impeachement of his wrong doing, as happened once to a Knight in this Realme of great worfhip fpeaking to the king. Nor in fpeaches with them to be too long, or too much affected, for th'one is tedious th'other is irkfome, nor with lowd acclamations to applaude them, for that is too popular & rude and/betokens either ignoraunce, or feldome acceffe to their prefence, or little frequenting

Kk ijʳ

(294)

their Courts: nor to fhew too mery or light a countenance, for that is a figne of little reuerence and is a
peece of a contempt.

And in gaming with a Prince it is decent to let him
fometimes win of purpofe, to keepe him pleafant, &
neuer to refufe his gift, for that is vndutifull: nor to
forgiue him his loffes, for that is arrogant: nor to giue
him great gifts, for that is either infolence or follie: nor
to feaft him with exceffiue charge for that is both vaine
and enuious, & therefore the wife Prince king *Henry* the
feuenth her Maiefties grandfather, if his chaunce had
bene to lye at any of his fubieĉts houfes, or to paffe
moe meales then one, he that would take vpon him to
defray the charge of his dyet, or of his officers and
houfhold, he would be marueloufly offended with it,
faying what priuate fubieĉt dare vndertake a Princes
charge, or looke into the fecret of his expēce? Her
Maieftie hath bene knowne oftentimes to miflike the
fuperfluous expence of her fubieĉts beftowed vpon her
in times of her progreffes.

Likewife in matter of aduife it is neither decent to
flatter him for that is feruile, neither to be to rough or
plaine with him, for that is daungerous, but truly to
Counfell & to admonifh, grauely not greuoufly, fincerely
not fourely: which was the part that fo greatly commended *Cineas* Counfellour to king *Pirrhus*, who kept
that decencie in all his perfwafions, that he euer pre-
uailed in aduice, and carried the king which way he
would.

And in a Prince it is comely to giue vnasked, but in
a fubieĉt to aske vnbidden: for that firft is figne of a
bountifull mynde, this of a loyall & confident. But the
fubieĉt that craues not at his Princes hand, either he is
of no defert, or proud, or miftruftfull of his Princes
goodneffe: therefore king *Henry* th'eight to one that
entreated him to remember one Sir *Anthony Roufe* with
fome reward for that he had fpent much and was an ill

beggar: the king aunſwered (noting his inſolencie,) If he be aſhamed to begge, we are aſhamed to giue, and was neuertheleſſe one of the moſt liberall Princes of the world.

And yet in ſome Courts it is otherwiſe vſed, for in Spaine it is thought very vndecent for a Courtier to Kk ijᵛ craue, ſuppoſing that it is/the part of an importune: therefore the king of ordinarie calleth euery ſecond, third or fourth yere for his Checker roll, and beſtoweth his *mercedes* of his owne meere motion, and by diſcretiō, according to euery mans merite and condition.

And in their commendable delights to be apt and accommodate, as if the Prince be geuen to hauking, hunting, riding of horſes, or playing vpon inſtruments, or any like exerciſe, the ſeruitour to be the ſame: and in their other appetites wherein the Prince would ſeeme an example of vertue, and would not miſlike to be egalled by others: in ſuch caſes it is decent their ſeruitours & ſubieéts ſtudie to be like to them by imitation, as in wearing their haire long or ſhort, or in this or that ſort of apparrell, ſuch excepted as be only fitte for Princes and none els, which were vndecent for a meaner perſon to imitate or counterfet: ſo is it not comely to counterfet their voice, or looke, or any other geſtures that be not ordinary and naturall in euery common perſon: and therefore to go vpright, or ſpeake or looke aſſuredly, it is decent in euery man. But if the Prince haue an extra-ordinarie countenance or manner of ſpeech, or bearing of his body, that for a common ſeruitour to counterfet is not decent, and therefore it was miſliked in the Emperor *Nero*, and thought vncomely for him to counterfet *Alexander* the great, by holding his head a little awrie, & neerer toward the tone ſhoulder, becauſe it was not his owne naturall.

And in a Prince it is decent to goe ſlowly, and to march with leyſure, and with a certaine granditie rather than grauitie: as our ſoueraine Lady and miſtreſſe, the

very image of maieſtie and magnificence, is accuſtomed
to doe generally, vnleſſe it be when ſhe walketh apace
for her pleaſure, or to catch her a heate in the colde
mornings.

Neuertheleſſe, it is not ſo decent in a meaner perſon,
as I haue obſerued in ſome counterfet Ladies of the
Countrey, which vſe it much to their owne deriſion.
This comelines was wanting in Queene *Marie*, otherwiſe a very good and honourable Princeſſe. And was
ſome blemiſh to the Emperor *Ferdinando*, a moſt noble
minded man, yet ſo careleſſe and forgetfull of himſelfe
in that behalfe, as I haue ſeene him runne vp a paire of
ſtaires ſo ſwift and nimble a pace, as almoſt had not
become a very meane man, who/had not gone in ſome Kk iijʳ
haſtie buſineſſe.

And in a noble Prince nothing is more decent and
welbeſeeming his greatneſſe, than to ſpare foule ſpeeches,
for that breedes hatred, and to let none humble ſuiters
depart out of their preſence (as neere as may be) miſ-
contented. Wherein her Maieſtie hath of all others a
moſt Regall gift, and nothing inferior to the good Prince
Titus Veſpaſianus in that point.

Alſo, not to be paſſionate for ſmall detriments or
offences, nor to be a reuenger of them, but in caſes of
great iniurie, and ſpecially of diſhonors: and therein to
be very ſterne and vindicatiue, for that ſauours of Princely
magnanimitie: nor to ſeeke reuenge vpon baſe and obſcure perſons, ouer whom the conqueſt is not glorious,
nor the victorie honourable, which reſpect moued our
ſoueraign Lady (keeping alwaies the decorum of a
Princely perſon) at her firſt comming to the crowne,
when a knight of this Realme, who had very inſolently
behaued himſelfe toward her when ſhe was Lady *Elizabeth*, fell vpon his knee to her, and beſought her pardon:
ſuſpecting (as there was good cauſe) that he ſhould haue
bene ſent to the Tower, ſhe ſaid vnto him moſt mildly:
do you not know that we are deſcended of the Lion,

(297)

whofe nature is not to harme or pray vpon the moufe, or any other fuch fmall vermin?

And with thefe exāples I thinke fufficient to leaue, geuing you information of this one point, that all your figures Poeticall or Rhethoricall, are but obferuations of ftrange fpeeches, and fuch as without any arte at al we fhould vfe, & cōmonly do, euen by very nature without difcipline. But more or leffe aptly and decently, or fcarcely, or aboundantly, or of this or that kind of figure, & one of vs more thē another, according to the difpofitiō of our nature, cōftitutiō of the heart, & facilitie of each mans vtterāce: fo as we may conclude, that nature her felfe fuggefteth the figure in this or that forme: but arte aydeth the iudgement of his vfe and application, which geues me occafion finally and for a full conclufion to this whole treatife, to enforme you in the next chapter how art fhould be vfed in all refpects, and fpecially in this behalfe of language, and when the naturall is more commendable then the artificiall, and contrariwife./

CHAP. XXV.

That the good Poet or maker ought to diffemble his arte, and in what cafes the artificiall is more commended then the naturall, and contrariwife.

And now (moft excellent Queene) hauing largely faid of Poets & Poefie, and about what matters they be employed: then of all the commended fourmes of Poemes, thirdly of metricall proportions, fuch as do appertaine to our vulgar arte: and laft of all fet forth the poeticall ornament cōfifting chiefly in the beautie and gallantneffe of his language and ftile, and fo haue apparelled him to our feeming, in all his gorgious habilliments, and pulling him firft from the carte to the fchoole, and from thence to the Court, and preferred him to your Maiefties feruice, in that place of great

(298)

honour and magnificence to geue enterteinment to Princes, Ladies of honour, Gentlewomen and Gentlemen, and by his many moodes of skill, to ferue the many humors of men thither haunting and reforting, fome by way of folace, fome of ferious aduife, and in matters afwell profitable as pleafant and honeft. Wee haue in our humble conceit fufficiently perfourmed our promife or rather dutie to your Maieftie in the defcription of this arte, fo alwaies as we leaue him not vnfurnifht of one peece that beft befeemes that place of any other, and may ferue as a principall good leffon for al good makers to beare cōtinually in mind, in the vfage of this fcience: which is, that being now lately become a Courtier he fhew not himfelf a crafts man, & merit to be difgraded, & with fcorne fent back againe to the fhop, or other place of his firft facultie and calling, but that fo wifely & difcreetly he behaue himfelfe as he may worthily retaine the credit of his place, and profeffion of a very Courtier, which is in plaine termes, cunningly to be able to diffemble. But (if it pleafe your Maieftie) may it not feeme inough for a Courtier to know how to weare a fether, and fet his cappe a flaunt, his chaine *en echarpe*, a ftraight buskin *al ingleffe*, a loofe *alo Turquefque*, the cape *alla Spaniola*, the breech a *la Françoife*, and by twentie maner of new fafhioned garments to difguife his body, and his face with as many countenances, whereof it feemes there be many that make a very arte, and ftudie who can fhew himfelfe moft fine, I will not fay moft foolifh and ridiculous? or perhaps/rather that he could diffemble his conceits as Kk iiijr well as his countenances, fo as he neuer fpeake as he thinkes, or thinke as he fpeaks, and that in any matter of importance his words and his meaning very feldome meete: for fo as I remember it was concluded by vs fetting foorth the figure *Allegoria*, which therefore not impertinently we call the Courtier or figure of faire femblant, or is it not perchance more requifite our

courtly Poet do diffemble not onely his countenances &
cōceits, but alfo all his ordinary actions of behauiour,
or the moft part of thē, whereby the better to winne his
purpofes & good aduantages, as now & then to haue a
iourney or ficknelfe in his fleeue, thereby to fhake of
other importunities of greater confequence, as they vfe
their pilgrimages in Fraunce, the Diet in Spaine, the
baines in Italy? and when a man is whole to faine himfelfe ficke to fhunne the bufineffe in Court, to entertaine
time and eafe at home, to falue offences without dif-
credite, to win purpofes by mediation in abfence, which
their prefence would eyther impeach or not greatly
preferre, to harken after the popular opinions and fpeech,
to entend to their more priuate folaces, to practize more
deepely both at leafure & libertie, & when any publique
affaire or other attēpt & counfaile of theirs hath not
receaued good fucceffe, to auoid therby the Princes
prefent reproofe, to coole their chollers by abfence, to
winne remorfe by lamentable reports, and reconciliation
by friends intreatie. Finally by fequeftring themfelues
for a time fro the Court, to be able the freelier & cleerer
to difcerne the factions and ftate of the Court and of al
the world befides, no leffe then doth the looker on or
beholder of a game better fee into all points of auauntage,
then the player himfelfe? and in diffembling of difeafes
which I pray you? for I haue obferued it in the Court
of Fraunce, not a burning feuer or a plurifie, or a palfie,
or the hydropick and fwelling gowte, or any other like
difeafe, for if they may be fuch as may be either eafily
difcerned or quickly cured, they be ill to diffemble and
doo halfe handfomly ferue the turne.

But it muft be either a dry dropfie, or a megrim or
letarge, or a fiftule *in ano*, or fome fuch other fecret
difeafe, as the common conuerfant can hardly difcouer,
and the Phifition either not fpeedily heale, or not honeftly
bewray? of which infirmities the fcoffing/*Pafquil* wrote,
Vlcus veficæ renum dolor in pene fcirrus. Or as I haue

Kk iiijᵛ

(300)

feene in diuers places where many make thēfelues hart
whole, whē in deede they are full ficke, bearing it
ſtoutly out to the hazard of their health, rather then they
would be fufpected of any lothfome infirmity, which
might inhibit thē frō the Princes prefence, or enter-
teinmēt of the ladies. Or as fome other do to beare a
port of ſtate & plentie when they haue neither penny
nor poſſeſſion, that they may not feeme to droope, and
be reiected as vnworthy or infufficient for the greater
feruices, or be pitied for their pouertie, which they hold
for a marueilous difgrace, as did the poore Squire of
Caſtile, who had rather dine with a ſheepes head at
home & drinke a crufe of water to it, then to haue a
good dinner giuen him by his friend who was nothing
ignorant of his pouertie. Or as others do to make wife
they be poore when they be riche, to ſhunne thereby
the publicke charges and vocations, for men are not
now a dayes (fpecially in ſtates of *Oligarchie* as the moſt
in our age) called fomuch for their wifedome as for their
wealth, alfo to auoyde enuie of neighbours or bountie
in conuerfation, for whofoeuer is reputed rich cannot
without reproch, but be either a lender or a fpender.
Or as others do to feeme very bufie when they haue
nothing to doo, and yet will make themfelues fo occupied
and ouerladen in the Princes affaires, as it is a great
matter to haue a couple of wordes with them, when
notwithſtanding they lye fleeping on their beds all an
after noone, or fit folemnly at cardes in their chambers,
or enterteyning of the Dames, or laughing and gibing
with their familiars foure houres by the clocke, whiles
the poore futer defirous of his difpatch is aunfwered by
fome Secretarie or page *il fault attendre, Monfieur* is dif-
patching the kings bufineſſe into Languedock, Prouence,
Piemont, a common phrafe with the Secretaries of Frāce.
Or as I haue obferued in many of the Princes Courts
of Italie, to feeme idle when they be earneſtly occupied
& entend to nothing but mifchieuous practizes, and do

14 (301)

bufily negotiat by coulor of otiation. Or as others of
them that go ordinarily to Church and neuer pray to
winne an opinion of holineffe: or pray ftill apace, but
neuer do good deede, and geue a begger a penny and
fpend a pound on a harlot, to fpeake faire to a mans face,
and foule behinde his backe, to fet him at his trencher
and yet/fit on his skirts for fo we vfe to fay by a fayned
friend, then alfo to be rough and churlifh in fpeach and
apparance, but inwardly affectionate and fauouring, as
I haue fene of the greateft podeftates and graueft iudges
and Prefidentes of Parliament in Fraunce.

    Thefe & many fuch like difguifings do we find in
mans behauiour, & fpecially in the Courtiers of forraine
Countreyes, where in my youth I was brought vp, and
very well obferued their maner of life and conuerfation,
for of mine owne Countrey I haue not made fo great
experience. Which parts, neuertheleffe, we allow not
now in our Englifh maker, becaufe we haue geuen him
the name of an honeft man, and not of an hypocrite:
and therefore leauing thefe manner of diffimulations to
all bafe-minded men, & of vile nature or mifterie, we
doe allow our Courtly Poet to be a diffembler only in
the fubtilties of his arte: that is, when he is moft artificiall,
fo to difguife and cloake it as it may not appeare, nor
feeme to proceede from him by any ftudie or trade of
rules, but to be his naturall: nor fo euidently to be
defcried, as euery ladde that reades him fhall fay he is
a good fcholler, but will rather haue him to know his
arte well, and little to vfe it.

    And yet peraduenture in all points it may not be fo
taken, but in fuch onely as may difcouer his groffenes
or his ignorance by fome fchollerly affectation: which
thing is very irkefome to all men of good trayning, and
fpecially to Courtiers. And yet for all that our maker
may not be in all cafes reftrayned, but that he may both
vfe, and alfo manifeft his arte to his great praife, and
need no more be afhamed thereof, than a fhomaker to

Ll ir

haue made a cleanly fhoe, or a Carpenter to haue buylt
a faire houfe. Therefore to difcuffe and make this point
fomewhat cleerer, to weete, where arte ought to appeare,
and where not, and when the naturall is more commendable than the artificiall in any humane action
or workmanfhip, we wil examine it further by this
diftinction.

In fome cafes we fay arte is an ayde and coadiutor
to nature, and a furtherer of her actions to good effect,
or peraduenture a meane to fupply her wants, by ren-
forcing the caufes wherein fhee is impotent and defectiue, as doth the arte of phificke, by helping the naturall
concoction, retention, diftribution, expulfion, and other
vertues, in a weake and vnhealthie bodie. Or as the
good gar-/diner feafons his foyle by fundrie forts of com- Ll iv
poft: as mucke or marle, clay or fande, and many times
by bloud, or lees of oyle or wine, or ftale, or perchaunce
with more coftly drugs: and waters his plants, and weedes
his herbes and floures, and prunes his branches, and
vnleaues his boughes to let in the funne: and twentie
other waies cherifheth them, and cureth their infirmities,
and fo makes that neuer, or very feldome any of them
mifcarry, but bring foorth their flours and fruites in
feafon. And in both thefe cafes it is no fmal praife for
the Phifition & Gardiner to be called good and cunning
artificers.

In another refpect arte is not only an aide and coadiutor to nature in all her actions, but an alterer of them,
and in fome fort a furmounter of her skill, fo as by
meanes of it her owne effects fhall appeare more beautifull or ftraunge and miraculous, as in both cafes before
remembred. The Phifition by the cordials hee will geue
his patient, fhall be able not onely to reftore the decayed
fpirites of man, and render him health, but alfo to
prolong the terme of his life many yeares ouer and aboue
the ftint of his firft and naturall conftitution. And the
Gardiner by his arte will not onely make an herbe, or

(303)

flowr, or fruite, come forth in his feafon without impediment, but alfo will embellifh the fame in vertue,
fhape, odour and tafte, that nature of her felfe woulde
neuer haue done: as to make the fingle gillifloure, or mari-
gold, or daifie, double: and the white rofe, redde, yellow,
or carnation, a bitter mellon fweete; a fweete apple,
foure; a plumme or cherrie without a ftone; a peare
without core or kernell, a goord or coucumber like to
a horne, or any other figure he will: any of which things
nature could not doe without mans help and arte. Thefe
actions alfo are moft fingular, when they be moft artificiall.

In another refpect, we fay arte is neither an aider nor
a furmoūter, but onely a bare immitatour of natures
works, following and counterfeyting her actions and
effects, as the Marmefot doth many countenances and
geftures of man, of which forte are the artes of painting
and keruing, whereof one reprefents the naturall by light
colour and fhadow in the fuperficiall or flat, the other
in a body maffife expreffing the full and emptie, euen,
extant, rabbated, hollow, or whatfoeuer other figure
Ll ijʳ and paffion of quantitie./So alfo the Alchimift counter-
feits gold, filuer, and all other mettals, the Lapidarie
pearles and pretious ftones by glaffe and other fubftances falfified, and fophifticate by arte. Thefe men alfo
be praifed for their craft, and their credit is nothing
empayred, to fay that their conclufions and effects are
very artificiall. Finally in another refpect arte is as it
were an encountrer and contrary to nature, producing
effects neither like to hers, nor by participation with
her operations, nor by imitation of her paternes, but
makes things and produceth effects altogether ftrange
and diuerfe, & of fuch forme & qualitie (nature alwaies
fupplying ftuffe) as fhe neuer would nor could haue done
of her felfe, as the carpenter that builds a houfe, the
ioyner that makes a table or a bedftead, the tailor a garment, the Smith a locke or a key, and a number of like,

in which cafe the workman gaineth reputation by his arte, and praife when it is beft expreffed & moft apparāt, & moft ftudioufly. Man alfo in all his actiōs that be not altogether naturall, but are gotten by ftudy & difcipline or exercife, as to daunce by meafures, to fing by note, to play on the lute, and fuch like, it is a praife to be faid an artificiall dauncer, finger, & player on inftruments, becaufe they be not exactly knowne or done, but by rules & precepts or teaching of fchoolemafters. But in fuch actiōs as be fo naturall & proper to man, as he may become excellent therein without any arte or imitation at all, (cuftome and exercife excepted, which are requifite to euery action not numbred among the vitall or animal) and wherein nature fhould feeme to do amiffe, and man fuffer reproch to be found deftitute of them: in thofe to fhew himfelfe rather artificiall then naturall, were no leffe to be laughed at, then for one that can fee well inough, to vfe a paire of fpectacles, or not to heare but by a trunke put to his eare, nor feele without a paire of ennealed glooues, which things in deed helpe an infirme fence, but annoy the perfit, and therefore fhewing a difabilitie naturall mooue rather to fcorne then commendation, and to pitie fooner then to prayfe. But what elfe is language and vtterance, and difcourfe & perfuafion, and argument in man, then the vertues of a well conftitute body and minde, little leffe naturall then his very fenfuall actions, fauing that the one is perfited by nature at once, the other not without exercife & iteration? Peraduenture alfo it wilbe gran-/ted, that a man fees better Ll ij^v and difcernes more brimly his collours, and heares and feeles more exactly by vfe and often hearing and feeling and feing, & though it be better to fee with fpectacles then not to fee at all, yet is their praife not egall nor in any mans iudgement comparable: no more is that which a Poet makes by arte and precepts rather then by naturall inftinct: and that which he doth by long meditation rather then by a fuddaine infpiration, or with great pleafure and facillitie then hardly (and as they are woont to fay) in fpite of Nature or Minerua, then which nothing can be more irkfome or ridiculous.

And yet I am not ignorant that there be artes and methodes both to fpeake and to perfwade and alfo to difpute, and by which the naturall is in fome forte re-lieued, as th'eye by his fpectacle, I fay relieued in his imperfection, but not made more perfit then the naturall, in which refpect I call thofe artes of Grammer, *Logicke*, and *Rhetorick* not bare imitations, as the painter or keruers craft and worke in a forraine fubiect viz. a liuely purtraite in his table or wood, but by long and ftudious obferuation rather a repetitiō or reminifcens naturall, reduced into perfection, and made prompt by vfe and exercife. And fo whatfoeuer a man fpeakes or perfwades he doth it not by imitation artificially, but by obferuation naturally (though one follow another) be-caufe it is both the fame and the like that nature doth fuggeft: but if a popingay fpeake, fhe doth it by imita-tion of mans voyce artificially and not naturally being the like, but not the fame that nature doth fuggeft to man. But now becaufe our maker or Poet is to play many parts and not one alone, as firft to deuife his plat or fubiect, then to fafhion his poeme, thirdly to vfe his metricall proportions, and laft of all to vtter with pleafure and delight, which reftes in his maner of language and ftile as hath bene faid, whereof the many moodes and ftraunge phrafes are called figures, it is not altogether with him as with the crafts man, nor altogither other-wife then with the crafts man, for in that he vfeth his metricall proportions by appointed and harmonicall meafures and diftaunces, he is like the Carpenter or Ioyner, for borrowing their tymber and ftuffe of nature, they appoint and order it by art otherwife then nature would doe, and worke effects in apparance contrary to Ll iij^r hers. Alfo in that/which the Poet fpeakes or reports of another mans tale or doings, as *Homer* of *Priamus* or *Vliſſes*, he is as the painter or keruer that worke by imitation and repreſentation in a forrein ſubieƈt, in that he ſpeakes figuratiuely, or argues ſubtillie, or perſwades copiouſly and vehemently, he doth as the cunning gardiner that vſing nature as a coadiutor, furders her concluſions & many times makes her effeƈtes more abſolute and ſtraunge. But for that in our maker or Poet, which reſtes onely in deuiſe and iſſues from an excellent ſharpe and quick inuention, holpen by a cleare and bright phantaſie and imagination, he is not as the painter to counterfaite the naturall by the like effeƈts and not the ſame, nor as the gardiner aiding nature to worke both the ſame and the like, nor as the Carpenter to worke effeƈtes vtterly vnlike, but euen as nature her ſelfe working by her owne peculiar vertue and proper inſtinƈt and not by example or meditation or exerciſe as all other artificers do, is then moſt admired when he is moſt naturall and leaſt artificiall. And in the feates of his language and vtterance, becauſe they hold aſwell of nature to be ſuggeſted and vttered as by arte to be poliſhed and reformed. Therefore ſhall our Poet receaue prayſe for both, but more by knowing of his arte then by vnſeaſonable vſing it, and be more commended for his naturall eloquence then for his artificiall, and more for his artificiall well deſembled, then for the ſame ouermuch affeƈted and groſſely or vndiſcretly bewrayed, as many makers and Oratours do.

The Concluſion.

And with this (my moſt gratious ſoueraigne Lady) I make an end, humbly beſeeching your pardon, in that I haue preſumed to hold your eares ſo long annoyed with a tedious trifle, ſo as vnleſſe it proceede more of your owne Princely and naturall manſuetude then of my merite, I feare greatly leaſt you may thinck of me as

the Philofopher Plato did of *Aniceris* an inhabitant of
the Citie *Cirene*, who being in troth a very actiue and
artificiall man in driuing of a Princes Charriot or Coche
(as your Maieftie might be) and knowing it himfelfe
well enough, comming one day into Platos fchoole, and
hauing heard him largely difpute in matters/Philo-
fophicall, I pray you (quoth he) geue me leaue alfo to
fay fomewhat of myne arte, and in deede fhewed fo
many trickes of his cunning how to lanche forth and
ftay, and chaunge pace, and turne and winde his Coche,
this way and that way, vphill downe hill, and alfo in
euen or rough ground, that he made the whole affemblie
wonder at him. Quoth Plato being a graue perfonage,
verely in myne opinion this man fhould be vtterly vnfit
for any feruice of greater importance then to driue a
Coche. It is great pitie that fo prettie a fellow, had not
occupied his braynes in ftudies of more confequence.
Now I pray God it be not thought fo of me in defcribing
the toyes of this our vulgar art. But when I confider
how euery thing hath his eftimation by oportunitie, and
that it was but the ftudie of my yonger yeares in which
vanitie raigned. Alfo that I write to the pleafure of a
Lady and a moft gratious Queene, and neither to Prieftes
nor to Prophetes or Philofophers. Befides finding by
experience, that many times idleneffe is leffe harmefull
then vnprofitable occupation, dayly feeing how thefe
great afpiring mynds and ambitious heads of the world
ferioufly fearching to deale in matters of ftate, be often
times fo bufie and earneft that they were better be vn-
occupied, and peraduenture altogether idle, I prefume
fo much vpon your Maiefties moft milde and gracious
iudgement howfoeuer you conceiue of myne abilitie to
any better or greater feruice, that yet in this attempt ye
wil allow of my loyall and good intent alwayes en-
deuouring to do your Maieftie the beft and greateft of
thofe feruices I can.

A Table of the Chapters in this booke,

and euery thing in them
conteyned.

(309)

Ll iiij^v

The Table of the fecond booke.

The Table of the third booke.

The names of your figures Auricular. Mm iʳ

THE ARTE OF ENGLISH POESIE

THE TABLE

FINIS.

(313)

APPENDIX I

VARIANT PASSAGES

The two passages respectively cancelled and revised while the work was in the press (cf. *Introduction*, p. ciii) run as follows. The text is based on B.M., C. 71. c. 16.

(*a*) And confulting vpon the affaires of the low countreis at this day, peraduenture her Maieftie might be thus aduifed: The Flemings are a people very vnthankfull and mutable, and rebellious againft their Princes, for they did rife againft *Maximilian* Archduke of Auftria, who had maried the daughter and heire of the houfe of Burgundie, and tooke him prifoner, till by the Emperour *Frederike* the third his father, he was fet at libertie. They rebelled againft *Charles* the fift Emperor, their naturall Prince. They haue falfed their faith to his fonne *Philip* king of Spaine their foueraign Lord: and fince to Archduke *Matthias*, whom they elected for their gouernor, after to their adopted Lord Monfieur of Fraunce, Duke of Aniou: I pray you what likelihood is there they fhould be more affured to the Queene of England, than they haue bene to all thefe princes and gouernors, lōger than their diftreffe continueth, and is to be relieued by her goodnes and puiffance. [Sig. Ee iᵛ, p. 206, ll. 2–16. Cf. present text, p. 245, l. 31–p. 246, l. 12, for the substituted passage.]

(*b*) transferred from thefe polifhers of marble or porphicite, who after it is rough hewen and reduced to that fafhion, they will fet vpon it a goodly glaffe, fo fmoth and cleere, as ye may fee your face in it, or otherwife as it fareth by the bare and naked body, which being attired in rich and gorgious apparell, feemeth to the common vfage of th'eye much more comely & bewtifull then the naturall. So doth this figure which therefore I call the *Gorgious*, polifh our fpeech & as it were attire it with copious & pleafant amplifications & much varietie of fentences, all running vpon one point & to one intēt: fo as I doubt whether I may terme it a figure, or rather a maffe of many figuratiue fpeaches, applied to the bewtifying of our tale or argumēt. In a worke of ours intituled *Philocalia* we haue ftrained to fhew the vfe &

(314)

application of this figure & al others mētioned in this booke, to which we referre you. I find none example that euer I could fee, fo well maintayning this figure in Englifh meetre (of the *Gorgious*) as that ditty of her Maiefties owne making paffing fweet and harmonicall, which figure beyng as his very originall name purporteth the moft bewtifull of all others, it asketh in reafon to be referued for a laft complement, and defciphred by the arte of a ladies penne, her felfe beyng the moft gorgious and bewtifull, or rather bewtie of Queenes: and this was th'action, our foueraigne Lady perceiuing how by the Sc. Q. refidence within this Realme at fo great libertie and eafe, as were skarce worthy of fo great and dangerous a pryfoner, bred fecret factions among her people, and made many of her nobilitie incline to fauour her partie: many of them defirous of innouation in the ftate: fome of them afpiring to greater fortunes by her libertie and life. The Queene our foueraigne Lady to declare that fhe was nothing ignorant in thofe fecret fauours, though fhe had long with great wifdome and paciencie diffembled it, writeth this ditty moft fweet and fententious, not hiding from all fuch afpiring minds the daunger of their ambition and difloyaltie, which afterward fell out moft truly by th'exemplary chaftife-ment of fundry perfons, who in fauour of the fayd Sc. Q.. dero-gating from her Maieftie, fought to interrupt the quiet of the Realme by many euill and vndutifull practizes. The ditty is as followeth. [Sig. Ee ij^r, p. 207, ll. 1–37. Cf. present text, p. 247, l. 5–p. 248, l. 12, for the substituted passage.]

APPENDIX II

TEXTUAL CORRECTIONS

The following corrections of errors in Field's edition have been made:

p. 2, l. 27	*then*	for	*them*
p. 5, l. 32	language	,,	lauguage
p. 6, l. 11	diſperſed	,,	diperſed
p. 7, l. 25	direction	,,	di ection
p. 11, l. 31	after	,,	aſter
p. 12, l. 5	*of*	,,	*oſ*
p. 12, l. 6	*the*	,,	*tht*
p. 12, l. 25	*Regi*	,,	*Rege*
p. 12, l. 28	*anum*	,,	*annum*
p. 15, l. 8	kings	,,	king
p. 15, l. 10	of	,,	oſ
p. 15, l. 35	of	,,	oſ
p. 16, l. 21	diſpatch)	,,	diſpatch(
p. 17, l. 6	*The hunte is vp*	,,	*The hunte it vp*
p. 17, l. 37	*Tirtæus*	,,	*Firtæus*
p. 19, l. 14	*Aphrodiſeus*	,,	*Aphrodiſcus*
p. 24, l. 23	but	,,	hut
p. 24, l. 30	as it conformeth	,,	as it is conformeth
p. 25, l. 31	recreate	,,	receate
p. 44, l. 28	*Oppianus*	,,	*Oprianus*
p. 49, l. 7	*Proroſtris*	,,	*Procoſtris*
p. 53, l. 27	*baſijs*	,,	*baſis*
p. 54, l. 20	theſe	,,	aheſe
p. 54, ll. 23–4	*Marphorius*	,,	*Marphorir*
p. 55, l. 25	ſame	,,	fame
p. 55, l. 32	*Nidificatis*	,.	*Indificatis*
p. 56, l. 3	bouche	,,	bonche
p. 56, l. 28	craftes	,,	catftes
p. 59, l. 23	tong, as	,,	tong (as
p. 60, l. 25	*Heywood*	,,	*Hoywood*
p. 65, l. 23	ſtaffe	,,	ſtaſſe
p. 65, l. 32	fift	,,	firſt
p. 66, l. 6	ſtaffe	,,	ſtaſſe
p. 72, l. 11	compoſition	,,	compotition
p. 76, l. 4	in	,,	id
p. 81, l. 8	is not	,,	it not
p. 85, l. 4	precipitation	.,	precipation
p. 86, l. 31	twelfth	,,	twefth
p. 87, l. 1	& diſtances	,,	& and diſtances
p. 89, l. 30	amiſſe	,,	a miſſe
p. 91, l. 28	*Anacreons*	,,	*Anacreens*

(316)

APPENDIX II

p. 95, l. 2	reuerſt	for	reueſt
p. 96, l. 30	*flame*	,,	*ſtame*
p. 97, l. 10	breadth	,,	breath
p. 98, l. 35	*things*	,,	*thiugs*
p. 102, l. 14	they be/vnfolded	,,	they/vnfolded
p. 102, l. 29	*lente*	,,	*lento*
p. 103, l. 11	onely, whoſe	,,	onely (whoſe
p. 104, l. 6	Argonauts	,,	Argonants
p. 104, ll. 19–20	conquerours	,,	conquerous
p. 105, l. 1	ſufficient	,,	ſuffificient
p. 105, l. 24	kings	,,	kins
p. 107, l. 17	dutie and	,,	dutie aud
p. 110, l. 4	of	,,	if
p. 110, l. 13	is by the	,,	is the by
p. 111, l. 6	after the	,,	af- the
p. 113, l. 25	maieſties	,,	maieſty
p. 119, l. 1	neceſſitie	,,	neceſſiitie
p. 120, l. 31	number	,,	member
p. 120, l. 33	*dēſpŏilīng*	,,	*dēſpŏilīng*
p. 128, l. 16	[*Amphimacer*]	,,	]*Amphimacer*]
p. 129, l. 28	*fountaines*	,,	*fountaiues*
p. 140, l. 18	ignorants	,,	ignorance
p. 141, l. 20	Æ-/gypt	,,	Æ-/gypt
p. 141, l. 23	Ægypt	,,	Ægypt
p. 144, l. 19	pronounced	,,	ponounced
p. 146, l. 6	anſwereth	,,	auſwereth
p. 151, l. 29	to be accompted	,,	to accompted
p. 155, l. 9	diſliking	,,	diſliking
p. 162, l. 1	[*remembre*]	,,	[*remembre*[
p. 165, l. 33	[*to fail.*]	,,	[*to ſhow.*]
p. 167, ll. 31–2	ſupplied, the Greekes	,,	ſupplied the, Greekes
p. 168, l. 9	and	,,	aud
p. 173, l. 18	The Greekes	,,	TThe Greekes
p. 189, l. 31	Gentlemā	,,	Gentlemē
p. 192, l. 13	would	,,	ould
p. 192, l. 27	and	,,	aud
p. 203, l. 3	*Copronimus*	,,	*Cepronimus*
p. 206, l. 14	emblē	,,	emble
p. 210, marg.	or the	,,	or the The
p. 215, l. 26	Partheniade	,,	Parthemiade
p. 215, l. 28	*ſeaze*	,,	*feaze*
p. 215, l. 31	Partheniade	,,	Parthemiade
p. 216, l. 7	of	,,	oſ
p. 216, l. 27	ſtudie and	,,	ſtudie aud
p. 217, l. 3	of Prince	,,	of of Prince
p. 218, l. 8	*libertie*	,,	*lihertie*
p. 218, l. 34	a ſecret	,,	a a ſecret
p. 222, l. 5	*or*	,,	*of*
p. 224, l. 13	particularly	,,	partitularly
p. 225, l. 29	*His*	,,	*My*
p. 228, marg.	rendrer	,,	rend
p. 234, l. 35	*eye*	,,	*eyes*

p. 238, l. 33	*Achilles* and	for	*Achilles* aud
p. 239, l. 22	ſleepe	,,	ſheepe
p. 239, l. 25	*Gryſyll*	,,	*Gryſyll*
p. 239, l. 28	thereunto	,,	therevnto
p. 251, l. 5	Barbarie	,,	Burbarie
p. 252, l. 28	dealing, our	,,	dealing (our
p. 260, l. 18	and/of	,,	and/and of
p. 265, l. 5	*Philiſcus*	,,	*Philiſeus*
p. 267, l. 17	vndecency	,,	vndeceny
p. 268, l. 5	beſt	,,	beft
p. 269, l. 13	*incontinentiæ*	,,	*incontinente*
p. 272, l. 13	his/miſtreſſe	,,	his/his miſtreſſe
p. 274, l. 26	pelfe)	,,	pelfe]
p. 277, l. 28	Philoſopher	,,	Philoſoper
p. 278, l. 20	Ægypt	,,	Ægypt
p. 283, l. 7	it	,,	is
p. 284, l. 21	For who would	,,	For who who would
p. 286, l. 1	according to the	,,	according the
p. 286, l. 18	ſeeme not onely	,,	ſeeme onely
p. 286, l. 18	deſpight	,,	deshight
p. 289, l. 7	*vuole*	"	*vuolo*
p. 289, l. 28	neuer	,,	ueuer
p. 306, l. 13	or	,,	of
p. 312, l. 52	Anachinoſis	,,	Anachmoſis
p. 313, l. 10	Parecnaſis	,,	Parecuaſis

APPENDIX III

THE SOURCES OF THE *ARTE*

On the immediate sources of the *Arte* the present editors can throw very little light. That there were sources for the work is, of course, obvious. The chapter on rhyming Latin verse (I, vii), for example, may have been incorporated *en bloc* from some earlier work; the anagrams in II, xii would appear to have been the stock examples of this kind of verbal ingenuity;[1] and the devices in the same chapter, like the spate of *apophthegmata*[2] which illustrates the chapters on Decorum (III, xxiii–xxiv), were plainly derived from a popular renaissance channel. It is also quite clear that a rhetorical manual was at hand when Book III was written. More precise definition of the *Arte*'s sources (with the exception of a number of contemporary verse collections) has proved impossible. Either the search for them has been attended by singularly bad luck or Puttenham's material had been so freely broken up and re-welded that it is impossible to arrive at any demonstrable proof of the channels through which it reached him.

In the absence of proof to the contrary it is, perhaps, legitimate to regard the *Arte* as, in the main, a testimony to independent judgment and original observation. It is, of course, a typical piece of renaissance criticism: its basis of historical information represented the *publica materies* of its age; its emphasis on rhetoric reflected the master-interest of renaissance education; and the problems it set out to solve were those of the vernaculars throughout Western Europe. The very nature of these last, however,

1 The same three examples appear in Du Bellay's *Défense* (II, viii) and in the section on Anagrams in Camden's *Remaines*. Du Bellay, Puttenham and Camden appear to be drawing on a common source rather than on one another.

2 Of the twenty-six *apophthegmata* and anecdotes of humanistic type which illustrate the final chapters of Book III all except four can be found in Erasmus' *Apophthegmata* which may be accepted as their most probable source, though indebtedness to this, rather than to some subsequent, compilation cannot be proved. From the same source Puttenham appears to have drawn some of the *apophthegmata* (such as the sayings of the elder Cato) which he versified to illustrate the Figures.

demanded of the critics who faced them a native intelligence which, though trained and directed by the past, must grapple unaided with the present. The manner in which Puttenham tackled this task establishes a measure for the self-reliance he was likely to show in covering the beaten track. The critic who was the first to note the French origin and name of the alexandrine, who had noticed the mid-century drama's inkhorn rhymes, who could so neatly trip up the slip-shod Turberville, and so effectively prick the bubble of 'solemne circumstance' in a stanza of Gascoigne's was not likely to prove less independent in dealing with the general principles of criticism or in handling the inheritance of the past. That the same originality was brought to bear on the more derivative sections of the *Arte* can be proved from the treatment of the Figures in Book III. Although no one textbook has been found which covers all Puttenham's ground, a comparison of the three whose range corresponds most closely to the *Arte*'s (the popular textbook of Susenbrotus, Sherry's *Schemes and Tropes* and Peacham's *Garden of Eloquence*) makes it possible to demonstrate what in this portion of the *Arte* was transmitted from its source (or sources) and what was not. Here Puttenham was dealing with a subject from which the life had gradually been ebbing since Quintilian's day, though the Figures had been augmented, illustrated and classified by generations of grammarians. He begins by refusing to fall into line with tradition and by re-organising the subject. He translates and adapts a great many stock examples from the accumulated store of the textbooks, but grafts a more fruitful branch to the venerable but decrepit tree by incorporating illustrations from the poetry of his own day; he also makes the Figures of genuine literary significance by using them as guides to the appreciation and detailed criticism of contemporary verse, in a manner never before attempted in English. It is manifestly erroneous to hope to apply successfully to work of this kind the methods of dissection which can be relied on to reveal the sources of most Elizabethan prose pamphlets.

Of the original observation put into Book II there can be no question, but Book I constitutes a problem. It is probably the least original book of the three, but the methods of re-organisation, adaptation and re-interpretation demonstrable in Book III render it quite possible that Book I reflects an almost equally personal approach to its subject. The name of Scaliger is generally associated with this book, but Book I of the *Arte* and the

Poetices have little more in common than the inevitable superficial resemblance of works covering the same ground. Puttenham's thesis of the correlated progress of poetry and civilisation and the slight interest he displays in prescribed form are so unscaligerian that it is difficult to believe that he could ever have handled the *Poetices*. Though he himself described Book I as taken from 'the best clerks writing in the same arte', he seems to have read them very subjectively. Renaissance 'clerks' like Jodocus Badius or Scaliger certainly would not have admitted responsibility for Puttenham's account of the early evolution of the Kinds, particularly of the 'foure sundry formes of Poesie Drāmatick reprehensiue'. There is in this book, moreover, enough of the rational, even materialistic, temper of Puttenham's mind to warrant the assumption that many of its conclusions were personal.

To the works which leap to the mind in reading the *Arte*— Quintilian's *Institutiones*, Castiglione's *Cortegiano* and Montaigne's *Essais*—no debt can be proved. Puttenham shares Quintilian's capacity for criticism that bestows on language a lively and living significance, but in view of the wide diffusion of Quintilian's material, it is impossible to demonstrate a firsthand acquaintance with the *Institutiones*.[1] Like Castiglione, Puttenham voices the courtier's point of view on society and the vernacular, but though parallel passages from the *Arte* and the *Courtier* might be quoted, they probably prove nothing more than similar environment and aim, and a common stock of renaissance examples, anecdotes and opinions. A number of small parallels between Montaigne's *Essais* and the *Arte* can be similarly explained.

Any mental picture of the kind of books Puttenham read can, therefore, be only sketchy, but its outlines and main features are sufficiently clear. Unless the *Arte* gives a very misleading picture of its writer's interests, Puttenham's bias is heavily marked. It is plain that he had no use for the portentous theological commentaries that swelled the more pretentious libraries of the period (such as Lumley's). In the *Arte* there is not a single reference to a father of the church or a mediaeval theologian. Its writer would undoubtedly have preferred a dictionary to all the volumes of Lyra or Gerson. His *penchant* in creative literature was clearly

---

[1] If Puttenham knew Quintilian's work, he certainly used as well some later textbook, since some of his Figures and examples represented late-Latin and early-mediaeval additions to the rhetorical tradition.

for a light and human touch: he had read the *Basia* of Secundus,[1] but there is no evidence that he knew Buchanan's *Jephthes*. His comparison of the 'wittie' conciseness of oriental verse with the 'long tedious descriptions' of which the poetry of his own country was only too full affords an index to his taste. He had a working knowledge of Greek, but his references to classical literature are very scanty when set beside the packed allusions of Wilson's *Arte of Rhetorique* or Ascham's *Scholemaster*. His 'humanism' was rather a matter of temperament and intellectual calibre than of bookish equipment. His mind drew its main stimulus not from books but from the exercise of its native curiosity and awareness, and was happiest in working out its own schemes and recording its contacts with the world of men and poets. Of works in the modern vernaculars[2] Puttenham was undoubtedly acquainted with Petrarch's sonnets and *canzoni*, Ronsard's *Odes* and Guevara's *Libro de Marco Aurelio*. His chief enthusiasm, however, was for the poetry of his own day and it is only in the field of Tudor poetry that a list of the books with which he had undoubtedly a first-hand acquaintance can be compiled with any confidence. The following lists cover the sources of verse quotations in the *Arte* that have been identified. References are to modern editions as easiest of access. Numerous variations between Puttenham's readings and the originals which seem to be mainly due to careless transcription have not been recorded. A great many of the lines and passages quoted remain unidentified: some of these were probably concocted *ad hoc* by Puttenham himself; others ring true as genuinely derived from contemporary sources which may one day be identified or may have perished with so much manuscript work of the period. One of the valuable warnings the *Arte* provides for the student of Elizabethan literature is the reminder of the mass of work which has been lost.

Appended to the account of original verse sources are a list of stock rhetorical examples, mostly incorporated as verse, in the *Arte* and notes on such further sources of Puttenham's illustrations as have been identified.

1 Puttenham's courageous and unqualified praise of Secundus' work (p. 53) is a striking example not only of the absence of theological and moralistic bias in his approach to poetry but also of his critical *flair*.
2 For complete lists of verse and prose writers referred to in the *Arte*, *v.* Index, *s.v.* Poet II (3), Poet III and Prose (2).

I. PRINTED SOURCES

arranged in order of date of publication

1. CHAUCER, *Works.*

Included in the early Chaucer canon were the apocryphal poems from which the following were derived:

p. 212 *O soppe of sorrow...* Henryson, *Testament of Cresseid,* 407–8; cf. Skeat, *Chaucerian and other Pieces,* p. 340.

p. 224 *When faith failes...* Anon.; cf. Skeat, *loc. cit.,* p. 450.

2. GAVIN DOUGLAS, *Eneados* (1553).

Douglas is the translator referred to on p. 273 who described Aeneas as 'by fate a fugitiue' (*v.* Douglas, *Works,* ed. Small, 1874, Vol. 2, p. 22).

3. TOTTEL'S *Miscellany* (1557).

References to the page numbers and opening words in the *Arte* are followed by references to the poems as numbered in Professor Rollins' edition (1928) with line references within the poem.

p. 71 *The smoakie sighes...* Anon., ccxiv, 1–10, omitting 5–6.

p. 72 *When raging loue...* Surrey, xvi, 1.
p. 123 *I finde no peace...* Wyatt, xlix, 1–2.
p. 123 *When raging loue...* *v.* under p. 72.
p. 123 *A fairer beast of fresher hue...* Surrey, cclxiv, 10.
p. 125 *What holy graue...* Surrey, xxix, 5.
p. 126 *Full manie that...* Surrey, xxx, 2.
p. 126 *Shed Cæsars teares...* Surrey, xxx, 4.
p. 126 *Th'enemie to life...* Wyatt, lxxxv, 1.
p. 126 *If amorous faith...* Wyatt, xcviii, 1.
p. 126 *Myne old deere enemy...* Wyatt, lxiv, 1.
p. 126 *The furious gone...* Wyatt, lxxiii, 1.
p. 129 *Like vnto these...* Wyatt, xcvii, 1–4.
p. 132 *Farewell loue...* Wyatt, xcix, 1.
p. 132 *When raging loue...* *v.* under p. 72.
p. 175 *For in her mynde...* Anon., cclxxviii, 207–14, omitting 211–2 (not in the first edition of the *Miscellany*).
p. 176 *The restlesse state...* Wyatt, lxii, 1–7.
p. 176 *If weaker care...* Wyatt, xliv, 1–6, omitting 5.

p. 180 *I lent my loue to losse...* Anon., cxcv, 1.
pp. 192–3 *Giue place ye louers...* Surrey, xx, 1–6.

p. 193 *But since it will...*	Anon., ccxxii, 37–42.
p. 194 *In winters iust returne...*	Surrey, xviii, 1–2.
p. 213 *Perdie I said it not...*	Wyatt, xci, 1–18.
p. 215 *My faith, my hope, my trust...*	Anon., clxxxiv, 33–4.
pp. 222–3 *Set me whereas...*	Surrey, xii, 1–14.
p. 229 *When fortune shall...*	Wyatt, lxxii, 3–6.
p. 229 *Accused though I be...*	Wyatt, lxxiv, 1–4.
p. 229 *And for her beauties praise...*	Anon., clxviii, 11–2.
p. 240 *When Cupid scaled first...*	[Vaux], ccxi, 1–22.
p. 241 *But as the watrie showres...*	Surrey, cclxv, 47–8.
p. 241 *Then as the striken deere...*	Surrey, cclxv, 21–2.
p. 255 *The smoakie sighes...*	*v.* under p. 71.

4. *King Edward IV and the Tanner of Tamworth* (1564–5).

p. 256 *I hope I shall be hanged to morrow*

This line represents a version of l. 172 of this ballad as recorded in Percy's *Reliques* (ed. Wheatley, 1891, Vol. 2, pp. 92–100)—

I trow I shall be hang'd to-morrowe.

The key-word of the line as quoted by Puttenham does not appear in existing printed versions of the ballad, all of which, however, are later in date than the *Arte*. Wheatley (p. 93) cites an example (from another ballad) of the use of *hope* for *fear* and perhaps in the lost ballad on the tanner of Tamworth entered to Griffith in 1564/5 the line ran as Puttenham quotes it. On the other hand, *sperare* for *timere* was a stock example of this vice of speech (*acyrologia*).

5. TURBERVILLE, *Epitaphes, Epigrams, Songs and Sonets* (1567).

References are to Chalmers' *English Poets*, 1810, Vol. 2.

p. 82 *O mightie Lord of loue...*	p. 604.
p. 177 *Of fortune nor her frowning face...*	p. 646.
p. 252 *O mightie Lord of loue...*	*v.* under p. 82.
p. 255 *A corrall lippe of hew*	p. 644.
p. 255 *A dongeon deepe...*	p. 640.
p. 256 *Her haire surmounts...*	p. 644.
p. 256 *The flouds of graces*	p. 644.
p. 257 *Nor Menelaus was vnwise...*	p. 649.
p. 259 *A misers mynde thou hast...*	p. 640.
p. 274 *Thou hast a misers minde...*	*v.* under p. 259.

6. GASCOIGNE, *The Posies* (1575).

References are to the pages of Cunliffe's edition (1907).

p. 182 *darke disdaine*	cf. first line of extract from Gascoigne quoted on p. 254.
p. 188 *The cloudes of care...*	p. 400.

p. 194 *The tenth of March...*	p. 333.
p. 212 *Why striue I with the streame...*	p. 370.
p. 212 *Ay me the dayes...*	p. 367.
p. 221 *Loue hope and death...*	p. 394.
p. 236 *To muse in minde how faire...*	p. 104.
p. 236 *I deeme, I dreame...*	p. 103.
p. 254 *The deadly droppes...*	p. 458.
p. 255 *And if I not performe...*	p. 414.
p. 258 *The tenth of March...*	*v.* under p. 194.

7. STANYHURST, *Aeneis* (1582).

Stanyhurst is the translator responsible for the words *trudge* and *tug* censured by Puttenham on pp. 273–4 (*Aeneis,* 1582, i, 7 and 16).

8. SOOWTHERN, *Pandora* (1584).

Collier (*Bibliographical Account,* 1865, Vol. 2, pp. 367–70) identified Soowthern correctly as the filcher from Ronsard's *Odes* denounced on pp. 252–3. All the gallicisms quoted on pp. 252–3 and the lines and phrases quoted on p. 253 are from Soowthern's dedicatory ode to the Earl of Oxford, based (as Puttenham pointed out) on Ronsard's dedication of his *Odes* to Henry II of France.

II. MANUSCRIPT SOURCES[1]

arranged in alphabetical order of authorship; surnames and titles are arranged on the same lines as in the Index

1. ANONYMOUS POEMS.

p. 72 *Now sucke childe and sleepe childe...*
These four lines are a version of the opening of an anonymous poem preserved in MS. Harl. 7392, fol. 31^r.
p. 173 *Mischaunces ought...*
p. 205 *What life is the liefest...*
pp. 205–6 *What life list ye to lead...*
p. 243 *Set the Giant deepe in a dale...*
There are four verse extracts in MS. Harl. 6910, fols. 159^v, 166^r and 166^v which correspond (for the most part very closely) with

---

1 This does not mean, of course, that Puttenham used the particular MSS. here referred to, but merely that the work was accessible to him only in MS. The references to MSS. containing poems quoted by Puttenham are not intended to be exhaustive and, where possible, references are to well-documented modern editions.

these, but, as MS. Harl. 6910 is certainly later in date than the *Arte* and as the verse extracts on pp. 205–6 seem to represent Puttenham's own versions of the well-known lines of Metrodorus and Crates (*v.* Professor Rollins' notes to nos. 151–2 of Tottel's *Miscellany*), the Harl. 6910 extracts were probably derived from the *Arte*.

2. SIR EDWARD DYER.

p. 169 *But now my Deere (for so my loue* . . .
ll. 9–10 of the poem beginning 'Before I dy, faire dame' preserved in MS. Harl. 7392, fols. 22^v–23^r. The poem is printed for the first time in a note, 'New Poems by Sir Edward Dyer', by Mr Bernard M. Wagner, *Review of English Studies*, October 1935, pp. 467–8.

3. SIR EDWARD DYER OR SIR ARTHUR GORGES.

p. 211 *Nor loue hath now the force* . . .
ll. 19–20 of the poem beginning 'But this and then no more' preserved in MS. Harl. 7392, fols. 27^v–28^r and printed for the first time in *R.E.S., loc. cit.*, pp. 468–9. Although Puttenham attributes this couplet to Dyer, MS. Harl. 7392 attributes the poem from which it is taken to 'GOR.' (*i.e.* Sir Arthur Gorges).
p. 227 *All you who read these lines* . . .
ll. 27–8 of the same poem. This couplet Puttenham attributes to 'Maister Gorge'.
p. 236 *But if my faith my hope* . . .
ll. 5–7 of the same poem. Puttenham attributes these lines to Dyer.
p. 237 *And as for you (faire one)* . . .
ll. 29–30 of the same poem. Puttenham mentions no author for this couplet.

Although the internal evidence of the poem from which these four extracts were taken renders it possible (and even probable) that it was Dyer's, the external evidence is, perhaps, slightly in favour of Gorges. Not enough of Gorges' work is extant to provide *criteria* for discussion of the poem's authorship.

4. QUEEN ELIZABETH.

p. 248 *The doubt of future foes* . . .
Preserved in MS. Rawl. Poet. 108, fol. 44^v, MS. Harl. 7392, fol. 27^v, B.M., MS. Add. 28635, fol. 105^v and printed in several nineteenth-century verse collections (*inter alia*, Hannah, *Poems of Sir Walter Raleigh and other Courtly Poets*, 1892, pp. 136–7).

The poem of Elizabeth's from which the couplet on p. 236 is quoted appears to be lost.

SIR ARTHUR GORGES, *v.* entries under (3) following Sir Edward Dyer.

5. EDWARD DE VERE, 17th Earl of Oxford.

p. 206 *When wert thou borne desire...*
The opening lines of the poem printed in *Brittons Bowre of Delights*, 1591 (no. 40); *v.* Rollins' edition, 1933, pp. 47, 94–8.

6. PUTTENHAM, *Partheniades* (B.M., MS. Cotton Vesp. E viii).

References are to the poem and line numbers of the MS. as edited by Haslewood, 1811 and Morfill, 1873 (cf. Introduction, p. xxxi, n. 1).

p. 182 *But in chaste stile...*	ii, 28–9.
p. 193 *Whom Princes serue...*	iv, 1–4.
p. 215 *O peereles you...*	xii, last 4 lines.
pp. 215–6 *Her heart is hid...*	vii, 47–50.
p. 217 *Than if there bee...*	vi, last stanza.
pp. 223–4 *Not your bewtie...*	xii, first 3 stanzas.
p. 234 *the paragon of Queenes*	prose heading to xv.
p. 234 *As falcon fares...*	xvi, omitting 5–6.
pp. 234–5 *Set rich rubie...*	xv, 9–20, omitting 15–8.
p. 243 *Nature that seldome...*	iv, last 5 lines.
p. 244 *Of siluer was...*	vii, 5–8, 13–6, 9–12, 25–8.
p. 256 *A cheere where loue...*	viii, 5–6.

7. SIR WALTER RALEIGH.

p. 201 *Yet when I sawe...*
The closing couplet of the poem beginning 'Calling to minde mine eie long went about'; *v.* Raleigh, *Poems*, ed. Latham, 1929, pp. 37, 141–3, and *The Phœnix Nest*, 1593, ed. Rollins, 1931, pp. 80, 178–80.

The lines attributed to Raleigh on pp. 198 ('In vayne mine eyes...') and 201 ('With wisdomes eyes...') appear to be from poems which are lost.

8. SIR PHILIP SIDNEY.

p. 203 *And all my life...*
The closing couplet of the poem beginning 'All my sense thy sweetnesse gained' first printed among the 'Certaine Sonets' appended to the 1598 *Arcadia* (pp. 486–7).

p. 217 *What medcine then...*
The closing couplet of the poem beginning 'The Loue whiche ys imprinted in my sowle', *Arcadia* (original), ed. Feuillerat, 1926, p. 219.

p. 225 *My true loue hath...*
    The first eight lines (*plus* refrain) of the poem beginning 'My true
    Loue hathe', *Arcadia* (original), ed. Feuillerat, pp. 179–80.

The reference on p. 244 to Sidney's 'description of his mistresse
excellently well handled...in his booke of *Archadia*' is probably to
the poem 'What Toungue can her perfections tell?', *Arcadia* (original),
ed. Feuillerat, pp. 223–6.

9. HENRY HOWARD, EARL OF SURREY.

p. 73 *Salomon Dauids sonne...*   *Ecclesiastes*, i, 1.

III. STOCK RHETORICAL EXAMPLES, APOPH-THEGMATA and TRADITIONAL VERSE

A considerable number of illustrations in the *Arte* which wear
the masquerade of Tudor verse from unnamed authors or of
original compositions of Puttenham's own prove upon investigation to be verse renderings of stock rhetorical examples. As
all but one of these can be found in Susenbrotus' *Epitome Tro-
porum ac Schematum*, this was very probably one of the main
sources of Book III, though indebtedness to Susenbrotus rather
than to some kindred compiler cannot be proved. The popularity
of the *Epitome* is attested by the number of sixteenth-century
editions, and references to its author by Nashe[1] and Lodge[2]
imply that his work was a school textbook and a recognised
authority. The number of rhetorical examples common to the
Arte, Sherry's two works (*Schemes and Tropes* and *Grammer and
Rhetorike*) and Peacham's *Garden of Eloquence* is best explained
as due to reliance on the same authority. Day, however, in the
section on schemes and tropes added to the *English Secretorie*
in 1595[3], drew on Puttenham since he paraphrased some of
Puttenham's original verse (e.g. his epigram on a dyer).

---

1 *Have with You* (*Works*, ed. McKerrow, Vol. 3, p. 64).
2 *Deafe Mans Dialogue* (appended to *Euphues Shadow*), p. 90 (Hunterian
Club edition).
3 We have been unable to find a copy of the 1592 edition of this work;
from the *S.T.C.* description (no. 6402) it would appear to have contained
this additional matter; the British Museum copy on which the *S.T.C.* description is based has been missing for many years.

The first of the following lists (A) covers verse illustrations in the *Arte* which can be identified, with some certainty, as verse renderings of textbook examples. These fall roughly into two classes. Some represent nothing more than fairly literal translation of short extracts from classical writers; their ultimate source is generally acknowledged and, frequently, the Latin example accompanies the English rendering. The second class consists of freer verse translation which has often been assimilated to the general context of Tudor poetry and is presented, for example, as a lover's lament or an extract from Puttenham's *juvenilia*. The second list (B) records illustrations which may have been suggested by stock rhetorical examples but cannot be positively claimed as derived from this source. As a fairly exhaustive search of Tudor verse, however, has failed to trace them to any other channel, it has seemed worth while to suggest a textbook origin.

(A)[1]

p. 164 *Faire maydes beautie (alack)*...	(*Ad Herennium*, iv, 27).
p. 164 *Either the troth*...	
p. 166 *Thus valiantly*...	(Justinus, *Hist. Phil. Epit.*, III, i, 9).
p. 175 *I came, I saw, I ouercame**	
p. 183 *Woe worth the mountaine*...	(From Euripides, *Medea*, V, iii, *via* Quintilian, V, x, 84; not in Susenbrotus).
p. 184 *After many a stubble**...	
p. 184 *I know you hate me not*...	(Virgil, *Ecl.*, iii, 74).
p. 187 *Stop vp your streames (my lads)**...	
p. 188 *It is my mother*...	(A very old riddle of wide distribution).
p. 199 *Our Christ the sonne of God*...	
p. 204 *Thou weenest thy wit**...	
pp. 204–5 *Wylie worldling*...	
p. 207 *The niggards fault*...	
p. 207 *The couetous miser*...	(Publilius Syrus, 'Tam deest avaro...').
p. 209 *If Poesie be*...	(*Ad Herennium*, iv, 28).
p. 209 *With pleasure if we worke*...	
p. 210 *Hye thee, and by*...	(Virgil, *Aen.*, iv, 381–3).
p. 210 *Goe now and giue*...	(Juvenal, *Sat.*, xii, 57–9).

1 Where stock examples are quotations from Latin prose and verse writers their ultimate source is given in brackets unless Puttenham's illustration is accompanied by the Latin; in the latter case its ultimate source is noted at the end of this appendix ('Latin quotations in the *Arte*') and the passage here is marked by an asterisk.

p. 211 *Was I able* . . . (From Ovid's lost play on Medea, *via* Quintilian, VIII, v, 6).

p. 214 *Is he aliue* . . . (Virgil, *Aen.*, iii, 339–41; the question is asked by Andromache concerning Ascanius, not by Aeneas concerning Orontes).

p. 217 *So huge a peece** . . .

p. 219 *A iollie man* . . .

p. 221 *It can not be* . . . (*Ad Herennium*, iv, 38).

p. 222 *Were it for grace* . . . (*Ibid.*, iv, 40).

p. 226 *Whether the cruell mother* . . . (Virgil, *Ecl.*, viii, 49–50).

p. 226 *Me thinkes that I* . . .

p. 227 *If my speech hap* . . .

p. 230 *I spake amysse* . . .

pp. 233–4 *No man can say* . . . (*Ad Herennium*, iv, 29).

p. 236 *Nature bids vs* . . . (From Terence, *Andria*, II, v, probably *via* Erasmus, *Adagia*, I, iii, 91).

p. 236 *The Prince that couets* . . . (A saying attributed by Quintilian, VIII, v, 3, to Domitius Afer).

p. 236 *Nothing stickes faster* . . . (Erasmus, *Adagia*, II, iv, 20; cf. Quintilian, I, i, 19).

p. 257 *For euer may* . . .

(B)

p. 170 *When we had climbde* . . . (Cf. Virgil, *Aen.*, iii, 662).

p. 173 *Weeping creeping* . . . (Cf. Ennius, *Ann.*, ii, 97).

p. 184 *O sinne it selfe* . . . (*hyperbole*)

p. 208 *His vertue made him wise* . . . (Cf. *Ad Herennium*, iv, 25).

p. 210 *His bent is sweete* . . . (Cf. *Ibid.*, iv, 15).

p. 213 *Enuy, malice* . . . (Cf. Romans, i, 29).

p. 216 *Many are the paines* . . . (*anteisagoge*)

p. 218 *He lost besides* . . .

p. 222 *Now gentill Sirs* . . . (Cf. *Ad Herennium*, iv, 40).

p. 227 *Tell me faire Ladies* . . .

p. 230 *I said it: but* . . .

All of these can be found in any sixteenth-century edition of Susenbrotus by reference to the relevant Figure or the Figure mentioned above in brackets.

There are as well a number of stock rhetorical examples (all in Susenbrotus and many derived ultimately from Quintilian) embedded in the prose explanations of the Figures in Book III[1]: e.g. the metaphorical use of *bark* (p. 178); 'loue by the name of *Venus*', etc. as an example of *metonymia* (p. 181); *taratantara* as an example of onomatopeic formation (p. 182); the illustration

---

1 This list is representative and not exhaustive.

of *allegoria* from Horace's 'O navis' (p. 187); the euphemism *virgineam dissoluit zonam* as an example of *synecdoche* (p. 196); the Hannibal illustration of *meiosis* (p. 220); the list of 'places vntrue' under *topographia* (p. 239); 'I...saw it with mine eyes' as an example of *pleonasmus* (p. 257) and the ambassadors illustration of *macrologia* (p. 257).

In a similar manner Puttenham translated, versified and adapted to his context a number of *apophthegmata* probably derived from Erasmus' *Adagia, Apophthegmata* and *Parabolae*. As these works, however, like the *Epitome* of Susenbrotus, were compilations which at once became the starting points for a fresh generation of compilers, no claim for direct reliance on them has been pressed. Most of the illustrations in this group bear somewhat obviously the marks of their kind but, where possible, Puttenham has grafted these slips into the stock of native verse so as to make them indistinguishable from his cuttings from contemporaries.

p. 200 *Feare many must he needs...*
A saying sometimes attributed to Publilius Syrus but to Laberius by Macrobius (*Sat.*, II, vii).
p. 205 *What life is the liefest...*
pp. 205–6 *What life list ye to lead...*
Both of these sayings are quoted by Erasmus, *Adagia*, II, iii, 49.
p. 209 *Brutus for casting out of kings...*
p. 209 *It seemes your offices...*
p. 209 *In trifles earnest...*
p. 212 *Must not (trowe ye)...*
p. 226 *Now is it not...*
All of these are in Erasmus' *Apophthegmata*; the first from Suetonius, the second, fourth and fifth from Plutarch's *Cato*, and the third from the *Moralia*.
p. 241 *As the shadow...*
p. 241 *The launce so bright...*
p. 242 *As true loue is...*
p. 242 *As the good seedes...*
p. 242 *A sage man said...*
p. 243 *After ill crop...*
p. 243 *It fares not by fathers...*
p. 243 *Set the Giant deepe in a dale...*
All of these are in Erasmus' *Parabolae*; the first, fourth, sixth and eighth from Seneca's *Epistolae*; the second and third from Plutarch's

Moralia; the fifth (a saying of Menedemus of Eretria, also included in the *Apophthegmata*) from the *Moralia* and the seventh from Theophrastus.

p. 246 *The Elephant is strong*. . .
  In Erasmus' *Apophthegmata*; from Capitolinus.

The following passages may be regarded as traditional:

p. 174 *Long beards hartlesse*. . .
  These lines are recorded as dating from Edward III's first campaign against the Scots: *v. The Brut, or the Chronicles of England,* ed. Brie (E.E.T.S., no. 131), Vol. I, p. 249. From this popular mediaeval chronicle, many times printed in the fifteenth and sixteenth centuries and generally known as 'Caxton's Chronicle', they were incorporated in the compilations of Fabyan and Holinshed.[1]

p. 208 *Peace makes plentie*. . .
  These lines, which Puttenham attributes to Jean de Meung, had apparently achieved the status of an 'olde sayde sawe' (Gascoigne, *Posies*, Dulce Bellum Inexpertis, stanza 9). Two fifteenth-century MS. versions are recorded by Wright and Halliwell, *Reliquiae Antiquae*, 1841, Vol. I, p. 315. Another rendering is preserved in B.M., MS. Add. 28635, fol. 7r. See also *Histrio-Mastix*, ed. Simpson, *School of Shakespeare*, Vol. 2, pp. 87–8.

IV. LATIN QUOTATIONS

A list of Latin quotations in the *Arte* which have been identified is appended below to help the reader's identification of index references.

p. 12 *Anglorum Regi*. . .   Schola Salernitana, *De Conservanda Bona Valetudine*, i, 1–6, omitting 4–5.
p. 14 *Quot cælum stellas*. . .   Ovid, *Ars Am.*, i, 59 *plus* a spurious line.
p. 15 *Carmina clarisonæ*. . .   Hucbaldus, *De Laudibus Calvitii*, Proemium, 1.
p. 15 *Laus tua non tua fraus*. . .
  These lines (the stock example of *versus retrogradi*) are included among the 'Pasquinatae' in T. R.'s *Deliciae Parnassi*, Dublin, 1700, Cap. i, 14, where they are described as 'Versus Ironici in

---

1 For our information concerning the source of these lines we are indebted to the kindness of Miss D. Everett.

Papae Laudem'. Confirmation of Puttenham's statement that the pope was Alexander has not been found. On the assumption that he was correct they have been indexed under Alexander VI.

p. 19 *Animam nō intelligere* . . . Aristotle, *De Memoria*, i.

p. 22 *O quantus artifex pereo!* Quoted in Erasmus, *Apoph.*, from Suetonius, *Nero*, 49, 1.

p. 22 *Frangatur potius* . . . Donatus, *Vita Virgilii*, xv, 58.

p. 52 *Sicut sponsa* . . . Cf. Psalms, xix, 5.

p. 53 *Ficenina licĕtia* Horace, *Ep.*, II, i, 145 ('fescennina . . . licentia').

p. 55 *Nocte pluit tota* . . . Donatus, *V. V.*, xvii, 69.

p. 55 *Hos ego versiculos* . . . *Ibid.*, xvii, 70.

p. 55 *Sic vos non vobis* . . . *Ibid.*

p. 100 *Hominem quadratū* Aristotle, *Eth. Nic.*, I, x (included in Erasmus' *Adagia*, IV, viii, 35).

p. 112 *Vanitas vanitatum* . . . Ecclesiastes, i, 2.

p. 119 *Arma uirumque* . . . Virgil, *Aen.*, i, 1.

p. 125 *Si volet vsus* . . . Horace, *A. P.*, 71–2.

p. 130 *Nil mihi rescribas* . . . Ovid, *Her.*, i, 2.

p. 147 *Multa renascentur* . . . Horace, *A. P.*, 70–2.

p. 155 *Ne quid nimis* A much-quoted saying of uncertain origin; *v.* Erasmus, *Adagia*, I, vi, 96.

p. 175 *Veni, vidi, vici* Suetonius, *Divus Iulius*, 37, 2.

p. 182 *Taratantara* Ennius, *Ann.*, ii, 35 (not Virgil); the juxtaposition of this with a quotation from Virgil in Susenbrotus may account for Puttenham's attribution.

p. 183 *Post multas mea regna* . . . Virgil, *Ecl.*, i, 69.

p. 186 *Qui nescit dissimulare* . . . The maxim of Lewis XI of France.

p. 187 *Claudite iam riuos* . . . Virgil, *Ecl.*, iii, 111.

p. 196 *Virgineam dissoluit zonam* Given as an example of *synecdoche* (with *soluit* for Puttenham's erroneous *dissoluit*) by Susenbrotus who, however, says nothing about 'the Poet').

p. 204 *Scire tuum nihil est* . . . Persius, *Sat.*, i, 27.

p. 205 *Optimum non nasci* . . . Cf. Erasmus, *Adagia*, II, iii, 49.

p. 217 *Tantæ molis erat* . . . Virgil, *Aen.*, i, 33.

p. 217 *Tantum relligio potuit* . . . Lucretius, *Nat. Rer.*, i, 101.

p. 272 *Sacras vestras occupationes* Suetonius, *Tiberius*, 27 (included in Erasmus' *Apophthegmata*).

p. 273 *Fato profugus* Virgil, *Aen.*, i, 2.

p. 274 *Insignem pietate* . . . *Ibid.*, i, 9–11.

p. 292 *Saltantem sobrium* . . . Cicero, *Pro Murena*, 6, 13.

p. 292 *Dolus an virtus* . . . Virgil, *Aen.*, ii, 390.

15   (333)

INDEX

This index is intended to cover (with reasonable fullness) references to people, works and topics in the *Arte*, with the exception of unimportant place names and a few common classical names, either mythological or legendary. The Introduction, whose main lines are indicated in the table of contents, has not been indexed; by thus eliminating editorial matter it is hoped that the index will provide an unblurred outline of what is actually in Puttenham's book. So far as possible the indexing of leading topics has been centralised: linguistic comments are classified under LANGUAGE; discussions of the kinds and forms of poetry (including drama), metre and style have been brought together under POET and (principally) POETRY. Under the latter have also been included (in one list) the Figures and Vices of style. This classification will, it is hoped, aid the approach to the book's material and provide a convincing conspectus of the range and variety of Puttenham's interests. *Obiter dicta* which reflect a particularly personal point of view are collected under PUTTENHAM. Greek words and names familiar in a Latinised form are indexed under the latter (*e.g.* the names of the Figures, Choerilus, Heraclitus). Well-known classical and non-European names are indexed under the most commonly used forms (*e.g.* Avicenna, Horace). Titles have been indexed in preference to surnames as these have proved in the majority of cases the most current forms (*e.g.* Anjou, Burghley, Surrey); only where the surname is more generally used than the title (*e.g.* Greville, Sackville) have cross-references been given. Italicised numbers denote topics, persons or works referred to, though not by name (*e.g.* all the references to Tottel's *Miscellany* are italicised). An asterisk indicates that additional or explanatory matter will be found in Appendix III. Information collected in Appendix III on the ultimate and (possible) immediate sources of quotations in the *Arte* has not been indexed save where such quotations were undoubtedly first-hand (*e.g.* English verse extracts) or were derived from sources which Puttenham must certainly have known and mentions elsewhere in the *Arte* (*e.g.* Juvenal, Ovid, Virgil). Names which are possibly incorrect, but whose correct forms have not been ascertained, are indexed within inverted commas. The fairly numerous corrections made in the proper names of Puttenham's anecdotes and *apophthegmata* have been determined by reference to relevant classical authorities (*e.g.* Philostratus, Plutarch, etc.). An index of the first lines of verse quotations is appended.

(335)

(336)

INDEX TO FIRST LINES OF
VERSE QUOTATIONS

This includes the opening lines of all English verse passages, single lines or parts of lines quoted in the *Arte* whether original verse or translation. The interruption of a verse extract by prose commentary or explanation has been disregarded and the first line only indexed (*e.g.* the epitaph on Sir John Throckmorton, p. 179). On the other hand, where two consecutive lines may conceivably be independent, both have been indexed (*e.g.* the two last lines quoted on p. 200). To avoid the *onus* of editorial discrimination between what was intended as verse and what was not, the editors have included in the term 'verse' all inset italicised lines. Sentences or phrases not inset which Puttenham describes as verse, or which have been identified as verse quotations, have been included with italicised page references. Where the extract quoted runs to more than one line the number of lines in the passage is given in brackets. Where geometrical poems are intended to be read backwards (*i.e.* beginning at the last line) the last (textual) lines have been indexed. To facilitate the finding of information concerning the sources of these extracts the following symbols have been used as cross references: * indicates original English verse whose author is either mentioned by Puttenham or identified in Appendix III; † indicates that the lines were either traditional or Puttenham's own translation, either acknowledged in the text or identified in Appendix III; P indicates verse, otherwise unrecorded, introduced as Puttenham's own; P*, extracts from *Partheniades*; P†, verse translation (identified in Appendix III) which, however, Puttenham leads the reader to suppose is of his own composition. Variations on lines or passages made to illustrate a prosodic or linguistic point have been indexed under the first form only in which they occur.

FIRST LINES OF VERSE QUOTATIONS